All About Child Care and Early Education

A comprehensive resource for early childhood educators

Marilyn Segal, Ph.D.

Betty Bardige, Ed. D.

Mary Jean Woika, M.A.

Acknowledgements

All About Child Care and Early Education is a collaborative effort.

JESSE LEINFELDER, Coordinator of Undergraduate Training at the Family Center of Nova Southeastern University, was the driving force behind this textbook. She convinced the authors of the importance of creating a textbook for students and practitioners that is practical, up-to-date and user-friendly, and that covers the entire birth to five age-span. Ms. Leinfelder read the manuscript line-by-line, page-by-page, from cover to cover, suggesting important changes and finding smaller errors in form and content that had to be corrected. Throughout the preparation of this book, Jesse Leinfelder has also been our most demanding critic and our best friend.

CHARLENE SWANSON, Coordinator of Continuing Education at the Family Center of Nova Southeastern University, is a guru on health and safety and a stickler for creating learning materials that take into account the characteristics of the adult learner. Like Jesse Leinfelder, Ms. Swanson read the text from cover to cover, exing out jargon and flagging passages that were unclear or too wordy. Mrs. Swanson is on a mission to rid the professional literature of jargonese and hard-to-interpret passages, and we are grateful for her red pencil.

KORI BARDIGE, an early childhood teacher who is currently getting her masters in early childhood special education, read our drafts through a teacher's eyes and provided many practical suggestions, tricks of the trade, and tips for beginning teachers. We are grateful for her good ideas and good sense and for her unfailingly cheerful assistance.

SUZANNE GREGORY and **JUSTIN KURUVILLA** have been the workhorses for this publication. With persistence and patience, they scanned in charts, put together pieces, coordinated input, typed revisions, formatted text, and kept track of our multiple drafts. In addition, they have had the good grace to apologize when rewrites were required for errors that could have been their fault but were more likely ours.

TONY CORBETT, Director of Marketing at the Family Center, has done an incredible job coordinating the production of the manuscript and keeping all of us on task.

We also wish to acknowledge the A.L. MAILMAN Family Foundation for supporting the development of this book.

Distributed by:

Gryphon House, Inc.
P.O. Box 217
Mt. Rainier, MD 20712

Cover Design:
Nova Southeastern University Office of Publications

Contents

Introduction

All *About Child Care and Early Education* is a comprehensive resource book for child care practitioners, including teachers, care givers, family child care providers, administrators, and directors. *All About Child Care and Early Education* provides practical suggestions for setting up classrooms, for developing curricula for infants, toddlers and preschoolers, for meeting children's social-emotional needs, and for working effectively with parents and staff. Child Development Associate candidates and other students preparing for roles as early childhood educators can use *All About Child Care and Early Education* as a primary text.

Research increasingly confirms what parents and caregivers have always known: the early years are a critical time for learning and for character formation. Those who teach and care for young children have taken on an awesome responsibility. Their work requires skill and training, creativity, intelligence, and lots of energy. It is also a great adventure. Each day, you share the wonder and delight of children who are discovering things for the first time.

The early years are a critical time for learning and character formation.

Come along. Let us show you the wonders of a child's world and the behind-the-scenes techniques that can make a world wonderful for children.

Section I, A Child Care Revue, provides a brief history of child care and early education and sketches future challenges for the field.

Section II, Setting the Stage, describes developmentally appropriate indoor and outdoor learning environments. It covers the CDA competency areas SAFE, HEALTH, and LEARNING ENVIRONMENT.

Section III, On Stage provides broad developmental overviews of infants, toddlers, and preschoolers, and then, in separate chapters, describes the typical sequence of development in particular domains and suggests methods of enhancing development at each stage. Each of the CDA competency areas PHYSICAL DEVELOPMENT, COGNITIVE DEVELOPMENT, COMMUNI-CATION, and CREATIVE is covered in a chapter.

Section IV, The Performers, focuses on emotional and social development. It covers the CDA competency areas SELF, SOCIAL, and GUIDANCE.

Section V, Behind the Scenes, focuses on the behind-the-scenes relationships and practices of adults that generate good outcomes for children. It covers the CDA functional areas PROGRAM MANAGEMENT, FAMILIES, and PROFESSIONALISM.

All About Child Care and Early Education combines the broad perspective of an early childhood professor and a policy expert with the practical know-how of practitioners who works with children on a daily basis. All curriculum, activities, and suggestions for classroom management have been field tested in private and subsidized child care centers serving children from a wide spectrum of ethnic and socioeconomic backgrounds.

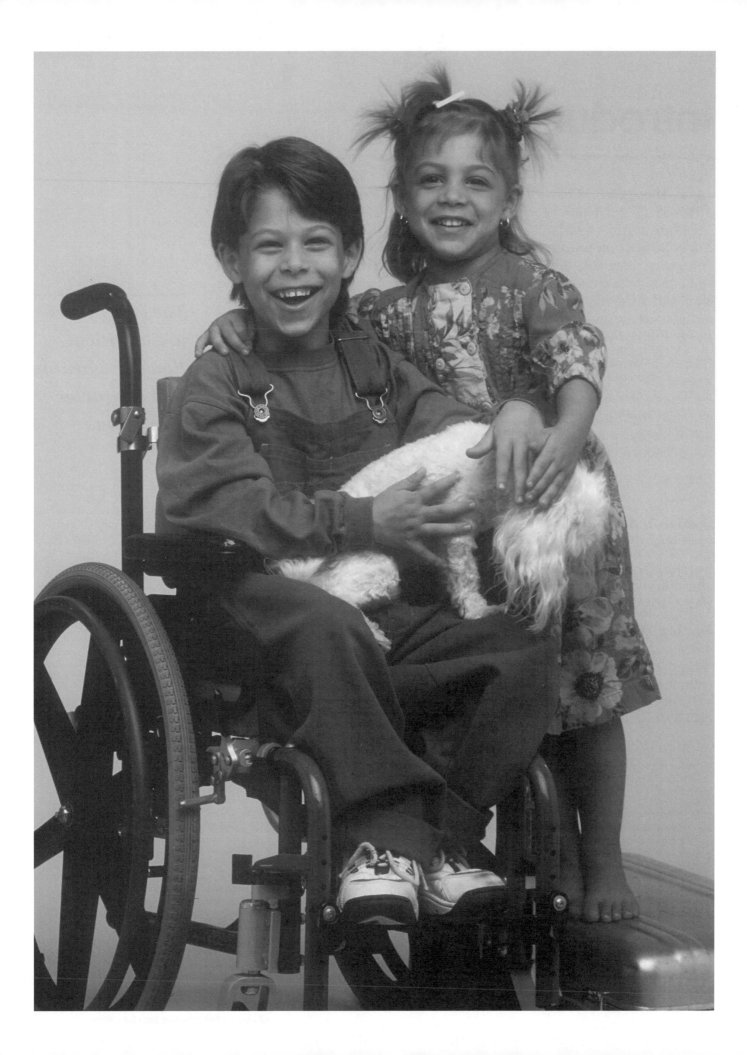

Section I:
A Child Care Revue

Miss Go-with-the-flow had just enrolled in a Child Development Associate course. She and some fellow students were looking through the textbook they were using for the course.

Miss Go-with-the-flow: "Why do textbooks always start out with history and theories? I've been a preschool teacher for eight years and believe me, nothing that goes on in my class has anything to do with theory. As far as I'm concerned all you need to be a good teacher is a good dose of common sense."

Miss Clock-Watcher: "I couldn't agree with you more. I sure don't know any theory and my kids don't give me any trouble. I know that kids love routine and I keep to a strict schedule. Every day we start out writing in our daybooks; then comes circle time, learning games, bathroom time, snack, outdoor play, bathroom, lunch, rest, free choice, circle time, and dismissal. When its time to make a transition I just flick the lights and the children automatically go to the next activity."

Miss Go-with-the flow: "Well the kids I work with don't like to be scheduled. They are free spirits, just like me. They choose what they want to do and if they're really into something like building a block structure, putting on a puppet show, or playing doctor, I am not about to stop them because it's bathroom time."

Although Miss Go-with-the Flow and Miss Clock Watcher insisted that you don't need theory to teach a class of preschoolers, these two seasoned teachers have very different ideas about the best way to operate a preschool classroom. Despite their insistence that their teaching techniques were based on common sense and not on theory, it is obvious that these teachers were making different assumptions about what is good for children. Although they did not realize it, these teachers were taking opposite sides on a theoretical issue.

Section I, A Childcare Revue, includes two chapters. The first chapter, Changing Perspectives, provides a brief history of child care in America and a description of the major childcare curriculum philosophies. The second chapter, Challenges Ahead, describes childcare challenges in the year two thousand and beyond. Our hope is that this theoretical overview will help practitioners to recognize the impact of theory on practice and will inspire them to play a role in shaping the future of early childhood care and education.

Chapter 1:
Changing Perspectives:
The American Scene

History of the Child Care Genre

Child care, meaning care for children outside the home by someone other than the child's parent, has a long history in America. Through the years, as the status and roles of women have changed, and as more women have joined the workforce, there has been an increased recognition that the provision of quality child care for young children must be a national as well as a family concern. As we trace the history of child care in the United States, we recognize a close link between the history of child care, the prevailing economic and social conditions, and the history of women in the workforce.

1828
The Boston Infant School is founded with the goal of providing a positive environment for children and for facilitating the entrance of women into the workforce. Children from the age of eighteen months to school age are accepted into the Boston Infant School.

1860
First kindergarten for English speaking children is introduced in Boston. In contrast to the Infant School, which emphasized physical care, the kindergarten emphasizes education for young children.

1880-1890
The day nursery movement begins in response to rapid urbanization and industrialization in the Northeast. The goals of these nurseries are child care for children and training and employment for their parents.

1920
Professionalism of child care providers becomes a major issue. Trained teachers place a major emphasis on education with a de-emphasis on support to parents.

The provision of quality child care for young children must be a national as well as a family concern.

1933

Government support for child care begins with the goal of helping teachers maintain their jobs.

1940-1945

Further government support is given to child care so that women can take jobs in defense factories.

1950-1960

Philosophy of the time is that mothers who can afford it should be in the house. Nursery schools are designed as half-day enrichment programs, many on the co-op model.

1965

Head Start begins as a key piece of the War on Poverty. It provides education and health services for children and leadership and employment opportunities for their parents. The goal is to give poor children a boost so that they will be ready to start school on a par with more privileged peers

1970-1980

Child care is increasingly recognized as being potentially beneficial for children, whether or not they are living in poverty. This change in thinking is brought about by the women's movement, by new research demonstrating the benefits of quality child care, and by the fact that many women seek the economic benefits of returning to work while their children are still young.

1980-1990

With an increasing number of women with infants and young children joining the workforce, the shortage of available, affordable, and quality child care reaches crisis proportions.

1990-2000

An overriding concern in this decade was the severe shortage of child care that parents could access and afford. This shortage was exacerbated by welfare reform, which forced welfare parents with young children to join the workforce.

An equally pressing concern was related to the quality of early child care. This concern was prompted by studies of the quality of child care in the United States and by what came to be known as the "brain research."

Well-designed studies of child care quality, based on a broad sampling of child care centers and family child care homes, found that the quality of most child care in the country ranged from mediocre to downright dangerous. Programs for infants and toddlers received the lowest ratings.

During the same period, research studies on brain development pointed out the important role of early experiences in shaping the structure and chemistry of the brain. According to this research, the quality of early experience can have a lasting influence on social, emotional, and intellectual development.

In response to these well publicized research studies, school readiness initiatives were launched throughout the country.

As we trace this brief chronology of child care history in the United States, we recognize that many of the child care issues we must grapple with in this millennium are older issues revisited. Is child care a benefit for children or simply a necessity for parents? Should child care be primarily custodial or primarily educational? Should infants be enrolled in child care? Should the government be responsible for supporting or subsidizing child care? Are child care workers a part of a professional community?

Recurring Themes: Theories of Child Development and Learning

While economic and social conditions have influenced the popularity of child care over the past century, the philosophic foundations of child care have been determined by psychological theory. The theoretical writings of several major psychologists and educators are responsible for the development of different models and practices.

The major theorists described in this introduction have provided us with a basic framework for understanding child development. They have enabled us to recognize the expected sequence of developmental events and, at the same time, have provided the rationale for individual differences. Most important, these theorists have provided guidelines for child development practitioners who are seeking to enhance children's well-being, knowledge, and competence.

Dr. Maria Montessori

Dr. Maria Montessori was an Italian physician who developed an interest in education in a somewhat round about way. As a young physician she was appointed as director of a state supported school for "mentally deficient" children. In this position she had the opportunity to take a close look at children's learning processes and came to recognize that learning for children is facilitated by the manipulation of concrete materials. When Dr. Montessori was appointed in 1902 to direct a "children's house" for the children of Italian laborers, she was able to put her ideas into practice.

Here are some of Montessori's ideas that have influenced child care practices.

- The early years are ideal for learning.

- Children learn best by the manipulation of concrete materials.

- Materials can be designed to promote learning of a specific concept.

- Educational programs for young children should be organized so that activities and objectives for learning move from less complex to more complex and demanding.

- Children need a variety of sensory experiences, including touch, taste, and smell, to develop their full capacities.

- Children appreciate beauty and order. With guidance and encouragement, children will learn to maintain a beautiful and orderly environment.

- Children are intrinsically motivated to learn and are capable of taking an increasingly more active role in planning and supervising their own learning.

- Parents are very important and should be involved in their child's education.

Arnold Gesell

The work of Arnold Gesell provided the theoretical basis for preschool programs in the United States during the middle years of this century. Dr. Gesell, a physician, believed that patterns of behavior unfold automatically during the course of the child's development in the same way that the child's physical growth and motor development unfold automatically. Gesell was one of the early leaders in the United States in the systematic study of young children's behavior. He and his colleagues at Yale spent many years observing and recording the behavior of infants and young children. Gesell's work provides teachers, parents, and psychologists with an outline of what to expect of normal children during the course of development. Gesell's writings have influenced child care practices in the United States in several important ways including the following:

- Children develop according to their own natural developmental timetable. Attempting to speed up maturation is a waste of time.

- Children should be provided with enriching experiences that are appropriate for their own level of development.

- Teachers should become familiar with developmental sequences so that they can provide individual children with appropriate experiences.

- Observing children at play is the most valid way of gathering information about their development.

Jean Piaget

Jean Piaget was a Swiss psychologist who began the systematic study of children's behavior in the 1920's. Though Piaget's teachings have had a dramatic effect on educational theory, his focus is not on education, but on the development of intelligence. Piaget describes and elaborates the following basic concepts:

- All children, beginning from infancy, pass through an orderly succession of developmental stages and substages. Their stage of development determines the way they interpret experiences, structure problems, and seek out solutions.

- The infant is in the sensori-motor stage of development. He understands his world by the actions he performs. The preschool child is in the pre-operational stage of development. In contrast to the infant, the preschool child recognizes that objects exist even when he does not touch them. He has developed his own system of symbols (images, props, and words) to represent objects in the real world.

- Learning takes place by the processes of assimilation and accommodation. When the child is introduced to a new phenomenon, she tries to understand it by assimilating it, or associating it with things that she already knows. As she gains experience with the new phenomenon, her way of thinking changes, or accommodates, to take into account the characteristics of the new phenomenon. This implies that children should be introduced to new experiences that are related to experiences they have already had but that also challenge their thinking in some way.

- Children are innately curious and motivated to learn. They do not require external rewards.

Based on this system of beliefs, preschools that ascribe to a Piagetian philosophy carry out the following practices:

- The teacher is seen as a facilitator. She arranges the environment and prepares lessons and experiences appropriate to the developmental level of the children in the class.

- Recognizing that the child learns by actively organizing and constructing the environment, the teacher provides concrete materials for the child to sort, order, and arrange.

- Concrete experiences are introduced before abstract concepts. For example, a child is given lots of experience with "floating" and "sinking" before learning scientific concepts like "density" and "displacement."

- Imaginative play is encouraged. Pretending is viewed as a way of developing a system of symbols to stand for real events and as a way of learning to take a different point of view.

- The child is given many opportunities to experiment with different media including water, sand, paint, clay, and play dough. Through manipulation, the child will make her own discoveries about the nature of reality.

- No external rewards are offered for the accomplishment of a task, and children are permitted to make choices about what they are going to do. Repetition of a task is encouraged if this is what the child wants.

B.F. Skinner

B.F. Skinner is a behavioral psychologist who has had a major influence on both therapeutic and educational practices. Skinner recognized that patterns of behavior are influenced by their consequences. Children who are rewarded, or "positively reinforced," for behaving in a particular way will increase the frequency of that behavior.

Children can learn new behaviors by successive approximation. By breaking a learning task into small segments and by careful use of rewards, a skilled adult can accelerate a child's learning. Negative behaviors that interfere with learning can also be brought under control by appropriate reinforcement. While punishment is ineffective because it creates anxiety, maladaptive behaviors can be reduced by lack of positive reinforcement or by rewarding incompatible behaviors.

Ideas generated by B.F. Skinner that have influenced practices in child care include the following:

- Learning is an observable and measurable change in behavior.

- Learning can be facilitated by breaking tasks down into small segments.

- Learning can be strengthened by repetition.

- It is important to reinforce good behavior rather than to punish negative behavior.

- Negative behavior is learned and can therefore be unlearned.

- Teachers who are concerned about a child's negative behavior need to take into account what happens after the negative behavior occurs. Is the child being rewarded in some way? For example, is she getting extra attention or avoiding having to do something she doesn't like?

- Negative behaviors can be eliminated by changing their consequences.

Erik Erikson

While Erik Erikson has not had a direct influence on the development of early childhood curriculum and practices, his focus on development as a lifelong process and his recognition of the importance of social interaction within each developmental stage has had a profound impact on our understanding of children and their parents.

Erikson described eight sequential stages of psychosocial development. At each stage, a child is faced with challenges or issues that need to be resolved. Children who successfully meet these predictable challenges develop emotional resources that help them to master the challenges of later stages.

The three psychosocial stages that the young child experiences are basic trust vs. mistrust, autonomy vs. shame and doubt, and initiative vs. guilt. Babies who are loved and well cared for develop a sense of trust in the people who love them. This feeling of trust is also associated with feelings of self-worth and confidence. The trusting infant becomes an exploratory toddler.

The second psychosocial stage characterizes the toddler between one and three years old. The major issue the toddler faces is autonomy vs. shame and doubt. Toddlers who master self-care tasks and who have had opportunities to make choices and explore new territory develop confidence in their own abilities. They learn the basics of self-control and overcome the feelings of doubt and shame that they experience when they are told "no".

Preschool children between three and six years old are in the third psychosocial stage, facing the crisis of initiative vs. guilt. As they interact with each other, they learn how to take initiative without being hurtful. Similarly, they gradually learn that the scary or mean things they imagine don't come true just because they think them. Children who have learned to be good playmates are ready for the challenges of the school age years.

Lev Vygotsky

Lev Vygotsky was a Russian psychologist who asserted that the course of development is shaped by a child's interactions with a social environment. According to Vygotsky, children construct knowledge in the context of social interaction. Adults as well as older children provide the scaffolding that enables children to reach higher levels of cognitive awareness.

Socially developed constructs such as language and symbols facilitate the construction of knowledge.

The Constructivists

The constructivist position incorporates both the Piagetian theory that knowledge is constructed by the child's hands-on experiences in the physical environment and Vygotsky's assertion that knowledge is constructed through social interaction. In other words, the child's level of cognitive development is determined both by the opportunities he is given to learn by doing and the opportunities he has to interact with responsive adults and peers.

Individual differences are seen as the result of children's different experiences with both the physical and social environment. New knowledge is best taught by taking into account children's different starting points and allowing them to learn together by discussing hands-on experiences with each other.

Selected Curriculum Models

The proliferation of early childhood curriculums based on different developmental theories illustrates the impact of theory on practice. In this section we feature some curriculum models that are used extensively throughout the country.

High/Scope

The High/Scope curriculum is based on Piaget's concept that children are active learners who construct their knowledge base through playing and experimenting with hands-on materials. High/Scope is a curriculum framework that describes educational ideas and strategies but does not rely on a specific set of materials.

A High/Scope classroom is set up with learning centers that invite children to explore the materials and engage in developmentally appropriate activities. The classroom schedule follows a "plan, do, and reflect" sequence, beginning with a group time where children are helped to plan their day. Following the planning session, children disperse to the different learning centers where they engage in self-initiated or group activities. The day ends with another whole group gathering, where children have the opportunity to discuss what they did and reflect upon what they learned.

The teacher is responsible for setting up the environment and developing the daily schedule. The schedule allots time for small group and large group activities. These activities are built around "key experiences" designed to promote the development of rational thinking within each curriculum area. The teacher is also responsible for assessing the development of each child and assuring that every child engages in activities that promote his continuing growth.

High/Scope places a major emphasis on teacher training. This training is designed to help teachers understand the rationale of key experiences and to plan for the incorporation of key experiences into each child's daily schedule. On-going in-service training hones the teacher's skills and provides him with new and creative curriculum ideas.

The Bank Street Model

The Bank Street model also reflects the point of view of the constructivists, with a special emphasis on the social aspect of learning. Its core beliefs are that children learn best when they like what they are doing and that children who feel confident and competent are motivated to learn and primed for intellectual growth. Children are encouraged to work in groups and to solve problems together.

Like High Scope classrooms, classrooms that adopt the Bank Street model are organized in interest centers, and the teacher's role is to set up a variety of interesting experiences and to facilitate the children's exploration, discussion, and reflection. Unlike High/Scope, however, there is no set curriculum or set of key experiences. Instead, teachers draw from a wide variety of sources to create classroom and community experiences that motivate children to ask questions, communicate ideas, and get excited about learning. Teachers help children to draw conclusions from concrete experience and engage in critical thinking.

The Reggio Emilia Approach

The Reggio Emilia approach, originated in a town in northern Italy shortly after World War II. Like High/Scope and Bank Street, it embraces the constructivist philosophy. It includes several features, however, that distinguish it from other constructivist models.

The Reggio Emilia approach stresses the importance of respecting children and discovering their amazing capacity. This begins with an emphasis on relationships. Children stay with the same teacher for several years. Teachers, parents, and other family members work together to nurture children's relationships within the classroom, the school, and the larger community.

Respecting children also means being genuinely interested in their ideas. Rather than being preplanned by the teacher, the Reggio Emilia curriculum, also known as the Project Approach, emerges from the children's interests and questions. Teachers carefully observe the children's spontaneous work and play, and bring in objects or experiences that they think will intrigue them. Together, teachers and children build long-term "projects" or investigations that bring forth and stretch the children's ideas. Children are encouraged to ask new questions, to discover the answers through active exploration, and to express their ideas in many different media.

Central to the Reggio Emilia approach is their definition of the teacher's role. The teacher is first and foremost a learner. Through careful observation and documentation of each child's work, he gains insights into children's unique ways of thinking and knowing. Teachers become increasingly more effective as they learn from the children they teach.

An equally important role of the teacher is as a facilitator. The teacher asks questions, makes comments, and encourages the children to question. He challenges children to explore their own ideas and carry out experiments. He helps children become close observers of their environment, paying special attention to different perspectives and details. He encourages children to represent their knowledge and ideas in spoken and written language, their own symbolic notation, drawing and painting, dance and pantomime, and various kinds of three dimensional modeling. As an art coach, he helps children learn new techniques, critique their own work, and re-do their work as their thinking develops.

The teacher finds creative ways of displaying the children's products so that children can appreciate their own and each other's, and so that parents and community visitors can know and appreciate what the children have been doing. Children often work together to create classroom displays and collective art projects that showcase their work and learning.

The concern with art and design goes beyond the children's work. The Reggio Emilia approach is also concerned with the way space is designed. It recognizes the importance of creating environments that are in harmony with nature and give children an appreciation of order and beauty. Interior spaces are carefully crafted to encourage creative expression. The environment is furnished with intriguing natural and recycled objects, carefully chosen and displayed to encourage children to create and experiment.

Direct Instruction

While few people believe that young children should spend their days sitting in desks, listening to teachers lecture, and filling out worksheets as instructed, many preschool teachers do give "lessons" for at least part of the day. Recognizing that young children enjoy and learn from imitation, they show them how to perform simple tasks such as setting the table or chanting the alphabet and more complex feats such as stringing beads in elaborate patterns, writing their names, making counting books, and spelling words. Often, teachers draw upon their own or the children's cultural traditions as they plan and carry out lessons. For example, they may use a "call and response" method derived from African-American or Afro-Caribbean culture to teach a color name or an arithmetic fact or to engage the children in a familiar story. "The Big, Bad Wolf said, 'I'll huff, and I'll puff, and I'll blow your house down.' What did he say, children?" "I'll huff, and I'll puff, and I'll blow your house down." This method is often used to reinforce important health, safety, and behavioral lessons. "What do we do when we feel angry?" "We use our words!"

Teachers who use direct instruction often follow a pattern of teach, repeat, reward. The individual child or group is praised for repeating the teacher's lesson or following her instructions correctly. Individual children may also be rewarded with gold stars or smiley faces on their hands or on their work.

When young children play "school," they often use a direct instruction approach, even if their own classrooms rely predominantly on other methods. They call their class to order and tell their pupils what to do. They quiz them to see if they remember what they have been taught, and write new lessons on the blackboard. They may even assign homework and give out stickers for good behavior.

Developmentally Appropriate Practice

Developmentally appropriate practice is a term coined by the National Association for the Education of Young Children (NAEYC) to describe ways of teaching and of organizing children's experiences that take into account the age and capabilities of each child. All of the methods described above can be developmentally appropriate—or not—depending on how they are implemented. For example, it would not be appropriate to ask a group of two-year olds in a High/Scope classroom to plan a whole morning or to spend a long time reflecting on what they learned from playing in the sand. It would be appropriate, however, to let the children choose between sand and block play, and to talk with them about what they are doing or how the sand feels. Similarly, it is not usually considered appropriate to give three-year olds formal lessons in how to read, whereas it would be considered inappropriate not to give these lessons to five and six-year olds who were interested in books but could not yet read on their own.

Berk, L.E. & Winsler, A. (1995). *Scaffolding children's learning: Vygotsky and early childhood education.* Vol. 7. Washington, D.C.: National Association for the Education of Young Children.

DeVries, R. & Kohlberg, L. (1987). *Constructivists early education: Overview and comparison with other programs.* Washington, D.C.: National Association for the Education of Young Children.

Edwards, C., Gandini, L. & Forman, G. (Editors). (1998). *The hundred languages of children: The Reggio Emilia approach-advanced reflections.* Greenwich, CT: Ablex Publishing Corporation.

Roopnarine, J.P. & Johnson, J.E. (2000). *Approaches to early childhood education.* NJ: Prentice Hall, Inc.

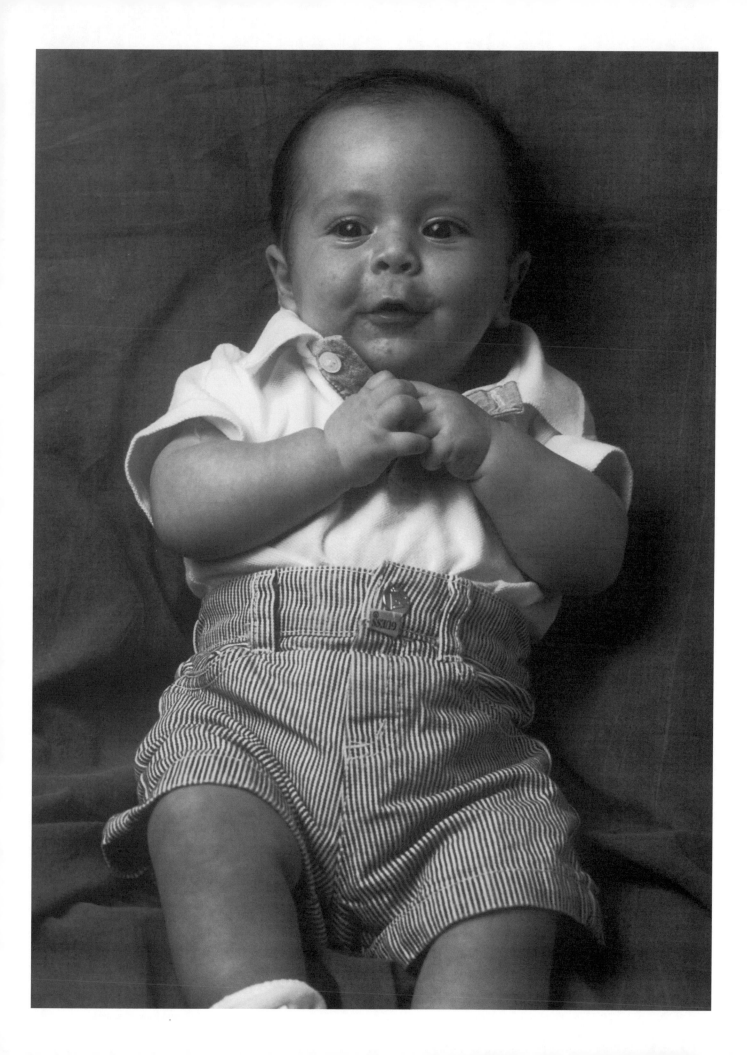

Chapter 2: Challenges Ahead

The year 2000 finds us on the threshold of a new era for child care providers. The signs of the times are loud and clear.

- More and more mothers are going back to work, so child care is becoming more of a necessity and less of an option.

- More and more parents are becoming knowledgeable about child care curriculums and about the intellectual potential of young children. Parents will continue to ask for a warm, safe, supportive climate for their children, but they will also ask for intellectual stimulation.

- More and more government agencies are taking a hard look at standards, training, and licensing requirements. The larger the use of child care facilities, the greater the need for regulation.

- More and more mothers of infants and toddlers are going back to work, making infant/toddler child care a priority need.

- More and more corporations are recognizing that providing child care benefits is in their own self-interest. More and more public schools are assuming responsibility for children under five.

- More and more educators are recognizing that there is no true distinction between quality child care and early childhood education. Quality child care assumes developmentally appropriate practices and supports the teaching of young children.

- More and more research regarding the effectiveness of quality child care is being published and distributed.

Child care providers have become increasingly more aware of their status as professionals. They are asking questions of their supervisors, and of themselves.

- What are my duties and responsibilities as a child care provider?

- What knowledge and skills do I need in my present position?

- What kinds of resources are available to help me acquire this knowledge and these skills?

- What kinds of career opportunities are open to me?

- What will the children in my care enjoy learning? How can I make sure that they will be ready to succeed in school?

- What kind of parent involvement should I seek out?

- How can I achieve this involvement?

- How can I, as a child care provider, serve as an advocate for children?

In the best of all possible worlds, high quality care and education beginning at birth would be the entitlement of every child.

Goals for the Future

In the best of all possible worlds, high quality care and education beginning at birth would be the entitlement of every child. In order to achieve this goal, we need to develop policies that will enhance the quality of child care as well as policies that ensure an adequate supply of accessible and affordable child care options.

Policies and Practices that Promote Teacher and Assistant Competency

- Enact licensing laws that require at least thirty hours of prescribed pre-service training for all teachers, assistant teachers, and personnel who do not have early childhood degrees or certification. This pre-service training must include information on child abuse, cultural competency, and anti-bias practices.

- Provide scholarships for all early childhood teachers seeking CDA's or advanced early childhood degrees.

- Provide all teachers and assistants with ongoing learning opportunities, including exposure to new research and curriculum ideas, reflection on their own practice, sharing of strategies with colleagues, and formal coursework.

Policies and Practices that Support and Retain Good Teachers

- Provide worthy wages and benefits to child care personnel at every level.

- Develop career lattices that are open to all child care personnel and subsidize training so that they can make lateral or upward moves within the early childhood field.

- Incorporate mentorship as a component of inservice education.

Policies and Practices that Upgrade the Skills of Child Care Directors

- Develop director credentialing systems in every state.

- Include director credentialing in the licensing code of every state.

- Develop national credentialing systems for child care directors.

- Develop a system for recognizing child care directors who complete advanced levels of training.

- Develop training programs for directors that focus on mentoring staff and continually upgrading their skills.

Policies and Practices that Assure the Quality of Programs

- Enact national or state licensing laws that restrict group size and maintain professionally recommended teacher/child ratios.

- Provide an incentive system within each state that rewards centers and homes that have been accredited by a system that meets or exceeds the standards set by the National Association for the Education of Young Children (NAEYC) and by the National Association for Family Child Care (NAFCC).

- Involve parents in envisioning what they want for children and helping professionals to design and maintain appropriate programs.

Family Friendly Policies and Practices

- Provide child care options that parents can select in accordance with their needs and preferences.

- Provide parents with opportunities to serve on policy committees with decision making power.

- Provide all parents with information on child care, including a description of the kinds of child care programs available to their children and a set of guidelines on how to find and select a high quality early childhood program.

- Enact national or state legislation that provides every child with health and dental insurance.

- Expand child care subsidies and scholarships to make high quality child care affordable to all families.

Policies that Protect the Rights of Children

- Develop programs within each state to provide developmental screening for every child.

- Provide assessment services for children who do not pass the screening test, and assure their access to early intervention programs or services.

- Develop systems within each state for determining school readiness, and use the results as a way of improving preschool and early intervention programs.

- Involve parents in the assessments, and in determining the programs and services that are right for their child.

The United States is largely a nation of immigrants, and its racial, cultural, and linguistic diversity continues to increase. By the year 2020, white children whose first language is English will no longer be in the majority. Many forecasters also expect that the gap between the life-styles of rich and poor children will continue to widen. New jobs in a new high-tech economy will demand new skills and higher levels of education. The role of the early childhood teacher will continue to become more important and more challenging.

What challenges do you see in your community or in your work and relationships with young children and their families? What new policies might be needed at the local, state, and national level to meet these challenges?

Greenman, J. & Stonehouse, A. (1996). *Prime times: A handbook for excellence in Infant and toddler programs.* St. Paul, MN: Redleaf Press.

Roopnarine, J.P. & Johnson, J.E. (2000). *Approaches to early childhood education.* NJ: Prentice Hall, Inc.

Section II: Setting the Stage

Miss Disgruntled was talking with her colleague, Mr. Coolheaded.

Miss Disgruntled: "What a day! I feel like going home tonight and never coming back."

Mr. Coolheaded: "You sound pretty upset. What's the matter?"

Miss Disgruntled: "What's the matter? Everything is the matter. Ever since we got our new director he's given me nothing but trouble. Yesterday, he came into my room with this whole long list of complaints. My cribs were too close together and I was endangering the health of the babies. My diapering supplies weren't close enough to the changing table. I had too much stuff on my shelves and I couldn't possibly keep them all sterile. A couple of boxes were in front of the doors and if there happened to be a fire I couldn't get the kids out fast enough."

Mr. Coolheaded: "I know what you mean. Mr. Striver is a real stickler when it comes to health and safety. Did you fix up the room?"

Miss Disgruntled: "I worked my butt off. I stayed here until eight o'clock last night rearranging the cribs, taking the toys off the shelves, throwing out the trash, and clearing off the shelf by the diaper area to make room for the diaper supplies."

Mr. Coolheaded: "Mr. Striver must have been happy when he saw your room in the morning."

Miss Disgruntled: "Happy? Not one word of thanks, you did a good job. All he said was that now if I wanted my room to a safe and healthy place for children I'd better make the room more attractive. Now what does making a room attractive have to do with health and safety?"

Mr. Coolheaded knew perfectly well what the director was trying to tell Miss Disgruntled, but he also knew that this was not the time to talk about it. Instead he said, "Go home and get a good rest and I'll help you with the room tomorrow."

Both Mr. Coolheaded and Mr. Striver recognized that a room that is uninviting might very well be a safety hazard for young children. All young children need to be in an environment that is attractive and home-like. Children need large spaces that are right for active play and smaller more intimate places for quiet play. In a well-designed classroom, the noise level is controlled, age-appropriate toys are in reach and displayed in an organized fashion, and there are places where children can gather in small groups and places where children can be alone or with one other friend. A well-designed classroom is a safe and healthy place where children can play and learn.

Chapter 3: Safe

Overview

Safe involves the prevention of injuries to children and to adults.

Rationale

The old adage, "Safety first," is especially true for those who are responsible for young children. Young children depend on adults to keep them safe; they do not yet have the knowledge, skill, or judgment to keep themselves out of danger. Therefore, it is the teacher's responsibility to create and maintain a safe environment while at the same time helping children to learn safety skills.

Although, as jobs go, caring for young children is relatively safe, teachers do need to be conscious of their own safety needs as well as the children's. Even a minor injury — such as a wrenched back or twisted ankle — can prevent a teacher from doing her job.

Objectives

1. To learn how to plan safe activities by taking into account children's developmental levels and likely behaviors

2. To learn how to create and maintain safe classroom and playground environments

3. To learn what to do in case of an emergency

4. To learn safe practices for taking children on field trips

5. To develop and model good safety habits

6. To learn how to involve preschool children in developing safety rules for their classroom

7. To learn how to develop a safety curriculum

8. To learn how to set up a safe environment for children with special needs

Miss Carefree felt good about the safety record of her classroom. "Since the beginning of the year," she boasted, "not one child in my class has gotten hurt. Keeping children safe is no big deal' she went on. "All you have to do is keep a good eye on the kids."

While good supervision is certainly the most important safety rule, if we are really committed to keeping children safe, we cannot rely on supervision alone. In this chapter we describe how teachers demonstrate their commitment to safety.

Objective 1: To learn how to plan safe activities by taking into account children's developmental levels and likely behaviors

The first rule of safety is prevention.

Miss Full-of-energy had been chided by the director, who told her that her classroom was out of control. "My classroom was not out of control," Miss Full-of-energy insisted. "When you came into the room they were playing follow-the-leader. It was just too bad that Kimberly bumped her head when she tried to jump off the chair, but she really didn't get hurt."

Miss Full-of-energy should be commended for wanting her class to have fun. At the same time, she should have realized that a rowdy, chair-climbing game of follow-the-leader is not appropriate for two-year olds. Two-year olds are great imitators. When one child performs a feat like jumping off a chair, the other children will want to do the same thing, even if they don't have the skill to do it safely.

The first rule of safety is prevention. A safety minded teacher must be aware of age-related norms and characteristics. She should also be aware of the characteristic behavior of the individual children. Kimberly was a daring child, although not physically adept. When another child performs a physical feat, Kimberly is bound to follow suit. Kimberly's fall from the chair was an accident waiting to happen.

Think about the young children you know, or skip ahead to the developmental overviews that begin Section III. Based on your observations or these descriptions, which of the following activities would be safe for preschoolers but not for younger children? Which would be safe for toddlers but not for infants? Which would be safe for children of all ages? Which would not be safe for children under six? Can you describe conditions or child characteristics that would make these activities safe or unsafe?

- blowing and watching soap bubbles
- a chase or tag game involving ten children
- dodge ball
- tricycle races
- drawing with chalk on a sidewalk
- Musical Chairs
- finger-painting with shaving cream

Developmental Picture

The infant 0-8 months:
- Is developing new skills day by day, like rolling over, reaching, putting things in her mouth, pulling on things and scooting

The caregiver:
- Childproofs the areas used by infants
- Never leaves infants unattended
- Provides clean protected floor space where infants can lay down, push up, roll over, crawl
- Provides safe toys infants can touch and mouth

The infant 8-14 months:
- Is learning new motor skills at a very fast rate, like scooting, creeping, pulling up, climbing, and toddling from place to place

The caregiver:
- Cleans and childproofs the areas and supervises closely
- Provides safe, low, and sturdy structures for babies to pull up on and climb on
- Provides appropriate outdoor surfaces for crawling and toddling such as blankets, clean sand, outdoor carpeting

The toddler 14-24 months:
- Is likely to develop a special interest in opening and shutting doors and drawers, picking up and mouthing small toys and objects, standing on top of things, or crawling into spaces that are hard to get out of

The caregiver:
- Safety proofs indoor and outdoor areas, making sure there are no dangers children can get into (thumb tacks, glass, sharp table edges, shelf units that can topple, loose rugs, etc)

The two year old:
- Is developing new motor skills such as walking up and down stairs
- Is apt to run or dart from place to place, but is not good at stopping
- Is curious and unable to identify dangers
- Is likely to imitate the feats of older children even when they are beyond his ability
- May be impulsive and dash into new places
- Investigates and experiments with throwing hard objects or hitting with sticks

The caregiver:
- Makes sure that there are no places in the classroom or on the playground where a child cannot be seen or can escape from

- Makes sure that the two year old has no opportunity to explore or play with dangerous things like matches, pills, poisonous plants, or cleaning fluids
- Recognizes that electric fans, balloons, plastic bags are potential dangers

The preschooler:
- Is frequently a risk-taker, especially with large muscle activities
- Is gaining the ability to consider safety and is ready to learn safety rules
- Learns safe practices through experiences
- Insistent about doing things for herself and may not like to hold hands while crossing a road, put on a safety belt, or let adults help when she is climbing down or jumping

The caregiver:
- Provides a safe environment with careful supervision
- Teaches safe practices and safety concepts

Objective 2: To learn how to create and maintain safe classroom and playground environments

Mrs. Happy-Go-Lucky was in great spirits. She had just made a tour of the infant-toddler room and it looked beautiful. There were pictures tacked up on all the walls at eye-level for the children. There were hanging plants with textured leaves that even babies could touch. There was a floor fan in the infant area that made the mobiles spin. There were jars of marbles on the table near the window that reflected the rays of the sun. There were pillows in the shape of turtles in every infant crib.

As you can imagine, Miss Happy-Go-Lucky was not so happy when her supervisor came to inspect the classroom. Can you identify five potential hazards that need to be removed?

A good beginning for thinking about the safety of a classroom or a playground is to identify the kinds of accidents that are likely to occur. In a classroom, children can get hurt by falling down, by having something fall on them, by bumping into something sharp, by getting an electric shock, by ingesting something harmful, by getting fingers pinched in doors or drawers, by getting cut with something sharp, by getting burned, or by being hit or poked by another child. Infants can suffocate on a surface that is too soft if they roll onto their stomachs and then can't turn their faces to get a breath. That is why parents and caregivers are taught to put infants to sleep on their backs and to provide firm surfaces for infants to lie on when they are awake. On the playground, children can get hurt by falling off something high, by falling on something sharp or hard, by colliding with something, by getting hit by something, by getting a part of their body caught or pinched, by eating or touching a poisonous plant, or by getting a splinter.

No matter how careful we are, we can not prevent all accidents. By looking at the kinds of accidents that can happen, we can recognize ways to reduce the risk.

Safety in the Classroom

Once you have thought about the kinds of accidents that can happen, take a close look at the classroom you work in and see if you can answer the following questions.

- Is all potentially dangerous material safely out of reach of children, even those who can climb? (This includes cleansing material, medicines, poisonous plants, sharp scissors or knives, matches, electric cords, hot drinks, etc.)

- Are all electric outlets covered?

- Are there no sharp edges on tables or ledges that children could run into?

- Is the floor clear of obstacles, loose rugs, and wet spots that could cause a child to trip or slip?

- Have you removed, secured, or cut any dangling cords that a child could get tangled in or pull on and cause something to fall?

- Are heavy pieces of furniture, including bookshelves, chests, high chairs, and folding tables, secure and stable so that they can not be tipped over by children who climb, push, pull, or swing?

- Do you know where the fire extinguisher is and how to use it and are you sure it works?

- Are all the toys in good repair and safe for the developmental age of the children in the class?

- Have objects that can be swallowed or have small parts been removed if there are children under three?

- Have you eliminated toy boxes or trunks with heavy lids that could trap children, fall on them, or pinch their fingers?

- Are the room dividers low enough so that you can see all the children at any one time?

- Are there appropriate precautions and adaptations for children with allergies, physical limitations, or other special health needs?

Safety on the Playground

Now it is time to go out to the playground and ask a second set of questions.

- Is the playground area securely fenced off with safety locks on all gates?

- Is the playground clear of broken glass and other debris?

- Are there railings and walk spaces on the top of slides to prevent falls?

- Are the S-hooks tightly closed on all swings? Are all swing ropes in good condition? Are swings made of soft, lightweight material so that a child who walks into an empty moving swing will not be hurt?

- Is there a minimum of 6 (and preferably 8) inches of sand, mulch, or grass under all climbing structures and swing sets?

- Is all equipment free of splinters, with no cracks, rusted areas, or loose screws and bolts?

- Is metal equipment shaded so that children cannot get burned?

- Is the playground surface smooth with no holes or protruding objects?

- Are the riding paths wide, gently curved, and marked for one way traffic?

- Has all broken equipment been removed?

- Has the playground been checked for poisonous plants?

- Is all play equipment anchored well in the ground and placed in an area with a "safety gate" around it? (Barriers to younger, inexperienced children should be placed around dangerous climbing structures, reserving them for only those children who are capable of getting around the barriers. Swings should be placed in an easily supervised area that is isolated from other playground traffic.)

- Are there appropriate precautions and adaptations for children with allergies, physical limitations, or other special health needs?

Complying With Safety Standards Set by the Licensing Bureau, the Fire Department, and Your Own Center

Mrs. Caution was visiting different childcare centers. She wanted to find a center where she could be sure her son would be safe. When she entered the classroom where her child would be placed she heard the director talking to the teacher. "Please move those boxes, Miss Careless. They are blocking the exit." Miss Careless immediately apologized. "I'll move them right after class," she promised. "I completely forgot that the fire department is coming tomorrow morning." Mrs. Caution decided she would find a different place for her son.

Every state establishes minimum safety standards for licensing childcare establishments. Although the stringency of these standards differs among states, all states require that childcare establishments adhere to fire safety standards and are monitored by the Fire Department on a regular basis. The purpose of standards is to protect children from harm. No one expects that there will be a fire in the childcare center and the chances of it happening are certainly slim. Unfortunately even slim chances do happen and when we are responsible for children's safety even the slimmest chance is too great a risk.

Objective 3: To learn what to do in case of an emergency

The only way to be sure that you know what to do in case of an emergency is to take a first-aid course. Use the following list as a refresher course.

First Aid Guidelines

The following first aid guidelines are provided by the Department of Health and Human Services, Center of Disease Control and Prevention, US Public Health Service. *http://www.cdc.gov/nicdod/hip/abc/policie5.htm*

In emergency-call 911. State the problem and give FULL address and telephone number. Note: The address, phone number, and directions to the center should be posted by all telephones.

Bleeding
• Apply pressure with a gauze pad for 10 to 15 minutes (use gloves). If bleeding continues or is serious, apply a large gauze and call 911 immediately.

Burns
• With or without blisters—place burned extremity in cold water, or cover burned area with cold wet cloths until pain stops, at least 15 minutes.
• Do not break blisters.

If burns are deep or extensive, call 911.
• Do not apply cold water.
• Cover child with a clean sheet and then a blanket to keep the child warm.

Fractures
Arm, leg, hand, foot, fingers, toes:
• Do not move injured part if swollen, broken, or painful.
• Call parent to pick up and take child to get medical care.

Neck or back:
• Do not move child.
• Keep child still.
• Call 911 for ambulance.

Head Injuries
• Keep child lying down.
• Call parents.
• Call 911 if child is:
  ▲ Complaining of severe or persistent headache
  ▲ Less than 1 year old
  ▲ Oozing blood or fluid from ears or nose
  ▲ Twitching or convulsing
  ▲ Unable to move any body part
  ▲ Unconscious or drowsy
  ▲ Vomiting

Choking
You should start CPR if:
- The child cannot breathe at all (the chest is not moving up and down).
- The child's airway is so blocked that there is only a weak cough and a loss of color.
- The child cannot cough, talk, or make a normal sound.
- The child is found unconscious.

Call 911 after starting rescue efforts.

DO NOT start CPR if:
- The child can breathe, cry, talk, or make a normal voice sound.
- The child has a strong cough. (A strong cough means there is little or no blockage)

CPR should be administered by a person trained in CPR.

Seizures
- Remain calm.
- Protect child from injury.
- Lie child on his or her side with the head lower than the hips, or on his or her stomach.
- Loosen clothing.
- Do not put anything in the child's mouth.
- Call 911 if seizures last more than 5 minutes or if they are the result of a head injury.
- Notify parents.

Nosebleeds
- Have child sit up and lean forward.
- Loosen tight clothing around the neck.

Shock
(A collapse of circulatory function caused by severe injury, blood loss, or disease-symptoms, including low blood pressure, pallor, and weak pulse.)
- Lie patient flat with legs elevated.
- Cover with blanket to avoid chill.
- Give water unless abdominal injury is suspected.

Broken Bones
- Call 911.
- Do not move the injured child.
- Splinting should be done by Emergency Medical Technicians.

Breathing Problems (Drowning)
- Use mouth to mouth breathing.
- For infants and small children:
  - Clear mouth and throat of any obstructions with your finger.
  - Place patient on back with face up; lift the neck; tilt head back.
  - Place your mouth over patient's mouth and nose.
  - Blow into baby's mouth in short spurts, twenty to thirty times per minute, removing your mouth after each puff to allow for exhaling.

Objective 4: To learn safe practices for taking children on field trips

Field trips can be great fun or absolutely disastrous. The outcome depends less on chance than on planning. The most important thing to plan for is the safety of the children. Here is a checklist that can help take the risk out of field trips.

- Visit the field trip site in person ahead of time.

- Get a signed permission slip for every child.

- Recruit parents to help you.

- Prepare the children for the field trip by describing where they are going, how they will get there, and what safety rules will be enforced.

- Pin an envelope on every child that has his or her name and the address and telephone number of the center in it.

- If you are going by car, make sure that there is a seatbelt for every person in the car, and a car seat for each child under three (or whatever your state requires).

- Bring along the permission slips, a first aid kit, and the emergency phone numbers of all the children.

- Make sure that each child has a buddy.

- Use the travel time to sing songs and tell stories.

- Count the children at least once every fifteen minutes and before moving to a new area.

Objective 5: To develop and model good safety habits

After a good two hours of extra work, Mrs. Happy-Go-Lucky completed the job of childproofing her classroom. She was standing on a little chair putting away the marbles when her supervisor returned to the room. "Get down from that chair this minute!" her supervisor insisted. "That's a good way to break a leg!" Poor Mrs. Happy-Go-Lucky. She wasn't allowed to leave the center until she studied the safe practices list.

Keeping Yourself Safe

Maintaining safe patterns of behavior includes much more than keeping your classroom and playground free of hazards. It also involves keeping yourself safe. Here is an adult safety checklist that one center compiled after keeping track of the kinds of accidents that had occurred there over the past several years.

- Bend your knees and use your legs rather than your back to lift heavy objects or children.

- Don't carry more than one child at a time.

- Dry the floor after washing it or after mopping up a wet spill.

- When using a sharp knife or tool, make sure that you will not be bumped or distracted by active children. If children are nearby, ask them to sit down and watch you or give them jobs of their own.

- Do not use or demonstrate child-sized furniture or equipment that is not designed to support an adult.

- Use common sense and don't take risks.

- Do not hesitate to ask another adult for help.

Keeping Children Safe

Young children are notoriously unpredictable. The safety-conscious teacher knows that he can not eliminate every danger or intercept every fall. But he can practice some basic safety habits and teach children to behave safely. The teacher can demonstrate his commitment to safety by:

- Supervising children at all times.

- Counting the children whenever you move to a new area, to be sure that none are left behind.

- Keeping the door to your classroom closed, though not latched. (You can put a bell or chime on the door to alert you when someone is leaving or entering.)

- Modeling safe behavior.

- Showing children the "safe way" to climb up or down, sit on a swing, carry something heavy or awkward, knock down a block tower, handle a tool, or use playground equipment.

- Not giving children foods that may cause choking. This includes popcorn, whole grapes, ice cubes, nuts, seeds, raw carrot rounds, hard candy, and corn chips.

- Planning and practicing fire drills.

- Releasing children only to those who are authorized to pick them up.

Helping Parents Follow Good Safety Practices

Many of the accidents and emergencies that occur at preschools involve parents, and occur during busy drop-off and pick-up times. A child may run into the traffic lane while his parent is talking to a friend or strapping his younger sibling into her car seat. A rushed parent may accidentally lock a child in a car, or give in to his pleas to sit in the front seat or stay out of his car seat. A child may wander into an unsupervised area while her parent is gathering her belongings.

To avoid these mishaps, you may want to make a safety discussion part of an early parent meeting, send home a safety flyer, or post reminder notices on the parent bulletin board or in other appropriate spots. Here are some points to cover:

- Young children should always ride in the back seat of a car, in safety-approved car seats that have been installed correctly. (You might invite a parent volunteer or police officer to do a safety check if parents are in doubt.)

- Children should be carried or held by the hand when entering or leaving the center.

- Everyone should take care to close the door slowly and firmly upon entering or leaving.

- Children can only be released to authorized persons.

- Drivers should follow a clearly marked one-way traffic pattern, if possible.

- Extra caution should be used when backing out of parking spaces.

- Parents are responsible for supervising their children if they use the playground when the center is not officially open.

If parents and staff feel it is necessary, you can station a staff person or parent volunteer outside during drop-off and pick-up times.

In addition, you will want to share general child safety information with parents. Parents of infants should be reminded of the "Back to Sleep" campaign to reduce Sudden Infant Death Syndrome by having babies sleep on their backs. All parents should be given information about local safety and first aid courses and product recalls. They should be reminded of the dangers of second hand smoke and of guns in the home. Parents should have opportunities to bring up any concerns that they may have.

Finally, you will want to help parents talk with their children about safety issues, especially if there has been an accident or a scare in your neighborhood. Brainstorm ways of reassuring the children and of teaching common-sense precautions without inducing fear.

Objective 6: To learn how to involve preschool children in developing safety rules for their classroom

Mr. Nose-to-the-Grindstone dropped into his daughter's pre-kindergarten classroom during morning circle time. The children were helping the teacher draw up a list of Safety Rules for the classroom. The redheaded boy suggested "no hitting or kicking." The class agreed that that was a good rule and it was added to the list. Next, the girl with a ponytail shouted out that she knew one. "Nobody should drop their peanut butter sandwich on the floor." The boy beside her chimed in. "That's a dumb rule. I don't ever eat peanut butter and jelly sandwiches. They are yucky." The teacher asked the group if it was all right to drop any kind of food on the floor. "Maybe you can't help it if you drop something on the floor. Like it could be an accident." The girl with the ponytail agreed. "Maybe we should say if you drop food or something on the floor you should clean it up." "And you shouldn't throw blocks at people," the boy in the red shirt added. "Good thinking," the teacher commented as she wrote down the two new rules. Mr.

Nose-to-the-Grind-Stone left the room and went right to the director. "You got to have a talk with that teacher," she told him. "Instead of teaching these kids something she has them sitting in a circle making up safety rules."

Despite Mr. Nose-the-Grind-Stone's assertion, the teacher was teaching the class something. First, she was helping the children think about behaviors that could cause someone to get hurt. Second, she was teaching the class that a safety rule is a way of preventing an accident. Third, and most important, the teacher recognized that children are likely to follow the rules that they have helped to create.

As you read this list of rules developed by a class of four-year-olds, think about which of these rules would be appropriate for your classroom and what other rules you would add:

...children are likely to follow the rules that they have helped to create.

Safety Rules for Classroom
(In the words of four year olds)

- No running.
- Sit on chairs but don't stand on chairs or on tables either.
- You shouldn't point things at people, like scissors.
- You don't leave the classroom unless your teacher says it's okay.
- You don't fool around with electric outlets or things like that.

Safety Rules for the Playground
(Also in the words of four year olds.)

- You have to sit in the middle of the swing and you can't stand up and you stop it before you get off.
- One at a time on the slide and you have to go down frontwards.
- You don't bump into people when you ride your tricycles.
- You don't say "ha-ha scaredy-cat" if somebody is scared to go on the jungle gym.

Objective 7: To learn how to develop a safety curriculum

In addition to childproofing the classroom, modeling safe behavior, and developing safety rules, teachers can help children become safety conscious by including safety lessons in their lesson plans. Here are some ideas.

Activity: Go on a safety walk.

Objective: To teach children to recognize and talk about potential hazards

Procedure: Give each child a red circle sticker. Ask the children to walk around the classroom (or the playground) and put the red sticker on anything that could be dangerous. In circle time, ask children where they put their sticker and what the danger is.

Activity: Play a "Freeze!" game.

Objective: To teach children to respond immediately to the word "stop"

Procedure: Make two parallel lines on the playground using crepe paper or yarn. Line children up on the starting line. When you say "go," ask children to begin walking toward the finish line. When you say "stop," all the children must stop on the spot. If children are in motion when you say "stop," they must go back to start. Add an element of cooperation by having children walk in pairs.

Activity: Read a story.

Objective: To teach children about safety

Procedure: Read children a safety story in circle time. Allow children to talk about experiences in which they have had to practice good safety.

Activity: Pretend Play 1

Objective: To teach children to dial 911 in case of a fire

Procedure: Turn your pretend play area into a fire station and encourage the children to play fire station. For props, use a telephone, fire hats that you could make as a craft, a bell, a length of hose, whistles, and some blankets. Help the children play out a scenario where a child sees smoke and dials 911. The call is received in the fire station. Someone rings the bell, the children get out the hose, rush to the fire, and put it out.

Activity: Pretend Play 2

Objective: To teach traffic safety

Procedure: Take the children for a safety walk on the playground. Pretend the path is a busy street. (If you do not have a path on your playground, make a path out of rope or mark one with chalk.) Use a yardstick with red on one end and green on the other as a signal. Teach the children to walk to the end of the road, wait until the light turns green, look both ways, and say "all clear" before they cross.

Activity: Safety Crafts

Objective: To reinforce awareness of safety

Procedure: Children can make fire hats, safety badges, or 911 signs to place by their home telephones. They can make a traffic light out of a quart-size milk carton by pasting red, yellow, and green squares of construction paper on one side. In circle time, use the craft activity to initiate a talk about safe practices.

Activity: Field Trip

Objective: To increase safety consciousness

Procedure: Take a trip to the fire station or the police station or invite a police officer or fire marshal to come to your center. Go on a safety walk in your neighborhood. Identify all the sights that have to do with safety. Examples include danger zone signs, stop signs, cross walks, and fire hydrants. Follow the field trip with a safety talk or lotto game in circle time.

Objective 8: To learn how to set up a safe environment for children with special needs

*P*rior to the opening day, the director of Open Arms Nursery School was telling the staff about the new children who were enrolled in their classes. "There are three children in your class," she told Mrs. Keep Safe, "who were not in the school last year. There's Jimo, who is Cornelia's younger brother, Jacques, whose family recently immigrated from Haiti, and Madeline, who is quite a self-sufficient child, although she is legally blind." Mrs. Keep Safe turned pale. "I would be happy to have Jimo and Jacques, but I must admit I am worried about having a blind child in my class. You know the children in my class are quite active, and I feel a blind child might get hurt. As far as I am concerned, my first obligation is to keep the children safe."

"You worry too much," the director responded. "I used to teach in a school where almost half of the children in the class had some sort of disability, and we had a perfect safety record. As a matter of fact, I just read an article. Children with disabilities in an inclusive school are less likely to get hurt than typically developing children. The article goes on to say that typically developing pre-school children are protective of children with handicaps, and are careful not to hurt them."

"Well, okay," Mrs. Keep Safe agreed. "I guess I'll give it a try."

The director of Open Arms Nursery School was absolutely right. Children with special needs are less likely to get hurt in a preschool setting than are typically developing children. Nevertheless, teachers or caregivers of children with special needs must remain continually vigilant and must anticipate the kinds of accidents related to a child's handicap that could occur, and take preventive measures.

Setting Up a Safe Indoor Environment

The kinds of modifications needed to make the classroom safe for a child with a handicapping condition depend very much on the nature of the handicap. Many children with handicapping conditions such as mild retardation or language delays do not require any special room arrangements. Children with physical or sensory limitations, however, may benefit from some adaptations. Modifications needed in the classroom may include raising or lowering a table, making a bathroom wheelchair accessible, and being extra careful that there are no sharp corners on the tables or shelves and that the doorways are barrier free.

In addition to the room arrangement, children with special needs may need special equipment or materials. Children who are visually-impaired may need a Braille computer, big books, or a magnifying glass. Children who are hearing-impaired may need hearing aids or language boards. Children who are physically challenged may need wheelchairs, standing tables, or chairs with special supports. Children with learning problems may need materials such as puzzles or pegboards that are likely to be used with younger children.

> *Children with special needs are less likely to get hurt in a preschool setting than are typically developing children.*

Setting Up a Safe Outdoor Environment

Like all children, children who have special needs benefit from active play. The kinds of modifications that you make on the playground depend upon the nature of the handicapping condition and the recommendation of the parent or therapist. Children who are physically challenged may need to have balance beams set in the ground so that they can practice balance without getting hurt, or tricycles with foot holders that make them easier to pedal.

With a visually-impaired child you may want to cordon off the area behind the swings or provide soft Nerf balls for playing circle games. Children who are hearing-impaired do not need special equipment, but you may want to use hand signals to give them directions.

Dodge, D.T., Koralek, D.G., & Pizzolongo, P.J. (1989). *Caring for school children.* Vol. 1. Washington, D.C.: Teaching Strategies, Inc.

Greenman, J. & Stonehouse, A. (1996). *Prime times: A handbook for excellence in Infant and toddler programs.* St. Paul, MN: Redleaf Press.

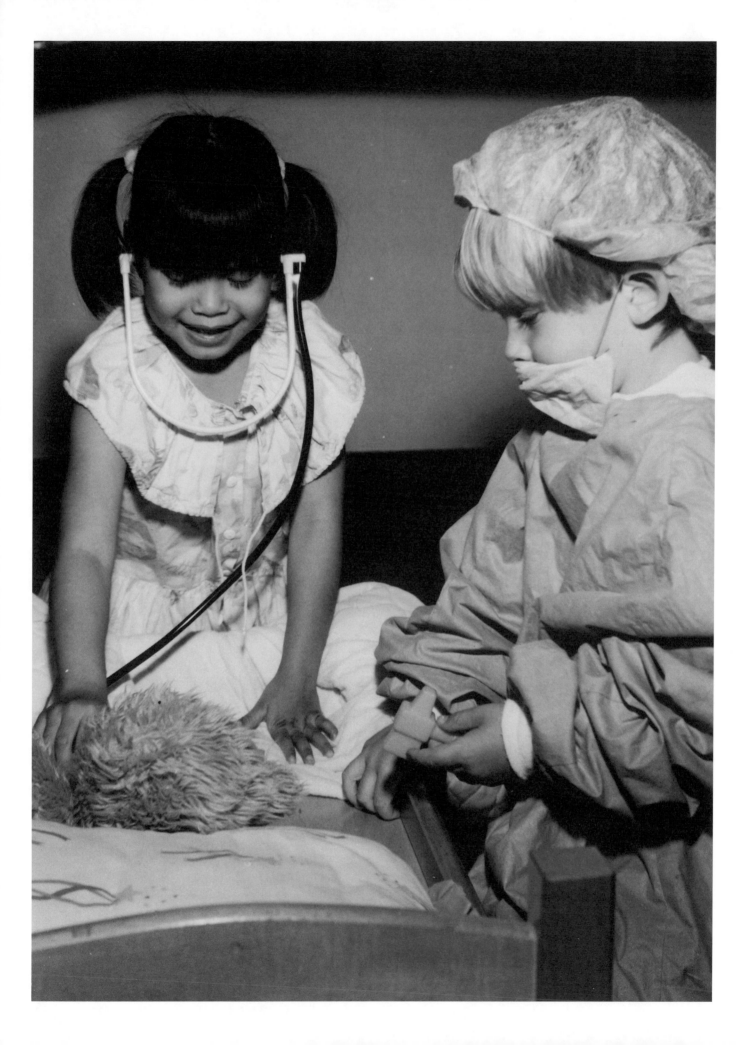

Chapter 4: Health

Overview

Often we think of health as simply the absence of disease. It is true that we can't stay healthy unless we learn good health habits that protect our bodies from illness — but we need to think of health in a larger sense. Being healthy means feeling fit and fine. It means having the internal resources to fight off illness or overcome the effects of physical insult; it also means having the energy and stamina to lead a productive life.

Rationale

Health is an important aspect of learning and development. Children who are healthy have the vigor they need for play, learning, and across-the-board development. Also, the more scientists learn about health, the more they become aware of the importance of behavior. Eating right, exercising, avoiding risks, practicing good hygiene and sanitation, and managing stress all contribute to long-term health. Habits acquired in early childhood tend to persist, so it is important to begin early. In addition, nutritional deficits and toxic exposure in early childhood can cause wide-ranging, lifelong problems.

The early childhood teacher promotes health within the classroom by:

- observing good health practices,
- conforming to health rules and regulations applying to her center,
- recognizing the signs and symptoms of illness,
- and by developing a program of health education that teaches children to value good health and to follow routines that maintain it.

Objectives

1. To develop a sound knowledge base regarding health, nutrition, and oral hygiene.

2. To carry out routine practices that prevent illness and promote good health and nutrition.

3. To establish guidelines/policies regarding how to handle health issues, including a record keeping system.

4. To incorporate activities that teach children and families about health, oral/dental hygiene, and nutrition.

5. To recognize indicators of abuse and/or neglect and follow the reporting policy mandated by your state.

6. To keep one's self healthy, and to model appropriate wellness behavior for children and their parents.

Providing a Healthy Learning Environment

Mrs. Good-Care was washing out the bathroom sink when her assistant came into the room. "What are you doing?" she asked. "Just cleaning up the bathroom," Mrs. Good-Care explained. "The janitor didn't come in this morning." "That's ridiculous!" the assistant insisted. "Cleaning the bathroom is not part of your job description."

Like any good early childhood teacher, Mrs. Good-Care did not consult her job description before she cleaned the bathroom. She realized that she was responsible for the well-being of the children in her class, and she wasn't going to let a job description keep her from protecting their health.

In this section, we look at different ways in which a classroom teacher safeguards the health of the children in her class by updating her own health knowledge, maintaining a healthy environment, teaching children about health and nutrition, and recognizing and reporting child abuse.

Objective 1: To develop a sound knowledge base regarding health, nutrition, and oral hygiene

While classroom teachers are not expected to be physicians, you do need to know some fundamental concepts about health and nutrition. Most importantly, in order to safeguard the health and well-being of the children in your class, you need to be able to share your information with parents. Your knowledge base should include the signs and symptoms of illness, recommended immunization timetables, and the daily nutritional needs of children under six.

Before you focus on the knowledge about health issues related to childcare, it is important to recognize the sequence of development relating to health and wellness.

Developmental Picture

The infant 0-8 months:
- Is dependent on others for meeting all basic needs
- Is likely to be alert and interactive during feeding and diapering
- Mouths objects to explore them

The caregiver:
- Helps infants establish a comfortable individual rhythm of sleeping, eating, waking, and playing
- Uses feeding and diapering times as an opportunity to play and interact with babies
- Maintains routines for sanitary diapering, disinfecting mouthed toys, and washing bedding and clothing

The infant 8-14 months:
- Is developing food preferences related to taste and texture and may push a spoon away
- Is interested in feeding himself and playing with food or throwing food on the floor
- Is learning from adult models
- Explores objects by touching, mouthing, and chewing on them

The caregiver:
- Provides time and support for practicing self care tasks
- Provides finger foods and encourages children to feed themselves
- Is careful to offer nutritious food, but not to force food
- Routinely cleans floors, equipment, and mouthed items
- Maintains sanitary diapering routines

The toddler 14-24 months:
- Is not usually ready to be toilet trained
- Is likely to enjoy handwashing
- May be insistent about self-feeding
- Continues to explore objects with all senses, including taste

The caregiver:
- Does not expect toileting skills, and maintains sanitary diapering routines
- Washes mouthed objects and maintains clean floors and play spaces
- Helps children wash their hands frequently
- Provides nutritious foods the child can eat easily with fingers or spoons, in a relaxed atmosphere
- Does not force foods or insist that a child eat

The two year old:
- Is at a good age for toilet learning, but may have accidents even when toilet learning has been achieved
- Enjoys having the ability to eat with a fork or spoon, wash her own hands, and brush her teeth with help
- Is anxious to do things all by himself
- Becomes listless or cranky and whiny when coming down with an illness

The caregiver:
- Makes toileting a routine activity for children who have begun toilet learning
- Makes sure every child has a change of clothes available
- Maintains a clean environment and washes toys after a child has mouthed them
- Recognizes signs of illness and separates the ill child from classmates

The preschool child:
- Is mastering self care
- Is capable of learning good health habits
- Accomplishes independent eating, handwashing, toileting, toothbrushing, and nose wiping
- Is likely to be frightened of going to the doctor

The caregiver:
- Provides ample opportunities to develop body image, to practice self care, and to develop good health habits
- Assures children nutritious foods, outdoor exercise, regular rest time, and a clean environment
- Isolates and sends home children with contagious diseases

Knowing the Signs and Symptoms of Illness

Some signs of illness like high fever or vomiting are unmistakable, while other signs are subtler and may be attributed to other causes.

Signs and symptoms to attend to:

Listlessness	Inactivity
Poor appetite	Moodiness
Urinating frequently	Excessive pallor
Tiring easily	Excessive thirst
Deep circles under eyes	Difficulty with vision or hearing
Chronic cough or runny nose	Hoarse voice
Pink eyes	Skin rashes, crustiness, or blotches
Nausea, vomiting, or diarrhea	Difficulty with breathing
Complaints of headache, stiff neck, or other pain	

Knowing About Contagious Diseases

Parents sometimes expect teachers to be all knowing. Although it is impossible to meet this kind of expectation, teachers can have a basic knowledge of the most common contagious diseases. They should also know how to obtain updated information from the local public health department, a pediatrician who consults to the center, and the Center for Disease Control (*www.cdc.gov*).

Common Contagious Diseases

Disease	Incubation Period	When it is "Catching"	Symptoms	Rash	Length of Illness	Prevention
Chicken Pox	4-21 days	1 day before rash & 6 days after rash	Fever Rash Itching	Individual spots beginning as water blisters spreading over whole body, forming crusts by 4th day	7-10 days	Varicella
German Measles	14-21 days	2 days before symptoms and 3 days after	Fever Slight cold Enlarged glands	First day-reddish purple-scarlet on the 2nd day	3-5 days	M.M.R. Vaccine
Measles	10-14 days	1 day before fever until rash disappears	Fever Cough Conjunctivitis	Reddish-purple spots running into each other from head downward	7-10 days	M.M.R. Vaccine
Mumps	12-24 days	1 day before swelling as long as swelling lasts	Fever Swelling under jaws	No rash-fever and swelling of face under jaws	7-10 days	M.M.R. Vaccine
Scarlet Fever	2-7 days	From first symptoms until 7 days later	Fever Sore throat Headache Vomiting	Pinpoint scarlet rash on body-not on face	7-10 days	None
Whooping Cough	7-14 days	From beginning of cough for 3-4 weeks	Cold Whooping cough Vomiting	None	4-6 weeks	D.P.T. Vaccine

Use this chart to help you answer the following questions that parents might ask:

"My child was exposed to measles last Saturday. If she is going to come down with measles, when would she first show symptoms?"

"My child had chicken pox. He's all better except for a couple of crusted-over spots on his forehead. Can he come back to school?"

"My child has a couple of red spots on her foot. Could that be the beginning of chicken pox?"

Center for Disease Control Immunization Guidelines, 2000

Approved by the Advisory Committee on Immunization Practices, the American Academy of Pediatrics, and the American Academy of Family Physicians.

Disease and Vaccine	First Dose	Second Dose	Third Dose	Fourth Dose/Boosters
Hepatitis B	At birth, if mother has been exposed; otherwise 2-4 weeks	1-6 months	6-18 months	
Diphtheria, Tetanus, Pertussis (DPT)	2 months	4 months	6 months	15-18 months, 4-6 years, then TD at 11-12 years and every 10 years thereafter
H. Influenza type B (HIB)	2 months	4 months		
Polio (IPV)	2 months	4 months	6-18 months	4-6 years
Measles, Mumps, Rubella	12 months	4-6 years		
Varicella (Chicken Pox)	12 months (if no history of chicken pox)			
Hepatitis A	2-12 years, but only in high-risk geographic areas			

Any dose not given at the recommended age should be given as a "catch-up" immunization at any visit when indicated and feasible.

Use the chart to help you answer the following questions that parents might ask:

"I went through the whole bit with shots and vaccination when Theresa was a baby. She is turning four pretty soon. I don't need to do anything else, do I?"

"I think Marvin has had all of his shots. At least they said he did at the health clinic, when he was six months old. He's 18 months now. We just got back from a year in Uruguay. Does he need any kind of booster shots or am I too late?"

Conditions or Diseases That Are Common in a Child Care Setting

HEAD LICE (Parasite)

Signs & Symptoms: Intense itching. Nits are most often found at the nape of the neck and over the ears.

Incubation Period: Re-treatment is generally recommended 7-10 days after the first application due to the hatching of more nits.

Treatment: A special shampoo, available over-the-counter or by doctor's prescription. Removal of the nits with the use of a fine-toothed comb.

Mode of Transmission: A parasite that is passed from person to person via personal items such as hats and combs.

Prevention: Do not allow children to share items that touch the hair, such as hats and combs. Clean rugs and bedding.

CONJUNCTIVITIS (Pink Eye)

Signs & Symptoms: Red, watery eyes, discharge, crusty eyes, sensitivity to light

Incubation Period: Usually 24-72 hours

Treatment: Prescription antibiotic

Mode of Transmission: Through contact with eye discharge

Prevention: Avoid touching the eyes. Frequent hand washing. Washing of towels and bedding. Avoid sharing of these items.

IMPETIGO

Signs & Symptoms: Flat, yellow, crusty, or weeping patch on the skin

Incubation Period: 5 days

Treatment: Washing of infected areas with mild soap and water. Doctor may prescribe an antibiotic or ointment.

Mode of Transmission: The infected person can easily spread the infections to other parts of her own body or to others by direct contact.

Prevention: Bathing daily with a mild soap. Keeping hands and finger nails clean. Frequent hand washing.

FIFTH DISEASE

Signs & Symptoms: A "slapped face" appearance rash. Fever and flu-like symptoms. The rash spreads to the trunk and extremities and may cause itching.

Incubation Period: Incubation is usually 4-14 days but can be as long as 20 days. Most contagious before the symptoms appear.

Treatment: No specific treatment.

Mode of Transmission: By direct contact of respiratory secretions and airborne droplets.

Prevention: Wash hands after touching any secretions from the nose or mouth.

HAND-FOOT-MOUTH DISEASE (Coxsackie Virus)

Signs & Symptoms: "Canker sore" like sores in the mouth and a rash on the bottom of feet, palms of hands, and sometimes the buttocks, sore throat and a mild fever.

Incubation Period: Usually 3-6 days. Most infectious for 7 days after development of the rash.

Treatment: No specific treatment

Mode of Transmission: Through the fecal-oral route or may be spread through respiratory secretions

Prevention: Hand washing. good personal hygiene.

ROTAVIRUS (Diarrhea)

Signs & Symptoms: Loose, watery stools, abdominal cramps, sometimes a runny nose and a cough

Incubation Period: 2 days

Treatment: Rest and a bland diet, avoidance of dairy products, plenty of fluid to reduce the change of dehydration

Mode of Transmission: Fecal-oral route

Prevention: Hand washing; disinfect surfaces and toys

PIN WORMS (Seat Worms)

Signs & Symptoms: Tiny white worms that cause itching and irritation of the anus

Incubation Period: After the egg is swallowed, it takes from 15-28 days for the worm to mature.

Treatment: Consult a physician.

Mode of Transmission: The eggs are passed from the anus to mouth. Children scratch the effected area where the eggs are, which then lodge under the fingernails.

Prevention: Hand washing and proper diapering and toileting procedures.

OTIS-MEDIA (Middle Ear Infection)

Signs & Symptoms: Pain, drainage from the ears, red ears, fever, tugging at the ears, irritability

Incubation Period: About the same as a cold

Treatment: Consult with physician. Chronic infection may be treated with the surgical placement of tube so that ear can drain.

Mode of Transmission: Virus or bacterial infection. Upper respiratory infections are usually spread by coughs and sneezes. Sometimes antibiotics are given. Some doctors have a wait and see attitude.

Prevention: Cover sneezes and coughs. Hand washing and the disinfecting of surfaces and toys.

SALMONELLA

Signs & Symptoms: Diarrhea, flu-like symptoms, stomach cramping, vomiting

Incubation Period: Several days to several months

Treatment: Usually no specific treatment. Seek doctor's advice in severe cases.

Mode of Transmission: Eating of infected foods, cross-contamination of foods, handling of reptiles such as iguanas and turtles.

Prevention: Proper preparation, cooking, handling, and storage of food. Proper hand washing after handling reptiles or other pets.

COMMON COLD

Signs & Symptoms: runny nose, watery eyes, sore throat, chills, cough, and malaise (blah feeling). Usually no fever unless complication has developed.

Incubation Period: Incubation is 12-72 hours, usually 24 hours.

Treatment: No specific treatment for illness. Treat the symptoms to make the infected person feel better. Rest. Drink plenty of fluids.

Mode of Transmission: Through direct contact with coughs and sneezes and indirectly through contaminated surfaces, hands and articles like tissues.

Prevention: Wash hands. Cover coughs and sneezes. Dispose of tissues properly. Wash surfaces and toys frequently.

HEPATITIS B (HBV)

Signs & Symptoms: Fatigue, loss of appetite, jaundice, dark urine, light stools, nausea, vomiting, abdominal pain

Incubation Period: Around 3 months

Treatment: No cure

Mode of Transmission: Infected mother to newborn through blood exposure at birth; exposure of cuts or mucous membranes to contaminated blood.

Prevention: Hand washing. Clean up and disinfect blood spills immediately, wearing gloves. Do not share toothbrushes.

STREP VIRUS

Signs & Symptoms: Sore throat, sometimes fever and tiredness. A rash may also appear. Swollen tonsils and lymph glands

Incubation Period: 1-3 days

Treatment: Doctor's prescription of antibiotics

Mode of Transmission: Contact with infected people

Prevention: Isolation of infected person for at least 25 hours after starting antibiotic

CHICKEN POX

Signs & Symptoms: Virus, slight fever, blisters that first appear on the face, back, under the arms, and on the "hot spots" on the body.

Incubation Period: 2-3 weeks. Children can return as soon as all of the lesions have crusted over and the sores are not wet or weeping.

Treatment: There is a vaccine for chicken pox. If children do get chicken pox, a fever-reducing medicine is usually suggested by a physician. Do NOT give aspirin — it can cause Reyes Syndrome, which can be fatal.

Mode of Transmission: Respiratory. Contact with infected people. Hands and surfaces that are contaminated through sneezing and coughing discharges, as well as airborne germs through the same transmission.

Prevention: Vaccine; isolation of infected person for six days after rash appeared and until all blisters have formed crusts or disappeared

BOTTLE MOUTH

Signs & Symptoms: Tooth decay
Treatment: See dentist.
Mode of Transmission: Infant's teeth are exposed to sugary liquids, formula, milk, or juices
Prevention: Do not let infants go to sleep with a bottle in their mouth. Wean from bottle at 12 months. Do not let infants carry bottle around in their mouth.

RESPIRATORY SYNCYTIAL VIRUS (RSV)

Signs & Symptoms: Similar to common cold. Half of the cases result in lower respiratory tract infections or otitis-media.
Incubation Period: Before symptoms appear to 1-3 weeks after the symptoms subside
Treatment: Treat symptoms. Severe cases may require hospitalization.
Mode of Transmission: Direct contact with infectious secretions.
Prevention: Hand washing; cleaning and disinfecting of surfaces and toys.

Knowing About Nutrition

Mrs. Easy-Going was talking with her four-year old's teacher. "My Melissa," she explained, "is a very fussy eater. Like most four-year olds, she hates fruits and vegetables. She also hates meat, milk, cheese, yogurt, and cereal. But don't worry if she doesn't eat lunch at school. I always stop on the way to school to buy her hash browns, and we get a big bag of french fries on the way home. She's perfectly healthy, and I don't want to make a big deal about food. "Is she allergic to anything?" the teacher asked. "No, she has no allergies; she just knows what she likes and what she hates."

Melissa's teacher assured Mrs. Easy-Going that they would not force Melissa to eat anything she did not want. True to her word, Melissa's teacher did not make a fuss over Melissa's lunch. She served Melissa a small portion of the school lunch every day, and explained to Melissa that she could eat as much or as little as she wanted. When Mrs. Easy-Going came to visit her daughter at lunch one day, she was surprised to find her eating a cheeseburger with a glass of milk. "I thought you hated cheeseburgers," Mrs. Easy-Going commented to Melissa. "I do," Melissa replied, "except I like the way they make them at school."

Melissa's teacher was concerned about providing pre-school children with a well-balanced and nutritional meal. At the same time, she respected Mrs. Easy-Going's child rearing philosophy, and agreed not to pressure Melissa into eating. She served Melissa a small portion of a well-balanced lunch on a daily basis and gradually introduced new foods to Melissa. When Melissa was introduced to the food pyramid in circle time, she developed a new interest in finding foods that she liked on different levels of the pyramid.

In order to meet the nutritional needs of children under six, we need to recognize the importance of the following facets of nutrition:

Identifying the daily requirements of the preschool child

Identifying the daily requirements of the preschool child requires knowledge of the food pyramid, which describes the six food groups and the number of recommended daily servings from each group. The following tables are taken from the USDA Dietary Guidelines for Americans 2000, 5th edition.

Bread, Cereal, Rice, & Pasta Group .... 6 servings daily
Vegetable Group .... 3 servings daily
Fruit Group .... 2 servings daily
Milk, Yogurt, & Cheese Group .... 2 servings daily
Meat, Poultry, Fish, Dry Beans, Eggs, & Nuts Group ...... 2 servings daily
Fats, Oils, & Sweets .... Use sparingly

What Counts as a Serving?

Bread, Cereal, Rice, & Pasta Group
- 1 slice of bread
- About 1 cup of ready-to-eat cereal
- 1/2 cup of cooked cereal, rice, or pasta

Vegetable Group
- 1 cup of raw, leafy vegetables
- 1/2 cup of other vegetables — cooked or raw
- 3/4 cup of vegetable juice

Fruit Group
- 1 medium apple, banana, orange, or pear
- 1/2 cup of chopped, cooked, or canned fruit
- 3/4 cup of fruit juice

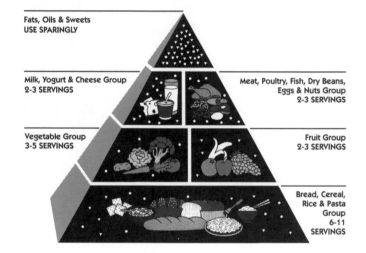

Milk, Yogurt, & Cheese Group
- 1/2 cup of milk or yogurt
- 1 1/2 ounces of natural cheese (such as cheddar)
- 2 ounces of processed cheese (such as American)

Meat, Poultry, Fish, Dry Beans, Eggs, & Nuts Group
- 2-3 ounces of cooked lean meat, poultry, or fish
- 1–1 1/2 cups of cooked dry beans or tofu
- 5 - 7 ounce soyburger or 2 eggs
- 4-6 tablespoons of peanut butter or 2/3 -1 cup of nuts

Note: Serving sizes for children ages 3-6 are the same as those for adults. For two-year olds, serving sizes should be smaller, except for milk.

Providing a pleasant environment during meals and snacks

- Bottle-feeding provides a special opportunity to hold a child in your lap and encourage closeness. Never prop the bottle.

- In some childcare centers, family-style serving (having the children select from serving bowls) is preferred. In other centers, particularly those where children bring in their own meals, each child is served individually. Family-style extends the time it takes to have a meal and, at the same time, provides the opportunity to use utensils and for the children to talk about the food with the caregivers.

- Have a comfortable conversation with the children as they are having their meal.

- Try not to rush the children — or leave them at the table too long.

Presenting meals to children that take into account their age and readiness

- Mealtime provides an opportunity to help children develop self-help skills.

- Encourage children to use the appropriate utensils or cups.

- Young toddlers can learn to use a spoon and drink from a "tippy" cup.

- Older toddlers can learn to use a fork with rounded tines and drink from a cup with handles

- Preschool age children can learn to use a dull knife and drink from a glass.

- Provide activities that allow children to help with simple food preparation. Some examples include: helping to set the table, pouring their drinks from small pitchers, and spreading jelly or cream cheese on a bagel, pita, or tortilla.

Avoiding food that could endanger a child's health

- Avoid food that could cause choking. Children 5 years old and under should not be given foods that they could choke on, such as hot dogs, raw carrots, and whole grapes.

- Avoid foods that could be aspirated, or sucked into the lungs. Children 5 years old and under should not be given foods that can be aspirated, such as popcorn and peanuts.

Recognizing that some children may have food allergies or sensitivities

- Maintain a list of children with food allergies or other allergies.

- As you plan menus or cooking projects, consult the food allergy list.

- Know how each individual child's allergy manifests itself and what to do in case of accidental exposure.

Involving parents in nutrition

- If parents provide snacks and/or meals, provide a list of suggestions to help parents select nutritious foods.

- Provide parents with a list of appropriate and inappropriate foods for bringing into the classroom for special events.

- Provide parents with a list of healthy snacks that they can give their children, such as:

Spreadable cheese	Bananas
Ice Slurpies	Whole wheat crackers
Thinly spread peanut butter	Cheerios
Thinly sliced or diced apples, pears, or peaches	Yogurt
String cheese	Rice pudding
Smooth cottage cheese	Quesadillas
Cut up grapes	Cooked peas

Promoting Good Oral Hygiene

- Provide healthy food for teeth, including calcium-rich foods like milk and crunchy foods like apples

- Limit the amounts of sugary/sweet/sticky foods.

- Explain to the parents that leaving a bottle in an infant's crib while she is falling asleep is likely to produce "bottle mouth," or rot a baby's teeth.

Objective 2: To carry out routine practices that prevent illness and promote good health and nutrition

The health practices that are most important for controlling the spread of disease in a classroom include:

- Following universal precautions
- Washing hands
- Washing and disinfecting surfaces
- Following appropriate procedures when changing diapers
- Maintaining a healthy indoor environment

Following Universal Precautions

Universal precautions are a set of strategies designed to protect people from infections that are spread through contact with blood or other bodily fluids. They should be followed without exception in child care settings, both for the protection of the caregiver and for the protection of the children.

- Avoid direct contact with bodily fluids including blood, urine, feces, vomit, saliva, and nasal/eye discharge.

- Use disposable gloves:
  - ▲ When handling body fluids
  - ▲ For food handling
  - ▲ When helping a child in the bathroom
  - ▲ When changing a diaper
- Clean up and disinfect any bodily fluid spills immediately.
- Avoid any contact with sources of bodily fluids, such as your eyes, nose, mouth, or open sores.
- Discard contaminated material in a tightly secured plastic bag.

Use Appropriate Hand Washing Procedures

Handwashing Sequence

- Gather all of the materials necessary.
- Remove jewelry—when possible, avoid wearing jewelry when working with children.
- Use soap and running water.
- Rub hands vigorously as you wash them.
- Wash back of hands, palms, wrists, between fingers and under fingernails.
- Rinse your hands well and leave the water running.
- Dry your hands with a single use towel.
- Turn off the water by using a paper towel, not your bare hands.
- Remember to wash the child's hands also, using the above procedure.

The information in this chart is from MITCH: Model of Interdisciplinary Training for Children with Handicaps. Module 8. Reprinted with permission of the Florida Department of Education and Dr. Carole Abbott, Project Specialist

Find fun ways to engage children in hand washing

The procedure for washing hands for children and adults is the same. The problem is that children aren't very good at judging how long to keep their hands under the water in order to rinse well. It also takes children time and practice to remember the sequence for washing hands.

Ways of helping children learn hand washing techniques include the following:

Sing a hand washing song with appropriate motions (to the tune of all around the mulberry bush).

This is the way I turn on the faucet,
Turn on the faucet, turn on the faucet.
This is the way I turn on the faucet,
Early in the morning

This is the way I lather my hands, etc.
This is the way I scrub my hands, etc.
This is the way I rinse my hands, etc.
This is the way I dry my hands, etc.
This is the way I turn off the faucet, etc.

Play a game called "Oops—I forgot!"

Procedure: Pantomime the sequence on hand washing. Leave out one step and see if the children can tell you what you missed.

Buy or create your own set of sequence cards on hand washing.
Let children arrange the cards in order.

Procedure: Put the cards in the wrong order and let the children correct your mistake. Omit one card and see if the children can tell you what is missing.

Put up hand washing sequence cards in the bathroom to serve as a reminder.

Set up a doll bath in the classroom.

Give a doll a bath in front of the children. Talk to the doll about the importance of washing its face first or making sure that you wash between the toes, etc. Give the children a chance to wash the doll, praising them for remembering the correct order and for making sure all parts get cleaned.

Cleaning and Disinfecting the Room and Materials

The director of Safeguard Child Care Center was taking new parents around to see the facility. "What makes our school so special," the director explained, "is the professionalism of our staff. We are very proud of the fact that our teachers are given job descriptions that recognize that teaching children is a full-time job. We have a secretary to manage the office, a bus driver to drive the bus, a cook to make the meals, and a custodian who comes in after school to clean up the classroom. Our teachers are not expected to wipe down the shelves or wash off toys that babies have mouthed."

The director was sure that all the parents on her tour would be impressed with her personnel policies. However, several of the parents were upset by the tour, and began asking questions.

- *What happens if a child messes up the floor in the middle of the day when the custodian isn't around?*

- *What happens if babies put toys in their mouths?*

- *Who is responsible for cleaning off the tables before and after snack time?*

Although the director thought that she was just being considerate of her staff when she relieved them of clean-up duty, it was easy for the parents to recognize that the children were being placed at risk.

Cleaning up in an early childhood classroom is an on-going responsibility that everyone must share. Messes must be cleaned up when they are made. Toys must be cleaned after they are mouthed. Here is a short quip about cleaning that will help you to remember the quick and easy solution to clean-up problems you will face during a normal day.

Keep-out germs-cut down on pollution
Spray every day with a fresh bleach solution
Mix water (1 gallon) with bleach (1/4 cup)
Sick rate will go down and attendance will go up!

Here are more guidelines for cleaning solutions:
- Make a fresh bleach solution every day (1/4 cup bleach to 1 gallon water).
- Dispense bleach from a spray bottle.
- Wipe all tabletops and toys that are mouthed on a daily basis.

Practicing Appropriate Toileting and Diapering Procedures

Diapering Sequence
- Have supplies ready including clean diaper, any needed clothing, and towelettes.
- Place fresh paper on the changing table. It is important to change the paper after each diaper change.
- Hold the child away from your body when you pick him up.
- Place child on changing table.
- Put on gloves.
- Remove soiled diaper.
- Place soiled diaper in a plastic lined container.
- Clean child with a towelette, wiping front to back.
- Diaper and dress the child.
- Wash the child's hands.
- Return child to a safe area.
- Remove table paper and discard it, touching only the uncontaminated side of the paper.
- Wash your hands.
- Clean and disinfect the diaper changing area, including the sink if it was used.

The information in this chart is from MITCH: Model of Interdisciplinary Training for Children with Handicaps. Module 8. Reprinted with permission of the Florida Department of Education and Dr. Carole Abbott, Project Specialist

Maintaining a Healthy Indoor Environment
- Keep the air in the room fresh and make outdoor activities part of the daily schedule

- Alternate quiet and physical activity to keep children active, alert, and healthy and to provide a time for children to rest or sleep.

- Space children's mats, cots, or cribs to reduce the spread of respiratory infections.

- Check state and local rules and regulations for additional requirements, such as lead free certification, ventilation requirements, and pest control guidelines.

Objective 3: To establish guidelines/policies regarding how to handle health issues, including a record keeping system

Maintaining Health and Immunization Records for Every Child

- The Center for Disease Control (CDC) publishes a recommended immunization chart on an annual basis that lists the types of immunizations required by law and lists the age for initial immunization and booster shots required. You should have verification of up-to-date immunization for every child, or a note from a physician stating the reason that the child has not been vaccinated.

- Require that verification of physicals be up-dated as required by the state and local enforcement agencies.

- Develop a system for maintaining physical and immunization records for children and a system of informing parents when they need to up-date immunizations and/or physicals. Maintain a health record for every child that includes: comments from daily health check, any unusual incidences or concerns, height, weight, alternative food plans, and allergic reactions.

Knowing the Guidelines Set by your Center for Excusing Children from Childcare Due to Illness

- Centers need to develop policies indicating when mildly ill children can and cannot attend childcare. Many children with mild illness can attend the center.

- Share these guidelines with parents.

- Know when to report communicable diseases and other conditions to the health department.

Objective 4: To incorporate activities that teach children and families about health, oral/dental hygiene, and nutrition

When we think about all the different things we would like young children to know about health and nutrition, it is difficult to know what to emphasize or even where to begin. One possible starting point is making a list of some of the basic concepts you would like children to learn in the course of the year. Next, develop lesson plans devoted to these concepts. You might want to do a theme or unit near the beginning of the year, or offer brief lessons on a weekly basis.

Basic Concepts About Health and Wellness

- Our bodies get strong when we get to sleep on time, get lots of fresh air, and eat healthy foods.

- Germs make us sick. When we wash our hands before we eat and after we go to the bathroom, we get rid of germs.

- Germs spread when we sneeze or cough. That's why we need to cover our mouths with our hands when we sneeze or cough.

- Cigarettes are not good for our bodies.

- We brush our teeth at least twice a day to keep them clean and healthy.

Basic Concepts About Nutrition

- Eating the right kinds of food makes us strong and healthy.

- Foods like candy and sweetened cereal are bad for our teeth.

- Foods that are high in protein like meat, fish, beans, and cheese make us strong and give us energy.

- Eating lots of fruit and vegetables gives us vitamins that keep us feeling well.

Suggested activities for nutrition

Activity: Pretend Play

Objective: To teach children to recognize healthy foods.

Procedure: Set up a restaurant in your classroom. Provide appropriate props such as chef hats, aprons, menus, trays, pads and pencils, pretend food, napkins, place settings, and a cash register. Join the play as the waitress or the parent so that you can talk about ordering healthy foods.

Activity: Craft

Objective: To teach children about the different food groups

Procedure: Help children construct their own food books by cutting pictures out of the newspaper or magazines or using labels from food packaging. Make separate pages or books for breads and cereals, dairy products, meats and meat substitutes, fruits, and vegetables.

Basic Concepts About Dental Care

- Brushing our teeth after every meal keeps them strong and healthy.

- The dentist is a special kind of doctor who helps us take care of our teeth.

Suggested activities for teaching dental care

Activity: No Cavity Collage

Objective: To teach children oral hygiene

Procedure: Draw a smiling face on one piece of tag board and a sad face on another. Ask children to bring in magazine pictures or wrappers that represent food that is good for your teeth and food that is not good for your teeth. Let the children paste things that are good for your teeth (e.g. picture of tangerine, a box top from a low-sugar cereal) on the happy face tagboard, and things that are bad for you on the sad face. This might include a candy wrapper, a box top from a highly sugared cereal, a stick of gum, or the wrapper from a sweetened dried fruit snack.

Objective 5: To recognize indicators of abuse and/or neglect and follow the reporting policy mandated by your state

Child abuse/neglect is a national problem. One out of every six persons is abused. Maltreatment, according to long-term studies, is associated with dropping out of school, violent crime, and unemployment. There is also evidence that children who have been abused are at risk for becoming child abusers when they become parents. Every childcare provider is obliged by law to report suspected abuse. If you suspect that a child in your center has been abused, follow the procedures for report by your center. If you are a family childcare provider, report directly to the abuse hotline in your state. Familiarize yourself with the following child maltreatment chart.

Type of Abuse or Neglect	Physical Indicators	Behavioral Indicators
Physical Abuse	Unexplained bruises, welts, burns, fractures, lacerations, and abrasions	Afraid of adults Afraid of parents and/or to go home Anxious about routine activities like sleeping, eating, and toileting Can be either aggressive or withdrawn
Emotional Abuse	Failure-to-thrive Lags behind other children in physical development Developmental delays	Habit disorders (sucking, biting, rocking) Withdrawn or aggressive Poor per relations
Sexual Abuse	Difficulty in walking or sitting Bloody underclothes, bruises or bleeding in genitalia, vaginal, or rectal areas Venereal disease or pregnancy (with teens) Wears clothing and/or make-up beyond their years	Unwilling to take off clothing Unusual sexual behavior or knowledge of sexual behavior beyond what children their age should know Poor peer and adult relations
Neglect	Poor hygiene Inappropriate dress Medical needs are not met Educational needs are not met Lack of supervision Abandonment Always hungry	Begging, stealing food, or taking food from the trash Asks to take food home Arrives early and is picked up late Constant fatigue or falls asleep in class Withdrawn

Objective 6: To keep one's self healthy, and to model appropriate wellness behavior for children and their parents

Miss It's-My-Business was called into the office by the director of the center.

Director: "I heard that you had a great meeting last night with your parent volunteer group."

Miss It's-My-Business: "They're a fabulous group of parents and we made some really exciting plans."

Director: "There is just one thing that concerns me. One of the parents said that when you went out for coffee after the meeting, you were smoking non-stop and..."

Miss It's-My-Business (interrupting): "I never smoke at school and I don't appreciate your telling me what I should do after school. If I want to ruin my health, it's my health and I'll do what I please."

Director: "I wasn't trying to interfere with what you do in your spare time. It's just that I would like to see you take better care of yourself. Remember, last year you had three attacks of bronchitis."

Although Miss It's-My-Business was miffed when the director complained about her smoking, it is important for all child caregivers to maintain their own health.

Most of us are fully aware of how to take care of our health.

- Eat nutritious meals.

- Maintain the weight level recommended for our height and body build.

- Get annual physicals and beneficial dental check-ups.

- Get prenatal care in the first trimester of pregnancy.

- Get enough rest and exercise and avoid getting over-stressed.

- Abstain from smoking, abusing alcohol, and taking illegal drugs.

- Make sure our immunizations are up to date. Child care workers in most states are required to provide evidence of negative TB tests or chest X-rays in addition to immunizations. We should also ask our health provider if an annual flu shot is advisable.

Unfortunately, the easy part is knowing how to stay healthy. The hard part is making a commitment to wellness, and living up to that commitment.

One way to convert our good intentions of maintaining a healthy lifestyle into commitment is to recognize the benefits that maintaining desirable health practices provides.

- When we feel well, we are happier, more energetic, and are better at coping with minor problems.

- If we practice what we preach, we are good models for children and parents. When Miss It's-My-Business smoked in a coffeehouse with parents from her center, she was sending a message that it is okay for adults to smoke when they are not in the child care facility.

- When we are committed to wellness, we are likely to have a better attendance record at work. If we ever want to change jobs or advance our careers, letters of recommendation that include a good record of attendance are bound to be helpful.

- Staying healthy is cost-effective. The cost of medial care continues to rise, so, in a very literal sense, it pays to stay healthy.

You should have health insurance. If you are an independent provider or if your center does not offer it, investigate state programs. Your local child care professional organization, union, or resource and referral agency may be able to help you track down resources.

Unfortunately, the easy part is knowing how to stay healthy. The hard part is making a commitment to wellness, and living up to that commitment.

Greenman, J. & Stonehouse, A. (1996). *Prime times: A handbook for excellence in Infant and toddler programs.* St. Paul, MN: Redleaf Press.

Kendrick, A.S., Kaufmann, D.B., & Stetson, C. (2000). *Winning ways to learn: 600 great ideas for children.* NY: Goddard Press.

Meisels, S.J., Marsden, D.B., & Stetson, C. (2000). *Winning ways to learn: 600 great ideas for children.* NY: Goddard Press.

Snow, C.W. (1998). *Infant development.* Upper Saddle River, NJ: Prentice Hall.

Chapter 5:
Learning Environments

Overview

A learning environment for preschool children is a place that is conducive to learning and is appropriate for the developmental level and learning characteristics of the children.

Rationale

The arrangement a classroom or family child care setting sets the tone for learning. The selection and set-up of play materials, the pictures on the walls, even the way the room is divided — all support beliefs about what and how children should learn. For example, puzzles and sorting toys on low shelves invite children to learn mathematical concepts through play. A pretend play area that can become a fire station, circus tent, grocery store, or café, invites children to learn about their world by playing together. Desks set in rows, with materials kept on high shelves, suggest that learning is serious business that should be controlled by the teacher.

Preschoolers need environments that are safe and welcoming, intriguing but not overwhelming. In a well-planned environment, babies will spend less time crying and more time exploring. Older children will spend less time wandering, fidgeting, or fighting and more time asking questions, working together, and mastering new skills.

Objectives

1. To set up an environment for infants that takes into account the behavioral characteristics and interests of infants at different stages

2. To set up an environment that takes into account the behavioral characteristics and interests of younger toddlers

3. To set up an environment that takes into account the behavioral characteristics and interests of older toddlers

4. To organize and equip preschool classrooms to promote different kinds of play and learning experiences and to reflect the interests, ability levels, and family backgrounds of the children

5. To organize and equip a learning environment for a multi-age or family childcare setting that includes children birth through five

6. To develop well-balanced daily schedules

7. To set up an outdoor play and learning environment

8. To ensure that the environment works for adults as well as for children

The chair of the parent advisory board from The Key to Growth Child Care Center arrived in the director's office full of excitement. "I just received the most wonderful news," the chair reported, "The Tot Toy Factory has agreed to give us the most fabulous contribution. They are giving us their complete display of over-sized cardboard Sesame Street characters. This place will look great with a giant muppet in every classroom!" The director of the center was in a quandary. On the one hand, she wanted to be gracious and accept this gift with enthusiasm. On the other hand, she wasn't so sure that her teachers would welcome the giant muppets. They were too big to fit into the classrooms without rearranging the learning centers. Thinking quickly, she came up with a perfect solution. "I am so appreciative of all that you have done for this center. You are always thinking of us. Instead of putting one muppet in each classroom, why don't we line them all up on the way out to the playground? They'll be a real conversation piece for the children."

The director didn't want to give up either her belief in the importance of parent participation or her belief in setting up an environment that expressed the philosophy of active learning that was so important to her and to her teachers. Fortunately, she found a quick solution that was consistent with both.

The Learning Environment for Infants

Objective 1: To set up an environment for infants that takes into account the behavioral characteristics and interests of infants at different stages

Ms. Shipshape had the infant room just the way she liked it. The cribs were lined up in a row on one side. The rattles were in a box that she could reach without stooping. The floor was clear. The walls were gleaming white. There wasn't a pillow in sight. Everything was disinfected.

"This is no place for a baby," said Mrs. Earthmother when she came to visit. "It's too sterile!"

Ms. Shipshape and Mrs. Earthmother each have a point. Babies do need an environment that is easy to keep sanitary. They also need to be in a space that is cozy, that looks and feels "like home," and that provides them with interesting things to look at and inviting places to explore.

Developmental Picture

The infant 0-8 months:
- Is limited in mobility
- Is attracted to interesting sights, sounds, and objects, and enjoys watching people
- Has individual particular needs for sleeping and eating
- Is likely to be startled or overstimulated by sudden noises or a room that is noisy, very bright, or filled with activity
- May "tune out," fuss, fall asleep, or be unable to sleep when over-stimulated
- May fuss or cry when bored
- Needs to spend some play time on his stomach on a firm surface so he can learn to roll over, crawl, and get into a sitting position

The caregiver:
- Provides a variety of perspectives by moving the infant about
- Brings experiences to the infant to look at, listen to, and touch
- Recognizes that infants have different levels of tolerance in terms of sound and visual stimulation and reads each child's cues
- Separates young infants from more active playmates
- Provides a quiet sleeping area
- Follows the infant's feeding and sleeping schedule, moving towards a regular rhythm

The infant 8-14 months:
- Is creeping, cruising, learning to walk and may be practicing walking and climbing skills
- Has favorite toys, and is interested in selecting her own toys
- Enjoys emptying and filling and holding soft cuddly things
- Is interested in exploring new spaces
- Can suddenly become overtired and/or overstimulated

The caregiver:
- Provides space and equipment for active movement indoors and out
- Divides the space so that infants can play in small groups
- Keeps toys on low sturdy shelves within reach
- Stores small items in see-through boxes
- Creates interesting "obstacle courses" for babies who are learning to crawl, cruise, walk, and climb
- Provides a reliable rhythm that meets babies' needs for frequent eating and resting

Basic Considerations for Setting up an Infant Room

- *Infants spend much of the day sleeping;* therefore the infant room should have a sleeping room or area with a crib for every child.

- *During their periods of wakefulness, infants learn best from their interactions with adults;* therefore the infant room should have well-equipped areas for changing and feeding that encourage adult-infant interaction.

- *During their wakeful periods, infants learn from playing with a variety of toys;* therefore teachers should be sure that every infant, when awake, has age appropriate toys to play with.

- *Infants as young as six months old enjoy interaction with other infants;* therefore the infant room should have a safe and easily cleaned area where two or three infants can play together.

- *The needs and schedules for an infant may change on a daily basis;* therefore it is important for every infant room to have a bulletin board where emergency telephone numbers, schedules, and instructions from parents are posted.

- *Infants are vulnerable to contagious illnesses and to over-stimulation;* therefore, if you have more than 8-10 children in a room, divide the room into two or more areas so that you never have more than ten bodies in a "room" together.

Equipping the Infant Room

Sleeping Area

An infant room must have one crib for every infant, but finding room for cribs can be a challenge. Some people solve the problem by putting the cribs on wheels and moving them aside when they are not in use. Others use the space under a crib for storage.

When in use, cribs should be at least eighteen inches apart and should be arranged so that the supervisor has full view of every infant. See-through cribs let caregivers look in and babies look out.

Generally, infants should have a separate area for sleeping, where the lights and noise level can be kept low. When a separate space is not available, you can use room dividers to create a quiet corner. A rocking chair in the sleeping area is useful for comforting fussy babies.

Changing Area

The changing table should be waist high with a safety strap, a washable surface, and at least a two-inch lip to prevent a baby from rolling off. Changing supplies, hot and cold running water, and a covered trash container should be in easy reach. A non-breakable mirror behind the changing table is fun for babies.

The changing table needs to be set up with the caregiver in mind. Items should be easy to reach and well-organized, to minimize the chance of skipping steps in proper diapering and hand-washing procedures.

Feeding Areas

The infant room should include places to warm bottles and to sit comfortably while bottle-feeding a baby. A quiet corner with a rocking chair is ideal. There should also be a comfortable, private space for nursing mothers.

Babies between six and twelve months are also eating solid food and may enjoy having meal times "at the table," especially if this is what they are used to at home. You can use high chairs, table-height feeding-chairs, or seats that attach to a regular table. Make sure they have seatbelts that can restrain a baby who suddenly learns to stand, and that they are sturdy enough so that they can't be tipped by a cruising toddler.

Bouncy Chairs and Swings

While bouncy chairs and swings give children the opportunity of seeing the world from a sitting position, they need to be selected carefully and used with caution. Bouncy chairs and swings should have safety belts, and should not be placed in doorways, where they would block emergency access. Confining babies in chairs or swings for too long a period deprives them of opportunities to learn new motor skills like rolling over, sitting, and crawling. Walkers with wheels should never be used in an early childhood setting — there is too much danger of colliding with another child, rolling over someone's fingers, getting tipped, or getting stuck.

Storage areas for infant supplies

Infants come with lots of supplies. You'll need places to store clean diapers, extra clothes, food, and perhaps even car seats for each child.

Play Areas

An infant room should have safe, easily cleaned areas where infants can play together. Low shelves, foam dividers, couches, a play yard or corral, and an empty wading pool can all be used to define intimate spaces or provide support for pulling up and cruising. Mirrors, busy-boxes, and laminated pictures can be mounted at different heights to intrigue babies who are learning to sit, crawl, stand, and walk.

Peep holes, hiding places (visible to an adult), crawling tunnels, large vinyl blocks, low windows, and different colors and textures on the floor help make spaces interesting for babies who are just learning to get around.

Put a sheet on the carpeted play area so that you can wash it daily.

Learning Materials

Shelf Toys

No infant should be left during wakeful period without access to age appropriate toys. Keep some of the toys where babies can get them themselves — on low shelves, in play areas and crawl spaces, or mounted on the wall or on the back of a shelf unit.

Here are some toys that are appropriate for babies in the following age groups:

- **Three to Six Months:** Rattles, soft squeak toys, cradle gyms, musical toys, washable dolls, or animals

- **Six to Nine Months:** Toy telephones, roly-poly toys, pop-up toys, colorful wheel toys, unbreakable mirrors, washable cuddle toys

- **Nine to Twelve Months:** Busy boards, fill and dump toys, rolling toys, large balls, soft blocks, cloth or cardboard blocks

Crib Toys

Although the amount of awake time that infants spend in their cribs should be minimized, age appropriate toys should be placed in or over every crib. Age appropriate crib toys include:

- **Three Months and Under:** Crib mobiles that attach to the side of the crib or hang from the ceiling, wind chimes, musical mobiles and see-through crib bumpers

- **Four to Seven Months:** Cradle gyms, see-through rattles, clutch balls, and teething rings

- **Eight to Twelve Months:** Busy-boxes, squeak toys, rattles, soft cloth dolls, clutch balls, pop-up toys, and mirror toys

Sensory Bin

Infants enjoy a variety of sensory experiences such as splashing water, finger painting with pudding, or rubbing their hands in cornstarch. A large dishpan is ideal for this kind of play. You can put it and the babies into an empty plastic wading pool to help contain the mess

Music Area

A cassette recorder, CD player, or record player is a must in an infant play area. "Easy listening" music, lullabies, nursery rhymes, and classical music provide satisfying listening experiences for infants and their caregivers. You might also encourage parents to record and share the songs or hums that they use with their babies.

Arranging the Infant Room

The way an infant room is arranged depends on how large the room is, how many infants there are, how many staff members are in the room at any one time, the age and mobility of the infants, and whether the room is single purpose (sleeping, eating, or playing) or multipurpose. Looking at the room with a "baby's eye view," you may see things you want to change as the babies develop new capabilities and interests. In every situation, however, there are some prime considerations for setting up an infant environment.

Arrange the room or rooms so that:

- There is a separation between awake and sleeping babies.

- Changing tables and feeding areas can be accessed easily from both the sleeping and the play areas.

- There is easy access to running water, refrigeration, covered waste disposal cans, and some type of food warmer.

- There is an adult "look out spot" with full visibility.

- The crib area has carpeted flooring for quiet and easy clean-up.

- The play area is enclosed and has a soft but washable surface.

- Toys and books are arranged on shelves with like toys grouped together.

- The CD, cassette, or record player is in easy reach for adults but out of reach of children.

- There is a two-foot wide walkway at all exits. Exits should be kept clear in accordance with fire safety laws.

- It works for the babies and for you.

Although the amount of awake time that infants spend in their cribs should be minimized, age appropriate toys should be placed in or over every crib.

The Learning Environment for Young Toddlers

Objective 2: To set up an environment for young toddlers that takes into account the behavioral characteristics and interests of young toddlers

Some Basic Guidelines for Setting up a Young Toddler Room

- *One to two-year olds spend long stretches of time in active play;* therefore, cots can be stacked, except during naptime, and the same room can be used for sleep and play.

- *The young toddler is developing her gross motor skills and needs opportunities to practice running, climbing, throwing, pushing, pulling, and carrying things around;* therefore the one to two-year old classroom should provide indoor slides, indoor climbing structures, riding toys, and rocking boats.

- *The young toddler needs different kinds of spaces — wide open spaces that let him explore space and small cozy places that make him feel comfortable and secure;* therefore create both a wide open space and cozy, crawl-in spaces such as playhouses, cartons, or corners.

- *Young toddlers are just learning to say "It's mine" and for the most part have not learned about sharing and cannot understand why some things, like toys, have to be shared while other things, like lunch and shoes, cannot be shared;* therefore make sure that most of the toys and equipment in the classroom are conducive to group play. Very attractive one-of-a-kind toys can initiate power struggles.

- *Young toddlers are delighted with rhythm, music, pictures, and books;* therefore make sure that your classroom has a tape player, a collection of tapes, attractive pictures at the child's level, and a library corner with indestructible books. A piano or a guitar and a teacher who can play it are a special asset.

- *Young toddlers tend to be exuberant and excitable and can make a shambles of a room in no time flat;* therefore the task of cleaning up should be simplified. Limit the numbers of small, loose toys that are kept within reach of children. Provide attractive containers for toys that make cleaning up fun. A carton "cage" or Noah's ark can be used as a container for toy animals. A corner of the classroom with lines drawn on the floor or marked on the carpet can be a parking lot for wheel toys. Colorful plastic laundry baskets make great storage containers for balls and beanbags.

- *Young toddlers are active and can be very noisy,* therefore, with the exception of areas that are used for eating, art, and water play, the one to two-year old room should be carpeted. Also, if it is possible, use acoustic tiles on the ceiling to absorb sound.

- *Young toddlers learn through active exploration;* therefore provide areas in the classroom where toddlers can finger paint, play with water and clay, experience different textures, and create different sounds. Create a texture wall where the children can feel different surfaces (hard, soft, smooth, rough, furry, slippery, bumpy) or a sound wall where the children can ring a bell, toot a horn, squeak a rubber animal, or beat a drum.

- *Young toddlers are creatures of habit and are disturbed by too many changes in their environment;* therefore once you have created an attractive and orderly classroom, change the basic layout as little as possible. One to two-year olds gain a sense of security by finding everything in its place. It is especially important for one to two-year olds to have their own special private space (a cubby or a shelf) that is never changed or disturbed.

Equipping a Young Toddler Room

Tables and Chairs

One to two-year olds enjoy sitting at tables and chairs, not only for eating, but also for sensory experiences, puzzle play, and art activities.

Specifications: Tables should be toddler size (16 to 18 inches high) with enough space for each child in the room. Trapezoid tables are desirable because they can be rearranged in interesting ways.

Looking at the room with a "baby's eye view" you may see things you want to change as the babies develop new capabilities and interests.

High Chairs

By one and a half, most children can eat comfortably at a low table and chair combination. For younger children who are still learning to feed themselves, however, it is best to have high chairs or table-height feeding chairs.

Specifications: A good rule of thumb is to have one high chair for every three children under the age of 18 months, but space limitations and individual preferences should also be considered.

Arranging the Young Toddler Room

The young toddler room combines some of the features of the infant room with some of the features of the older toddler room. Like infants, young toddlers need a place to sleep, place to eat, a place for diaper changing, and a place to play.

Like older toddlers, younger toddlers need larger places for active play, a place for imaginative play, a quiet place for reading a book, playing with manipulatives, or playing alone or with a friend, and a place for sensory play.

Before you can decide where to put the different areas in your room, you first need to look at the givens in your room.

- Windows provide light and views, but also take up wall space. You may want to put tables for eating and art activities in front of the windows, saving your walls for other activities.

- Doors need to be kept clear as emergency exits. Closet doors that open out create a dead space in the room.

- Carpeted areas are best for active play and circle time activities and for other activities where children sit on the floor. Tiled areas provide easy clean-up for feeding, sensory play, and art activities.

- Electrical outlets determine where you will put the CD player, cassette tape player or record player, bottle warmer, refrigerator, and microwave oven.

- Corners are ideal for quiet play.

- Built in furnishings determine your storage spaces. Since you want to limit the amount of toys in the room at the same time, you will need plenty of storage for toys, art materials, and other equipment. Remember to provide storage for your personal belongings, as well as for the children's.

- Use high wall space for a parent information board and for posting emergency plans and phone numbers. Use child level wall space for sound and texture boards, mirrors, photos of the children and their families, a flannel board, and for displaying the children's creations.

Next, make a rough diagram that indicates the placement of major furnishings and equipment taking into account all of these fixed features.

Setting up and Equipping Activity Centers

Your room should include these basic areas:

Greeting Area

The greeting area should include a place where children can store their personal belongings such as a cubbie. Parent boards are most visible in this area, as are teacher boards.

Eating, Sensory Play, and Creative Art Area

This area will include toddler-sized tables and chairs, high chairs if needed, storage for art and craft supplies, and at least one chair that you can sit in comfortably. Ideally, the eating area should also include a small refrigerator, a microwave oven, running water with disposable paper towels, and a covered garbage can.

Toileting/Diapering Area

Most children under two are still in diapers so you should include a changing table, a diaper bin, and a storage unit for clean diapers and supplies. Access to hot and cold running water is a must. You will also need potty chairs if you do not have access to small toilets for those children who are ready to give up diapers.

Pretend Play Area

Early pretending is very simple, with a strong imitative quality. Children replay experiences that are most familiar such as driving, sleeping, cooking, and eating. A doll sized stove, sink, table, high chair, and crib encourage early pretending. Make sure, too, that there is a place for doll tea set, cooking utensils, play food, and, of course, ethnically appropriate dolls. A nice addition to the pretend area is an unbreakable mirror with dress up jewelry, ties, scarves, purses, carry-alls, and a "steering wheel" chair.

Active Play Area

Climbing Structures: Because young toddlers spend much of their day practicing their motor skills, the choice of climbing structures is critical. The size and number of climbing structures that are placed in the room depend on several factors:

- How much space you have
- How many children are using the space
- How well-equipped your playground is
- How much outdoor time the weather permits

Desirable climbing structures include:

- **Slides:** A slide is an important piece of basic equipment. A good indoor slide has a crawl space underneath and is designed so that the stairs are easy to mount.

- **Rocking Boat:** A rocking boat that converts to a staircase is a particularly desirable structure. It provides opportunities to practice different motor skills and at the same time encourages cooperative play.

- **Special Structures:** Ramps, wedges, tunnels, and platforms can provide further practice in motor skills. Again, it is important to remember that the young toddler needs room to move around. A desirable climbing structure that takes up too much space is really not desirable.

Blocks: Blocks can be either the large cardboard bricks, large nesting blocks, or vinyl covered shapes.

Push/Ride-on Toys: Young toddlers are also on the move. Cars and trucks that can be ridden, pushed, and pulled keeps young toddlers busy.

Music: Every young toddler room should include a cassette tape recorder, CD player, or record player. This should be placed on a relatively high shelf along with the tapes, CDs, or records and, if the equipment is not battery operated, an electric outlet. One to two years olds should not have access to this equipment. Rhythm instruments also require a storage bin out of reach of the children so that their use is controlled.

Quiet Play Areas

Cuddle-up structures: Young toddlers need closed, protected, quiet space just as much as they need space to move around in. Cushions wedged in a corner, a beanbag chair, and an empty television cabinet lined with carpet are some ideas for private space.

Reading Corner: Cuddle-up spaces can also double as reading corners. Place cuddly stuffed animals in the cuddle-up area and a small book display rack within easy reach.

The Learning Environment for Older Toddlers

Objective 3: To set up an environment that takes into account the behavioral characteristics and interests of older toddlers

*M*r. Stickler had just read a book on setting up a toddler environment. He loved their suggestions on open space and interest centers and decided to set up his room exactly like the diagram in the book. When he completed the task, he asked the director to come in and admire it.*

The director was at loss for words. She congratulated him on his hard work and told him the room looked great, but there was one small problem. She didn't see the cots.

Mr. Stickler explained that he put the cots in the empty room across the hall. "I arranged the room exactly like the diagram in the book you lent me," he told her proudly. "I didn't have room for everything, so I decided I would just put the cots down the hall and bring them back for naptime."

"You need to put the cots back in the classroom," the director explained gently. *"Unfortunately, our toddler room isn't nearly as large as the one in the book, and you can't simply follow a diagram. Try rearranging the room, leaving space for the cots."*

As you read about the suggested layout for a toddler room, you will undoubtedly have the same problems as Mr. Stickler. If you do not have enough room to follow all of our recommendations, you will have to make compromises. But try not to be a Mr. Stickler. Keep the essential furnishings in the room and work around them.

Characteristics and Interests of Older Toddlers

- *Older toddlers are practicing emerging motor skills and enjoy running, jumping, twirling, and marching to music;* therefore the classroom needs open spaces where children engage in active circle time activities.

- *Older toddlers are interested in exploring different kinds of spaces;* therefore the classroom should include a variety of different space experiences such as a tunnel, a pit, a platform, a bridge, a two-level townhouse, and/or an indoor climbing structure.

- *Older toddlers enjoy quiet cozy spaces;* therefore the classroom should include a comfortable hideaway spot. It may be a corner with cushions and bolsters, a carton to crawl into, a playhouse, or a hideaway reading corner.

- *Older toddlers are beginning to learn about sharing and turn-taking;* therefore the classroom should include some toys for side-by-side play and some toys like blocks and wagons that encourage cooperation.

- *Older toddlers enjoy constructive play;* therefore the classroom should have a carpeted block area where children have easy access to unit and cardboard blocks.

- *Older toddlers are interested in creating with different kinds of materials;* therefore the classroom should have access to fluid and pliable materials like, water, sand, easel paint, clay, and crayons.

- *Older toddlers are becoming more sophisticated in their pretend play;* therefore the classroom should contain play structures, props, and dress-up material for maxi-pretending and small representational objects, like toy animals, vehicles, and dolls for mini-pretending.

- *Older toddlers are experiencing a rapid growth in language skills;* therefore the classroom should be well stocked with culturally and thematically appropriate picture books, audiotapes, prints, and photos that encourage receptive and expressive language.

Equipping the Older Toddler Room

Tables and chairs

Older toddlers enjoy sitting at tables for snacks, mealtime, arts and craft activities, and manipulative play.

Specifications

- *Size:* Tables for older toddlers should be approximately eighteen inches high; chairs should fit under the tables, allowing enough space for leg room.

- *Number:* Because older toddlers enjoy meal or snack times together, it is important to have a chair and room at a table for every child.

- *Shape:* The shape and size of the tables depends on how the classroom is arranged. If the same tables are used for snack time, art, and manipulative activities, it is important to have small tables that can be moved. Rectangular or trapezoidal tables work better than round ones for arts and crafts, and can be put together and taken apart in different configurations.

Structures

Toddlers love to climb and explore, both alone and together. A loft with a ladder serves several purposes. It challenges toddlers to climb up, gives them a bird's eye view, and provides spaces above and below where two or three friends can have private playtime. At the same time, it presents endless possibilities for pretend play. Add a blanket — it becomes a tent for camping or for a circus performance. Add a steering wheel — it's a car, a truck, an airplane, a boat, or a rocket ship.

Make sure the loft is sturdy enough and the railings high enough to support jumping toddlers.

Shelves and Room Dividers

Because older toddlers enjoy a room that is organized into play centers, it is important to have enough shelving, book racks, and room dividers to section off the classroom.

Materials and Toys

Pretend Play Props and Equipment

The amount and type of pretend play equipment depends both on budget constraints and on the size of the classroom. A well-equipped older toddler classroom will include six types of pretend play equipment:

- Equipment for kitchen play, including a stove, refrigerator, sink, high chair, mop or broom, and table and chairs

- Equipment for store or puppet play including a puppet stage which converts into a grocery store, post office, or bank

- Equipment for doll play including a crib, carriage, blanket, and a dresser or box with doll clothes

- Dress-up play equipment including a mirror and appropriate storage for costumes, shoes, and jewelry

- Equipment for "driver" play, such as a shopping cart or doll carriage, a riding toy or steering wheel, chairs that can be lined up to make a train, and a large box or laundry basket the children can climb into and use as a boat, racing car, or jeep.

- An assortment of miniature play sets such as a farm, zoo, restaurant, doll house, garage, train, and fire station, with the accompanying props and miniature characters

The Learning Environment for Preschool Aged Children

Objective 4: To organize and equip preschool classrooms to promote different kinds of play and learning experiences and to reflect the interests, ability levels, and family backgrounds of the children

Two preschool teachers from different schools were having dinner together. Miss Free Thinker, who worked in the Creative Workshop Preschool, began the conversation.

Miss Free Thinker: "Boy, am I glad it's Friday. School begins on Monday and I spent most of the week moving furniture and arranging the shelves. I do feel it was worth it. I needed to add the pretend play area and the Science Discovery area. Now the room looks great."

Miss Discontent: "Well, you know I took a job at the College Prep Preschool and we never have to change the room arrangement. The teacher sits at the desk in front of the room and children sit at tables, two children per table, facing the teacher's desk."

Miss Free Thinker: "Do you like that arrangement?"

Miss Discontent: "Personally, I hate it, but it goes along with the philosophy of the school. The director believes that the best way to get children ready for success in school is to teach them academics and that you arrange the room like an elementary classroom. It sets the right tone."

Miss Free Thinker: "Do you agree?"

Miss Discontent: "I told you, I hate it, but that's the way the director wants it, and the parents are all right there behind her. So, as long as I stay in the school, I am not going to rock the boat."

We cannot argue with Miss Discontent. If she is planning to keep her position as a teacher in the College Prep Preschool, she is obligated to endorse its philosophy and to set up her classroom like a traditional 2nd grade.

All About Childcare and Early Education is built on the philosophy that children are active learners who do best in environments that encourages exploration, imagination, and creativity. The suggestions for organizing learning environment provided in this chapter are a reflection of this philosophy.

Characteristics and Interests of Preschool Children

Just as an infant and toddler classroom is designed to meet the special needs of the very young child, a preschool classroom must take into account the social, emotional, and intellectual characteristics of the three, four, and five year olds and the cultural backgrounds of children in the class.

- *The preschool child appreciates a beautiful classroom;* therefore the classroom should be inviting and attractive. If there is a choice, the walls should be painted in a neutral or light pastel color, with pictures and materials providing the color. Shelves are critical. Even the best-equipped classrooms are often short of shelf space. Shelves serve the double function of dividing space into discrete areas and providing a place where toys and learning materials are accessible to children.

- *The preschool child enjoys an orderly classroom;* therefore materials should be arranged and coded so that everything in the classroom has its appropriate place. An ideal plan is to color code or picture code the shelves and materials so that it is easy to remember where everything belongs.

- *The preschool child needs a variety of social experiences with large groups, small groups, and individually;* therefore the classroom should provide a variety of spaces for each. These may include:

  - Large group space: A circle on the carpet, individual mats that can be placed in a circle on a carpet, and round or trapezoid tables facilitate large group interaction.

  - Small group space: Interesting areas where the space is defined by lofts or corner enclosures encourage children to interact in small groups.

  - Individual space: Private, all by myself time can be provided by a reading corner with a rocking chair or beanbag chair, a telephone booth structure, or even a large carton with a fuzzy rug on the bottom.

- *The preschool child likes to feel at home.* The careful choice of family photos on the wall, materials such as play foods that are familiar to her, dress up clothes that resemble the clothes that the adults she knows are likely to wear, dolls that look like the children in the classroom, and rhythm instruments that are used in the ceremonies she attends make a child feel that the classroom is an extension of her home and a part of her neighborhood.

- *Preschool children need help in learning to be considerate of each other;* therefore a classroom should be arranged to make it easy for children to be considerate.

  ▲ Noisy areas — music, block play, and pretend play — should be separated from quiet areas — library corner or problem solving areas.

  ▲ Bookshelves should be used to control the traffic flow so that children won't upset each other's work.

- *Preschool children are ready to make activity selections;* therefore whether a preschool classroom is large or small, it is important for it to be organized into learning or interest centers. Both the number and the type of interest centers depend on the size and configuration of the classroom, the objectives of the curriculum, the staffing pattern, and the age and characteristics of the children.

- *Preschool children enjoy working at tables;* therefore tables and chairs should be placed in the art and snack area and in some of the work areas. Children may enjoy using tables for practicing writing, putting puzzles together, setting up scenes with miniature figures, and playing math or language games.

- *The preschool child needs opportunities to pretend;* therefore every preschool classroom should provide spaces and the equipment for imaginative play. Housekeeping equipment, a dress-up corner, a mirror, a telephone, dolls, and dishes are basic requirements. Other items can be added to reflect the children's interests, home cultures, and favorite stories, and the themes that the teacher has introduced.

- *A preschool child must have experience with music and art;* therefore the classroom should be equipped with a CD, tape, or record player; a variety of music including marches, folk songs, and nursery rhymes; simple musical instruments; and a place where children can sit or march in a circle. For art, there should be tables and chairs, a sink, a non-carpeted floor area, and plenty of eye-level wall space where the children's work is attractively displayed. Easels, drying racks, and magic marker boards are desirable.

- *Preschool children need opportunities to play with blocks and to work with a variety of construction toys;* therefore every preschool classroom should have a block area where children can learn to construct. Block play helps children develop their imagination and creativity and, at the same time, teaches mathematical and spatial concepts. Miniature figures, toy animals, cars and trucks, and small balls encourage children to build pretend worlds and raceways.

- *Preschool children are developing their language and communication skills;* therefore a preschool classroom should provide space and materials that encourage language development. Picture books, display counters, eye level wall treatments, puppet stages, elevated platforms, mirrors, cameras, and tape recorders can all be used to encourage language development.

- *Preschool children are ready and eager to learn new concepts;* therefore a preschool classroom should include spaces and materials for manipulative play, problem solving, and science exploration. The traditional preschool science and discovery corner should not be simply a display area, but should provide opportunities for hands-on experiences. It should include:

  ▲ Science and Discovery — pets (check with health department), plants, sink and float activities, magnet challenges, shells and rocks that can be classified, a scale, prisms, magnifying glasses, color paddles and a sand table.

  ▲ Manipulative Play and Problem Solving — a variety of materials that encourage sorting, ordering, number skill development, and pattern making, such as number puzzles, peg boards, table blocks, picture puzzles, counting games, stacking toys, color and shape games, sequencing boards, beads, and sewing cards.

Arranging the Preschool Classroom

The Big Picture

In order to meet the different needs of the preschool child, it is important to take a very broad look at the way the space is utilized. Specifically, we need to consider three facets:

- How can we use space to control group size?
- How can we separate noisy and quiet spaces?
- How can we control traffic flow?

Using Space to Control Group Size

We have said that children need opportunities to spend time in large groups, in small groups, and by themselves. A carefully engineered classroom provides areas that invite different size groups. A circle in the middle of the floor is an invitation to form a large group. A table for two or three, an interest area set off by bookshelves, a loft, or a playhouse invites children to cluster in small groups. "All by myself" places can be created by a book corner with a rocking chair, a small carton "house", or a beanbag chair that faces the wall.

Separating Noisy and Quiet Areas

In a well-designed classroom there is a separation of noisy and quiet activities. Activities like reading, problem-solving, and language skills that require concentration are on one side of the classroom. Noisy activities like block building, climbing, and music are placed on the other side. Art and imaginative play, which are relatively quiet activities that do not require excessive concentration, can serve as buffers.

Controlling Traffic Flow

In a toddler classroom, where children are not very good at negotiating corners, we are careful about not placing furniture in a place where toddlers may be running. With older children, we do just the reverse. We use the placement of furniture to discourage follow the leader games and encourage the formation of small groups. We can also use the placement of furniture to discourage children from interfering with each other. A block area that is arranged as an interest area, with only one space for exiting and entering, is a safe place to build a structure.

Other factors to think about in arranging a three to five year old classroom are:

- What kind of floor covering to use

- What kind of work and play surfaces work best

- How to make the best use of wall space

- What to use as interest center dividers

Floor Covering

Floor covering is an important consideration in designing a preschool setting. A low pile carpet is great for most of the classroom, but a linoleum type floor covering is best for the "messy activity" areas. The sink area, snack area, art corner, and science and discovery area should be set over linoleum or similar floor covering for quick, easy clean up. Smaller pieces of carpet can be used to define specific playing areas, where a child can take an activity and be on his own private "island." (Alternatively, if the entire floor is carpeted, vinyl remnants can be placed in messy areas.)

Work & Play Surfaces

Thought should be given to open space areas (versus tables) near display units. Some activities work better at tables then on the floor and vice-versa. Table work is often approached more seriously by children and should be encouraged with activities requiring concentration and problem solving. To direct traffic to table or floor space, simply place a table close to shelves displaying table work activities and leave open floor space near other activities. Don't be too concerned about separating table from floor activities. Children will often make these distinctions according to their own set of rules.

Setting up Interest Centers

An interest center is a defined classroom area that can accommodate three to six children. Some interest centers, like a block area or art table, remain the same throughout the year. Others, like a "firehouse," puppet stage, or "science museum," may change with the curriculum units and the children's interests. Some, such as a woodworking center or cooking center, may be open only when you have extra help.

The traditional preschool science and discovery corner should not be simply a display area, but should provide opportunities for hands-on experiences.

Here are some interest centers that work well in most preschool classrooms. You, the children, and their families will certainly add others.

Imaginative Play Center

Type of Space: Semi-enclosed, carpeted, shelving for play materials, place for mirror, clothes rack and play structure (2-story house).

Pretend Play Area

Type of Play	Benefits	Equipment and Materials
Doll Play	• Consolidating experiences • Encourages care and empathy	Multicultural dolls, doll bed, carriage, high chair, dresser, blanket, clothes, bath, diaper set, feeding set, bibs, changing table, toilet
Kitchen Play	• Encourages cooperative play • Provides practice in playing a grownup role • Encourages helping behavior	Telephone, stoves, sink, refrigerator, small table and chairs, dishes, silverware, pots and pans, table cloth, placemats, pot holders, oven mit, baking utensils, toaster
Cleaning & Housekeeping	• Encourages helping behavior • Provides practice in playing a grownup role • Develops new skills	Brooms, mops, dustpan, carpet-sweeper, scrub brush, feather duster
Store	• Creates feeling of power • Invites cooperative play • Develops number skills	Cash register, balance scale, paper bags, play money, stamps, empty cans, boxes, play food
Doctor/Nurse	• Helps children cope with fears • Gives children feelings of power • Encourages cooperation	Stethoscope, thermometer, throat sticks, Band-Aid box, sling, diploma, eye chart, blood pressure cuff, flashlight, doctor and nurse uniforms, empty medicine bottles, spoons, prescription pad, pencil, bag, syringe

Dress-Up Play Area

Type of Play	Benefits	Equipment and Materials
Dress-up	• Provides practice in role playing • Encourages creativity • Builds self confidence • Provides practice in dressing and undressing	Firefighter and police hats, masks, mirror, purses, wallets, keys, 'credit cards', suitcases, clothing racks. Clothes: shirts, dresses, capes, shawls, scarves, robes, ties, belts. Footwear: slippers, boots, shoes.

Constructive Play Area

Type of Play	Benefits	Equipment and Materials
Constructive	• Encourages creativity • Promotes cooperation • Develops numerical concepts • Improves small muscle development • Promotes language	Unit blocks, large Lego sets, bristle blocks, giant dominos, farm fences, small vehicles, people, zoo and farm animals

A carefully engineered classroom provides areas that invite different size groups.

Move and Grow Center

Type of Space: Large and open-relatively noisy. Furnishings: Carpeted, storage space for large equipment-and shelving for rhythm instruments. Place for piano and CD, tape or record player.

Gross Motor Activity Area

Type of Play	Benefits	Equipment and Materials
Gross Motor Activity	• Develops large muscle skills • Provides an outlet for energy • Provide opportunities for group play	Tumbling mat, walking board, balance beam, hope scotch or number line, skipping rope, bean bags, large sit-on trucks, train

Music Area

Type of Play	Benefits	Equipment and Materials
Music	• Develops an appreciation of music • Improves coordination and rhythm • Develops listening skills • Provides opportunities for self expression	Piano, rhythm instruments, CD, tape or record player, CD's tapes or records, scarves, songbooks

Create and Discover Center

Type of Space: Large noisy. Furnishings: Uncarpeted sink, tables and chairs, shelves for craft materials, table for science and discovery displays, sand and water tables, hot plate.

Science and Discovery Area

Type of Play	Benefits	Equipment and Materials
Sorting and Classifying	• Encourages children to ask questions	Rocks, shells, beans, nuts, seeds, small containers, magnifying glass, mystery boxes, labels
Encouraging Investigation	• Help children use their senses for investigation	Water table with sieves, basters, funnels, pitchers, bottles, measuring cups, egg beater
Manipulation	• Provides opportunities for sensory play and investigation	Sand table with sifter, different shaped containers, scoops, shovels, spoons
Discovery	•Develops problem solving	Magnets and metal objects, sink and float tub ,lab book
Sharpening the Senses		Kaleidoscope, color paddles, sound and smell containers, prisms, touch beads
Growth Center		Pots, seeds, shovels, ruler, graph paper
Pet Center	• Develops nurturance and responsibility	Goldfish, hamster, ant farm, guinea pig, pet care books, notebook

Cooking Area

Type of Play	Benefits	Equipment and Materials
Cooking	• Provides opportunities to use all the senses • Helps Children to learn about food and nutrition • Develops small muscle coordination • Stimulates language and concept • Helps children follow directions	Heat source-stove, hotplates or electrical pans. Refrigerator and sink (ideal but not essential). Other kitchen equipment: Table and chairs, pots and pans, cooking utensils, recipe board, chef hat and smocks, cleaning materials, food and recipes, large paper for displaying recipes

Creativity Area

Type of Play	Benefits	Equipment and Materials
Painting	• Encourages exploration in a variety of media	Easels, brushes, paper, rollers, paints, drying rack or clothes line
Art	• Develops artistic sense • Develops a sense of personal accomplishment	Clay, scissors, scrap materials, paste, tape, wallpaper, books, magic markers, crayons, colored tissues, cookie cutters, chenille stems, stamps and inkpads, sponges, screen, tooth brushes, hole punches, craft sticks
Weaving	• Encourages exploration with materials	Weaving loom, yarn
Collage		Cloth and carpet samples, wall paper books, ribbons, scraps of paper, buttons and beads, feathers, old magazines and catalogs, recycled items (berry baskets, meat trays, egg cartons, boxes, paper towel rolls)
Wood Working		Scrap pieces of wood, dowels, safety glasses, wood glue, hammer and nails, vise, sandpaper, paints, patterns and diagrams

Circle Activity Area

Type of Play	Benefits	Equipment and Materials
Circle Activity	• Provides a place for opening and closing activities • Develops language and listening • Provides opportunities for participating in large group activities	Carpet squares for each child to define individual spaces, projector and film strips, peg or flannel board for language activities, weather charts, picture roll calls, birthday charts

Table work is often approached more seriously by children and should be encouraged with activities requiring concentration and problem solving.

Play and Learn Center

Type of Space: Relatively quiet-carpeted-shelving for materials, small table and chairs, and computer (optional).

Reading and Writing Readiness

Type of Play	Benefits	Equipment and Materials
Visual Skills	• Develops visual skills related to reading	Inset puzzles, beads, string and pattern matching cards, picture dominoes, lotto games, block design sets, sequence puzzles
Auditory Skills	• Develops listening skills related to reading	Rhyming cards and letter sound games
Learning Alphabet	• Encourages work alone and completing a task	Tactile letter board, alphabet puzzles, alphabet cards, magnetic letter board
Writing Readiness	• Learns to use simple computer programs to make books, pictures, notes, and items for pretend play • Practices motor skills for writing • Develops concepts of print and symbol correspondence	Wooden tool sets, sewing cards, lacing shoes, geo-form boards, dressing frames, lock box, writing utensils, templates, stencils, slate and chalk, pencils, paper and crayons, word processing and picture-making software
Reading	• Develops an appreciation for stories and pictures	A collection od different books from an appropriate bibliography (big books, multicultural, teacher made and child made, cassette tapes or CD's that go along with books (read along books), a quiet corner with comfortable pillows, child sized couches or rocking chairs, camera and film, pictures, posters, puppets

Number Readiness

Type of Play	Benefits	Equipment and Materials
Counting	• Develops concepts of number and sets that prepare the child for learning mathematics	Cubes, buttons, counting frame, abacus, bead-o-graph, color and count sorting box combination, Montessori beads, computer and board games
Learning Sets and Numerals	• Helps child make discriminations on the basis of shape, weight and size	Number cards, peg numbers, unifix cubes, magnetic numerals and boards, dominoes
Learning about Shape and Size	• Introduces basic numerical concepts relating to measurement and quantity	Geometric shapes, fit-a-square set, fit-a-circle set, nesting toys, stacking squares, Montessori cylinders, pink tower, long stair, broad stair
Learning about Measurement, Time and Money		Balance scale, play money, see-through clock, yard stick rulers, tape measure, nesting measuring cups and rice weight tablets

Language and Concept Development

Type of Play	Benefits	Equipment and Materials
Vocabulary Development	• Increases vocabulary • Learns classification skills • Learns about patterns and relationships • Develops problem solving skills	Picture cards, occupation match-up cards, lotto games, classification skills, category cards, touch and match sets, feel tablets, color boards, color tablets, computer stories and story-telling software
Pattern Relationship		Spatial relationship cards, play tile sets, parquetry blocks, peg boards
Problem Solving Skills		What's missing games, puzzles, attribute blocks, computer-based treasure hunts

Wall Décor

In most classrooms, wall space is at a premium. Walls are taken up by a sink, by doors, by windows, by shelves, and by storage units. This means that all available display wall space has to be used wisely.

Here are some suggestions:

- Make sure that you have posted all items required by the licensing bureau. They are likely to include:

  ▲ A fire escape plan
  ▲ Emergency telephone numbers
  ▲ A daily schedule

- A high priority in using wall space is to demonstrate children's products. Make sure that the products are hung at the child's eye level in an attractive display.

- Use some accessible walls for conversation starters. These can be posters, photographs taken on field trips, interesting things that children have said, flannel boards or blackboards, and displays relating to what the children are investigating. If your classroom is divided into interest centers, tie in the wall decoration with the purpose of the interest center. (The housekeeping wall could have a mock window with an outdoor scene, or, when it changes to a doctor's office or veterinary hospital, a sign saying ("The doctor is in.")

- Display photos of children and their families in places where children can point to them and talk about them.

- Put up words. Put children's names on their cubbies, family photos, and artwork. Label interest centers with the current theme. Post appropriate reminders such as "Close door gently."

Interest Center Dividers

Use low furniture to define areas. Make sure that the furniture is sturdy. In some areas it is useful to have double-sided bookcases.

Other Essentials

For Health and Safety

- A place for toothbrushes and drinking cups (for a full day program)
- A fire extinguisher
- A place to post the fire evacuation plan
- A place to keep health records and emergency numbers
- A place for tissues and paper towels
- Waste paper baskets
- An out-of-reach place for cleaning products
- A locked cabinet for medication
- A drinking fountain at children's height or a water bottle for each child

For Personal Possessions

- A special "cubby" for each child
- A place for you to keep plans, records, and personal items
- A place for cots, mats, and blankets
- Some private hideaway, or soft spaces where children can be alone.

From the Drawing Board to the Classroom

Whether you are arranging a classroom for the first time or simply rearranging, begin your task with a paper and pencil. (It is much easier to erase a line then to move a piano.)

- Draw the outline of your room, putting in doors, windows, fixed furniture or partitions, electrical outlets, sink, closets, etc.

- Using circles, lay out your classroom areas remembering to:
  - ▲ Put art activities on a non-carpeted floor near the sink.
  - ▲ Put the music center or any interest center requiring electrical power near an electrical outlet.
  - ▲ Separate quiet and noisy areas.

- Walk through your classroom with your fingers. Is there any problem with traffic flow?

- Make an inventory of materials to go in each interest area. Are the areas the right size?

- Put down the paper and move the furniture.

Objective 5: To organize and equip a learning environment for a multi-age or family childcare setting that includes children birth through five

Spring had sprung at Growing Together Family Day Care, and the children couldn't wait to get outside. "Here's your coat, Jomo, said four-year old Luis to his two-year old friend. Let me help you put it on."

Outside on the playground, Luis and Jomo turned over rocks together, looking for bugs and sprouts. Luis drew an L in the damp earth, then showed Jomo how to make a J. "That gives me an idea," said their teacher. "How about planting our garden in the shapes of our initials, instead of just in straight rows?"

Today, many parents are choosing family childcare because they like its home-like atmosphere. They like the idea that brothers and sisters can be together, and that their children will have playmates of different ages. Many centers are also experimenting with "multi-age" grouping. They put infants, toddlers, and even preschoolers together, as they would be in a family, so that the younger children can learn from the older ones and the older children can experience the joy of helping to take care of younger ones.

Multi-age grouping presents the teacher with unique challenges. How can she set up a room to accommodate such a range of developmental needs? How can she structure the environment to get the most benefit from multi-age grouping?

One way to begin is to block out some key areas:

- a gathering place for the whole group

- a cubby or personal storage space for each child

- sleeping spaces

- protected floor space for babies and young toddlers, with sturdy furniture for cruising and climbing

- an active play area for older toddlers and preschoolers

- some places in lofts and on tables where older children can draw, build, display collections, and work with puzzles and games without interference from the babies

- spaces for cooking, eating, music, pretending, reading, and looking after pets that everyone can share

Add some special spaces where children can be alone or spend time with one or two friends — a box house, a quiet corner with a beanbag chair or soft pillows, a rocking boat, or a loft. Don't forget about the adults' needs: a rocking chair, places for planning and record keeping, comfortable seating, safe and efficient set-ups for diaper changing, food preparation, and - in a home- daily chores and maintenance.

Use low furniture to define areas.

Next, make sure that each area is furnished appropriately, with safe toys that the children can reach. Young babies like to watch older children, so make sure you have an easy way of moving them from place to place, and keep some of their toys within reach. Toddlers like to imitate, so make sure there are items they can use for "cooking," building, reading, art, active "sports," and other activities that the older children will be involved in.

Stock up on items with broad age appeal, such as balls, soap bubbles, rubber animals, sensory play and art materials, dolls, and riding toys like wagons that children of different ages can use together. Store some of the toys in bins, baskets, and other containers so that you can rotate them easily to maintain children's interest. Keep popular toys where children can get at them and put them away easily. You might set up appealing storage spaces such as a "garage" for cars and trucks under a small table, a "basket" for balls or bean bags, or a "doll house" on a shelf for miniature figures.

Finally, assess each room or area at different heights. What interesting things can a baby see from an infant seat or from the floor? Where can a crawler go and what can she get to play with? Where can a young toddler pull up to a stand? What is within his reach? What will stimulate conversations among the older children and encourage them to play together? Will the younger children be able to "participate" in the older children's games and activities? Is the area safe for all of the children who will use it?

Objective 6: To develop a well balanced daily schedule

With more parents in the workforce, children's time has become more scheduled. For many children, weekdays involve getting up early, going to one or more child care placements, and returning home late in the day. Most child care centers and family child care homes now operate 10-13 hours a day; some have evening and/or weekend hours as well.

When children are spending significant portions of their waking hours in a child care facility, it is important to establish a daily routine that meets their developmental needs. Although activities will change from day to day, there needs to be a basic schedule that is flexible but predictable.

Planning the Infant's Day

Mrs. Davis was looking for a child care center for her six month old baby. She found the Wee Care Center in the telephone book and made an appointment to visit.

Mrs. Carer (the child care provider): "Oh, yes. We have a fine staff here. We feed our babies on demand and keep them dry and clean at all times."

Mrs. Davis: "That sounds like just what I'm looking for. What sort of activities do you have for the babies when they are awake?"

Mrs. Carer: "Activities? I told you already that we feed our babies on demand and keep them clean and dry at all times. Oh, I know you might have read about infant curriculums in some of those fancy books, but you can bet your bottom

Today, many parents are choosing family childcare because they like its homelike atmosphere.

dollar the people who wrote those books never changed a baby's diaper! If you want to run a real good nursery you sure don't have time for fun and games!"

Mrs. Carer has obviously not been reading the "fancy books" she complains about, and has not kept up with the research on infant brain development. If she has no time for "fun and games," she may be caring for too many babies. In any case, she needs to rethink her schedule so that she has time to talk and play with each baby and engage the babies in simple activities. Much of the "fun and games," of course, will take place during routine care. As she changes diapers, gets babies up from a nap, feeds and soothes them, and puts them to sleep, Mrs. Carers can take the time to talk with the babies, tickle their tummies, play simple body awareness games, help them pull up into a sitting or standing position, point out interesting sights, and sing songs.

Setting up a simple, basic schedule and spending some time planning for each day could help Mrs. Carers make the time she needs for other activities.

Some Hints on Planning the Day for Infants

Routine and Flexibility: Within a childcare setting, as at home, it is important to let young infants follow their own feeding and sleeping schedules. At the same time, babies will be more playful and less fussy when their schedules are somewhat predictable. Dividing the day into segments that follow a consistent pattern helps young infants to develop more regular eating and sleeping patterns. Older infants will tend to be more flexible and can begin to adjust to a common eating and sleeping schedule. Infants should be assigned to a specific caregiver so they can establish a relationship with one significant person who knows their schedule and can read their cues.

Indoors and Out: Infants enjoy spending time each day outside, as long as weather permits. Riding toys, pull and push toys that need space, and small climbing structures are appropriate for the twelve to eighteen month group. Infants who are not walking can be placed outdoors on quilts along with their toys. A patio area, covered with linoleum or indoor-outdoor carpet, provides a nice play area. Messy sensory experiences - such as playing with water, soap bubbles, or cornstarch - can be conducted outside to minimize clean up.

Quiet and Active: Balance quiet times (playing soothing music, rocking, or reading) with more active periods.

Special Times: Set aside a special time every day for a sensory activity.

Movement/Music Time: This should be a regularly planned time so that infants are exposed to music each day.

Books and Language Activities: Set aside a quiet time for looking at books and doing language activities to insure this important area is not neglected.

Infants should be assigned to a specific caregiver so they can establish a relationship with one significant person who... can read their cues.

A Basic Schedule for Infants

Arrival Time
Caregivers exchange information with parents and help each baby get comfortable.

Mid Morning Playtime (on floor)
Sensory activities, reading, music and movement, play with toys and with caregiver

Outdoor Time
Outdoor play and sensory activities.

Lunch (for infants who are on solid food)

Nap Time (for older infants)

Mid-Afternoon Playtime (on floor)
Music, singing and movement games, reading, playing with toys and with caregiver

Afternoon Walk

Late Afternoon
Start to organize each infant's belongings for the trip home. Complete daily report.

Departure
Parents arrive to pick-up the infants. Time for communication between caregivers and parents.

With infants, most activities will be individual, but some group times can be planned. Here are examples of planning sheets for group activities:

Weekly Planning

Dates: _____

Activity	Monday	Tuesday	Wednesday	Thursday	Friday
Greeting	Hello song Pat-A-Cake See-saw Wheels on bus	Hello song Trot-Trot to Boston Wheels on bus	Hello song Who has a Nose See-saw Pat-a-cake	Hello song Exercise song See-saw Trot-Trot	Hello song See-saw Pat-a-cake
Sensory	Bubbles	Bubbles	Cornmeal	Cornmeal	Cornmeal
Music	Music & Movement	Music & Movement	March music	March Music	Lullabies

Planning the Day for Toddlers

Young toddlers are very busy trying out new motor and language skills. They need lots of watching as they learn to walk, run, and climb, and lots of individual attention as they try to make their wants and discoveries understood with grunts, gestures, and newly learned words. Participation in group activities, like circle time, is likely to be sporadic and brief. Still, a regular schedule, with lots of repetition of favorite activities, provides a comforting rhythm to the day. Rituals like "hello" and "good-bye" songs help young toddlers mark time and place and provide a sense of security.

Older toddlers also do best with a predictable schedule, and enjoy learning routines. Rituals at the beginning and end of the day help them feel secure and in control. A comfortable, predictable balance of active and quiet activities helps keeps their natural energy and exuberance within bounds. With their short attention spans and insatiable curiosity, two-year olds tend to flit from one activity to another. At the same time, they may resist transitions that they do not initiate. You can play music or sing special songs to help the children know when it is time to join the circle, clean up, eat, take a nap, or get ready to say good-bye.

Most toddlers will be able to follow a common schedule when it comes to eating and nap times, but they will still be on their own time schedules when it comes to getting drinks of water, diaper changing, and — for some— learning to use the toilet.

...a regular schedule, with lots of repetition of favorite activities, provides a comforting rhythm to the day.

A Basic Schedule for Toddlers

Arrival Time
Caregivers exchange information with parents and help each toddler get comfortable.

Hello Song; Circle Time (for children who are interested)

Morning snack or breakfast

Mid Morning Playtime
Music and movement experiences, reading to individual or small groups of children, free play in activity centers

Outdoor Time

Lunch

Nap Time

Mid Afternoon Playtime
Music and movement experiences, reading to individual or small groups of children, free play in activity centers

Outdoor Time

Late Afternoon
Start to organize the children's belongings for the trip home. Complete daily report.

Departure
Parents arrive to pick-up the children. Time for communication between caregivers and parents

Developing a Daily Schedule for Preschoolers

Mrs. Curtis came to visit the day care center. She found the teacher, Mr. Owens, sitting with a small group of children reading a rainbow story. In the center of the room four children were sitting in a rocking boat singing, "Row, Row, Row, Your Boat." Several children were trying on old clothes at the far end of the room. In another corner a boy was sitting by himself building a giant block tower. When Mr. Owens spotted his visitor, he finished the rainbow story and suggested that the children go to the drawing table and color their own rainbow.

When all the children had found the crayons they wanted, Mr. Owens welcomed his guest to the classroom.

Mrs. Curtis looked amazed. "How do you ever do it?" she asked. "You have fourteen children in this classroom and every child seems busy and happy. I've got three kids at home and my house is always in a state of turmoil."

"I've been at it for some time," Mr. Owens replied modestly.

Although Mr. Owens made light of his accomplishment, keeping a room full of five-year olds productively involved in a variety of tasks is not an easy feat. It requires a teacher who is confident, well organized, and adept at engineering a classroom. Let us look at some of the ingredients of good classroom management.

- Developing a Daily Schedule
- Implementing the Daily Schedule
- Planning for a Rainy Day
- Transition Time

Whether you are a family child care provider taking care of four children or a childcare center teacher with a class of fourteen, the place to begin good management is with a daily schedule. A schedule is not a curriculum or a daily plan. It does not describe the crafts, lessons or activities that have been scheduled for the day. It does, however, describe the timetable that you follow, on a daily basis, throughout the year.

A daily schedule must take into account the philosophy of the program, the age of the children you are working with, the size of the group, the length of the day, the children's patterns of arrival and departure, and the physical set up of the child care facility.

Philosophy
A daily schedule is a reflection of the philosophy of the center. A program that stresses academics will set aside large blocks of time for structured lessons or for play-based activities that promote academic skills. A program that stresses the development of creativity in art, music, and movement will provide time slots in the daily schedule for these activities. A program with a religious orientation may block out time for prayer or religious teaching. A program with a major focus on physical health and nutrition may provide blocks of time for health checks, personal care, and the preparation and serving of nutritious snacks.

Age of the Children
All preschool children, whether they are a year old or five years old, are still developing their ideas about time. Most cannot yet read a clock or even understand what we mean by minutes and hours. The best way for children to understand time is through routine events. Events that mark off the day include meal times, snack time, circle or whole group meeting time, playground time, and nap time. Because children perceive time as passing at a much slower rate then adults do, for them a day is very long. Time markers help them

to realize that a day goes by in an orderly way and that going home time will come and can be counted on. The younger the children, the more important it is to have distinct and predictable time markers.

A second way in which a daily schedule takes into account the age of the children is in the amount of time devoted to group activities. Very young children have short attention spans and cannot be expected to participate in a group experience for more then ten or fifteen minutes.

Length of the Day

A schedule for a full or extended program is necessarily quite different from the schedule for a half-day program. For a short period of time, children and adults enjoy a fast-paced program with quick changes in activities and little time spent in making transitions. For a full day program, it is better to increase the duration of activities and take more time moving from one activity to the next. It is also critically important to provide a balanced day, alternating quiet activities with activities that are faced paced and active.

Implementing the Daily Schedule

Having a workable schedule posted on the wall is a good step — but it is only that. By far the greater challenge is making the schedule work.

Here are some guidelines:

- Make sure to differentiate between setting up a daily schedule and developing plans. A daily plan describes the curriculum to be implemented during the time slots indicated on the schedule.

- Make your daily plans at least a week in advance, so that you can make necessary phone calls, purchase supplies, or prepare the materials needed.

- Read plans for the next day before you leave the center and make sure you have all the materials you need.

- Begin each day by talking to the children about what they are going to do.

- End each day by going over with the children what they have done and talking about plans for the next day.

Planning For a Rainy Day

No matter how carefully we plan and how well we have thought out our curriculum, there are always days when our greatest plans must be canceled or our favorite ideas must be scrapped. It rains for the picnic, there is a three alarm fire when the firefighter is suppose to come, or the exterminator came on the wrong day and no pets are allowed in the classroom. The bus for the field trip is late, lunch is taking longer to cook than usual, or the visitor you invited is stuck in traffic, and you find yourself with extra time on your hands and a class full of restless children. Whatever the problem, it happens to all of us, and we should be prepared.

The best quick fix solution for unexpected waiting time is a repertoire of familiar songs with appropriate variations. Some suggestions are provided in Chapter 9: Creativity.

While a song or finger play is appropriate for filling up a five minute waiting space, there will inevitably be emergency situations with longer time slots to fill up. The best way to prepare for a "rainy day" is to have an emergency daily plan with all the appropriate materials put away on the top shelf. These Surprise Boxes can turn a disappointing day into a special one.

...provide a balanced day, alternating quite activities with activities.

Unbirthday Party: old greeting cards, stickers, glitter, old party hats, tissue paper or foil and ribbons (children can wrap toys from the classroom for the presents), birthday candles (can be stuck in clay, cheese, or Jell-O as well as real cakes or cupcakes), rice cakes with peanut butter or jelly and sprinkles. *Let the children help prepare an unbirthday party for the class. Sing "Happy Unbirthday."*

Let's Go to the Beach: shells, pebbles, driftwood, picnic cloth or blanket, story books about sea animals, pails, shovels, and sand molds, "picnic basket" or "cooler." *The children can set up a beach scene or make a sandcastle at the sand table, make sand castles from play-dough and decorate them with shells, draw or paint beach scenes and glue on real sand and shells, pack the cooler with pretend food, spread out the blanket, and listen to a beach story. For a change, you can serve lunch or snack on the picnic blanket instead of at the table.*

Edible Art: recipes and ingredients for peanut butter play-dough, chocolate syrup drawing or finger painting (on wax paper), alphabet pretzels, or edible faces (children can make these by decorating paper plates or buttered rice cakes with bits of fruit and vegetables, pieces of cereal, or small crackers). *You don't have to save these for a rainy day.*

Old Favorites: Toys, books, puzzles, and games that the children had seemed to be finished with. *Children will enjoy rediscovering their old toys and will know just what to do with them.*

Valentines: Heart cutouts, doilies, stickers, rubber stamps, envelopes, glitter, gold and silver pens, mailbox. *Any day can be Valentine's Day.*

Train Ride: Train book, engineer's cap, whistle, pictures of exotic places. *Put on the cap, line up the chairs, blow the whistle, and call "All Aboard." Sing some train songs. Let the children take turns suggesting places to go. Make some suggestions yourself. You might go to a baseball game, the zoo, a faraway or nearby city, or an imaginary place. Pretend to ride the train to the destination, then talk about what you see or get out and pantomime the action.*

Transition Times

Moving from one activity to the next needs special consideration. A typical crisis in a classroom occurs when the whole class is ready to go outside except for one child who hasn't put the last touches on a craft or the last piece in a puzzle. Here are some ways of avoiding transition time problems:

- Sing a special song or ring a bell five minutes before the end of an activity so that the children have time to get ready.

- Make clean-up time fun by having everyone join in singing a clean up song.

- Sing a marching song or play train (children place their hands on the shoulders of the child in front) when you go to the playground or to a different room.

- Don't insist on a perfect line up. Children are not very good at it.

- Find fun ways of moving in a line such as tip-toeing, walking with hands in the air, putting hands on heads, or singing a counting song.

Scheduling and Planning for a Multi-Age Group

In scheduling the day for a family child care home or a multi-age group at a center, there are several questions that need to be asked first. Some of these are:

- How many children are present?
- How many caregivers will care for the children?
- What are the ages of the children in care?
- What are the hours that the children will be in care?

Having infants and toddlers in care would lead to a schedule where children eat, are diapered, and nap on their own individual schedules, with scheduled times for outdoor play or carriage rides.

Having preschoolers in care would require scheduling of large blocks of time for child-directed play. Meals/snacks, outdoor play, and naps/rest times would be scheduled at approximately the same time everyday.

The schedule for homogeneous groups in family child care could look very similar to center based child care schedules.

For mixed aged groupings, whether in center-based or family care, the provider needs to schedule those activities that need to get done in the day according to the needs of the children. Those activities would include:

- Activities associated with the arrival of children

- Preparing and having meals and snacks: Older children can help with the setting of the table and some simple preparation. At the end of the meal/snack, the children can assist in the clean up. Bottle-fed babies have individual schedules for feedings.

- Preparing for and nap/rest time: Children take naps or rest depending on their individual needs. Babies may be awake during this time if they recently have awakened from a nap.

- Providing time for pretend play and child-directed play: Most of the day should be spent in child selected and directed play. This allows you to change activities when children seem to be flagging and to bring babies in and out of the older children's activities as appropriate.

- Providing for music and creative arts: Music activities and art/sensory activities especially lend themselves to mixed age groups, so try to offer them when the older infants and toddlers will be awake.

- Reading and literacy promotion: Daily experiences with books and other literature need to be planned for all age groups. This should occur several times in the day.

- Projects with wide age appeal: Thematic explorations that may extend over a period of time, such as putting on a play or rhythm-band concert, visiting a zoo or farm and creating a mural or setting up a mini-zoo, celebrating a holiday, or planting a garden.

- Diapering and the use of bathroom would be taken care of as needed.

- Observing children for program planning: Plan time to observe each child on a regular basis.

- Preparing for children's departure: Just before the scheduled departure of the children, the caregiver must prepare the children and gather their belongings.

- Keeping of records and other administrative duties: Records and other required administrative duties also need to be taken care of. This could typically happen when the children are napping, after the children leave, or at a set time if there is more than one childcare provider.

- Giving individual attention to children: Children of all ages need individual attention. Be sure to schedule time for private conversations with each child. Try to also find time when you can follow the child's lead as you play together.

Other considerations would include:

- Balancing of active and quiet activity

- Balancing whole-group activities like story-reading, outings, cooking, some pretend play and art/sensory activities, music, and parachute play with age-specific needs like sports, puzzles, games, and lessons

- Making schedules dependable but flexible

- Time for the caregiver to share ideas with the parents

Objective 7: To set up an outdoor play and learning environment

Although the amount of time devoted to outdoor play is dependent both on the age of the children and the weather conditions, every child care center should provide opportunities for children to spend part of each day outdoors.

MUSTS for the outdoor play area include:*

- Forty-five square feet of space for every child over two years.
- A five-foot fence that completely encloses the play area with child-proof latches on the exits.
- Adequate shade.
- Safe play equipment.
- Adequate space between pieces of play equipment
- Soft surfaces under the climbing structures.

Please check the regulations for your particular state.

Play Area for Infants and Toddlers

Infants enjoy spending a part of the day outdoors. They can be placed in carriages, strollers, baby swings, or oversized playpens. Spreading a blanket on the ground can allow for sensory play outdoors for the infant. Crawling around on the blanket, feeling the warm breeze, watching the world around them, and watching soap bubbles are all enjoyable activities for the infants.

Toddlers love the opportunity to play outside. Outdoor play provides a chance to release energy, initiate games, and practice emerging motor skills and social exchanges with other youngsters. A toddler play area should include the following types of play opportunities:

Wheel Toy Section

Wheel toy play is particularly desirable for toddlers because it combines opportunities to practice motor skills with opportunities for pretending. A wheel toy area works best where there is a circular path that children can ride around. It also is an excellent idea to include a "service station" where wheel toys can be washed, oiled, fixed, and filled with gas.

Climbing Structures

Climbing structures for toddlers should take into account the fact that toddlers may not be fully aware of their own capabilities and limitations. In selecting toddler structures, we cannot assume that the child's natural fear will keep her out of danger. A toddler who is learning to climb may climb to the top of a structure without concern about getting back down again. Make sure, therefore, that the height and construction of a structure minimizes the danger of a fall. Also, make sure that climbing structures are placed on soft surfaces. Eight inches of sand is ideal.

Many climbing structures have swing sets attached. In general this is not a good idea. If the swing set is used in the toddler area, it should be a reasonable distance from other structures and the swings should be made of soft material. Toddlers do not recognize the danger of running behind a swing.

Sandboxes or Sand Tables

Although one to three year olds enjoy playing and digging in a sandbox or a sand table, there are some problems that require special supervision.

- Toddlers are likely to throw sand in each other's eyes or take a bite of their sand-cakes.

- It's difficult to convince toddlers to keep sand inside the sandbox or sand table.

- Sandboxes can be breeding grounds for pinworms. (Sand tables are unlikely to present this problem.)

- Sandboxes and sand tables must be covered when not in use.

Despite these disadvantages, sand boxes and sand tables provide young children marvelous opportunities to fill and empty, to sieve, to pour, to experiment, and to pretend. If you have enough staff to maintain a sandbox, it deserves a place on the toddler playground.

Play Area for Children Three to Five

In designing playgrounds for children between three and five years old, we should consider the kinds of play that these children will engage in. The three kinds of play that these children enjoy are play for mastering motor skills, construction play, and representational play.

Play for Mastering Motor Skills

Because of space and noise tolerance, the playground is the most logical place for gross motor activity. As children run, climb, swing, and balance, they are learning to control their bodies, to understand spatial relationships, and to master a host of important motor skills.

The following structures and equipment can foster motor skill development:

Structures
Jungle gyms	Slides
Swings and tire swings	Tunnels
See-saws	Log Walks
Basketball hoops	Swinging gates
Balance beams	

Equipment
Balls	Hoops
Tricycles	Wagons
Riding Toys	Nerf bats

Construction Play

A second type of outdoor play that children enjoy is construction, where children experiment and create with different media. Construction play can take place with liquid, semi-liquid, or solid materials. The following structures and materials can be used creatively in many construction play activities:

Wheel toy play is particularly desirable for toddlers because it combines opportunities to practice motor skills with opportunities for pretending.

For creating and exploring with liquid or semi-liquid materials
- Water tables
- Sand boxes
- Clay-soil digging areas

For creating and constructing with solid materials
- Large hollow blocks
- Cardboard cartons
- Planks
- Milk cartons
- Crates

Representational Play

A third type of play that occurs on the playground is representational. This play parallels the imaginative play of the indoor environment. Children vent frustrations, express feelings, and work out problems as well as engage in social interaction with other children (perhaps even more so in this wide-open environment). Although children will use climbing structures and the constructive materials for imaginative play, their pretending can be enhanced by inclusion of some key props.

Climbing area
- Steering wheel on a "car"
- Telephone
- Row of stumps (for seats on a train or bus)

Sandbox
- Cars, trucks, bulldozers, back hoes, and boats (various sizes)
- Rubber animals, people
- Empty containers
- Shovels
- Kitchen utensils, pots, pans

Water Play
- Empty containers
- Baby dolls with soap
- Objects that float/sink

Gasoline Stations
- Large oil cans with rubber hoses
- Toy tools to repair cars
- Money box with plastic coins to pay for gas

Play House

Children love child-size space. A well-equipped playground for young children should include a playhouse with a telephone and a shed that can be used for both imaginative play and storage. Because eating is so important to young children, pretend routines often revolve around this activity. A picnic table with tableware is an excellent play house prop for encouraging pretending.

Science and Discovery

The outdoors is the perfect setting for science and discovery. Children have a natural curiosity for nature and living things. Nature walks and listening to nature can add to the sensory experience of the outdoors. Simple equipment that can enhance this experience includes: magnifying glasses, bug catchers or plastic jars, binoculars, butterfly nets, tools for digging and raking, and paper and writing instruments to document the discoveries.

Objective 8: To ensure that the environment works for adults as well as for children

When asked what keeps them working in child care, the first thing most teachers and caregivers say is "the children." Experienced professionals talk about the importance of their work. They enjoy watching young minds and personalities unfold and find that each day brings new discoveries and surprises. They know they are providing an important service to families and to society. Yet, when pressed, these professionals often give another reason for staying in jobs that pay relatively low salaries: "I love the people I'm working with and the atmosphere of the workplace."

Child care centers and family child care homes can be special places for adults as well as for children. But this doesn't happen by itself. It requires conscious effort to make spaces comfortable for child care workers and welcoming for parents.

Spaces for Adults

Most child care centers have some spaces that are designed for adults: an office, a teachers' room and/or parent room, adult-size bathrooms, and a kitchen/work area that is off limits to children. These spaces should be clean, bright, and cheerful, with comfortable furnishings, windows, attractive wall displays, plants, bulletin boards, and reading materials. Fresh coffee and snacks invite adults to linger and encourage communication. A few toys and children's books in these areas help to welcome parents whose younger children are not in the center or who would like to spend some time with their child outside of the classroom.

Classrooms, though designed for children, also need to be set up with adults — teachers, parents, and classroom visitors — in mind. Each room should have:

- Comfortable seating for adults: a rocking chair in an infant or young toddler sleeping area, places to sit while feeding or eating with children, seating with back support for reading to children, and chairs that visitors can use

- A desk or other work and record-keeping station, conveniently located to allow simultaneous supervision of children who are playing or sleeping

- A secure place for the teacher's purse or briefcase and other personal belongings

- Displays of children's work and words that let parents know what is happening in the classroom
- Pictures of the children's families and artifacts that represent their home cultures
- Pictures and artifacts that are meaningful to the teacher
- Inspirational posters, favorite quotes, and visionary messages that inspire adults who care for young children and reflect their wisdom
- Words in the children's home languages; notes to parents in their home languages when possible
- A bulletin board where teachers and parents can post and exchange information
- A telephone

A learning environment for young children should be a place where their teachers, caregivers, and parents feel at home. The environment you create will be a reflection of who you are — your philosophy of teaching and learning, the things you love and want to share, and what you find beautiful, engaging, calming, and inspiring. It should be a place where you like spending time, a learning environment for adults as well as for children.

Bredekamp, S. (Editor). (1993). *Developmentally appropriate practice in early childhood programs serving children from birth through age 8.* Washington, D.C.: National Association for the Education of Young Children.

Brickman, N.A. & Taylor, L.S. (Editors). (1991). *Supporting young learners: Ideas for preschool and day care providers.* Ypsilanti, MI: High/Scope Press.

Bronson, M.B. (1995). *The right stuff for children birth to 8: Selecting play materials to support development.* Washington, D.C.: National Association for the Education of Young Children.

Curtis, D. & Carter, M. (1996). *Reflecting children's lives: A handbook for planning child-centered curriculum.* St. Paul, MN: Redleaf Press.

Greenman, J. & Stonehouse, A. (1996). *Prime times: A handbook for excellence in Infant and toddler programs.* St. Paul, MN: Redleaf Press.

Lally, J.R., Griffin, A., Fenichel, E., Segal, M., Szanton, E., & Weissbourd, B. (1995). *Caring for infants and toddlers in groups: Developmentally appropriate practice.* Washington, D.C.: Zero to Three.

Pawl, J.H. (1990). *Infants in day care: Reflections on experiences, expectations, relationships.* Washington, D.C.: Zero to Three.

Phillips, C.B. (Editor). (1991). *Essentials for child development associates working with young children.* Washington, D.C.: The Council for Early Childhood Professional Recognition.

Section III: On Stage

*M*rs. Try-My-Best, a family childcare provider, was having dinner at a restaurant with a friend.

Mrs. Try-my-Best: "Sorry about being late. I was talking to one of my parents about her baby and she wouldn't let me go."

Friend: "Was she complaining about something?"

Mrs. Try-My-Best: "No, she is a very nice parent and she almost never complains. But she wanted me to tell her about her baby and no matter what I told her she kept asking me the same question."

Friend: "What was the question?"

Mrs. Try-My-Best: "How is my baby developing? It was strange. I told her how well he was sitting by himself and how he had just learned to pass a toy from one hand to the other. But whatever I told her she would say, " No, that's not what I'm asking. I just want you to tell me about my son's development."

Although Mrs. Try-My-Best could not figure out what this parent was trying to find out, her question is quite legitimate. Knowing how well a child is doing in several domains of development does not answer the question of how well that child is developing. Domains of development are interdependent. In order to master a task like picking up a spoon on demand, the child must have the language ability to understand what he is expected to do, the cognitive ability to recognize which object is a spoon, the physical ability to pick up the spoon and the psychological motivation to do it. A child's developmental level refers to the total range of his capacities and resources at a particular point in time.

In this text we describe several domains of development: physical, cognitive, language, imaginative or creative, emotional, and social. Each of these domains is described in its own chapter. The emotional and social domains are touched on in this section, but described in more detail in the next. This approach allows us to focus on the expected developmental sequences in each domain and to suggest activities to reinforce existing skills and encourage the development of emerging skills at each stage. The downside of this approach is that it does not provide a wide-angled picture of the expected developmental status of children at different ages. In the developmental overviews that follow, we present a global picture of child development at age points from birth to five.

Developmental Overview: Birth to One Year Olds

Following an infant's development in the first year of life is an exciting experience. Infants change from week to week, from day to day, and sometimes from minute to minute. Like busy scientists, they are continually seeking out new information, performing experiments, and testing out new ideas. Over time, infants discover new things about themselves. They discover ways to kick with their legs, grasp with their hands, and make interesting sounds with their mouths. They discover that people are useful, that language is important, and that an object that is hidden from sight continues to exist. In fact, many behavioral scientists feel that the foundations for all later development — physical, psychological, and social, are established within the first year of life. This means that the kinds of experiences we provide for babies are extremely important and can have a lifelong impact.

Before zeroing in on the kind of curriculum that would be appropriate for babies, let us look at the characteristics of babies at different ages so we know what to expect.

Birth to Three Months

Although we may think of a newborn baby as being fragile and helpless, the infant comes into this world with an impressive set of built-in reflexes and adaptive behaviors. He looks into his mother's eyes and attends to the sound of her voice. He closes his eyes in response to bright lights and reflexively grasps a finger when it is placed in his palm. Within the first three months, a baby will make connections between feelings, sights, and sounds. When he hears the sound of a rattle, he will search for it with his eyes. When he sees a smiling face, he will respond with a smile and a coo.

From birth to one month old, babies respond more to what is happening inside them than to what is happening outside. If they are kept clean, dry, and well fed, placed in a comfortable crib, and soothed when something disturbs them, they do not require outside stimulation. During the next two months, there is a gradual turning outward — an awakening to the world outside. The baby who is held, rocked, sung to, smiled at, and loved begins to make some early connections between the sound of mother's voice and the smile on mother's face or the sensation of being rocked. Babies who are played with, cuddled, and soothed are learning to associate the presence of a caregiver with a sense of well-being. Children who do not receive this kind of nurturing continue to tune out the outside world.

Our goals and activities during these early months are designed to help the infant develop her emerging capacities. We help her to focus her eyes and follow moving targets. We encourage the baby to listen and respond to different sounds. We provide special exercises to help infants relax and gain muscle tone. An alert caregiver recognizes the infant's needs. There is a time when the infant needs stimulation and a time when soothing is more appropriate. We try to recognize and respond to the baby's rhythm, to adjust our activities and routines to each infant's individual needs.

Three to Six Months

From three to six months old, the infant is learning to explore the world with her hands as well as with 'her eyes. Learning to reach out is dependent on having something to reach for. If the baby has an interesting gym strung across her crib, she will bat at it, watch it jingle in response to the batting, and bat at it again. This tendency to repeat an action that creates an interesting effect shows the infant's first intuitive recognition of her own ability to affect her environment.

At about the same time the baby is making discoveries about her emerging ability to make things happen, she is also discovering things about her social world. She has learned to smile and coo at a caregiver and to expect a cooing response, and is developing her first "conversational skills." With appropriate experience she will learn to draw the caregiver into an interaction, to "coo" back and forth taking turns with her partner, and to imitate simple cooing sounds.

During these next three months, infants become more responsive and less irritable. Their interest in environmental exploration increases. Important developments include social smiling, hand watching, hand play, the gradual development of increasingly precise reaching skills, interest in playing with toys, rolling over, and, by the end of the sixth month, progress in learning to sit. This is an important time for face to face interaction between the infant and the caregiver.

Suggested activities for caregivers during the three to six month period are designed to give the baby an opportunity to practice those new and emerging skills.

Motor activities enhance balance and muscle strength in preparation for crawling and sitting, Activities with rattles and squeak toys encourage manipulation and hand-eye coordination. Language and "cooing" games encourage infants to make new sounds and engage in social interaction.

Six to Nine Months

By this time the baby has begun to use a pincer grasp, to drop things on purpose and then look for them, to bang objects on a hard surface, and to transfer things from hand to hand. He is beginning to have a crude notion of object permanence (something continues to exist even though we can't see it) and can imitate simple actions (like banging) that he has already learned. In the next three months the infant's notions about objects will become more sophisticated, and, by the end of the ninth month, he will begin to look for hidden objects. The infant will add many more sounds to his vocabulary and will begin babbling (mamma, dadda, babba). He will start to respond to a few specific words like his name or "Hi" and may begin to show a wariness of strangers. During this time period, most babies prefer sitting up and they begin to use some method of crawling. The pincer grasp is now used successfully to pick up small objects and finger foods. The baby can drink from a cup with help and will hold his own bottle.

Activities during this period are designed to help infants become more sophisticated in their ability to manipulate objects. We provide the infant with a variety of toys that are different in shape, size, texture, and in the sounds they make. How many different things will the infant do with a toy? Does he know that a soft rubber toy is for squeaking and a rattle is for shaking? Do his hands work together when he plays with a toy? As we give infants experience with finger foods, we help to refine their pincer grasps. We suggest dropping games as an aid in learning releasing skills. During this period, the infant is learning to recognize the patterns and rhythms of language. We introduce songs and nursery rhymes to give infants exposure to the special qualities of language.

Nine to Twelve Months

This is a time when we see many rapid developments. The baby understands more and more specific words, such as "mommy," "no," "bottle," etc. He becomes interested in looking at books and may start pointing to specific objects. The baby's babbling starts to sound more and more like true speech; some babies during this time will start saying words. The baby's imitative skills improve and he begins to imitate new actions. The infant learns to wave bye-bye and play pat-a-cake. At first these gestures are imitative-caregiver waves and baby waves. But after a while the baby responds to the verbal command. The baby may also learn to imitate a simple social action like "making nice" to a doll and putting a hat on his own head.

His interest in objects shifts from simple manipulation to performing tasks with the objects, like dropping them into a container, throwing, or rolling. He learns to use a new method of exploration, poking with a finger, and will begin to actively explore objects within his reach.

The baby is now really on the go. He creeps quickly on all fours, pulls himself to a standing position, and cruises sideways along the furniture. This new ability to move through space carries the potential danger of moving away from mother or trusted caregiver. Fortunately the baby recognizes his caregiver's face, even from a distance, and is able to keep a close watch on her whereabouts. For the baby between nine and twelve months, his mother or caregiver becomes the base of operations. The baby will explore freely as long as his caregiver is in sight.

Activities during the 9-12 month period are designed to teach understanding of specific words, to encourage the development of object permanence, and to help infants learn to imitate simple actions. We also work on simple self-help skills and on providing opportunities for infants to explore their rapidly developing motor capacities.

Developmental Overview: One to Two Year Olds

Between 12 and 24 months, babies develop at greatly varying rates. Each baby seems to have her own special strengths. Some babies are very social; they like to "talk" and interact a great deal. Others are more interested in their toys. Some babies are concentrating on learning to talk and are not in such a great hurry to run or climb. Others never have the time to stop to talk. They are always on the move — running, climbing, and manipulating.

During this time period, most babies will learn to walk steadily. They will attempt to run and they will begin to walk up and down stairs. Self-help skills will improve. By 24 months the child should be able to use a cup and spoon fairly well and to help in the dressing process by pulling off his socks, raising his arms, or picking up his foot so his shoes can be put on.

In addition to practicing emerging motor skills, babies between twelve and twenty-four months have become interested in exploring and experimenting. They are continually searching for objects with moving parts, for things that fit into other things, or for things that can be poured, spilled, carried, or somehow transported around. They enjoy toys that can be pushed, or pulled, or wheeled around, toys that can be stacked, pounded, or lined up, and toys that respond to their manipulations by making interesting sounds.

At the same time that children show an interest in sound-making toys, they are also likely to expand their own sound-making repertoire. Sometime during the second year, expressive babble language is converted to meaningful words. Most children by eighteen months have a meaningful vocabulary of fifteen words. By two years old, their vocabulary may include as many as 200 words.

More importantly, the one to two-year old is showing quantum leaps in receptive language, that is the understanding of spoken words. The one-year old can show you eyes, nose, mouth, and ears, point to photos of different family members, and follow short, one-word commands. In the course of the second year there will be a rapid expansion of receptive language and an emerging capacity to listen to stories, watch a video tape with a story line, and follow a two step command. Paralleling the emergence of receptive language is an emerging capacity to imitate behavioral sequences. One to two-year olds will jabber on a toy telephone, wipe up a spill, place a key in a lock, smear their faces with make-up, sweep with a broom, or lap up the water from the cat's dish. This imitation of familiar actions is evidence of a child's capacity to think in symbols and is the precursor of pretend play.

Another important development in the second year of life is the emergence of self-awareness. The child is becoming increasingly aware of himself as an "actor." If you laugh at something he does, he will promptly do it again to produce another laugh. He is also sensitive to the fact that some of the things that he wants to do are prohibited by adults. When an adult tries to curtail his explorations with a "no," he is likely to persist in what he is doing until he recognizes that he does not have a choice. The fact that the baby can now choose between conforming and not conforming puts a new strain on the adult. Parents and caregivers are likely to be torn between encouraging exploration and independence and teaching caution, obedience, and responsibility. An overriding concern is that a baby who hears "no" too many times may lose interest in exploring, thus limiting his opportunities to learn.

Developmental Overview: Two to Three Year Olds

The period from two to three is known as "The Terrible Two's." The "no" of the toddler has become a convincing temper tantrum and the two-year old is described as ornery, stubborn, and impossible to live with. The two-year old child, for the most part, has earned her reputation. This is a period in which the child is continually exerting authority. The "no's" of the two-year old are not simply a way of saying "I don't want it" or "I won't do it." The "no's" are a way of declaring her right to make decisions. The two-year old wants to do it by herself, even when doing it by herself may not be in her best interest.

For the most part, the tantrums of the two-year old disappear as long as they are ignored. After all, it is not really worth having a tantrum if no one is going to pay attention. A few children at this age, however, have tantrums as a reaction to being tired, and leaving them alone doesn't change the behavior. For these children it is usually a good idea to take them out of the situation, hold them quietly but firmly, and invite them back to play when the screaming stops.

Two year olds have learned to run and would much rather run than walk, even when they are tired. Although they can run forward at a good pace, most two-year olds have not learned how to negotiate a turn or run around a corner. When two-year olds are running on the playground, some bumps and falls are to be expected. Emerging motor skills for two-year olds include jumping with feet together, riding a tricycle, walking up and down stairs alternating feet, and sliding down a slide at an accelerated pace. Throwing and catching skills are just beginning to emerge.

An important development in two-year olds is the emergence of constructive play. Two year olds love to make castles and sand-cakes, packing sand into a mold, turning the mold upside down, and marveling at their creations. They are learning also to build towers and rows of blocks, scribble with a crayon, and propel a wheel toy across the floor.

The most remarkable developmental phenomena at two years old is the capacity think in symbols. This new capacity manifests itself both in the emergence of pretend play and in the mastery of language. The two-year old represents her thoughts and ideas in imitative actions, pretend play routines, and in a rapidly growing vocabulary.

Another dramatic development at two years old is the emergence of pretend play. While the one to two-year old pretend play is largely imitative, the two-year old is quite capable of acting out an assumed role or talking for miniature characters.

Developmental Overview: Three to Four Year Olds

Three-year olds have broadened their view of the world. Their ideas of time and place have undergone interesting transformations. They are beginning to grasp the complexities of their social world and to recognize the difference between real and pretend. Typical questions include "Where do birds sleep at night?," "Were there dinosaurs when you were a baby?," and "Are the people on television real or pretend?"

Past time is divided into the immediate past, yesterday, last week and last month, and a long time ago like when their parents were young. Future is divided into tomorrow, soon, and "when I get big." Although they may not know the names of the seasons, three-year olds are beginning to make associations. They might remember summer as when it's hot and you go on vacation and fall as when the trees turn color, when you go trick or treating, or when you watch football on television. Space, like time, is divided into categories. Some places are near and you can walk to them. Some places are too far to walk to. Some places are really far away, like Africa or the moon. There are also categories of people like children, teenagers, people who are old and work at jobs, and people who are very old and don't do much at all. Things can be living or not living, people and animals can be alive or dead, and things can be real or pretend.

By three or three and a half the turbulence of the two's has passed and a quieter child emerges. The three-year old is able to focus on a task for several minutes and to interact in a positive way with other children. By three years old the child has expanded her repertoire of emotional responses. She can be sad or pensive. She can be jealous, wary, or frightened. She can be contented, jolly, or exuberant. She is also more tuned in to the feelings of others. Pleasing adults is becoming increasingly more important to her, and praise or affection is becoming a powerful reinforcer. Although the three-year old is less apt to throw temper tantrums than the two year old, her behavior can disintegrate when she is tired or hungry.

Developmental Overview: Four to Five Year Olds

The four-year old child is becoming increasingly aware of herself as a member of the peer group. Much of her day is spent establishing and maintaining her position with her peers. The four-year old uses her growing facility with words to praise or to put down other children, to call attention to her own accomplishments, and to convince the group to adopt her ideas. The four-year old is interested in playing with other children and will use threats and promises to win a friend or gain entry into a group. "I'll be your best friend," or "I won't be your friend," are frequent refrains in a preschool.

Separation of the sexes is a common phenomenon among four-year olds. On the whole, boys tend to gather in larger groups than girls and their play is noisier and more active. Out on the playground they require plenty of space to move around. They enjoy all varieties of play and are particularly fond of monster or superhero play.

Girls are more likely to gather in groups of two or three. When a third or fourth child moves in on the play, we may see an active effort made to exclude the intruder. Four-year old girls, on the whole, do less running around than four-year old boys and spend more of their time involved in conversation.

Although four-year olds of both sexes are learning to take turns and share their toys, arguments over possessions take place continually. Frequently, disputes that begin verbally end with a push, a punch, or a skirmish. For the most part, children do not really hurt each other in these skirmishes, but adult supervision is an important safeguard.

Four-year olds love to learn new things, like pumping a swing, naming all the dinosaurs, counting up to 20, or playing games on the computer. They believe in what they see, hear, and touch. If the juice in their friend's glass looks like it's more than the juice in their own glass, then their friend has more juice even if the juice was poured out from same-sized cans. If they heard a monster make growling noises under their bed, then there is a monster under their bed even though their father says they are just imagining it. Four-year olds are very curious, and their favorite word is "why."

Developmental Overview: Five to Six Year Olds

Five-year olds seem older than four-year olds in many ways. Like four-year olds, they love to learn new things, but they are likely to be more persistent about mastery. If they are drawing a rainbow, a house, or a self-portrait, they will work for quite a while until it's just the way they want it to look. Like four-year olds, they love to pretend but their pretending is more elaborate. They gather props before the pretending begins; when they act out a pretend scene, the events take place in a logical sequence. If they are putting on a performance, they will set the stage, make the tickets, and put on their costumes before the performance begins. The performance is likely to include an announcement of what is going to happen, some sort of act or acts, and an elaborate ending with lots of bows and the expectation of applause.

Five-year olds are interested in using and interpreting symbols. While some five-year olds are faster than others in learning the mechanics of reading and writing, most five-year olds are serious about wanting to learn. They like to choose from a menu in the restaurant, read the signs on the road, make lists of things they need to buy, and write their names on their books or their drawings. They can work out simple problems in their head and can grasp the concept of adding and subtracting, though they are likely to count on their fingers before they come up with the right answer.

Five-year olds who have the opportunity to use a computer love interactive programs. They are able to understand and apply the rules of a game and enjoy reading, writing, and number activities where the computer lets them know if they have the right answer. Favorite computer activities include programs where you have to solve problems, programs where you can arrange characters on the screen to create your own imaginative story, and programs that help you make drawings, paintings, birthday cards, or invitations.

Five-year olds are even more likely than four-year olds to enjoy playing with their same gender peers. Kindergarten children are quite likely to make playground plans before the day begins. Their choice of friends is likely to be made on the basis of shared interests. Girls and boys who like active play will choose to play on the climbing equipment, play running and chasing games, play some sort of ball game, or race around the playground on a vehicle. Girls and boys who like quieter play are more likely to play in the sand, hunt for bugs or lizards, put on a performance, or huddle with a friend and just talk. Girls are more likely than boys to engage in quiet play.

Chapter 6: Physical Development

Overview

Physical development refers to the development of gross motor or large muscle skills like crawling, walking, and batting and of fine motor or small muscle skills involved in tasks like eating, writing, cutting, and drawing.

Rationale

Because young children are always on the go, the parents and teacher are apt to relax about their physical development. You might hear them say "Just let them run around and play and they'll get all the exercise they need."

It is true that all children have their own developmental time table, and that children will sit up and walk and run according to this time table no matter how we arrange their environment. But physical development involves a lot more than learning how to walk and run. Physical development is an important facet of the whole developmental process. The child's mind and body work together. The development of motor skills contributes to the development of social and emotional skills, language, and problem solving skills. The teacher plays an important role in supporting physical development by preparing the environment and by providing a variety of appropriate equipment, activities, and opportunities.

Objectives

1. To recognize expectable sequences in small and large muscle development in infancy and describe materials and activities that enhance this development.

2. To recognize expectable sequences in small and large muscle development in young toddlers and describe materials and activities that enhance this development.

3. To recognize expectable sequences in small and large muscle development in older toddlers and describe materials and activities that enhance this development.

4. To recognize expectable sequences in small and large muscle development in preschoolers and describe materials and activities that enhance this development.

5. To identify appropriate activities and to enhance the physical development of children with special needs.

Ms. Braggart and Mr. Doubtful were both seated in the waiting room of their babies pediatrician's office. Their babies, who were approximately the same age, were playing on the floor with some of the same kinds of toys. Mr. Doubtful noticed that his baby was not getting around as well as Ms. Braggart's baby and asked, "How long has your baby been crawling that well?" "About three weeks," answered Ms. Braggart. "My baby is very intelligent; he is almost pulling up to a standing position on the furniture. Soon he will be walking all over the place." Mr. Doubtful was very concerned about his baby because he was barely getting up onto his hands and knees to crawl. He thought to himself, "I will have to talk to the doctor about this. I hope my baby will be as smart as hers."

In the first four sections of this chapter on physical development, we describe the developmental sequences, environments, and activities that facilitate the development for infants, young toddlers (1-2 years old), older toddlers (2-3 year olds), and preschoolers (3-5 years old). While the attainment of developmental milestones is a critical component of healthy development, there is no reason to assume that children who acquire motor skills at an accelerated rate will be equally advanced in the acquisition of other facets of development. Nor can we assume that children, who are advanced in one area of physical development such as growth, will be ahead of schedule in the acquisition of motor milestones such as walking.

Objective 1: To recognize expectable sequences in small and large muscle development in infancy and describe materials and activities that will enhance this development

During the first twelve months of life, the infant learns important motor skills. He learns to hold his head without support, to turn from side to side, to turn from stomach to back and back to stomach, to hold his head when he is pulled to a sitting position, to reach or grasp, to pull to a sitting position, to cruise holding on to furniture, and, perhaps, to walk. Motor development occurs so quickly during the first year of life that the observant caregiver sees almost daily changes.

Developmental Picture

The infant 0-6 months:
- Is born with all the basic movements
- Turns towards sounds
- Follows moving objects
- Practices movements such as lifting head, supporting self with arms, then rolling over and sitting
- Increases in the ability to explore and discover through mastery of small muscle skills such as bringing hand to mouth, reaching, swatting, grasping, raking, and using an immature pincer grasp to pick up small objects

The caregiver:
- Provides infants the opportunity to practice emerging skills in large and small motor development
- Uses caregiving times as opportunities to encourage infants to practice motor skills
- Provides infants the opportunity to kick and move their arms while lying on their backs
- Allows infants to spend time on their abdomens so that they can practice lifting head and chest and watching moving objects
- Provides a variety of safe positions for practice that use all muscles
- Provides appropriate toys and environments to encourage large and small muscle development

The infant 8-12 months:
- Is learning to use motor skills to achieve desired goals
- Crawls, creeps, pulls to standing, cruises, walks with help, rides scooting toys, and walks alone in a predictable sequence
- Enjoys mastering motor skills and wants to share accomplishments
- Is always on the move
- Uses objects to hold, mouth, bang, drop, pick-up, turn, put together

The caregiver:
- Identifies the motor skill that the infant is trying to master
- Provides opportunities for each infant to practice emerging skills
- Provides safe spaces, furniture, and equipment for large muscle activity
- Provides many safe and interesting objects for manipulation and sensory exploration

Infants need to practice new large muscle skills. Barriers need to be created so that the space is safe and older infants are not tumbling onto the younger infants playing on the floor.

Activities that Enhance Large Muscle Development

Birth to Three Months

- **Massage:** Gently rub the baby's arms, legs and body

- **Change Baby's Position:** Make sure the infant is sometimes placed on his back, sometimes on his stomach. At times the infant can be propped up in an infant seat.

- **Rolling Over:** Help the infant learn to turn over by rolling him back and forth. Bend one knee and arm and gently roll.

- **Kicking:** Place a cradle gym over the infant's feet to encourage the development of reciprocal kicking.

- **Reaching out:** Place baby on his stomach and hold a toy a few inches in front of him to encourage stretching.

Three to Six Months

- **Reaching and Grasping:** Hold a rattle out for the baby to encourage reaching and grasping.

- **Turning From Side to Side:** Attach an attractive toy or mobile to first one side of the crib and then the other. Baby will turn from side to side in order to look at the toy.

- **Pull Ups:** Pull baby slowly to a sitting position, giving only as much head support as the baby needs.

Six to Nine Months

- **Come and get it:** Hold a toy in front of the infant and encourage him to retrieve it. Make sure the infant is allowed to be successful. To help children get started crawling, let them push with their feet against your cupped hands.

- **Sitting up:** Make sure the infant spends time sitting up, even if he has to be propped by pillows.

- **Finger food:** Help infants develop the pincer grasp by offering finger foods like cereal rings, bits of cheese, and macaroni.

Nine to Twelve Months

- **Pulling up:** Make sure there are low shelves or places the infant can use to pull himself to a standing position.

- **Ball games:** Roll a ball back and forth. Play retrieval games. Hang the ball on a string and show the infant how to bat it.

- **Walking:** Give the beginning walker something that can be pushed and used as a walker. A riding toy with raised handle works well.

- **Feeding:** Encourage infants to use a cup and spoon.

- **Tunnel crawl:** Encourage the infants to crawl through a tunnel.

Walkers in the Early Childhood Setting

- Contrary to popular belief, infant walkers do not promote early walking.

- Walkers are dangerous if children placed in them can fall down stairs or get to objects that had been previously out of reach

- Walkers limit the amount of time infants can practice cognitive skills

Activities and Materials to Enhance Small Muscle Development

Birth to Three Months

- Shake toys like rattles with handles for holding (Beginning rattles with handles are better than dumb-bell type rattles.)

- Toys and materials with textures for feeling

Three to Six Months

- Toys for handling and mouthing

- Objects for visual tracking such as mobiles that spin, plate puppets, fish in a tank, soap bubbles, wind-up cars, and pendulums

Six to Nine Months

- Squeeze toys like a rubber ducky for hand strength

- Activity boards that require the infant to hold onto, poke and pull

- Place cereal rings on highchair trays so that the infant can practice picking it up with a raking motion

- Stuffed animals and soft dolls for building hand strength

Nine to Twelve Months

- Simple finger plays like pat a cake and "Where is thumbkin?"

- Place cereal rings or macaroni on highchair trays so that the infant can practice using finger and thumb opposition (pincer grasp)

- Provide blocks and objects for filling and dumping from buckets

- Provide sensory experiences like painting with pudding

Objective 2: To recognize expectable sequences in small and large muscle development in young toddlers and describe materials and activities that enhance this development

Young toddlers spend much of their waking time practicing their motor skills. When they accomplish a new feat like walking backwards, climbing stairs, or doing a somersault, they not only perform the new feat over and over again, but they find new ways of making it more difficult. The one to two-year old who has learned to walk downstairs holding on to your hand will insist on walking down by himself, carrying his teddy bear.

Developmental Picture

The younger toddler 12-24 months:
- Is developing new skills like squatting, pushing, pulling, climbing, walking, running
- Is able to drop toys into a bucket
- Enjoys bouncing up and down in time to music and tries to perform simple finger plays
- Enjoys rolling a ball back and forth
- Is practicing small muscle skills like stacking blocks, turning pages of a book, or putting large pegs in a peg board

The caregiver:
- Provides opportunities for each child to practice acquired skills and develop emerging skills.
- Provides toys for practicing large muscle skills like large balls, pull toys, riding toys, and sturdy push toys
- Provides toys for developing small muscle skills like blocks, stacking toys, large peg boards, and pounding benches
- Engages in back and forth ball play
- Plays recorded music that encourages movement

Toys and Structures That Promote Motor Skills

The increase in large motor skills between one and two years of age is attributable in part to improvements in balance. Emerging motor skills include stepping onto a stool, backing into a chair, going from sitting on the floor to standing without getting on hands and knees, propelling a riding toy, and going down a slide. Walking and running skills continue to improve in subtle ways. As hands are not needed for balance, the toddler is able to carry a large toy, lift up a small suitcase, push a play vacuum cleaner or a lawn mower, or control the pace of a pull toy by walking frontwards or backwards.

Small motor skills, like gross motor skills, are expanding rapidly from one to two years of age. Children are learning to master cups, spoons, and forks with only a little spilling. They are also learning to turn a handle, pound with a hammer, use one finger to point and probe, zip a zipper, open and close doors, and turn dials on and off on radios or television sets.

Suggested Activities to Encourage Large Muscle Development

- Provide toys that encourage pushing, like cornpoppers, carpet sweepers, or toy lawn mowers. For safety reasons, look for push toys that have knobs or handles.

- Provide sturdy riding toys like sit-on-top-of cars or trucks that children can propel with their feet.

- Provide rocking boats that convert to stairs to give children practice with balance and coordination.

- Provide toddler slides that allow children to practice climbing stairs and experience momentum.

- Provide movement and music activities that increase body awareness, encourage imitation, and provide motor skill practice.

- Provide safe places for toddlers to climb up on in the classroom and outdoors. Toddlers will find unsafe places to climb if they are not offered safe places. It is a good idea to have a small climbing structure right inside the room so that toddlers are not climbing on the cubbies and the tables.

- Children of this age enjoy picking up and carrying items around. Some of these items could include balls of different sizes and lightweight blocks.

- Tunnels for crawling through not only give a child practice with motor skills but also give the child a quiet place to go to when he needs to be by himself.

Activities and Materials to Develop Small Muscle Skills

- Provide busy boards, lock boards, and dressing frames to for practicing small muscle skills

- Provide pounding benches that give children practice with wrist action and eye-hand coordination

- Encourage children to play with toys that have cranks that turn, like a music box or a jack-in-the-box.

- Provide materials that help children strengthen their hands and fingers, like pop-beads and squeeze toys

- Offer children drawing materials like paper and large crayons for scribbling

Objective 3: To recognize expectable sequences in small and large muscle development in older toddlers and describe materials and activities that enhance this development

Mrs. Overprotective was giving some last minute instructions to Absolome's teacher, "And remember, I do not want Absolome out on the playground. Why, I can just see him climbing up on the jungle gym and getting hurt. My Absolome is a very active boy, and I am proud to say he has never had so much as a scratch. His Dad and I see to that."

...children, like adults, need variety and change of pace.

Although we can understand Mrs. Overprotective's desire to keep her son safe, keeping an active, healthy two-year old from practicing motor skills is not a good idea. It is far better to risk a few scratches and bruises than to tell a two-year-old that he can't jump, can't run, can't climb, or can't scoot around on a ride-on-toy.

Developmental Picture

The older toddler 2-3 years old:
- Is learning to go up and down the stairs
- Is proud of physical accomplishments and insists on being watched and praised
- Is likely to get wound up and overactive
- Is developing small muscle skills
- Tears paper, glues, scribbles with a crayon, and enjoys easel painting
- Enjoys big toys and equipment like slides, bounce toys, and wagons
- Experiments with throwing different objects like balls, blocks, and puzzles

The caregiver:
- Provides toys and equipment that encourages children to play together
- Provides toys that encourage active play, such as big balls, hoops, and ride-on toys
- Provides toys and materials that develop small muscles such as play-dough, large beads to string, pitchers for poring, and paper for wadding and tearing
- Alternates quiet and active play so that the children are not over-stimulated
- Supervises closely during jumping, climbing, and going up and down stairs

Activities and Materials That Promote Large Muscle Development

- **Rope train:** Two-year olds love to run around the playground, but the running around can easily get out of control. Tie two or three skipping ropes together and then tie ribbons or pieces of cloth at equal intervals along the rope about a foot and a half apart. With each child holding on to a section of the rope, lead the toddlers around the playground at a fast walk or a slow trot.

- **Obstacle Course:** Obstacle courses work well with two-year-olds so long as the obstacles are easy to master. One way to create an obstacle course is to lay a ladder flat on the ground.

- **Bullfrog:** Create a "pond" by making a circle with a long skipping rope. The children line up on the outside of the circle. When the bullfrog (teacher) says "ribbit ribbit," all of the little frogs have to jump over the rope and into the pond. When the bullfrog (teacher) says "turn around," the children jump out of the pond.

- **Provide large motor equipment:** Provide equipment like ride-on toys, push toys, and transportation vehicles, age appropriate climbing structures and slides.

- **Outdoor ball play:** Provide large balls for kicking, throwing, catching, and trapping

- **Music and movement:** Children enjoy moving to recorded music while they play rhythm instruments

- **Blocks and construction materials:** Children can build with a variety of blocks. Other construction materials, such as pieces of cardboard and paper towel spindles, and miniature props can extend this play. For example, add animals to the blocks and the children may build a corral or use a blocks as "hay" for the horse.

Activities and Materials That Encourage Small Muscle Development

- Children this age are just really starting to use manipulatives that can be put together and taken apart, like large put-together building blocks sets.

- Children enjoy tearing paper they can glue onto other sheets of paper. Other types of art materials that encourage small development include big crayons and paper, easels and large brushes, beginning scissors for snipping paper, and chalk for use on paper or outdoors on the sidewalk.

• Place the baby dolls in the water table with some sponges and washcloths. As children wring out the sponge and wash cloth, they will develop their hand strength.

Objective 4: To recognize expectable sequences in small and large muscle development in preschoolers and describe materials and activities that enhance this development

Mrs. Matthews had decided to place Billy in Little Follies Play School. She was just finishing an extended visit with Billy's teacher, Miss Janice, and was giving her some last minute instructions. "And, by the way," she continued, "I don't want Billy spending too much time outdoors playing. That playground looks very dusty and I don't want to take chances with his allergies. Furthermore, I am against all the stress you people place on sports. I want my Billy to grow up with a good mind and I don't care a bit whether or not he grows up to be an athlete!"

The following day Billy arrived in school. Much to Miss Janice's surprise, Billy got along well with the other children. When playground time arrived, he ran out enthusiastically with a group of active boys and joined them in a space explorers game on the jungle gym. At the end of the playground period, he was red-faced, dusty, and full of happy chatter.

Billy's mother arrived to pick him up. Mrs. Matthew's first words were, "Oh, I see you let him go out on the playground."

"Yes," Billy added with great gusto. "And I climbed on the jungle gym and I was Darth Vader and I jumped off the jungle gym and I – " Mrs. Matthews had a dark look in her eyes as her son prattled.

Miss Janice decided not to be defensive. "Yes, Mrs. Matthews, I did let Billy go out on the playground. He had a very good time and it did not bother his allergies. Billy is an extremely well coordinated youngster and he enjoys active play. You know that, contrary to what many people believe, bright children are usually healthier and more athletic than less bright children. Intellectual development and physical development frequently go hand in hand."

Mrs. Matthews was interested. All of a sudden she forgot about Billy's allergies and dusty clothes.

Miss Janice was quite correct. The development of motor skills is a critical component of a good preschool curriculum. The very fact that children spend so much of their time practicing motor skills suggests the importance of physical development. Furthermore, children themselves attach great importance to motor skill achievements. Parents who accompany their preschoolers to the playground or a swimming pool are constantly bombarded with cries of, "Watch me, Mommy." "Look at me, Daddy." Each new motor achievement is a source of pride for young children. In planning activities to develop gross motor skills, it is important to remember that children, like adults, need variety and change of pace. They need to have free play activities where there are opportunities to socialize and make up rules, as well as guided activities where they listen to and follow directions. They need to have slow paced activities where energy is channeled and faster paced activities where energy is expended.

Developmental Picture

The preschool child 3-5 years old:
- Is proud of physical accomplishments and insists on being watched
- Is aware of the motor skills that other children are mastering
- Likes to jump and climb but is not aware of the risks
- Is learning new small muscle skills such as scribbling, pretend writing, cutting and gluing, coloring and painting
- Is learning new motor skills including climbing, jumping, throwing and catching, peddling a tricycle, pumping a swing, hopping on one foot, and galloping
- May engage in competitive rough-and-tumble games involving sliding, racing, jumping, balancing, and swinging, without regard for safety

The caregiver:
- Recognizes that preschool children like to be on the move and require large, open spaces to play
- Recognizes that stopping a movement or staying still is a major challenge for a preschool child and knows they may have trouble sitting still
- Recognizes that supervision is an essential because most preschoolers are not safety conscious
- Provides children with a variety of opportunities for indoor and outdoor motor activities on a daily basis
- Provides opportunities to engage in quiet as well as active activities
- Provides many opportunities to develop small muscle skills such as scribbling, lacing, wadding and tearing paper, pasting/gluing, cutting with scissors and with plastic knives

Motor skill development is important in the preschool for many reasons. As children learn to control their body in space and master motor feats along with their peers they are:

- Developing body awareness
- Improving balance
- Learning about position in space
- Improving throwing, catching, and jumping skills
- Engaging in imaginative activities that foster creativity while enhancing large muscle skills

Large motor skills in the preschool years can be categorized in several ways:

Balance

Balance skills can be broken down into static-non-movement and dynamic-movement.

- **Static-non-movement** includes those activities that require standing, reaching while standing still

- **Dynamic-movement** includes those activities that require crawling, walking, running, marching, or climbing

Coordination

- **Expressive Movement:** Expressive movements are typically seen in music and gymnastic type activities where the children could make their own interpretation of the dance, music or gymnastic movement. The movement can express mood, feelings, or concepts.

- **Integration:** Following directions or putting together what you hear or see with what your body does. An example of this kind of activity would be playing Simon Says.

Developing Body Awareness

A good way to develop body awareness is to lead the children in action songs. "This Old Man" is a good one to use.

This old man, he played one. He played nick-nack on my thumb, etc.
This old man, he played two. He played nick-nack on my shoe.
This old man, he played three. He played nick-nack on my knee.
This old man, he turned red. He played nick-nack on my head.
This old man, he liked deers. He played nick-nack on my ears.

See if the children can add any rhymes. Other action songs and rhymes include "Miss Polly Had a Dolly," "Simon Says," "Brown Girl in the Ring," "Skip To My Lou," and "Head and Shoulders."

Activities for Improving Balance

- **Cross Over the Stream:** Use carpet strips or pieces of tag board as stepping stones. Play Follow the Leader across the stream, cautioning the children about getting wet.

- **Toe the Line:** Draw a chalk line or place masking tape on the floor securing each end with masking tape. Ask the children to walk on the line like little mice. When the children have learned to walk forward on the line, vary the activity —

  ▲ Walk backwards
  ▲ Walk sideways
  ▲ Walk on tip toes
  ▲ Walk with your eyes closed

- **Walk the Plank:** Repeat Toe the Line activities using a plank or balance board.

Activities for Learning About Position in Space

- **Obstacle Course:** Set up an obstacle course by weaving a string in and out of the tables and over and under chairs. Encourage the children to follow the course.

- **Formation:** Draw a circle out of chalk or make a circle out of strips of tape. Distribute red and yellow ribbons to the children, giving every other child the same color. Explain that when the music stops, red ribbons take a giant step into the circle and yellow ribbons take a giant step out of the circle. When the music starts up again everyone takes a giant step back to the circle and walks around it. Make the activity more difficult by playing faster music.

- **Recorded music and musical instruments:** Children will naturally start to move when they have musical instruments and hear marching music.

Activities for Improving Throwing, Catching, and Jumping Skills

- **Circle Game with Large Ball:** Seat children in a circle with their legs spread apart. The teacher rolls the ball to each child and encourages the child to roll the ball back. At first roll the ball to the children, going from left to right. When the children have become adept at catching and returning the ball, play the same game with the children standing in a circle.

- **Tether Ball:** Place a rubber or beach ball in a bag or net and hang it from the ceiling. Let the children bat at the ball with a Nerf bat.

- **Bean Bag Toss:** Let children toss a bean bag into a waste paper basket or carton. When they become skilled at this, draw a clown with a large mouth on the side of the carton and let the children "feed the clown".

- **Crossing the Stream:** Give two children the task of holding the ends of a skipping rope. Let the children jump over the rope when it is in the floor. Gradually raise the height of the rope.

Activities for Enhancing Large Muscle Skills

Encourage the children to play a variety of pretend motor activities such as:

- Jogging in place
- Swimming in place
- Hop like rabbits
- Roll over like a dog
- Do the bicycle on your back
- Pretend to fly a kite
- Play skating in a circle
- Fly around the room like birds
- Crawl like a baby
- Kick like a baby
- Kick a pretend football
- Pretend to catch a high ball

Circle Time Activities that Encourage Body Awareness

Pass the Shoe

Equipment: Each child takes off one of their shoes for passing.

Directions: Players sit in a circle and sing the song as they pass their shoe to the right. When the children receive their shoe back they stand up and clap.

Sung to the tune of London Bridges

Pass the shoe from me to you, me to you, me to you:
Pass the shoe from me to you, and do just as I do!

Little Sally Walker (An African-American ring game)

The children form a circle with one child in the middle. "Sally" or "Sal" kneels in the center of the circle and acts out the words to the song. The other children in the circle walk around as the song is sung. "Sally" or "Sal" shakes toward the child that they chose next to be in the circle.

Little Sally Walker sittin' in a saucer.
Rise Sally rise.
Wipe your weeping eyes,
Put your hands on your hips and let your backbone slip.
Ah. Shake it to the east. Ah. Shake it to the west.
Ah. Shake it to the one that you love the best.

We're Going to Kentucky, We're Going to the Fair

The children hold hands to make a big circle. Then they drop hands to have their space in the circle. One child is chosen to be in the center. The song is sung and the child in the center performs the moves as directed in the song. During the last line in the song the child in the middle closes their eyes to spin around. The person they stop on has their turn in the center.

We're going to Kentucky. We're going to the fair,
To see the Senorita with flowers in her hair.
Oh! Shake it, Shake it, Shake it.
Shake it till you stop,
Turn around and turn around until you make a stop.

Activities and Materials that Enhance Small Muscle Skills

- Materials and activities that practice finger isolation and finger strength include: beads for stringing, peg boards, geo-boards (rubber band boards), lacing materials.

- Put a clothesline with clothespins in the dramatic play area. Children will be able to develop their pincer grasp and develop finger strength as they hang up clothes on the clothes line.

- Provide a basket with different sized plastic jars and their lids. Children will develop their wrist swivel as they put the lids on the jars.

- Making play-dough and then playing with it helps children to develop hand strength. Be sure to include a variety of objects that children can use for rolling, shaping, cutting, molding, stamping, and poking into the play-dough.

- Give the children tongs to pick up small objects and transfer them into a container. Suggested objects include pom poms or ping pong balls.

Outdoor Activities for Improving Motor Skills

The playground is especially appropriate for gross motor activities that require space, equipment, or climbing structures. The following types of equipment are especially desirable:

- Wheel toys and riding path
- Climbing structure that is safe and provides space for several children and encourages imaginative play
- Planks and large blocks that the children can use to create their own structures
- Small tires or spindles that can be rolled
- Larger tires that can be used for jumping
- Beach balls and playground balls
- Hula Hoops
- Jump ropes
- Tire swings
- Tunnels
- Balance beams and log walks

Organized Outdoor Activities

Red light, Green light

Children form a line. When the caller says "green light," they run forward. When the caller says, "red light," they freeze.

Punchinello

The children form a circle with one child in the middle who is Punchinello. During verse one. Punchinello makes a motion as the children in the circle clap and sing the song. During verse two, the children copy the motion that Punchinello had made. In the third verse Punchinello, chooses another child to be in the center to become the new Punchinello.

What can you do, Punchinello funny fellow?
What can you do, Punchinello funny you?
We can do it, too Punchinello funny fellow.
We can do it, too Punchinello funny you.
You choose one of us, Punchinello funny fellow.
You choose one of us, Punchinello funny you.

Ring-Around-the-Rosy

Children hold hands in a circle and dance around to the familiar chant. On "all fall down," they stop and sit down abruptly.

Freeze

This game can be played with or without music. The players begin to move around the pre-designated area. At the signal to "freeze" or when the music stops, players try to stay as still as possible. When the signal to "melt" is given or when the music is turned back on, the players begin to move around again.

Follow the Leader

One child is chosen to be the leader. The children line up behind the leader and follow her actions.

The Teacher's Role on the Playground

Helping children with minor motor delays to improve their skills.

Playground time offers a good opportunity for teachers to work with children who are mildly delayed in terms of motor skill development and need special instruction and/or encouragement. Children who are not well coordinated may shy away from active physical play. In order to identify children who could benefit from physical activities, identify children on the playground who seldom engage in active play. Play a game like "Monkey Say, Monkey Do," where children have to imitate your actions. First, ask the children that you have selected to imitate everything you do. Jump, bounce and catch a ball, balance on one leg, march heel-to-toe, or touch your toes. Give each child in the group an opportunity to choose a stunt that you and the group have to imitate.

When you return to the classroom, check off the names of the children who were in your selected group. Put a star beside the children who had difficulty imitating the activities that you demonstrated. While the rest of the group may have selected quiet play because they prefer it, the children who had difficulty with motor skills could be avoiding active play for fear of failure. This second group of children may need some special time on a daily basis to practice motor skills. Planned physical activities for the identified children should include

Playground time offers a good opportunity for teachers to work with children who are mildly delayed in terms of motor skill development and need special instruction and/or encouragement.

activities that allow them to practice skills that they have already achieved and activities that help them develop new skills appropriate for their age. Use a checklist of physical skills to chart their progress.

Plan a daily outdoor activity, which focuses on physical skills that need strengthening. Your list of activities may include:

- walking on a board to improve balance
- running games to improve skill and stamina
- obstacles courses to improve coordination and motor control
- climbing structure activities to improve coordination, balance, and upper body strength
- ball play to encourage eye-hand coordination, thrust, and aim
- hula hoop games with the hula hoops on the ground to encourage jumping skills

Objective 5: To identify appropriate activities that enhance the physical development of children who have special needs

Mrs. Protect had come to school to observe her daughter, Merissa, who has cerebral palsy. It was mid-morning and she was surprised to find Merissa on the playground. The children were sitting in a circle on the ground, tossing a playground ball around the circle. Mrs. Protect was worried; Merissa wasn't good at catching and perhaps the ball would hit Merissa in the face. Just as her worry was surfacing, the ball hit Merissa's nose. Mrs. Protect expected that Merissa would burst into tears, but Merissa just started laughing and all the children joined in. Needless to say, Mrs. Protect was proud of her daughter and delighted with the teacher.

An Individualized Educational Plan (IEP) determines the types of intervention that the classroom teacher is responsible for implementing for children with diagnosed handicapping conditions. However, it is up to the classroom teacher to modify the recommended activities for children with special needs so that these children can participate as much as possible in the group activities that other children are enjoying.

Here are examples of some ways in which a teacher can include children with special needs in physical activities:

- If an infant or toddler has difficulty with sitting or balance, place her on the floor inside a rubber tube or swim ring so that she can join the other children in floor play.

- If a child is in a wheelchair, adjust the height of the table so that she can join the other children in craft or clay activities that encourage small muscle development.

- If a child is on crutches, has poor balance, or is visually impaired, make sure that the furniture is not out of place, so that the child has a clear path to anywhere in the room.

- If a child is unable to stand, play movement games during circle time where the children are sitting on the floor and the physically challenged child can perform the arm and hand movements along with the other children.

- If a child is physically challenged and cannot use the playground equipment, plan activities that the child can participate in like digging for gold (rocks) in the sandbox or catching bubbles.

- If a visually impaired child wants to play in a group game, try a three-legged race. Each child chooses a partner and the teacher ties the left leg of one child to the right leg of his partner. Visually impaired children do well in this game because they have had practice in trusting other children to take the lead.

Helping other children join you in 'safe keeping' children with special needs

Talk to the children about ways of helping children who have a handicapping condition. Your first suggestion should be that you should not try to help a child with a disability unless he asks for help or seems to be in trouble. Suggest to the children that they should take special care when they are running, swinging, or riding a wheel toy, so they do not bump into a child who has poor balance or cannot see them or hear them.

Fortunately, young children are usually quite trustworthy when they know that a child has a problem.

Bredekamp, S. (Editor). (1993). *Developmentally appropriate practice in early childhood programs serving children from birth through age 8*. Washington, D.C.: National Association for the Education of Young Children.

Bronson, M.B. (1995). *The right stuff for children birth to 8: Selecting play materials to support development*. Washington, D.C.: National Association for the Education of Young Children.

Curtis, D. & Carter, M. (1996). *Reflecting children's lives: A handbook for planning child-centered curriculum*. St. Paul, MN: Redleaf Press.

Diffily, D. & Morrison, K. (Editors). (1996). *Family friendly communication for early childhood programs.* Washington, D.C.: National Association for the Education of Young Children.

Dodge, D.T., Koralek, D.G., & Pizzolongo, P.J. (1989). *Caring for school children.* Vol. 1. Washington, D.C.: Teaching Strategies, Inc.

Meisels, S.J., Marsden, D.B., & Stetson, C. (2000). *Winning ways to learn: 600 great ideas for children.* NY: Goddard Press.

Snow, C.W. (1998). *Infant development.* Upper Saddle River, NJ: Prentice Hall.

Torbert, M. & Schneider, L.B. (1993). *Follow me too: A handbook of movement activities for three-to-five-year-olds.* NY: Addison-Wesley Publishing Company.

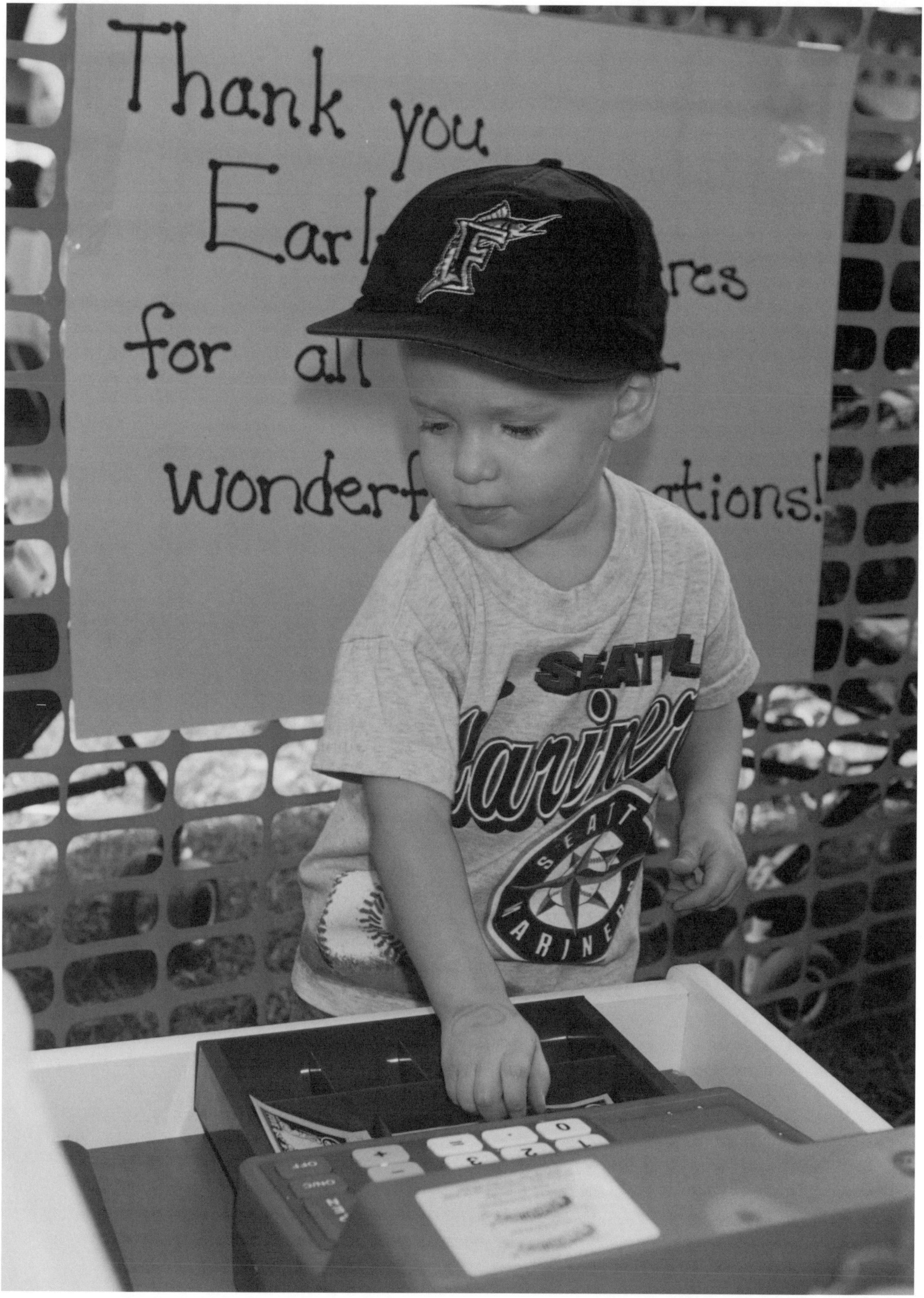
Thank you
for all

Chapter 7:
Cognitive Development

Overview

Cognitive, or intellectual, development refers to the child's growing ability to give meaning to experiences, to reason, to acquire knowledge, and to problem solve.

Rationale

As the child interacts with the environment, she discovers how things work. As she interacts with people, she acquires patterns, and language, information, and ideas. As she tries to make sense of her experiences, she develops new concepts and modifies her old ways of thinking.

Although what each child learns is unique, their underlying concepts are developed in a predictable sequence. Each new step provides the foundation for the next.

Objectives

1. To recognize expectable sequences in cognitive development in infancy and describe materials and activities that enhance cognitive development.

2. To recognize expectable sequences in cognitive development in toddlers and describe materials and activities that enhance cognitive development.

3. To recognize expectable sequences in cognitive development in two to three years olds and describe materials and activities that enhance cognitive development.

4. To recognize expectable sequences in the acquisition of cognitive skills in preschool children and describe materials and activities that support the attainment of sorting, ordering, counting and pattern identification skills, and conceptual thinking.

5. To learn how to create a preschool environment that encourages exploration, curiosity and critical thinking.

6. To learn techniques for introducing meaningful themes into preschool classrooms.

Ms. Get-Them-Ready was teaching her four-year olds a lesson on colors. She held up a card with a turquoise square on it. "This color is turquoise. What color is it, class?" "Turquoise." She held up a second card. "And this is chartreuse. Can you say that?" A parent who happened to be visiting asked Ms. Get-Them-Ready why she chose those particular colors to teach. "Oh," replied the teacher. "They're on the kindergarten readiness test. I want to make sure that all my kids get a perfect score."

If Ms. Get-Them-Ready really wants her students to be ready for kindergarten, she should worry less about the test and more about helping them develop their minds. Preschool children are naturally curious, and colors are just one of the things they notice. Choosing wallpaper for the dollhouse, comparing the colors of leaves collected on a nature walk, mixing paints, planting a garden, designing outfits for paper dolls, stringing beads in a pattern, making "rainbows" with a prism or hose, and playing sorting games all provide opportunities to talk about colors in a meaningful way. Activities like these build on children's interests, deepen their knowledge, and enhance their cognitive development. Young children who are given opportunities to explore and investigate, solve problems, make discoveries, and develop new thinking skills are primed for success both in school and in life.

> *Babies are born with a built-in need to take in new information and make sense out of their world.*

Objective 1: To recognize expectable sequences in cognitive development in infancy and describe materials and activities that enhance this development

Allison's mother agreed to take care of her six-month old son when she went back to work. When Allison dropped her son off at her mother's on her first day back to work, she gave her mother a long list of instructions. One instruction was underlined in red. "After his ten o'clock nap, spend 15 minutes showing Timothy flash cards with words. Begin by showing the flash card with 'cat', 'cake', and 'mouse.' Mrs. "C" looked over the list of instructions. "I am delighted to take care of Timothy. What is this about showing him flash cards? Six-month old babies, no matter how bright they are, should not be taught how to read." At first Allison was not at all sure that her mother was right about the flash cards. But then she had second thoughts. "Maybe mother is right," she told her husband that night. "When we show Timothy flash cards he watches our faces and smiles, but he never looks down at the cards."

Babies are born with a built-in need to take new information and make sense out of their world. In the beginning, an infant experiences sounds, sensations, sights, smells, and tastes as loosely connected experiences. Over time, the baby discovers connections between these experiences. She recognizes that the sound of her own cries is followed by the appearance of her mother's face and the comfortable feeling of being held in her mother's arms. She learns to anticipate sequences of sensations, and her world becomes more predictable.

Developmental Picture

The infant 0-6 months:

- Is unique in terms of temperament, coping ability, and developmental timetable
- Is working hard to make sense out of the world—by listening, watching, and touching
- Is programmed from birth to engage in interactions with parents and/or caregivers
- At 4 or 5 months old makes interesting things happen again
- Puts together sensations and information from different senses
- Shows interest in new information
- Gets accustomed to familiar sights and sounds

The caregiver:

- Recognizes and adapts to each infant's unique temperamental characteristics
- Discovers ways of enabling infants to experience sensations, sounds, feel, tastes, smells, and sights
- Responds to each infant in a predictable way
- Recognizes that different infants have different thresholds of responsiveness and responds to each infant's need for more or less stimulation

The infant 6-12 months:

- Learns through exploration and discovery
- Anticipates new events based on past experience
- Recognizes that people can affect objects and other people
- Imitates actions and expressions
- Empties and fills, opens and shuts, pushes and pulls, pokes and prods
- Points to an interesting object and expects the caregiver to look at it
- Looks at objects that the caregiver points to or looks at
- Uses simple tools such as shovels, spoons, or drum sticks
- Demonstrates awareness that objects are there even if they are out of sight by playing peek-a-boo or finding toys covered by a blanket

The caregiver:

- Identifies and reinforces infants' interests and capabilities
- Shares the joy and excitement of new learning and new discoveries
- Provides opportunities for infants to experiment with dropping objects into a container
- Plays games that the infant enjoys like peek-a-boo or "Where did teddy go?"

Activities to Encourage Problem Solving Skills
Birth to Three Months

Although babies spend much of their time sleeping in the first three months, they also have periods of quiet wakefulness when they are alert and ready to learn. Babies learn to put together information they receive from different senses. Within the first three months they make connections between sounds they hear, sights they see, and sensations they feel. They will learn to search with their eyes for the source of a sound, or respond to a smiling face with a smile and a coo.

- **Look and Stare:** Hold a brightly colored object in front of the infant and see if he can focus his eyes on it.

- **Tracking:** Hold a bright toy 12 inches in front of infant, slowly moving it from side to side. When the infant has learned to track the toy, move it vertically and then in a circle.

- **Grasping:** Place a small article in the baby's hand and allow him to grasp it. Change hands.

- **Sound search:** Shake a bell or rattle behind and above the child's head. Give him time to turn his head to see what made the sound.

Three to Six Months

Between three and six months old, babies are learning to reach out and grasp for toys. They are making connections between actions and outcomes. They shake a rattle, hear its tinkle, and purposefully shake it again.

- **Rattle shake:** Give the infant a rattle and show him how to shake it to make a sound.

- **Wristband:** Make a wristband for the baby to help him "discover" his hands.

- **Banging:** Give the infant a rattle to bang on a hard surface.

- **Reaching activities:** Give the infant lots of opportunities to reach. Hold out objects, dangle objects on ribbons, put a cradle gym within the infant's reach.

- **Kicking activities:** Place the cradle gym near the baby's feet so he can make it move by kicking.

- **Peek-a-boo:** Play a peek-a-boo game with baby.

- **Toy manipulation:** Give the infant a soft squeak toy.

Six to Nine Months

By now, babies are making fine discriminations relating to people and toys. They greet familiar people with smiles and babbles, and turn away from strangers. They play with a toy in different ways, in accordance with its attributes. They test a new toy in a variety of ways, looking at it from all sides, shaking or banging it, and even tasting it.

- **Squeaks:** Show the infant how to make a squeak toy work.

- **Cause and Effect Activity:** Give the baby a cause and effect toy, like a pop-up or musical toy that responds when he pushes down a key or lever.

- **Learning Scheme:** Give the baby a wooden spoon and a pie tin. Show him how to use the spoon to bang the tin and make an interesting sound.

- **Batting:** Give the infant a roly-poly clown toy to bat back and forth.

- **Hidden object:** Partially hide a favorite toy and see if the infant can find it.

- **Bell ringing:** Give the infant a bell to ring.

- **Block tower:** Build a block tower and let the baby knock it down.

Nine to Twelve Months

During the nine to twelve month period, babies develop a new repertoire of problem-solving skills. With increased memory power, they develop the ability to hold in mind the image of an object and to recognize that objects continue to exist even when they are out of sight and out of touch. Recognizing that someone can be there even when they cannot see her, nine to twelve month olds initiate a game of peek-a-boo by hiding under the blanket. When caregiver hides one of their toys under a blanket, they will lift the blanket and joyfully recover the toy.

- **Dropping games:** Give the infant objects to drop into different size containers. Once the infant has mastered this, cut a round hole in the plastic lid of a coffee can and show the infant how to drop a ping-pong ball through the hole.

- **Ball Play:** Play a rolling game with the infant. Say "I roll the ball to baby and she rolls it back to me."

- **Reaching Challenge:** Hold a plastic tray upright with a toy behind it. See if your baby tries to reach the toy by reaching around it, or by trying to go through the tray.

- **Hidden object game:** Hide a toy under a small cloth and let the infant retrieve it. Next use two and then three cloths. Try hiding the object in the infant's clothes and inside boxes.

- **Emptying game:** Fill a box with interesting objects. Let the infant empty the objects from container.

Objective 2: To recognize expectable sequences in cognitive development in young toddlers and describe materials and activities that enhance this development

Pedro and his wife Rosita shared the care of their daughter Maria. Pedro was always telling people how easy it was to take care of a baby. When Maria was a year old and walking, he began changing his mind. Maria would not stay in one place. All she wanted to do was toddle around the house pulling at lamp cords, pulling books and magazines off the shelves, and turning the house upside down. By the time his wife arrived home at noon to take over his shift, Pedro was always exhausted. "She's a handful all right," he would admit to his wife as he hurried off to work.

One to two-year olds are active and curious. They are continually on the go — prodding, exploring, and investigating. Although they often cannot communicate with words, toddlers are continually asking questions and trying to find out the answers.

- What sorts of things are inside Mommy's purse or inside the garbage can?
- What does the dog's water taste like?
- How many stuffed animals can fit inside the toilet?
- For how long can I keep pulling the tissues out of the box?
- What happens when I take the top off of the perfume?
- What could I reach if I climbed up on the kitchen stool?

While parents and other caregivers can appreciate the scientific spirit of the young toddler, for the sake of safety and cost containment, her explorations must be limited. The challenge that caregivers face is to provide toddlers with problem solving activities that are age appropriate, safe, and feasible.

Activities That Encourage Problem Solving

- Play hide and seek games with objects and toys. Hide favorite toys under one or several hollow blocks or hide a toy inside your pocket and let the children find it.

- Place large beads inside a large container. The children will have to tip over the container in order to retrieve the beads.

- Provide a sloped board for wheel toys. One to two-year olds will learn to let the wheel toys roll down the slope.

- Place toys in boxes with different kinds of lids. One to two-year olds will learn to remove the lids in order to retrieve the toys.

- Give the children pots with lids to play with. See if they can put the right lid on each pot.

- Make a "house" from a large appliance box. Cut a door that children can open and close and windows that they can peek in or out of.

- See if toddlers can figure out how to climb into a large box or laundry basket and how to climb out.

- When a toddler is sitting in a high chair, attach a ribbon to a toy. The child will toss the toy over the high chair and pull it up with the ribbon.

- Demonstrate ways of using hollow blocks for stacking as well as nesting.

The challenge that caregivers face is to provide toddlers with problem-solving activities that are age-appropriate, safe and feasible.

Developmental Picture

The young toddler:
- Imitates actions that she sees the caregiver do like sweeping, stirring, or hugging a toy animal
- Is beginning to engage in pretend activities like going to sleep, eating a cookie, or talking on the phone
- Knows where to find a favorite toy even when it is not in sight
- Can help with simple tasks like putting toys away, passing out crackers, or wiping the table
- Plays with toys in appropriate ways, like putting together a stacking toy, zooming a miniature car across the room, or using a stick to beat a drum or play a xylophone

The caregiver:
- Provides housekeeping materials like dishes, plates, spoons, play food, brooms, and mops that encourage simple pretending
- Initiates pretend play like going shopping or serving a pretend meal
- Places toys on shelves in categories—e.g.: puts manipulative toys together, picture books together, cars and trucks together
- Asks children for help with simple tasks
- Provides toys that challenge each child

Objective 3: To recognize expectable sequences in cognitive development in older toddlers and describe materials and activities that enhance this development

Jack, age two and a half, walked into his family day care home dragging a pink and black jump rope. "'Nake," he said, as soon as he saw his caregiver. "Oh," she responded. "I see you brought your snake. Is he hungry?" "Yes," said Jack. "Want s'ghetti." "Here's some spaghetti, Snake," the caregiver responded, feeding the snake from an imaginary bowl. "No," said Jack. "Me do it."

Older toddlers, like younger toddlers, are learning about their world through exploration. Their needs to explore, to find out, and to do things their own way and by themselves dominate their play activities. But despite the fact that two-year olds are self-willed and on the go, we can also see the beginning of task-oriented behaviors. The two-year old will systematically complete a simple puzzle, sort toys according to color, place a round ball in a shape box, or fill up a pegboard with pegs.

Developmental Picture

The older toddler:
- Is interested in sorting objects according to color or shape
- Can string large beads, stack 3-4 blocks to make a tower, and complete an inset puzzle with 4-10 pieces
- Recognizes when something is out of place or doesn't belong
- Enjoys playing with toys that present a challenge
- Uses an object to represent a different object (e.g., pretends a block is a cookie)
- Enjoys playing with other children and copying their actions, but is probably not ready to share toys

The caregiver:
- Encourages children to sort things into categories
- Encourages pretend play
- Color codes shelves so children can help with pick-up
- Provides a variety of materials and toys that encourage exploration, manipulation, and problem solving

Problem Solving Activities

Bean Pouring and Sorting: For children above the age of two-and-a-half, where swallowing is no longer a problem, bean pouring and sorting is an excellent activity. Individual small trays and scoops work best. Different color beans can be used for sorting activities.

Nature Corner: Provide trays of shells, rocks, or pine cones of various shapes and sizes. Encourage children to name the objects, to talk about the likes and differences they notice, and to arrange the objects in pleasing ways. Increase children's interest by adding magnifying glasses.

Exploring Textures: Collect materials with a variety of textures, such as fabric swatches, pieces of wood, stones, sandpaper, sponges, jar tops, plastic, and bark. Ask children to find things that are rough and smooth, heavy and light, hard and soft, thick and thin. Children can have fun finding matches and opposites.

Salt tray: Fill a shallow tray with salt. Children will enjoy drawing circles, lines, and eventually letters with their fingers.

Nature walks: Increase the fun by making a nature bracelet. Put a piece of tape, facing sticky side out, around each child's wrist. During the walk stick blades of grass, seeds, flowers, gravel, and bark on the tape. Collect leaves, rocks, bark, etc. in a bucket. When you get back, you can sort the materials and make collages, paint rocks, or do leaf printing.

Planting activities: Plant seeds in dirt, sponges, or water. Talk about how they grow. Look at roots, stems, and leaves. Smell the flowers. A fun toddler activity is to give each child a paper cup and let her punch holes in the bottom and decorate it with markers or paste scraps of paper on it. Let each child put dirt in her cup and plant seeds. (Note: Radish seeds and bean seeds are good choices because they sprout and grow more quickly than other seeds.)

Weighing and measuring: A small balance scale gives children experience comparing different weights.

Animals: Although it requires extra effort, classroom animals such as fish, rabbits, or gerbils, help children learn about animals' needs and the responsibility of caring for another living thing.

Magnets: Put out magnets and a tray of metal and nonmetal objects. Let children discover what objects can be picked up.

Sinking and floating experiments: Put out a tray of objects and a bowl of water. Let each child pick up an object, guess what will happen, and try it out. Put all objects that sink on one tray and all objects that float on another.

Color paddles: Transparent colored paddles or colored gels give children experience with mixing colors.

Objective 4: To recognize expectable sequences in the acquisition of cognitive skills in preschool children and describe materials and activities that support the attainment of sorting, ordering, counting, and pattern identification skills, and of conceptual thinking

Mrs. Push-and-Pull was visiting the Sunny-Isles child care center prior to enrolling her three-year old. After a tour of the center in which she saw the art area, the dramatic play house, the music and rhythm room, and the block building corner, Mrs. Push-and Pull was feeling very ambivalent. "It's a beautiful center and the children seemed happy and all that but I want my Angelica to learn academics," said Mrs. Push-and-Pull. "She's a very bright child, you realize. She already knows how to count to ten, and she can pick out all the letters in her name."

Mrs. Push-and-Pull is not very different from many parents. She wants her child to do well in school, but she doesn't realize that getting ready for school involves much more than counting by rote and recognizing the letters of the alphabet. Real understanding of letters and numbers rests upon the understanding of key concepts and the development of thinking skills.

Developmental Picture

The preschool child:
- Is eager and excited about learning new things and making new discoveries
- Is interested in finding out how things work and what things change into and how they can be transformed
- Is interested in nature and natural phenomena
- Is discovering how things are alike and different, and what things belong together
- Is interested and ready to learn about counting and creating sets of objects up to ten
- Is able to understand concepts and make generalizations and is ready for a thematic curriculum
- Enjoys sorting things out and making collections
- Tries out different ways of making objects move, change, or fit together
- Learns from watching adults and other children and imitates what he sees
- Remembers things that happened in the past and anticipates what will happen in the future

The caregiver:

- Provides opportunities for children to learn through hands-on experience
- Provides children the time and space to manipulate, explore, and experiment
- Provides opportunities for children to learn about things outside of their immediate experience
- Allows children to try things their own way, to make mistakes, and to try again
- Provides children with a variety of experiences with plants and animals
- Provides children with opportunities to learn about counting, arranging items into sets, size, shape, and ways to measure
- Introduces familiar themes like transportation , families, weather, and building things

Understanding Basic Properties of the Real World

Vanessa's grandmother bought her two beautiful new dresses for her birthday. The day after her birthday, Vanessa wore one of the dresses to pre-school. "What a beautiful dress!" her teacher commented as soon as Vanessa walked into the room. "Red dress," Vanessa repeated. "That's right. It's a red dress. You are learning your colors." The next day Vanessa wore the other new dress to school. "Red dress," Vanessa repeated, as she proudly showed her dress to her teacher. "No, Vanessa, it's not a red dress. This dress is blue." Vanessa was disappointed and confused. The last time she called a new dress "red," the teacher was happy. Today she called a new dress "red" and the teacher was sad.

Vanessa's problem with learning color names is a very common one. She could remember the word red and connect it with dress, but she did not know what aspect of the dress red stood for. The guess she made was perfectly logical from her point of view. The most special thing about her dress was its newness, so red, she decided, meant "new".

Before children can name the color of an object, they have to figure out what we mean by color. Actually, color is a complicated concept involving several insights.

- Red, green, blue, etc. are all names of colors.

- Color is a property of objects, just the way size and shape are properties of objects.

- The answer to "What color is it?" must be one of the color names. It cannot be a size name like big or a shape name like square.

- Colors that look different sometimes have the same name (light blue and dark blue), while colors that look similar sometimes have different names (dark blue and purple).

Categorizing objects according to color is one of the many ways in which young children learn about real world objects. In this section we are concerned with the development of thinking skills that help a child acquire concepts about the physical world. These skills include sorting objects into categories, placing objects in a logical sequence, learning about number relationships, and identifying properties.

Sorting Objects into Categories

In a manner of speaking, the very youngest infants categorize experiences. Newborn infants are programmed to discriminate between voices and other sounds. By six weeks old they respond differently to voices, showing a preference for the sound of their mother's voice over the voice of a stranger. During the infancy period these sorting skills become more sophisticated. Children learn to recognize familiar faces, a skill that requires comparing the new face that they see with an earlier memory of a face.

Preschool children continue to develop more sophisticated sorting skills. As they play with objects and look at pictures, they put like objects together and discover pictures that match. Sometimes this ability to recognize a match creates a problem in the family. The toddler may make a fuss if the cup he is drinking from doesn't match the other cups or if a sibling receives a present that does not exactly match his.

When children have become proficient in matching objects and pictures, they are ready to sort objects on the basis of their properties, such as color and shape. We see children group objects together that are the same color, but have different shapes, or group objects like "toy cars" together even though their colors and sizes are different. In performing a sorting task, children may start off with the notion of color or shape but lose the basis of the sort as the task continues. In other words, children may begin to put red objects in a pile but then add a green triangle because it looks like the red triangle that they placed in the pile.

We have been talking so far about sorting objects according to the way they look. It is also possible to sort objects into non-visual categories, such as where they belong, how they are used, or what they are called. Some toys belong in the house and some toys stay outside. Some food goes on the shelf and some food goes in the refrigerator. Some clothes are for cold days and some clothes are for hot days. Some kinds of foods are called fruits and some kinds of foods are called vegetables. Through everyday experience, children continually learn new ways of categorizing objects and events.

Activities to Develop Sorting Skills

Matching
Matching Things
> *Materials:* Cardboard tray with pairs of small objects (small cars, blocks, little people, balls)

What to do: Pick up one object from the tray. Ask the child to find one that is just the same. If the child selects an object that is different, say, "That one is not the same. I will help you find one that is just the same. Here it is. We found one that matches."

With a small group: Give each child in the group one of a pair of like objects. Pass the tray around to the group. Let each child select an object that is the same as the one he or she has.

Matching Pictures
Materials: Make sets of matching cards by cutting pictures out of two identical catalogs. Laminate or cover with clear contact paper.

What to do: Follow the same procedure used with a tray of small objects. When several children have the concept of matching, place trays with sets of pictures within reach on the shelf so that the children can play alone.

Activities Involving Sorting by Color
Activity #1
Materials: Peg board with pegs of different colors.

What to do: Let the children help you arrange the pegs so that each row is a different color.

(If the three-year olds have difficulty with the idea of making a row, cover most of the board so that only one row is visible at a time.)

When children have become adept at arranging pegs in color rows, play "Guess What's Wrong" and "Guess What's Missing" with individual children or small groups. In "Guess What's Wrong," the children close their eyes as two pegs are switched and then guess which two have been moved. In "Guess What's Missing," one of the pegs is removed from the color rows and the child guesses what color it is.

Activity #2
Materials: Slip-on clothespins, can or box, colored tape or construction paper.

What to do: Cover section of the rim of the can or box with different colors. Paint the clothespins to match. Children place clothespins around the rim, matching the colors

Activity #4
Materials: Counting bears, milk cartons, construction paper

What to do: Make red, green, yellow, and blue 'houses" by covering small milk cartons with construction paper. Cut a door in each house. Have the children help the different colored teddy bears find their "own" houses.

Activity #4
Take children on a color walk through the classroom or outdoors. Have them point out and name "all the things that are blue," etc.

Other Sorting Activities

Activity #1

Materials: Two sheets of tag-board, one cut in a circle and the other cut in a square. Catalog cutouts of round things and square things (plates, clocks, boxes, blocks)

How to play: Give children turns finding round things and square things to fit on the circle and the square.

Activity #2

Materials: Cut out a large tag-board hand and foot. Cut out pictures from a magazine of things that go on a hand (gloves, mittens, rings) and things that go on feet (socks, stockings, shoes and boots).

How to play: Let the children place the cutouts on the hand or foot.

Activity #3

Materials: Plastic farm animals and zoo animals and a sandbox.

How to play: Help the children build a farm on one side of the sandbox and a zoo on the other side. Let the children place each animal in either the zoo or the farm.

Activity #4

Materials: Make books that are shaped to represent a concept (a truck could stand for transportation, a fruit bowl could stand for fruit and a suitcase could be used for clothes). Shaped covers are cut from construction paper. The books can be put together by lacing with yarn, stapling or using paper fasteners.

How to play: Let children sort through old magazines and catalogs to find pictures for their books.

Activity #5

Make a classroom "museum" to display objects that children have collected or made. These can be rocks, shells, leaves, seedpods, toy cars or toy animals, clay creations, photographs, jar tops, small balls, bead necklaces, or anything that the children find intriguing. Have the children work together to arrange their objects in boxes or on shelves so that similar things are grouped together. Help them label the displays.

Discovering Order and Sequence

At the same time that children are learning to put things into categories, they are also learning about order. A child who sorts a box of buttons into small buttons, medium size buttons, and big buttons is also learning to put things in order according to size. When we think about ordering we usually think about ordering in space according to size or ordering in time according to clock units or calendar units. Actually, any quality we can think of, any adjective that is used to modify a noun, implies the possibility of ordering. A heavy object can be somewhat heavy, heavy, or very heavy. A flower can be pretty, very pretty, or beautiful. An odor can be mild, strong, or overpowering.

When preschool children first place objects in order of size, it may be accidental. They push three blocks together in ascending order and decide that it looks like a staircase. Children are able to recognize order by the way something appears before they understand the logic of order. Understanding the logic of order implies the recognition that each element has more of a certain quality than the element that precedes it and less of the quality than the object that comes after it. Before children can understand the logic of order, they need to have many different opportunities to arrange objects according to different dimensions.

Activities to Develop Ordering Skills
Activity #1
Materials: Stacking blocks or a stack of cans (Make sure there are no rough edges.)

How to play: Demonstrate ways of stacking the blocks or cans together or making a tall tower by beginning with the largest block or can.

Activity #2
Materials: Stacking toys

How to play: Demonstrate how to place rings on the spindle so that the larger rings go on the bottom and the smaller layer on top.

Activity #3
Materials: Table blocks of varying length

How to play: Demonstrate several different ways of building a block staircase.

Activity #4
Materials: Objects that involve matching and ordering (sets of cups and saucers of different size, plastic bottles with lids, dolls of different sizes with doll clothes)

How to play: As children play freely with these objects, they learn to recognize that the smallest cup fits on its smallest saucer, the next size cup on the next size saucer, etc..

Activity #5
Materials: Sequence puzzles. Buy or make puzzles that require sequencing according to size. Puzzles can be made that require double sequencing. Example: out of tagboard create a puzzle with dolls and ladders. The smallest doll gets the highest ladder.

How to play: Let the children complete the puzzle by trial and error. After a while they will recognize the appropriate order.

Learning Number Skills

Johnny, a sturdy three-year old, stood up in the middle of the room and slowly looked around. Grandma and Grandpa smiled encouragingly. Mother nodded her head and said, "Go on, Johnny, let's hear you count." Johnny counted loudly to ten. At the end of this recital there were kisses, hugs, applause and extravagant praise. Johnny laughed delightedly.

The next day at pre-school, Johnny had another "counting" experience. "That's right, Johnny, one, two, three," the teacher said as he touched each cookie on the plate. "You have three cookies."

Johnny picked up the cookie the teacher had labeled "three" and proudly carried it over to the table, repeating, "Three! Three!"

"No, no, Johnny," he is told, "that is one cookie." Johnny is confused. He looks back and sees "one" still on the plate.

> *Counting is an enormously complicated idea that takes a long time for children to master.*

Counting is an enormously complicated idea that takes a long time for children to master. When a child has learned to recite his numbers (count by rote) he has taken the first of many steps. We have already talked about ways in which young children develop concepts about the physical world by sorting and ordering. A numeral, such as "three," has two meanings. On the one hand, it refers to a set of three items. This is called its "cardinal" meaning. On the other hand it stands for the third item in a sequence. This is its "ordinal" meaning.

When children learn to sort into groups and order objects along a particular dimension, they are gaining basic insights that will help them learn to count. In the story of Johnny and the cookies we see how easy it is for a child to be confused about the ordinal and cardinal meaning of numbers. An even more common problem that children have is moving from counting by rote to counting objects. Counting by rote or learning a number chant is easy for children. It is a social game that adults enjoy playing with children. Counting objects, however, involves a critical concept that is difficult for children to grasp — one-to-one correspondence. One-to-one correspondence means that each object or item gets one and only one count. If a teacher has to help a child count by placing the child's finger on each item as it is counted, the child has not yet learned one-to-one correspondence.

Activities to Develop Number Skills

Learning to Count by Rote: Singing number songs or counting as a group in the classroom teaches the child counting order. Until the child has learned the other counting skills, it is better not to teach him a counting rhyme or chant that goes beyond ten.

Learning One-to-One Correspondence: Give children turns passing out cookies or napkins. Help them understand that each child gets one and only one cookie or napkin.

Matching Numerals to Sets: Cut out pictures that have several objects in them. Glue each picture on a large card. At the bottom make a circle and glue a washer on it. Make matching circles with numerals on them and magnets on the back. The child counts the objects and matches the correct circle to the picture.

Number Puzzles: To help children understand the ordinal meaning of numbers: Give children practice filling a bead counter. Provide one of one color, two of a second color, three of the third color, etc. When children first start working with a bead stacker, you may want to paint the stacks to match the beads.

Match Up: Begin a row of block houses. Ask the children to put one roof on top of each house or one tree beside each house.

Creating Sets: Let children create set books or posters. A book of the "two set" would include pictures of things that come in two's (two eyes, a pair of shoes, a cup and saucer, a set of twins)

Go Fishing: Make a fishing pole from a dowel, a stick, or the small cardboard tube from a coat hanger. Make the line from string or yarn and the hook from a pipe cleaner. Glue a magnet on the hook. Make construction paper fish and put staples or paper clips on them. On the back of each fish, write a number. The children take turns "catching a fish" and calling out the number they have caught. Then let the child place his or her fish on the correct counter in the fish market. The counter is a piece of tag board with a pocket on the bottom. It is color coded to match the fish. For example, if the fish with the numeral 3 on it is blue, then it is placed in the third pocket, which is also blue.

String Along: Hang a clothesline low enough for the children to reach easily. Provide clothespins and ten cards with a number on each card. Have the children hang the cards up in order from "1 " to "10".

Take Your Share: Pass around a tray of crackers or a basket of crayons. Ask children to take three crackers or four crayons.

Crowd Control: Post a sign in each interest area or play center indicating the number of children who can play in the area. E.g. a sign with the numeral four and four dots or stick figures.

Hide and Count: Play guessing games with a small group of children. Put down five or more chips and let the children count them. Then, remove several chips when the children have their eyes closed. Ask them how many chips are hiding in your hand. Give the children a chance to play the games with you as the guesser or let them play the game with each other.

Number Talk: Use numbers and number concepts in everyday conversations with children. Talk about how many days are left until a special event, how many children are usually in the group and how many are missing on a particular day, how many places to set when guests are expected, the shapes and sizes of blocks and buildings, how long a trip will take. Have children help you count out crackers for snack, put the blocks away in order of size, pour in the right amount of each ingredient in a recipe, or measure an area for a new carpet or bulletin board.

Everyday Math: Set up a play store, fast food restaurant, veterinary clinic, or gas station. Include a cash register and appropriate measuring instruments such as a scale, a yardstick, a tape measure, a thermometer, or a tire gauge. Introduce number concepts and problems when you join the children's play.

Sing Along: Make songs and finger plays with numbers part of your regular routine. When children have become proficient at counting forward and backward, introduce rhymes like "Two, four, six, eight, who do we appreciate?" that involve counting by twos.

Pattern and Counting Books: Include counting books, books about size and shape, books with hidden, camouflaged, "wacky," or out of place objects to find, and stories with repeating or cumulative (add an element each time) patterns in your library. Encourage the children to read them with you and with each other, and to make their own variants of favorite books.

Algebra 1: Teach children addition by giving them real life problems, e.g. at snack time six children are sitting around the table. Take out four crackers. Ask the children if you took out enough crackers. When the children say "no," ask them how many more crackers you need. If they answer 2 — say, you are right. We have six children, so we need 6 crackers. Four crackers plus 2 more crackers equals six crackers. If they answer five, take out one more cracker and pass five crackers out. Then say, "oops" I have six children. I need another cracker. Four plus two equals six.

Discovering Relationships

The more experience children have with manipulating real world objects, the more proficient they become at putting objects into categories. At the same time, manipulating real objects helps children recognize ways in which objects relate to other objects. A child playing with a toy car and a plank discovers that the speed at which the car rolls is determined by the angle of the plank. A child bouncing a ball discovers that the height of the rebound is related to the force of the downward throw.

Discover Spatial Relationships

Children learn about spatial relationships by fitting things together and taking them apart. Puzzles, wooden blocks, interlocking blocks, and toys that come apart and fit back together are useful materials to develop this skill. Here are some other things you can do:

- Provide materials in the house area that can be put together and taken apart — jars and lids, several sizes of plastic containers and tops, pots and pans with matching lids.

- As a class project, draw a large map of the room, building, or playground. The class decides where to place cutouts representing furniture and equipment. During the discussion include some of the following words: next to, beside, between, in front of, behind, close to, far away, under, over, up, down.

- As a small group activity, give each child an empty milk carton or small box, scissors, glue, and a tray of scraps to decorate with fabric, construction paper, tissue paper, wallpaper, sandpaper, etc. Let each child decorate his box as he chooses and then describe to the group what he has done. The teacher may have to help by asking some questions. ("Did you put anything inside?" "What is next to the red paper?")

We have talked so far about very concrete ways of sorting, ordering, and exploring spatial relationships. These concrete activities lay the groundwork for more abstract thinking.

Science Concepts

When we talk about sorting, ordering, and counting, we are describing the basic building blocks of a science curriculum. Scientists categorize plants, animals, minerals and other physical phenomena according to shared attributes. They discover the order in which things happen in time or occur in space. They discover ways in which one set of phenomena or events relates to another set of phenomena or events. As preschool children are given opportunities to sort out and manipulate objects and materials, they are learning the basic skills of the scientist.

There is one aspect of scientific thinking that we have not yet mentioned. The scientist uses what she knows to discover what she does not know. She develops a hypothesis and then carries out experiments to see if this hypothesis is correct. In other words, the scientist continues to ask "if-then" kinds of questions. "If-then" questions are difficult for young children to ask in an abstract way, but they do ask these questions in a concrete way. The child who places the plank on more of an angle to see if the marble will slide down faster is asking an "if-then" kind of question. A scientific environment for young children provides many different opportunities for "if-then" investigations.

Suggested Materials to Invite Scientific Investigation
- Water table containing funnels, sieves, a water pump, see-through containers of different sizes and shapes, ladles, basters, clear plastic tubing, soap bubbles, food coloring, soda straws.

- A balance scale with dishes of small objects that can be placed on the pans.

- A standing magnifying glass with a basket next to it full of interesting material to look at (shells, rocks, cones, bark, nuts, postage stamps).

- A large magnet with a basket of steel and non-steel materials.

- A water tub with a tray of objects, some that float and some that do not float.

- Different kinds of clay, play-dough, and plaster, some that harden and some that stay soft.

- Toy cars and small balls; planks or tubes; blocks that can be used to raise one end of the track

- Different colors and kinds of paint

- Unusual materials to make like "oobleck" (cornstarch, water, and food coloring), soapsuds clay (beat 3/4 cup soap powder and 1 tablespoon warm water with a hand mixer), Jell-O, and glue paint (Elmer's glue mixed with food coloring).

Sparking a Child's Interest in Science

Young children often develop intense interests in scientific information. For example, they may get interested in dinosaurs and want to learn all of their names, become fascinated with stars and planets, or want to learn all there is to know about snakes. It is a good idea to include science picture books and nature guides in your library to spark and build on children's interests. Encourage children to learn by direct observation and by making predictions as well as from books. For example, they might plant seeds, make drawings of what they think the plants will look like under and above the ground, then make books of drawings showing how the plants look at different stages.

Sparking a Child's Interest in Social Studies

Sometimes when we think of social studies, we think of geography, history and political science. Young children cannot think about things that are remote in time and space, nor can they think about things that involve abstract principles or systems. They are interested in things that are happening and people that are making things happen in their immediate world. The social studies curriculum, like the science curriculum, must deal with the concrete and the immediate. It must provide children with opportunities to categorize people and events, to find out about the order of things, and to discover relationships. It must build on student's knowledge of their own families and communities to teach them about other people, places, and times. Through song and celebration, it should help children appreciate their own heritage and that of others.

Here are some sample themes that can be included in a social studies curriculum:

Family Unit

Because a child's family, no matter what the size or composition, is the most important thing in her life, a social studies unit on the family is always appropriate.

Suggested Activities

- **Create Family Albums:** Let children bring in pictures of different members of their families. Create family albums in which different color pages are used to show different generations. Construct a family tree using family pictures.

- **Make Individual Books Called "All About My Family":** An "All About My Family" book can contain pictures of things the family does together (plays ball, eats dinner, watches TV). You can include holidays the family shares and places the family goes together (the supermarket, a restaurant, the beach).

- **Bring Families into the Classroom:** Place photographs of the children and their families where the children can study them. Ask families to bring in recipes or special foods, songs, nursery rhymes, games, and other elements of their heritage that they would like to share with the children.

- **Study Families Around the World:** Collect pictures and books that show families from different cultures or different parts of the world. Choose pictures that show ordinary events — eating, sleeping, taking children to school, styling hair, washing clothes, or reading together. Have children identify similarities and differences among the pictures. For example, you might have several pictures of a child helping a mother, all showing two people carrying food. Children might notice the differences in foods, containers, and clothing. If you use cutouts from calendars and magazines, children can make books or bulletin board displays showing how families are alike and different.

- **Build a Multicultural Library:** Be sure that your library includes both books that reflect the children's family heritages and books about families with different structures and cultures.

Transportation Unit

Children are very interested in all kinds of vehicles and a unit on transportation provides limitless opportunities for interesting activities.

Suggested Activities

- **Truck Day:** Invite people with different kinds of trucks to come to your school. Talk about ways in which the trucks differ from each other and help the children discover reasons for the differences. (Some trucks have double sets of back wheels; some have attachments like snowplows, trailer hitches, or flashing lights.)

- **Field Trips:** Take a bus ride, a trolley ride, or a train ride with the children. Visit an airport, a bus terminal, or a train station. Take a walk around the school and see how many different kinds of transportation you see. Did you see bicycles, motorcycles, buses, delivery trucks, moving vans, and garbage trucks?

- **Pretend Play:** Create an airport in the classroom in the imaginative play corner. Include as props a scale, suitcases, tickets, luggage tags, purses, wallets, money, etc. You might also add a "plane" (this can be as simple as a row of chairs or pillows, with a joystick or steering wheel and painted control panel for the pilot), some tools for the mechanics, food and trays for the flight attendants, and a wagon to bring gas, luggage, and supplies to the plane. Read the children books about airplanes and help them role-play airplane trips.

- **Music Time:** Sing songs about different kinds of transportation ("The Wheels On The Bus," "Row, Row, Row Your Boat," "I've Been Working On The Railroad," "Yankee Doodle," "Jingle Bells").

- **Craft Time:** Make trucks out of cracker boxes by letting the children glue on wheels and cut out or paste on windows. Make a license plate for the back of the truck. Construct a train in the classroom by cutting out large cardboard boxes. Put chairs in the boxes so children can sit on the train and look out of the windows as they sing a train song or pretend to take a train ride.

- **Mural:** Cover a wall with large sheets of paper and draw on some roads. Have children make (or cut out) pictures of vehicles, houses, stores, gas stations, and other places in the "city." Help them glue them onto the mural.

- **Book Corner:** Make transportation books in which the child cuts out pictures of trucks, boats, airplanes, cars, etc. and glues them into the book. Or make trip books that show a picture of a place and of the kind of transportation you would take to get there. Read these along with library books about transportation, trips, and vehicles.

Other Ideas for Social Studies Units

The possibility of developing social studies themes that are interesting and important to children is almost endless. Social studies themes may be developed around:

- The places people live
- The jobs people do
- The kinds of stores we have in our city
- Places we like to visit (the farm, the beach, the zoo, etc.)
- The holidays we celebrate
- Babies
- All kinds of machines
- Things that go up in the air
- What happens to a letter?
- Different kinds of clothes
- Pets and other animals

Once you have decided to develop a theme for your classroom, invite the children's parents to help you think of different ways of expanding it.

Objective 5: To recognize the value of a preschool environment that encourages exploration, curiosity, and critical thinking

Annabelle had just enrolled Amelia, her six-month-old infant in the College-Bound Academy for pre-school children. She was excited about the school and couldn't wait for her husband to come home so she could tell him all about it. "It is an unbelievable place," she told her husband Peter as soon as he walked in the door. "Even the three year olds can count to a hundred and name every state in the union! It's so cute to see those little tots sitting quietly at their desk trying to copy a big 'A'." Annabelle's husband was not impressed. "What happened to good old-fashioned play?" he asked.

The learning environment created in a preschool is a reflection of the school's philosophy. A behaviorally oriented preschool views children as consumers of knowledge. The teacher is responsible for presenting the children with carefully designed lessons in accordance with a preset curriculum. The room arrangement and the materials placed in the classroom are determined by this curriculum. In contrast, a preschool with a developmental or constructivist orientation views children as active learners who construct knowledge through their own activities. The teacher designs a classroom environment that invites children to explore, experiment, and make their own discoveries.

When parents like Annabelle and Peter can't agree on the choice of a preschool, the problem may well be that they have different ideas about how children learn. Annabelle believes that her daughter should spend her time in preschool learning academic skills that are taught by the teacher. Peter believes that his daughter will be happier and will learn more if she is allowed to play with her peers and choose what she wants to do. Although it may not be true for every child, most early childhood professionals agree that children who attend a preschool that encourages play and discovery will do better when they enter first grade than children who attend a preschool with a highly structured academic curriculum that allows little time for play.

The learning environment created in a preschool is a reflection of the school's philosophy.

Objective 6: To recognize ways of introducing themes that are meaningful to preschool children

Several teachers from the Wee Care Preschool were meeting informally after school. Their director had just distributed a list of themes that she wanted the teachers to introduce into all the preschool classrooms. She made it clear that she wanted them to incorporate these themes into all the learning centers; reading, writing, art, music and movement, science, number skills, and imaginative play. The list of themes included All About Me, Far Away Places, Plants and Animals, My Five Senses, and Imagination. The teachers thought it wasn't a bad idea, but when they tried to figure out how to do it they found themselves getting silly. "I have a great idea for teaching kids about smell!" one teacher exclaimed. "First we'll spray each of the learning centers with different spray bottles. Then we'll blindfold the children and let them smell their way to the learning center they decide to go to." "That idea," a second teacher commented, "absolutely stinks." By this time all the teachers were laughing so hard that they couldn't do any more work.

Educators have different opinions about the value of themes in a preschool classroom. Educators who are strong proponents of themes give the following arguments:

- Themes are a way to help children grasp a new concept.

- Themes are a way to integrate the curriculum. Children are introduced to the same concepts in different contexts or learning centers. The experiences he has in different learning centers build on each other and the whole becomes greater than the sum of its parts.

- Themes are a way to introduce new materials and activities in each interest center.

- Themes provide a way to involve parents in the classroom. and strengthen the bonds between home and school.

- A theme provides a way of connecting the experiences children have outside of the classroom with the experiences they have in the classroom.

- Themes give teachers a way to express their own creativity.

- Children have fun with themes.

Educators who are opposed to themes give the following reasons:

- Using the same theme in every interest area is silly and restrictive. For instance, there is no good reason to believe that children are going to learn more about life on a farm because they are singing *Old MacDonald Had a Farm* or putting a cow puzzle together.

- The selection of themes is usually made by the teacher or the director, with no input from children.

- Themes can interfere with learning. For instance, if the teacher has been using Montessori beads to teach a sequence of counting skills, changing from counting beads to counting miniature cows is distracting rather than productive.

- Themes are likely to encourage take-home craft projects where the teacher does most of the work. Instead of engaging in process art where they are free to use art materials to express ideas and feelings, children are taught how to put a craft together that relates to the theme of the week.

Most early childhood educators do not take an all or nothing approach to the use of themes. They believe that themes make good sense as long as they are used properly. Here are some of the criteria teachers use in making decisions about themes.

- The theme should be built on the spontaneous interests of children.

- The theme should not have a predetermined end date. Children should be allowed to investigate a theme for as long as their interest lasts.

- Themes should be extended into only those facets of the curriculum where there is a natural fit.

Once a theme has been selected, it is up to the teacher to discover different ways in which the theme can be expanded. A theme like "the wind," for instance could lead to an investigation of what causes the wind to blow, a creative movement activity like pretending you are taking a walk with a strong wind blowing in your face, or an art activity like drawing a picture of clothes on a line blowing in the wind. Children could experiment with blowing soap bubbles, making waves in the water table by blowing through a tube, flying paper airplanes, throwing light scarves into the air, making wind with a fan, blowing into and across bottles of different sizes, making wind chimes, and watching clouds on still and windy days. Their investigations might lead to a new theme, such as "flight," "weather," or "musical instruments."

Bredekamp, S. (Editor). (1993). *Developmentally appropriate practice in early childhood programs serving children from birth through age 8.* Washington, D.C.: National Association for the Education of Young Children.

Bronson, M.B. (1995). *The right stuff for children birth to 8: Selecting play materials to support development.* Washington, D.C.: National Association for the Education of Young Children.

Curtis, D. & Carter, M. (1996). *Reflecting children's lives: A handbook for planning child-centered curriculum.* St. Paul, MN: Redleaf Press.

Diffily, D. & Morrison, K. (Editors). (1996). *Family friendly communication for early childhood programs.* Washington, D.C.: National Association for the Education of Young Children.

Dodge, D.T., Koralek, D.G., & Pizzolongo, P.J. (1989). *Caring for school children.* Vol. 1. Washington, D.C.: Teaching Strategies, Inc.

Meisels, S.J., Marsden, D.B., & Stetson, C. (2000). *Winning ways to learn: 600 great ideas for children.* NY: Goddard Press.

Snow, C.W. (1998). *Infant development.* Upper Saddle River, NJ: Prentice Hall.

Chapter 8: Communication

Overview

Communication is the sharing of thoughts, feelings, and ideas through language or through non-verbal means such as gestures, facial expressions, and art.

Rationale

Language, a uniquely human accomplishment, is the basis of much of our thinking as well as our communication. It is the primary way we receive the accumulated wisdom of humankind and communicate with people remote to us in space and time. Language is also the way we communicate with ourselves, recalling past events, working out problems, planning ahead, and keeping our impulses in check. We urge children to think before they act, just as we urge children to "use their words" to control the behavior of others. We think about school as the time when children learn reading, writing, and arithmetic. We can think about preschool as the time when children develop the language skills underlying these school-related achievements. Language development begins at birth, as the baby and her caregivers communicate with gaze, sounds, and touch. Teachers and caregivers provide children with many opportunities to learn communication skills, to use verbal and nonverbal means to communicate their own ideas and feelings, and to understand the ideas and feelings of others.

Objectives

1. To recognize the relationship between language development and real world experiences.

2. To describe the expectable sequence of communication skills in infants and suggest ways to support their development.

3. To describe the expectable sequence of communication skills in young toddlers and suggest ways to support their development.

4. To describe the expectable sequence of language skills in older toddlers and suggest ways to support their development.

5. To describe the expectable sequence of language skills in preschool children and suggest ways to support their development.

6. To learn ways of reading to children that encourage active participation and engender a love of books.

7. To describe early literacy skills and describe activities that promote these skills.

8. To describe the small muscle skills that are used in writing and suggest activities that develop these skills and provide the child with opportunities to practice writing.

9. To select books that foster empathy, promote prosocial behavior, counteract bias, and support bilingualism.

The hardest part of learning language is not learning how to repeat a word but learning the connection between the spoken word and a real world object or event.

Objective 1: To recognize the relationship between language development and real world experiences

Three-year old Jennifer was having a family dinner with her parents, grandparents, and great-grandparents. She tuned in to the adults' conversation about the approaching hurricane. "If it doesn't change course, the eye will pass right over us." "But they say it might turn north and miss us completely." "We'd better stock up anyway." "Cheese is good for hurricanes." All of a sudden, Jennifer began to cry. "I'm scared of the hurricane." "Do you know what a hurricane is?" her mother asked. "Yes," said Jennifer with conviction. "It's a one-eyed monster that eats cheese and doesn't know where it's going!"

Having no experience with hurricanes, Jennifer put together a logical explana= tion based on her prior knowledge. Like a typical preschooler, she interpreted words literally and personified the storm.

The hardest part of learning language is not learning how to repeat a word but learning the connection between the spoken word and a real world object or event. The toddler learns to say "dog" when the family dog licks his face or when he gives it a biscuit. After a while the toddler will use the word "dog" to stand for any member of a category of animals that have some of the features of his dog. He may use the word "dog" to label all the four-legged animals he sees, whether they are dogs, horses or elephants. Later he will refine this category and will reserve the label "dog" for animals that have four legs, bark, and wag their tails.

In order to learn a language, a child must first grasp the concept that a word can stand for a particular object, person, or action, or for a category of objects, people, or actions. In toddlerspeak, "Car" can stand for Daddy's car, any car, or any vehicle with wheels. "Daddy" can stand for his Daddy or for every other man whether or not he is somebody's father. "Down" can stand for "put me down," or where the ball went after he rolled it off his high chair. Children can also learn ways of refining a category by using descriptive words. A child might use "big dog" to label a dog that is bigger than his own dog or a four-legged animal that is bigger than a dog. She might say "box juice" for juice that comes in boxes or "Mommy paper" for papers she is not supposed to touch.

By the time a child is two years old, he is likely to speak in short sentences that describe a relationship between a familiar object and action, or between a person, object, and action or location. "Baby crying." "Daddy bye-bye car." Before long a child will acquire a much larger vocabulary that includes nouns, verbs, pronouns, adjectives, adverbs, and prepositions. He will also learn to use language for many different purposes: to request, direct, ask questions, describe, joke, talk to himself, or invite interaction. But throughout the preschool years, the language a child uses and the concepts he is able to grasp are built on what he sees and experiences in real life, in picture books, and in stories that he can imagine and visualize.

Objective 2: To describe the expectable sequence of communication skills in infants and suggest ways to support their development

...even before they understand the words, babies can be soothed or excited by different tones of voice.

Gina, a teenage mother, had just dropped her baby off at the Cuddle and Croon Child Care Center and was talking to her friend Gilda. "Gilda, you'd never believe it," she muttered. "You know that child care center where I drop my kid? Well, they're a little touched in the head. There are two old ladies who sit there holding the little babies in their laps and talking to them. 'How are you today, sweetie pie? Should we play a little game of pattycake?' I bet they're expecting those babies to understand them. Just listening to them is a blast!"*

Despite Gina's uncomplimentary remarks, the caregivers at Cuddle and Croon have a very good understanding of language development in young children. They realize that infants, from the moment of birth, tune in and attend to language. They know that, even before they understand the words, babies can be soothed or excited by different tones of voice. They know that the high-pitched "baby talk" or "parentese" that adults tend to use with babies is especially engaging. They recognize that in the first year of life, infants are developing critical communication skills - distinguishing and repeating the sounds of their language(s), carrying on babble conversations, and recognizing the difference between a playful tone and a serious tone that means "stop." They realize that in the second and third year, babies who have been involved in lots of back and forth conversation will burst into language, understand single words and phrases, and speak in one word, two word, and finally three or four word sentences.

Beginning at birth, infants have a repertoire of communication skills — both verbal and nonverbal. Infants communicate through cries, coos, facial expressions, movements, and autonomic signs. Caregivers who know an infant well can read the messages in babies cries. They can differentiate between the rhythmic, intense cry that means, "I'm hungry," the sharp cry that means, "I'm in pain," and the whiney cry that means, "I'm not comfortable." They can also read a baby's autonomic signs. They know that when a baby hiccups, tenses her body, tightens her lips, screws up her face, stiffens her body, or curls her toes, the baby is saying "I am over-stimulated or overwhelmed and I need to be soothed."

During the first year, the baby will learn ways of communicating through purposeful nonverbal signs. He will lift his arms to signal, "pick me up," push away your hands to signal "I don't want that," point with one finger to tell you to look at something, turn or shake his head to tell you he doesn't want what you are offering. As caregivers interpret and respond to a baby's signs, the baby learns the value of conversational exchanges.

Caregivers need to provide opportunities for the infant to hear language as part of all daily routines...

Developmental Picture

The infant 8-14 months:
- Tunes in to words and phrases such as "bye-bye", "uh-oh", "patty cake", "up"
- By 12-13 months, begins to use recognizable words such as wa-wa, mamma, da-da, down, ba-ba
- Uses recognizable words or strings of sounds that sound like talking
- Recognizes the difference between playful or soothing words and words that signal disapproval, and may stop what she is doing when she hears "no" or "hot"
- Uses language to initiate and maintain contact with parents and caregivers

The caregiver:
- Communicates individually with every child at every opportunity
- Maintains eye contact during conversations
- Responds to children's interest in objects and events using words and gestures
- Engages children's interest in objects and events using words and gestures

Activities to Encourage Language and Imitation

Language learning is not confined to just special times or special activities. Language is a part of our daily experience. Caregivers need to provide opportunities for the infant to hear language as part of all daily routines, including diapering, rocking, and feeding, as well as playing. When you are with an infant, describe what is happening, what you are doing, and what the infant is doing. Speak slowly and in short sentences, varying your pitch and sound level. In addition, find time to engage with the baby in purposeful activities that promote her language development.

Birth to Three Months

- **Talking with baby:** Talk softly to the baby as you hold or feed him.

- **Sing a lullaby:** Sing a lullaby as you put the infant to sleep.

Three to Six Months

- **Face to face interaction:** Hold baby directly in front of you. Talk to him and encourage him to coo back. Talk-pause-talk-pause. Try making the same cooing sounds as the baby. If the baby looks away, it may not mean that he wants to end the conversation. Most babies need to take breaks when they are engaged in a cooing conversation.

- **Picture show:** Let the infant explore and touch large pictures.

Six to Nine Months

- **Let's babble:** Make some of the sounds you know the baby can make and see if he will imitate you.

- **Imitating banging:** Begin banging with your hands on a hard surface and see if the infant will bang with you. When he does, say "bang, bang, bang." Once the infant has mastered this activity, see if he will imitate you when you bang with a spoon.

- **Clapping:** Clap your hands and encourage the infant to clap his. Once he can imitate clapping, see if he will clap when he's given the verbal command.

- **Waving:** Substitute waving for clapping in the above activity.

- **Body parts:** Use a large doll with clear features. Show the baby how to point to the eyes, ears, nose, mouth. Next, teach him to point to his own body.

- **Blowing:** Blow on baby's tummy. Let the baby watch your face and see if he will pucker his lips.

- **Smelling:** Pick up a flower, sniff it, smile, and then hold the flower in front of the baby.

Nine to Twelve Months

- **Object Show:** Place two objects in front of the baby. Say "Show me the shoe," "Show me the plate" Later, add more objects.

- **Look at a picture book:** Ask the infant to point to specific pictures.

- **Songs, Chants, and Nursery Rhymes:** Songs, nursery rhymes, and chants give infants the opportunity to hear language. Repetition at this age is important and songs help the infant become more aware of the rhythms, patterns, and inflections of a particular language.

• **Family Album:** Ask parents to put together books of family pictures. See if the baby can point to family members when you say their names.

Objective 3: To describe the expectable sequence of communication skills in young toddlers and suggest ways to support their development

Between one and two years old, children are learning to communicate with words. At first, a single word will stand for a whole sentence and the caregiver will know from the context what the one word means. "Cookie" may mean "I want a cookie," or "My cookie fell on the floor." After a while, the toddler will put together two words and the meaning is easier to interpret. "Gimme cookie." "That-a cookie." While learning to use words is an important development, it is only one aspect of the language skills that toddlers are learning.

A second aspect of language learning is receptive language or the ability to assign meaning to words and sentences. Both expressive and receptive language are based on the recognition that a word is a symbol that stands for something else. Toddlers who enjoy pretend play often invent their own symbols. When a toddler who is pretending to cook takes a bite of a block, he is creating his own symbol. The block, like the word "cookie," becomes the symbol of the object cookie. By supporting pretend play we are fostering language development.

Developmental Picture

The toddler 14-24 months:
- Is developing a single word vocabulary that usually ranges from 50 to 100 words
- Enjoys picture books about familiar things
- Is learning to make the sounds of pets and farm animals
- Puts together two-word phrases such as "baby cookie," "mommy home," or "daddy push"
- Can follow a one-step command such as "Bring me the keys" or "Give Nana a kiss"

The caregiver:
- Responds appropriately to toddlers' requests
- Provides opportunities for toddlers to follow simple directions
- Recognizes that toddlers learn language at different rates
- Reads picture books, naming the pictures or talking about the pictures in their own words
- Repeats and expands the child's language. E.g., when a toddler says "Mommy bye-bye" the caregiver says "Yes, Mommy went bye-bye."
- Provides toddlers with many experiences that match an object with its name

Activities to Encourage Language and Imitation

Picture games: Play games involving pointing to and labeling specific pictures and objects.

Doll games: Give the one to two-year old a doll (or a stuffed animal)and the appropriate props. Ask him to hug the doll, kiss the doll, put the doll to sleep, wipe the doll's nose, rock the doll, feed her, and put her in her crib. Show him how to brush the doll's hair and give it a bath.

Picture albums: Make picture albums with pictures of familiar toys, objects, and people.

Retrieval games: Send the children on "errands." Say, "Get the doll," "Bring me the ball," etc.

Puppets: Introduce puppets. Show children how to make them talk.

Picture matching games: Between 20-24 months, many children like to match pictures. They also like to match an object with a picture of the object.

Sensory games: Water and ice cubes, bubbles, shaving cream, and crinkly paper invite children to explore and at the same time provide opportunities to learn and practice new words.

Picture Books: "Read" to the children. Help them point out and label familiar pictures or items.

Telephone games: Encourage two-way conversation by talking with children as they play with a toy telephone..

Nursery rhymes, songs, and chants: Give toddlers many opportunities to participate in music experiences.

Pretending: Encourage pretending by introducing simple props such as a doll or stuffed animal, doll-size pots, dishes and utensils, a wallet or old purse, a small brush, and a play telephone, and by joining the child in play.

Both expressive and receptive language are based on the recognition that a word is a symbol that stands for something else.

Objective 4: To describe the expectable sequence of language skills in older toddlers and suggest ways to support their development

Although children cannot learn a language unless they hear it spoken, learning a language involves much more than the imitation of adult speech. The foundation of language is real world experiences. Babies associate names with the most important people in their life: Mama, Dada, Nana, Papa, siblings' names, the most important objects: cookies, blankie, car, and the most important actions or experiences: bye-bye, up, hot. As soon as a toddler masters the concept that a spoken word can stand for an experience, he is poised for a second discovery. Putting two words together is a way of describing a relationship. "Big ball" can mean that the ball is big or I want the big ball. "Daddy car" can mean that the car belongs to Daddy or Daddy is in the car.

When toddlers advance from the two-word stage to the three-word stage, their language is much less ambiguous. "That-a big ball" means that is a big ball. "Gimme big ball" means I want you to give me the big ball. "That Daddy car" means the car belongs to Daddy. "Daddy bye-bye car" means that Daddy drove away in the car.

When toddlers are able to use three word sentences, they are able to carry on a conversation. They can ask questions, give orders, make comments, describe feelings, provide information, and play with words. As toddlers expand their vocabulary, become more fluent, and speak in longer sentences, their language becomes more than a tool for talking about real world experiences. It also becomes a tool for expanding their knowledge of the world beyond the horizon of their direct experiences.

> *As toddlers expand their vocabulary, their language becomes more than a tool for talking about real world experiences. It also becomes a tool for expanding their knowledge.*

Developmental Picture

The two-year-old:
- Is rapidly expanding her vocabulary
- Enjoys rhymes, picture books, and books with repetition
- Speaks in 2 and 3 word sentences
- Can follow a simple 2-part command, such as "go to the table and bring me a napkin"
- Uses words to communicate wants and needs, to share interests, and to initiate interactions
- Asks "where" and "what's that" questions

The caregiver:
- Repeats with brief expansion when children begin to communicate with words
- Provides opportunities for children to hear nursery rhymes and songs
- Reads books with children with a simple and familiar story line
- Names and describes objects and experiences to develop children's vocabularies

The understanding of language and the ability to communicate ideas, feelings, and needs is an evolving process. During these early years children need many opportunities to hear language and to practice using language. At two years old, most children understand simple commands and can put a few words together. By three they have learned to speak in sentences (maybe even paragraphs) and can understand a simple story. While preschools may have a special time of the day and a special area of the classroom set aside for language, language learning is an ongoing activity. It takes place in the classroom, on the playground, in the bathroom, and at the lunch table. In every area there should be many opportunities for children to hear language and to practice emerging language skills.

Materials That Encourage Language Development

- Books: hard cardboard pages, simple story and picture books

- Picture cards: DLM cards, homemade cards, matching cards made from catalogs, and cutout pictures or stickers placed on index cards

- Common objects: small animals, miniature cars, trucks, trains, small dishes, dolls, etc. Make an object box and continually change the objects.

- Puzzles with pictures of common objects

- Old typewriters or computer keyboards

- Printing stamps: You can get a transportation set, a food set, etc.

- Lotto games: Present one card at a time and you have a fairly simple matching activity.

- Puppet theater

- Wall posters with interesting pictures

- Polaroid camera

- Writing materials — pens, paper, envelopes, stickers, postcards, old greeting cards, index cards, scrap paper, chalkboard

In every area there should be many opportunities for children to hear language and to practice emerging language skills.

Activities to Encourage Language Learning

Although language occurs in every area of the classroom, it is helpful to have a special area devoted to language learning. It is also important to recognize conversational techniques that encourage language learning and to initiate activities in the classroom that increase a child's understanding, production, and appreciation of language. Here are some activities and techniques that work well with two-year olds.

Everyday Conversation

Make a special point of carrying on a conversation with every child at least three times a day. Before beginning the conversation, position yourself so that you are on the same level as the child and establish eye contact. Remember, it is only considered a conversation if you and the child are sharing information and there is a back and forth exchange of ideas.

Teacher: *"Look at that! You have a new pair of sneakers."*
Child: *"New shoes."*
Teacher: *"Yes, you have new shoes. I'll bet you are a fast runner with your new shoes on."*
Child: *"Bobby runs fast."*
Teacher: *"Your brother Bobby is a fast runner. Did he get new shoes too?"*

Farm Animal Game

Hold a toy farm animal behind your back and engage one or more children in a game. "I am holding an animal behind my back — that says "moo" — It is a _____."

As the children fill in the word "cow," show them the miniature cow. Repeat the game with a pig, horse, lamb, chicken, etc. Let the children have a turn picking up the animal, making it's sound, and letting you or the other children say it's name.

"Let's go shopping" game

(This game works best with two to four children)

Put play foods on a tray and give each child a paper bag. Each child has a turn choosing an item, e.g. banana, cookie, hot dog, apple, pizza, tomato. He names the item as he places it in his bag. If he can't name the item, let the other children help him.

Describing your actions

Talk about what you are doing as you prepare for an activity. "We are going to play with peanut butter play dough. I am going to give each of you a ball of peanut butter. A ball for Pedro, a ball for Maria, etc.

Describing their actions

For children who are slower with language learning, increase their understanding of language by describing what they are doing.

"You have made a block tower. Oh, you're putting the yellow block on the top."

Object boxes

Use object boxes as story starters in circle time. Children choose an object from the box — a toothbrush, a shoelace, a toy car, a Band-Aid, etc. As children select the items, they say something about them. Some children may just name the object while others will tell a short story.

Puppets

Introduce puppets in a variety of ways. You can use puppets to talk to the children or you can let the children talk for the puppets.

Taking Pictures

Take photos of field trips, special days, or of routine events. Encourage the children to sequence the photos and retell the events.

Sharing Books

Look at picture books with the children. Good books for two-year olds:

- are simple and repetitive. Books with rhymes, repetition, and "choruses" are particularly appropriate.
- are filled with illustrations of high quality with clear detail and bright colors.
- have themes that are familiar to the children.
- can be retold by the child by looking at the pictures.

Two-year-olds like books that have lots of things they can learn the names of.

Two-year olds also like books that have lots of things they can learn the names of, like all kinds of cars, trucks, and machines, all kinds of animals, Richard Scary's books, *Good Night Moon,* Spot books and other books where you have to find something hiding, and some of the Eye Witness books that have lots of photographs of different objects. The children can learn lots of details that can then be incorporated into pretend play. Here's an example:

Miss Love-Kids took the children on a field trip to a nearby park. Several children were climbing on the toy train. "What kind of train is this?" Miss Love-the-Kids asked. " 'team engine," said Jacob, who insisted that Miss Love-the-Kids read his favorite train book nearly every day. "See tender?" he said, pointing to the car attached to the engine. "I'm glad we have a tender to carry fuel for our steam engine," said the teacher. "We need coal to keep the fire hot." "I get coal," said Maisha, as she scooped up a handful of grass and sprinkled it on the "tender." "Go fast." Ralph grabbed the wheel and turned it vigorously back and forth. "Me engineer," he said proudly. "All aboard!"

Two-year olds learn new words eagerly and easily, perhaps more rapidly that at any other time in their lives. As they expand their vocabularies, they are building a firm foundation for reading. In fact, many researchers believe that helping children develop a rich vocabulary at two, three, and four is one of the most important things we can do to promote success in reading and in school.

Here are some other things you can do to help two-year olds build a foundation for literacy.

Two-year-olds learn new words eagerly and easily, perhaps more rapidly than at any other time in their lives.

- Provide children with many opportunities to see you read and write and to imitate reading writing in their play. They might use tickets or menus, ask you to write their names or other words on their drawings, "write" (with scribbles) a card or letter and "read" it aloud, play "office," or follow along as you point out the title of a favorite book or their name on a cubby.

- Encourage children to handle books, and to "read" on their own. As they imitate your reading, children will practice holding a book right side up and turning pages from front to back. They may even point to words as they read if they have seen you do this.

- Let children be the ones to get their favorite books for story time. It is surprising how many two-year olds can recognize their favorite books, cereal boxes, videos, and even signs. They notice the way the words look long before they can read.

- Help children act out simple stories they have read or special experiences they have had, or play them out with miniature figures and props. Ask questions to expand the play or move it forward.

- Engage in word play with children. For example, they might enjoy making up nonsense words and repeating rhymes like "Anna banana" or simple tongue twisters like "Peter, Peter, Pumpkin Eater" and "Peter Piper picked peppers."

Objective 5: To describe the expectable sequence of language skills in preschool children and suggest ways to support their development

*J*ust *before a recent election, Jamie, age four and a half, explained how the process works:*

"Well, you see, there are these two people named George Bush and Al Gore. They are going to have a race and the one that wins gets to live in Washington in a white house. It's not a race in cars; it's just a running race."

This anecdote points up two aspects of children's language. First, it shows how much in tune children are with the language that is spoken around them. Obviously, Jamie does not understand what an election is, but he has picked up some key words and is able to repeat them. Second, it shows how children interpret the language they hear in a very concrete way. Jamie did not recognize the metaphorical interpretation of either running a race or of living in the White House.

Ways to help preschoolers enhance their spontaneous language

Psycholinguists, who study the stages of speech development in young children, point up several facets of early speech that are important to parents and caregivers.

- Children do not parrot back the words they hear. Their language is an original creation or construction.

- Children have their own grammar or consistent word order that is not the same as adult grammar.

- When children listen to adult speech they tune into its meaning and not its form.

Correcting a child's grammar does not make sense because the child is focused on the communication and does not recognize that there are correct and incorrect ways of expressing the same meaning. The same thing is true about correcting pronunciation. The child attends to the meaning of a sentence, not to the way it sounds. Correcting a child's pronunciation is completely ineffective. Here is an example of a conversation between a mother and a child.

Abbie: "Mommy! Mommy! My pusgetee keeps slipping off my fork."
Mommy: "Abbie, you mean your spaghetti keeps slipping off your fork."
Abbie: "That's what I said, it keeps slipping—see?"
Mommy: "Say 'spa'."
Abbie: "Spa."
Mommy: "Now say 'get'."
Abbie: "Get."
Mommy: "Now say 'tee'."
Abbie: "Tee."
Mommy: "Now say 'spa-get-tee'."

Abbie: "Spa-get-tee."
Mommy: "Very good! You said it perfectly."
Abbie: "But Mommy, my pasgetee falled off again. Can I use my fingers?"

Although an adult cannot improve a child's pronunciation or grammar by correcting his speech, the adult does play a critical role in helping a child develop language.

- The adult provides the child with real world experiences, which are the basis of language development. These experiences include opportunities to manipulate objects, to practice motor skills, to experience a variety of sights and sounds, to visit new people and see new places, to hear stories, poems, and songs, and to see and create pictures.

- The adult uses words in a meaningful context so that the child can discover that words stand for real world things or events.

- The adult serves as a good speech model, exposing the child to correct grammar and pronunciation. If we accept children's language and avoid the pitfall of correcting pronunciation and grammar, the child, in time, learns to speak correctly. It seems that children have an innate ability to abstract the rules of grammar and articulation and apply these rules to their own original sentences. When Abbie complained because her "pasgetee falled off" the fork, her use of the word "falled" demonstrated how much she already knew about language. Abbie recognized that the "ed" sound at the end of a word was a way of indicating that something happened in the past. Abbie made this kind of connection: "I kick the ball today." "I kicked the ball yesterday." "I fall down today." "I falled down yesterday." Abbie had never heard her parents use the word "falled." Her use of the word was a logical application of a rule. It will take several years for Abbie to realize that there are exceptions to rules and to know when these exceptions apply.

- Adults model not only the form of language for children but also uses of language. As they listen to adults use language in a variety of ways, children learn that language is used to:

  ‣ Give commands or directions
  ‣ Ask questions
  ‣ Provide information
  ‣ Describe things that happen
  ‣ Greet people
  ‣ Express how you feel
  ‣ Tell jokes and stories
  ‣ Sing songs and have fun

- Finally, and most important, adults serve as good listeners and good audiences. They provide an emotional climate that encourages children to share information and feelings.

Although an adult cannot improve a child's pronunciation or grammar by correcting his speech, the adult does play a critical role in helping a child develop language.

Activities to Promote Language Development

Conversation

One of the most effective techniques to encourage children's verbal expression is, perhaps, one of the least used by adults. It is simply to listen quietly and attentively when a child is speaking and to talk with him, not at him. When an adult has an attitude of respect for the child as an individual who has something interesting to share, the exchange is mutually rewarding and reinforcing. One way to extend this technique to a group setting is to have a planning time at the beginning of the day to discuss the activities for that day. The children may have some ideas the teacher hasn't thought of. At the end of the day, have a "recall" time to talk about what has happened that day —both good and bad. It is a time to share memories, ask questions, and express feelings.

...listen quietly and attentively when a child is speaking and talk with him, not at him.

Story Time

One of the favorite activities of both teachers and students is "Story Time." Each class has its own favorites that it never tires of hearing over and over. Once children become familiar with the story, it can be presented in different ways, with the children becoming more active participants.

- Make puppets from paper bags, paper plates, socks or mittens to represent the characters in the story.

- Use props that the children can manipulate to act out the story as the teacher is telling it.

- Use a cassette recorder to record the child as he says the lines of his character and then intersperse the recording with the telling of the story. For example, record the Big, Bad Wolf saying "I'll huff and I'll puff and I'll blow your house down," and when you get to that point in the story let a child push the button for the dialogue.

If your story time is not successful, ask the following questions:

- Did I pre-read the book?

- Was it appropriate for the age and interest level of the children?

- Was it too long?

- Did I allow interaction with the children? Did we discuss the illustrations? Did I ask questions? (e.g., What do you think the wolf found when he opened the door?)

- Was the setting appropriate? Were the children comfortable? Was the room quiet? Were there many distractions?

- Did I paraphrase if the language was too difficult?

- Did my voice, facial expression and body language reflect the mood of the story?

Reading from books is important because it allows children to see how the written word is a symbol that has a specific meaning. It is also important for the children to see that we can make up interesting stories as we use our imaginations.

Other Language Experiences or Activities

- Display several large pictures cut from magazines and mounted on brightly colored paper. (The National Geographic magazine is an excellent source for language stimulation pictures.) The children take turns choosing a picture. At first, the teacher tells a story about the picture. Then she gradually encourages the children to help with the story as she asks questions and incorporates their ideas and suggestions into the story. Soon the children will be able to tell a story themselves with little prompting. This is a good language activity for a small group of children.

- A field trip not only provides new experiences that can expand language, but also gives the children an opportunity to participate in detailed planning before the trip and critical evaluation after the trip.

- Provide opportunities for interaction among the children. Give a specific task to two or three children, which will involve cooperative planning (e.g.. cleaning and setting tables for a special snack to welcome a visitor or celebrate an occasion).

- Encourage children to express their feelings by using paper plate puppets with expressions of anger, sadness, fright, happiness, surprise, excitement, etc. With older children, prepare a chart with a slot for each child's name. As the child comes into the classroom in the morning, he places his name on the chart and beside his name he places a circular disc with a face that describes his feelings — happy, sad, angry, etc. At the end of the day at Good-bye Circle Time, each child is given a chance to change the face beside his name if his feelings have changed.

- "My Story": The teacher interviews the child using the cassette recorder. She then translates what the child has said about himself into short, simple sentences on large poster sized newsprint, leaving room at the top for a Polaroid picture of the child. The stories are mounted on the wall to be read and reread. This activity can also be done in book form, with the child providing illustrations.

Building A Classroom Environment That Promotes Language Development

We cannot compartmentalize language activities. There is no area in the classroom that cannot be used in some way to expand the child's vocabulary or encourage him in expressive speech. Here are some examples:

- The block and car area is especially effective as children experience over, under, inside, outside, between, around, beside, on top of, smaller, larger, big, little, long, short, fast, slow. You can expand children's language by encouraging them to build a wide variety of structures and environments — castles, hospitals, factories, farms, zoos, circuses, sports arenas, museums, garages, space stations, and theme parks. Add books, miniature figures, signs, and other props to encourage new ideas. You can help children expand their vocabulary as they build, e.g. "Your zoo is getting so big. But where do the people go if they are hungry? Do you need a refreshment stand?" Encourage children to tell the class about their structures before knocking them down.

- The imaginative play area gives children the opportunity for role-play. Even normally quiet children often become more talkative in a pretend situation. You can vary the area to reflect the current classroom theme, or add items that reflect the children's cultures. For example, the kitchen can become a Mexican restaurant, a cafeteria, a pet hospital, a grocery store or bodega, part of the fire station, or the galley of a ship.

- Music activities can be used to develop the child's ability to listen and to imitate. Songs and finger plays enrich children's language.

- Sensory activities involving smelling, tasting, and especially touching provide wonderful opportunities to extend children's vocabularies. As they play with a variety of interesting materials, you can help them learn words like "salty," "crunchy," "squeaky," "fluffy," "silky," "goupy," "sticky," "jiggly," and "crinkly" to describe their experiences.

- Even gross motor activities like climbing and sliding provide opportunities to expand children's vocabularies as you comment on their feats or talk together about how they plan to approach a new challenge.

- A table or area can be set up in the classroom that focuses on a theme (zoo animals, community helpers, etc.) or a question (How do we get milk? Where do letters go?). The children can have an active part in planning and producing the display.

Here are some special tools or props that can be placed in the classroom that foster expressive language.

- Telephone in the house area

- Cassette recorder that the children can operate by themselves

- Puppets, toy animals, dolls, and related props

- Sets of sequence pictures that the children can put together and use to tell a story

- Wordless books

- Mystery objects — These can be parts of machines, artifacts from other places or times, unusual plants or plant parts, crystals, natural sponges, pumice stone — anything out of the ordinary that will intrigue and puzzle children and prompt discussion.

Simply stated, successful language experiences give children an opportunity to express themselves and their ideas in their own way. A good teacher can stretch and expand these expressions without stifling creativity or spontaneity.

Objective 6: To learn ways of reading to children that encourage active participation and engender a love of books

Reading to children is a very special art.

Carla Caring, the director of the Caring About Children pre-school, was supervising a new teacher. In an after school conference with Ms. Caring, the teacher described several activities she had planned for circle time. The activities sounded appropriate, but Ms. Caring was disturbed about the fact that the teacher had not allotted time for reading to the children. "What books are you planning to read in circle time?" she asked the teacher. "I have decided not to read to the children," the teacher explained. "The children in my class don't like to be read to. Yesterday when I read them a book they did everything besides listening." "That's unusual', the director commented. "Most children love to be read to. Maybe they just didn't like the book you were reading." Ms. Caring picked up two books with attractive pictures on their covers. "Here, these books just came in. Read them to the children in your morning circle time."

The next day the director made a point of visiting the new teacher's class during circle time. The teacher was sitting in a low chair with the children sitting around her. She was holding the book in her hands and reading to the children word by word without letting them see the pictures. The director was not at all surprised when two of the children started squabbling. "I've got to teach this teacher how to read a book," the director said to herself.

Reading to children is a very special art. Some teachers are like pied pipers. As soon as they pick up a book the children gather around them. Other teachers need to learn techniques for reading to children that will keep them interested and involved.

At the next teacher's meeting Ms. Caring asked the teachers to talk about some of the techniques they use when they read to children. Here are some of their suggestions.

- Be sure to read the book to yourself before you read it to the children. This way you can figure out how to introduce the book and you can also figure ways to keep the children engaged. With some books you may decide to tell the story in your own words rather than reading the text. With other books you may decide to begin by showing the children the illustrations and asking them to tell you what they are looking at.

- When you read to children, make sure to position the book so that everyone can see the illustrations. If some children want a closer look, pass the book around.

- It is especially important to read with expression and enthusiasm. Vary your pitch, volume and inflections to maintain the children's interest. Use different voices when they are appropriate for different characters.

- Don't be in a hurry. Encourage children to ask questions and talk about the story or the illustrations.

- Reread the books that children really enjoy. When a book has a refrain, encourage the children to join in. If some children have memorized the book, give them a chance to read along with you. Try hesitating in the middle of a line and see if the children can finish it.

- Encourage children to guess how the book will end.

- See if the children can think of a different ending for a story.

- Let children retell the story in their own words, act out the story, or draw a picture about the story.

- When you finish reading a book place it on a low shelf where the children can reach it.

- Let the children choose the books they would like you to read.

- Make books with the children and encourage them to read the books to you.

- When reading to babies or toddlers, choose a time when you can be with just one or two children and can hold them on your lap. Choose sturdy books with lots of pictures that the child can point to, or with different textures for the child to feel. Stop when a child looses interest.

Objective 7: To provide a description of literacy skills and describe activities that promote these skills

The following conversation was overheard at the supermarket checkout line:

Parent: "Have you heard what they say about that preschool over on Maple Street?"

Parent: "No, what about it?"

Parent: "Well, they claim that over 50% of the four year olds are reading by the end of the year and almost all the children can read before they begin first grade."

Parent: "Wow, that sounds terrific! You know, Janie is only three, but I think I'll call about enrolling her."

Parent: "Good luck! They say the waiting list is so long that parents are filling out applications for admission as soon as their baby is born. I also heard that children who can't keep up with the work are kicked out."

Unfortunately, many parents judge the value of a preschool by how much reading is taught. We disagree with this measure, although we share with parents the belief that reading is important. After reviewing a large body of research on how children become good readers, a panel of experts commissioned by the National Academy of Sciences concluded that a preschool language and literacy foundation is important for later reading success. This foundation involves all kinds of experiences with stories, conversation, word play, books, and other meaningful print (signs, notes, lists, directions, etc.). Its most important component is a rich vocabulary; in whatever language or languages the child speaks. Providing the range of experiences that build a strong foundation is more important in the long run than simply teaching children to recite the alphabet or read simple books.

A good preschool, from our point of view, provides children with daily opportunities to "read" or look at books and to sing songs, listen to stories and poems, and tell or act out stories as they play with toys and with their friends. It paves the way for fluent reading by providing experiences that:

- Increase the child's use of language.
- Increase the child's knowledge base.
- Promote enjoyment of books and stories and motivation to read.
- Show children the many different ways that adults use reading and writing in their daily lives.
- Encourage children to communicate through "writing" and drawing, and to incorporate reading and writing into their play.
- Help the child associate printed and spoken words.
- Help the child develop specific skills that are related to reading success — phonological awareness (recognition of the sounds that make up words), print concepts (such as right to left reading and spaces between words), and letter naming.
- Help the child feel good about herself and confident that she can learn new things.
- Teach the child to follow directions.
- Help the child to attend to a task until it is completed.

Let's take a closer look at how we can provide these experiences by creating an environment that supports literacy, through shared reading, and through skill-building activities. Promoting self-confidence, motivation to learn, and ability to follow directions and complete tasks will be covered in more detail in later chapters.

An environment that support language development goes a long way toward promoting literacy.

Creating an Environment that Supports Literacy

An environment that supports language development goes a long way toward promoting literacy. As mentioned earlier, this language-rich environment should include:

- Interesting spaces and props that invite socio-dramatic play

- Intriguing objects and pictures that invite questions and conversation

- Toys, games, and puzzles that children use in pairs or small groups

- Blocks, sand, miniature figures, cars and trucks, and other toys that invite children to build things together

- Puppets, sequence cards, a tape-recorder, costumes, and other elements that encourage children to tell a story or "put on a show."

An environment that supports literacy is also rich in meaningful print. There will be:

- children's names on cubbies, artwork, displays of photographs, and charts showing "jobs" like feeding classroom pets or helping with snack

- captions for bulletin board displays

- signs that show where toys go or provide directions for adults and children to follow

- a calendar or schedule

- charts related to what children are learning

- reminder notes

- information for parents and classroom visitors

In addition, many teachers use chart paper and markers to post:

- words to children's favorite songs, chants, poems, and finger plays

- intriguing things that children have said

- recipes

- big books showing the text of favorite stories so children can read along or point to words as they are spoken

- children's questions and ideas about a new theme or project

- each child's contribution to a group story about a field trip or other experience

- weather reports

> *An environment that supports literacy is also rich in meaningful print.*

Finally, an environment that supports literacy incorporates books, writing materials, and meaningful print into many classroom areas. For example, you may see:

- a library or quiet reading corner

- paper and pencil and even computers in dramatic play areas so that children can "write" shopping lists, prescriptions, menus, tickets, train schedules, office work, checks, notes, secret codes, captains' logs, and e-mail

- boxes, cans, and other labeled food containers in the kitchen, restaurant, or store

- science books, nature guides, and writing materials in the science area so that children can identify found objects, "write" lab reports, make drawings to record their observations, and "do research"

- story books in the doll corner for reading to the babies

- a sign that says "Save" that children can put on their block constructions

- greeting cards, envelopes, letter and picture stamps, and book-making materials in the art area so that children can create books, letters, cards, notes, props for pretend play, and comic books or cartoons that tell a story

- a computer that children can use to play reading and writing games and to create books, letters, cards, notes, and props for pretend play

- a "museum" or labeled display related to a theme children are studying

- traffic signs for tricycles or miniature vehicles

- a book-making and repair area

Shared reading activities should occur daily in every preschool classroom.

Shared Reading

Shared reading activities should occur daily in every preschool classroom. They provide opportunities for children to enjoy, tell, and retell stories and to expand their language. They also provide opportunities for children to connect the spoken with the written word, to learn the conventions of print, to develop listening comprehension skills, and to see themselves as part of a community of readers and writers.

Here are some shared reading activities that preschoolers enjoy:

Story time Discussions: As you read to children, encourage their involvement in the story and attention to details by asking questions:

- ask children to recall what happened before

- ask children to look at the pictures and predict what will happen next

- ask children what they think a character wants or will do

- ask children to explain or guess the meaning of a word that may be unfamiliar

- ask children about how they think the characters feel, what they can do to solve their problems, or why they are acting in a particular way

- ask children if they have had experiences like those of the characters in the story

- ask children to repeat or retell their favorite parts

Circle Time Charts: Some teachers like to begin the day with a Circle Time Chart. A Circle Time Chart is used to talk about and write down special things that will happen in the course of the day. A creative teacher can draw a picture along with the words. If Circle Time Charts are dated, teachers can use them to talk about past events.

Experience Stories: Plan a field trip or nature walk for the children in your class. Take pictures of places or events along the way. Let the children help you create a picture book by placing the photos in the correct order. Ask the children to talk about each picture, and write their words underneath or on the facing page. Read the experience story with the children.

Choral Reading: Print the words to a favorite chant or finger play on a large piece of chart paper. Point to the words as the children say them with you.

Dictation: Let a child dictate a sentence or two, and write down his words exactly. Then read them back together.

Skill-Building
Phonological Awareness

Phonological awareness is awareness of the sounds that make up words. Being able to break words into component sounds and put sounds together to make words help children to "sound out" and spell new words. Here are some fun activities to develop phonological awareness.

Name Clapping: Sing songs using the children's names. For example: "Hello, Costanza, How are you? How are you today?" Have children clap out the syllables as they say the names: two for "Sameer," three for "Costanza," four for "Alexander."

Silly Songs: Teach the children songs that involve rhymes and sound play:

- "Ring Around the Rosie"
- "The Ants Go Marching"
- "This Old Man"
- "There Was an Old Lady Who Swallowed a Fly"
- "Anna, Anna, Bo-Banna, Banana Fanna, Fo-Fanna, Fi Fie Fo-Fanna, Anna" (substitute each child's name for "Anna")

The Sound Game: Say a compound word such as "lunchbox," "orange juice," or "playground" and ask a child to repeat it. Then ask her to "say it again" without one of its parts. For example, "Say 'lunchbox.' Say it again but this time don't say 'box.'" Once children have mastered the game with compound words, you can make it more challenging by taking away just a syllable (say "table" but don't say "ta") or just the first or last sound (say "stamp" but don't say "st;" say "lunch" but don't say "ch.")

Rhyme Cards: Make a set of rhyming picture cards — cat/ hat, shell/ bell, key/ bee. Color code the backs so that rhyming cards match. Encourage children to find the rhyming pairs. The four or five year old can also identify words that have the same beginning or ending sounds.

Invented Spelling: Using letter stamps, a computer, or their own attempts at writing, have children write words by writing letters for the sounds that they hear. Some children like to write notes to friends; others like to write captions for their drawings or make books or journals. If the child wants you to, you can ask her to read what she wrote "her way" and then write the words underneath "the way I write it."

Print Concepts

By the time they get to preschool, most children already know a lot about print. They may recognize some favorite cereal boxes, store logos, and even books and videos. If they have been read to frequently, they can probably hold a book right side up and turn its pages from front to back. They may even realize that the reader reads the words rather than the pictures and may correct a reader who doesn't read every word of a favorite book they have memorized.

Most preschool children are ready to master more advanced print concepts, such as naming letters, recognizing words, and following along.

Letter Naming

By the time they start kindergarten, children should be able to name some letters. Usually, the ones that most interest them are the letters in their names. Here are some fun ways to help children who are interested learn the names of letters.

Name Games: Help children identify the letters in their names and find them in different contexts, such as on food labels or on signs in the classroom. Children might also learn to recognize the first letter of each others' names. You might point out the first letter in a book title and ask, "whose name starts like this?"

Letter Stamping: Many children enjoy playing with rubber stamps and stamp pads, or with homemade stamps cut from potatoes, sponges, or cucumbers. Use stamps with letters as well as ones with simple shapes. Another fun way to stamp is to roll out a slab of clay or play-dough and make impressions with cookie cutters, rubber stamps, plastic letters, and found objects. Encourage children to talk about their stamp pictures. Help them name the letters and shapes they used.

Keyboard Play: Let children play with an old keyboard or typewriter. If you have a computer in your classroom, use any word processing program, with the font size set on 18 point or larger. At first, children will enjoy typing random letters and "reading" back what they wrote. Later, they may try to type particular letters, write their names, and ask you to help them write names of friends and family members.

Letter-of-the-Week Books: Make individual books for each child by folding and stapling several sheets of paper. Select a letter of the week for each child to cut out and place on the cover of his book. Talk about different objects that start with the letter of the week. Have children draw or cut out pictures of things beginning with that letter.

Word Recognition Games

Children who can recognize familiar signs and logos and can pick their own name out of a group may enjoy some of these word recognition games:

Labels: Label objects in the classroom. Read the labels out loud to the children. Every once in a while, take a label away. See if the children can put it back in the correct place.

Lotto Games: Buy or make a set of lotto boards with pictures of familiar animals or objects on one side of the cards that fit on the lotto board. When you read the lotto cards to the children, show them the word before naming the object or animal.

Word Puzzles: Make a series of word puzzles by backing pictures of familiar objects with the name of the object, then cutting them in half to form a two-piece puzzle. Mix the pieces from several of these puzzles in a storage tray. Let the children complete the puzzles on the word side. If they select the pieces that go together, they can turn the puzzle over to see the picture.

Word Banks: Put familiar words on index cards with pictures on the reverse side. As children learn to read a word, they place the card in their word bank.

Reading Along

One of the first things a reader needs to know is where to begin. When you read to children, show them where the words begin. Point out the first few words so that children can see that a printed word corresponds to a spoken word, that there are spaces between words, and that reading (in English and other languages written with the Roman alphabet) goes from left to right and top to bottom.

Children who are beginning to read for real can follow along as text is being read. Allow children who are ready to "help" you read by moving a finger under the words. These children might also help out in shared reading time, using a pointer to point to words on a chart as you read them aloud.

Technology can be a real boon to beginning readers. *Living Books* and similar computer programs highlight words as they are read. Other programs allow children to select words or rebuses (pictures that can be changed to words) to use in their writing, and will read back what the child has written. You can also make tape recordings of familiar storybooks, and encourage children to read

Technology can be a real boon to beginning readers.

along with the tape. (Make sure to clap or say, "turn the page" at the end of each page.

There is no magic age at which a child is ready to learn to read. Because each child is a unique individual, the age will vary and will be influenced by the following factors:

- His understanding of and ability to effectively use language
- His development of gross and fine motor skills
- His social and emotional development
- His background of experiences
- His interest in reading and his desire to learn
- The opportunities he is given to learn to read

Objective 8: To describe the small muscle skills that are used in writing and suggest activities that develop these skills and provide the child with opportunities to practice writing

Getting Ready to Write

Even more than reading, writing requires the development of skills that are related to maturation. Children develop their large muscle skills before they develop small muscle skills. Even if a two- year old knew how to form letters and numbers, he would be unlikely to have the small muscle skill or the eye-hand coordination needed to control the pencil and make the appropriate strokes.

In order to write with a pencil, the child must have the strength and muscle control to hold the pencil firmly between her thumb and first two fingers. Just as important, she must be able to swivel her wrist, control the fine movements of her fingers, and coordinate the movements of her fingers and hand with the movement of her eyes.

The following activities help children develop and practice these pre-writing skills.

Activities for Developing Pre-Writing Skills

Dressing Frames or Books: Provide dressing frames or "Dress Myself" books that give children practice in pulling up zippers, doing up snaps, lacing, and buttoning.

Sewing Cards: Make sets of sewing cards by cutting up old greeting cards into interesting shapes and punching holds around the outside. Use yarn for threading, making sure to put tape around the ends to make it easier for children to thread.

Lock-Boxes: Create a lock box with different kinds of latches and bolts.

Screw and Bolt Activity: Place nuts and bolts in a box and let children practice putting them together.

Rice for a Change: With a large pair of tweezers, let children transfer rice from one container to another.

Practical Life Activities: Children develop strength and coordination by washing tables, drying dishes, or polishing silverware.

Spinning: Provide children with spinning toys, like small tops or dreidels.

Bead Stringing: Provide children with opportunities to string increasingly smaller beads.

Clay: Encourage children to mold clay into different forms using rolling pins, cookie cutters, and plastic knives.

Peg Boards, Tinkertoys, Lock Blocks, Bristle Blocks, etc.: Provide children with a variety of put- together toys and encourage building.

Puzzles: Provide children with alphabet inset puzzles.

Sandpaper Letters: Encourage children to trace letters with their fingers in the sand and to make letters out of clay or pretzel dough.

Template Activities: Provide opportunities for children to create designs using templates of different shapes.

Tracing: Let children trace their own name by placing see through paper over their name on a small clipboard.

Creating Initials: Using an ice box cookie recipe, let each child create his or her initials.

Sponge Play: Let children use a sponge or eye dropper to move colored water from one container to another. Children can have fun mixing colors to make colors they like.

Play Writing: Encourage children to engage in activities that are related to writing, including making greeting cards, mailing pretend letters, writing birthday invitations, or making signs for the classroom.

Objective 9: To select books that foster empathy, promote pro-social behavior, counteract bias and/or promote bilingualism

A grandparent was buying books for her two-year old grandson. "My grandson loves the books where pictures pop up, but he tears them up in no time flat. Do you have any of those nice strong cardboard books?" she asked the salesperson. The salesperson showed her to a large display of books with cardboard pages. "Did you have any particular books in mind?" she asked the grandmother. "Oh, he's too young to understand what it says in the book," the grandmother explained. "Just find me a couple of nice sturdy books with lots of pictures."

We would agree with this grandmother that books with pop out pictures or movable parts are apt to be torn up if they are left in the hands of a toddler. At the same time, durability is not the only criteria we should use when selecting books for young children. Here are some other suggestions:

Selecting Books

- Choose books that are well-written, with language that is pleasant to read and repeat. Get in the habit of reading book reviews before you buy a book written by an unknown author. Look for books that have won a children's book award or that have been recommended by recognized authorities.

- Choose books with beautiful or playful illustrations. These may be drawings, photographs, paintings, or collages. The popularity of some of the all time favorites like *Winnie the Pooh, Madeleine, Goodnight Moon,* and *Curious George* is due as much to their illustrations as their stories.

- Choose books with anti-bias themes and books that are representative of different cultures.

- Choose books that show people of different races. If most of the children in your class are white, try to have about half of your books about people include people of color. If the majority of your students are non-white, try to have about three-quarters of your people books show people of color. Be sure there are some white faces as well.

- Avoid books with gender or age stereotypes.

- Select different types of books to create a rich and varied library.
  - ▲ Animal books
  - ▲ Books about everyday events
  - ▲ Fantasy books
  - ▲ Books about everyday problems
  - ▲ Books that describe feelings, like love or fear
  - ▲ Books about mischievous animals or children
  - ▲ Books about children from faraway places
  - ▲ Adventure stories
  - ▲ Silly books
  - ▲ Books that invite participation

▲ Books with refrains that are easy to remember
▲ Rhyming books
▲ Non-fiction books about favorite topics such as dinosaurs, space, sports, and dance
▲ Books with surprise endings

The books we read to children influence their feelings, their learning, and their actions. Even before children can follow a story line, they are influenced both by the illustrations we show them and by the words that we use to talk about the illustrations. If we select books where the doctor is always male and the nurse is always female, or where the grandmothers are always sitting in a rocking chair, we are exposing children to gender and age stereotypes. If we talk about feelings as we point to the illustrations, —"The puppy is sad; he wants his Mommy" — we encourage feelings of empathy.

The books we read to children influence their feelings, their learning, and their actions.

When children are able to follow a story line, we can select stories with a message we would like to share. There are many children's books about children with a disability, children with different skin colors, and children from different cultures that help children respect and appreciate differences. There are also children's books that encourage sharing, being a good friend, helping out, accepting a new baby, using words instead of hitting, or following rules that keep you safe. Often, the authors use animal characters so that children can recognize the point of a story without feeling put down.

Before you select books to read with the children in your class, think about whether there is an immediate message you would like to send. Is someone in the class about to get a baby sister or brother? Is a dental hygienist coming to your school to teach children about teeth brushing? Has a new child come into your class who you've been told is a biter? Has their been a recent article in your hometown newspaper about a child who drowned in a swimming pool or who ran into the street to retrieve a ball and was hit by a truck? Have the children been taunting a new girl in the school because she always wears a pretty dress?

Next, make a list of the kinds of messages you would like to send to the children during the course of the year. Once you have compiled the list, organize it into logical categories. You may want to include in your categories books that encourage children to be kind to each other, to take care of the environment, to appreciate their family, to learn how to share and take turns, to avoid bias, to cooperate, to follow health and safety rules, and to learn about different cultures. Try to find one or more books appropriate for children of different ages that fall into each category you select.

If you have children in your class who hear languages other than English spoken at home, look for books in that language and books that are bilingual. Invite family members to share songs and nursery rhymes in their home language with the class or to help you make some simple books or tapes. Encourage parents to read to their children in their home language as well as in English. Children may learn sophisticated concepts more easily in their first language. Also, in order to maintain the advantage of knowing two languages, they should hear both informal spoken language and more formal literate language in their mother tongue.

Bredekamp, S. (Editor). (1993). *Developmentally appropriate practice in early childhood programs serving children from birth through age 8.* Washington, D.C.: National Association for the Education of Young Children.

Brickman, N.A. & Taylor, L.S. (Editors). (1991). *Supporting young learners: Ideas for preschool and day care providers.* Ypsilanti, MI: High/Scope Press.

Bronson, M.B. (1995). *The right stuff for children birth to 8: Selecting play materials to support development.* Washington, D.C.: National Association for the Education of Young Children.

Burns, M., Griffin P., & Snow, C. (1999). *Starting out right: A guide to promoting children's reading success.* Washington, D.C.: National Research Council.

Diffily, D. & Morrison, K. (Editors). (1996). *Family friendly communication for early childhood programs.* Washington, D.C.: National Association for the Education of Young Children.

Dodge, D.T., Koralek, D.G., & Pizzolongo, P.J. (1989). *Caring for school children.* Vol. 1. Washington, D.C.: Teaching Strategies, Inc.

Meisels, S.J., Marsden, D.B., & Stetson, C. (2000). *Winning ways to learn: 600 great ideas for children.* NY: Goddard Press.

Schickendanz, J.A. (1999). *Much more than ABCs: The early stages of reading and writing.* Washington, D.C.: NAEYC.

Snow, C.W. (1998). *Infant development.* Upper Saddle River, NJ: Prentice Hall.

Chapter 9: Creativity

Overview

Creativity means many things and each of us has his own definition. For some it means artistic talent, for others a passion to...

- produce the original
- appreciate beauty
- discover joy
- mold a product that is unique, beautiful, or inspiring
- solve problems
- seek out the unusual

Creativity and talent are not the same thing. Talent is the ability to perform easily and well in a particular area. Creativity is a more generalized trait that enables the individual to find new ways of arranging materials, asking questions, or solving problems. It is up to the teacher to structure an environment that nurtures and supports each child's innate creative spark.

Rationale

Whatever our definition, all of us recognize that creativity is a highly desirable characteristic that we want to encourage in children. The child who is considered creative is treasured at home and in school. The bright child learns whatever we teach, but the highly creative child goes beyond our teaching and makes discoveries on her own.

This unit focuses on providing opportunities for children to exercise their creative abilities, to appreciate the creativity of others, and to explore and experiment with a variety of media, not only through art, music, and dramatic activities, but in all aspects of the program. It demonstrates ways in which teachers can provide children with an array of experiences that stimulate exploration and provide opportunities for children to express their creative ideas.

Objectives

1. To use a variety of teaching techniques to encourage children to think and act creatively.

2. To recognize ways in which children birth to five express their creativity at each developmental stage and identify caregiver behaviors and techniques that foster the development of creativity.

3. To describe materials and activities that encourage infants to explore and experiment.

4. To describe sensory, music, movement, art, building, and pretend play activities that encourage toddlers to express their creativity.

5. To describe music, movement, art, building, story telling, and dramatic play activities that encourage preschool children to express their creativity.

Manuel was a new student at the Magic Years Preschool. The teacher of the four-year-old group, Miss Try-Hard, had met Manuel's parents when they enrolled him in the school. They described their son as a good kid who marched to the tune of a different drummer. They were convinced that what he needed was a teacher with a firm hand who would keep him out of trouble. Miss Try-Hard, who had expected the worst, was surprised to find that Manuel was a delightful kid. He had a fantastic imagination, and the other children gravitated to him. One day he taught the class how to make paper airplanes and they pretended to put on an air show. On another day he organized a safari on the playground. Some boys climbed on the jungle gym and pretended they were riding in a swamp buggy. Several girls pretended to be wild animals and raced around the playground screeching, roaring, and growling. "Manuel could be the teacher," Miss Try-Hard told the director. "Just about every day he comes up with a creative idea."

Manuel was lucky to have Miss Try-Hard as a teacher. Miss Try-Hard loved creative ideas and she was flexible enough to let the children set their own agenda. She wasn't upset when Manuel rearranged the classroom so that the airplanes had a place to land, and she enjoyed the cacophony when the children became wild animals racing through the jungle.

In this unit, as we explore the different facets of creativity, we recognize that a truly creative teacher does not have to be an artist, musician, or star performer. The essential characteristic of a creative teacher is the ability to recognize, value, and support the different ways in which children express their creativity.

Objective 1: To use a variety of teaching techniques to encourage children to think and act creatively

The Funsters were half an hour late for their appointment with the director of the Creative Preschool. They wanted to see the school in action before they made the decision to enroll their twins. They apologized to the director for being late but hoped that they could still see the school. "I would be happy to show you the school," the director responded. "Unfortunately, the children just went home, but you will be able to see how the rooms are set up."

When they went into the toddler room, everything was in perfect order. There was a section with puzzles and manipulative toys, a block area, a child size kitchen equipped with doll-size appliances, play food, pots and pans, and two brooms, and a music area with a cassette player and a set of rhythm instruments. Mrs. Funster remarked to the director, "This is incredible. This room doesn't look as if even one toddler was in it, let alone fourteen. Either your teachers are speed wizards or the children aren't allowed to play with the toys!"

Mrs. Funster was wrong. In actuality, the toddler teachers were quite laid back and a half hour before dismissal every toy in the room was out of place. The lead teacher was also very creative. She had a puppet that she called "Alexander the Great," and had convinced the children that the classroom belonged to Alexander. Alexander loved to share his toys with children, but he couldn't go to sleep at night unless every toy in his room was exactly where it belonged.

A truly creative teacher, in addition to fostering the creativity of children, finds creative ways of guiding children's behavior and of helping children learn. She is a teacher who invites children to question, who likes children who are spunky, who enjoys humor, and who values individuality and diversity. She is also a teacher who has a talent for finding many different ways of getting across a new concept, for recognizing and building on children's interests, and for asking questions or presenting problems that have more than one right answer. A creative teacher invites children to try out new ideas without being fearful of failure.

Think about the activity suggestions in the previous chapters. What physical, cognitive, and language activities foster creativity in children? Which ones also engage the teacher's creativity?

Objective 2: To recognize ways in which children birth to five express their creativity at each developmental stage and identify caregiver behaviors and techniques that foster the development of creativity

Miss Efficiency, the director of the Growing Children Preschool, was developing a curriculum framework for her Center. Her goal was to identify the major curriculum categories for each age group so that teachers could develop their own curriculum plans. At a staff meeting, she asked the teachers at what age they felt that creativity should be introduced as a curriculum area. While most teachers agreed that creativity should be considered as a curriculum area for the three and four year olds, one toddler teacher insisted that creativity was a trait that children were born with and that teachers should foster creativity at every age level. As the teachers continued the discussion, they came to the conclusion that, if you define creativity as the push to explore and discover, creativity begins at birth.

Developmental Picture

The infant 0-8 months:

- Is keenly sensitive to sensory information from the moment of birth
- Uses new information to learn about the world
- Distinguishes between new and familiar information, and can tune out information that is too overwhelming
- Enjoys listening to different kinds of music, experiencing rhythmic movement, and looking at colorful displays or designs

The caregiver:

- Provides a variety of things for the infant to look at, such as mobiles, pictures, and designs, and a variety of experiences with touch and sound
- Enjoys playing with infants, and shares their delight in toys, actions, and sounds
- Plays different types of music (cheerful, rhythmic, soothing)
- Dances or sways to music while carrying the infant; sings to the infant

The infant 8-14 months:

- Is an active experimenter, trying out new ways of playing and interacting
- Tries out a variety of actions on the same object, such as hitting, banging, shaking, tasting and dropping
- Tries the same actions on a variety of new objects, noticing the ways that different objects react (some objects bounce when dropped while other objects; and with a crash, thud, or splat)

The caregiver:

- Recognizes the ways an infant is playing and exploring and provides toys and objects that support the baby's interests
- Provides infants with different objects and combinations of objects that encourage safe and fun play
- Plays with the infant; sensitively following the child's interests

The toddler 14-24 months:

- Experiments with different ways of playing with the same object—drops, rolls, kicks, and squeezes an item like a Nerf ball
- Enjoys using a crayon to make a mark
- Plays with sand and water in a variety of creative ways
- Responds to music with body movements

The caregiver:

- Provides opportunities to play with sand and water with a variety of toys such as pails, shovels, sieves, plastic containers, pitchers, rakes, and toy boats

- Provides the opportunity to listen and respond to different kinds of music: lyrical, fast, slow, classical, modern
- Provides opportunities for early art experiences, such as finger painting, making marks with crayons, playing with play-dough

The two year old:

- Is beginning to understand representations, such as knowing that a doll represents a baby or that a drawing of a dog represents a real dog
- Uses blocks to make a tower, a road, or a house
- Enjoys things that are beautiful, like music, flowers, butterflies, and paintings
- Experiments with different scribbles or different ways of finger painting
- Listens to music and invents dances; enjoys marching to music and being part of a rhythm band

The caregiver:

- Provides opportunities for children to look at paintings, hear different kinds of music, watch different kinds of dancing
- Allows children to play with toys in different ways, such as putting blocks in the frying pan or filling a pail with a variety of small objects
- Provides opportunities for singing, dancing, playing with clay, building with different kinds of blocks, and pretending

The preschool child:

- Enjoys creating with different materials, such as finger paint, water colors, tempera, collage, Play-Doh, or clay
- Is more interested in the process of creating than the product
- Is intensely interested in and committed to her own creations and is unlikely to welcome interference
- Enjoys telling stories and making up songs
- Uses drawing as a way to tell a story
- Enjoys making up rhymes or playing with words
- Enjoys different kinds of dramatic play, including "macro play" where he is the actor, and "micro play" where he tells a story with miniature objects

The caregiver:

- Provides children with opportunities to create in a variety of media
- Gives children the freedom to create in their own way rather than directing their productions
- Provides opportunities to participate in different musical experiences such as singing, dancing, activity records, and rhythm band
- Encourages individuality, but recognizes that children often enjoy copying each other
- Provides opportunities to experience excellent art, music, poetry, and prose
- Provides different kinds of props that encourage pretend play

Objective 3: To describe materials and activities that encourage infants to explore and experiment

*M*rs. Kid-Me-Not was observing in the infant room in the Hope County Child *Care Center. She nudged one of the caregivers. "Hey there Ms. Kootsey, do you see what Patsy is doing? You better clean her up, she's got her fingers in Jell-O and she's spreading it all over the table." "It's okay," Mrs. Kootsey explained, "Patsy is having fun 'finger painting" with Jell-O. She likes the feel of Jell-O and she is particularly interested in the way it looks when she spreads it out on the table. Our little Patsy is an artist in the making!"*

> *Because exploration is the wellspring of creativity, an infant curriculum should provide opportunities for a wide variety of sensory experiences.*

Although spreading Jell-O around the table may seem unrelated to any form of art, providing young children with different sensory experiences is the beginning step in encouraging creativity. When we give infants and toddlers opportunities to experience and experiment with different textures and consistencies, or when we allow young children to experience and experiment with rhythm, melody, and movement, we are laying the ground work for creative expression.

Activities to Encourage Sensory Exploration

Because exploration is the wellspring of creativity, an infant curriculum should provide opportunities for a wide variety of sensory experiences. Here are some activities that are appropriate for infant programs:

Texture Rub: Get swatches of different textured fabrics. Let babies handle the fabrics. Play a tickling game where you rub the material on different parts of the infant's body.

Bubbles: Blow bubbles for the infants. The younger babies can watch them move. Older babies can reach for, grasp, pop, and finally run after them. (You can make your own bubble solution by mixing 1 cup of Joy, Dawn, Sunlight, etc. dish soap with 1 cup of water. If you add 1/4 cup of glycerin, bubbles last longer.)

Cornmeal Play: Put some cornmeal out in a large, low basin. Encourage the babies to touch it and play in it. Later, add a variety of implements: spoons, cups, rubber spatulas, toy trucks, and a sieve or funnel.

Spaghetti Pull: This is an excellent activity for developing fine motor skills. Place a tray of wet spaghetti in front of the babies and let them have fun.

Finger painting: Most babies between nine and twelve months old love to finger paint. You can make your own finger paint by mixing some liquid starch with powdered tempera paint. Put in tight containers and let infants paint on their high chair trays.

Sand Play: Clean sand can provide older babies with hours of fun.

Colored Acetate Fun: Give each infant pieces of colored acetate and play a peek-a-boo game.

Sound exploration: Provide infants with a variety of sound makers: rattles, squish toys, bells, and musical balls. Let the babies experiment with similar and different sounds.

Music for Babies

Setting the Mood: Play soothing lullabies during going to sleep and feeding times. Play faster, upbeat music when the babies are wide-awake. Play all different kinds of music – classical, jazz, Reggae, soft rock, and simple folk songs, as well as music written for babies.

Moving to Music: Pick babies up and dance with them. Also encourage them to wave their arms and bounce up and down or to imitate your movements when you play dance music Play their favorite dance tunes frequently.

Music Making: Between nine and twelve months, infants are ready for drum play. At first, babies will use their hands to beat a drum. After a while, they discover that hitting the drum with a stick (a short handled wooden spoon or a rubber spatula is safe) will make a delightful sound.

Marching Band: Play children's songs and encourage all the infants to shake a rattle or musical instrument to the music. Put on a marching beat and bang the drums (a drum made out of an oatmeal box or coffee can works just as well) or march in a circle.

Action Songs for Baby Play

Babies need and enjoy one-on-one play with their caregiver. Make the most of this one-on-one time by engaging babies in back and forth chants or action songs. Here are some songs and chants that every baby enjoys.

Pat-a-Cake

Pat a cake,
Pat a cake baker's man,
Bake me a cake as fast as you can,
Roll it (roll it in baby's hands), knead it, and, Mark it with a B and put it in the oven for baby and me.

How Big Is Baby?

How big is baby?
So big! (lift up baby's hands)

Trot Trot to Boston

Trot trot to Boston
Trot trot to Lynn
You better watch out or you might fall in (tilt baby backwards and bounce him up)

Bicycle Baby
(for leg bicycle exercises)

Bicycle, bicycle baby
Bicycle, Bicycle girl (or boy)

See Saw

See saw up and down (child's name) is going to town.
See saw side to side (child's name)'s going for a ride.
See saw bumpity bump (child's name)'s getting ready to jump!

Objective 4: To describe sensory, music, movement, art, building, and pretend play activities that encourage toddlers to express their creativity

Toddlers enjoy listening to music, "dancing" to music, and creating music on their own.

M *rs. Artlover was deciding on a child care placement for her daughter. She described to the director of a center the kind of place she was looking for. "I would like my child to have a creative learning experience," she explained. "I am not hung up on academics. She'll learn to read and write soon enough when she gets to school. But I do want my daughter in a center where she will be immersed in artistic activities When I read your brochure, I was impressed by the fact that beginning with toddlers you offer lessons in music, art, ceramics, dancing and dramatics. Could you talk more about these?"*

Although we recognize the importance of introducing children to creative arts at an early age, we do not agree with the introduction of formal artistic lessons. Young children need opportunities to explore and discover their own talents. Creativity is not something that you teach a child. It emerges spontaneously as children play with materials and engage in activities that encourage observation and self expression.

Activities that Encourage Sensory Exploration

Sensory activities are usually favorites with toddlers. They provide opportunities for children to heighten their sensory awareness, to practice many fine motor skills, and to expand their language skills. Additionally, they encourage a great deal of social interaction.

Water Play: The ideal place for water play is in a water table. To prevent children from getting too wet, have them wear plastic smocks. If you don't have a water table, use a large dishpan or tub.

Cornmeal Play: Place cornmeal in a large, low basin. Give children coffee scoops, cups, and sifters. To vary the activity, add small cars and farm animals and encourage the children to make roads and mountains.

Jell-O Play: Cut stiff Jell-O into cubes and let the toddlers have fun picking it up in their hands.

Rice Pouring: The advantage of rice is that, while it can get messy, it is very easy to vacuum. The same kinds of implements and activities suggested for cornmeal and water work well with rice.

Smell Jars: Use film cans with holes punched in the tops. Soak cotton balls in extracts (such as vanilla, peppermint, orange, and almond), perfume, and water mixed with a spice such as cinnamon or ginger. Stuff a ball in each can and shut the lid. Make two sets so you can do matching activities.

Musical Activities for Toddlers

Toddlers enjoy listening to music, "dancing" to music, and creating music on their own. Because toddlers are sensitive to the moods that music creates, caregivers often use records or songs to signal a transition. In many child care centers, there is a special song for circle time, for clean up time, and for saying good-bye at the end of the day. Another common practice is to play soft music at nap time.

Listening to Music

One to two-year olds enjoy music most when the tune and the song are familiar. Like a favorite doll or stuffed animal, a favorite song is something you play over and over again and never get tired of listening to. Songs that are enjoyed by young toddlers include:

"Twinkle, Twinkle Little Star"
"Happy Birthday to You"
"All Around the Mulberry Bush"
"Frére Jacques"
"Old MacDonald"
"London Bridge"

Dancing To Music

Dancing to music for a one to two-year old means bobbing up and down when the music plays. Because toddlers love the familiar, it is a good idea to play up-beat music, like disco or rock, that they have heard at home.

Creating Music

One to two-year olds are not very good at singing words, but they love to clap their hands in time with the music. They also enjoy playing percussion instruments like drums, sticks, and shakers.

Movement and music activities, like art activities, are expressions of creativity and help children to become more aware of their bodies, to develop their ability to take the initiative, and to learn specific concepts. Songs and finger plays give children the opportunity to hear the structure and rhythm of language and to have fun with words.

Songs, Finger Plays and Poems
Honey Bunny
(to the tune of "Frére Jacques")

> *Honey Bunny, Honey Bunny*
> *Nice and soft, nice and soft (stroke arm)*
> *We love to feed you carrots (pretend to feed carrots)*
> *We love to feed you carrots*
> *Hop away. Hop away. (put up two fingers & have them hop)*

Raindrop Song

> *Raindrops fall with a pitter, patter, pat, pitter, patter pat, pitter, patter, pat. (make finger go up & down) Raindrops fall with a pitter, patter, pat-making all things grow. (raise cupped hands)*

Six Little Ducks

> *Six little ducks that I once knew (hold up 6 fingers) Fat ones, skinny ones, big ones, too (use 2 hands to show size)*
> *But the one little duck with the feather on his back (put one hand on back) ,*
> *He led the others with a quack, quack, quack. (put heels of hands together and move fingers apart and together like a beak opening and closing)*
> *Quack, quack, quack.*
>
> *Down to the river they would go (point over shoulder)*
> *Widdle-waddle, widdle-waddle, to and fro (put hands together and move them back &forth)*
> *But the one little duck with the feather on his back,*
> *He led the others with a quack, quack, quack,*
> *Quack, quack, quack.*

Variations on Traditional Songs
The Wheels on the Bus Go 'Round and 'Round
Variations: After going through the routine things, put a cat on the bus that goes meow and a ghost on the bus that goes boo. Let the children come up with new ideas.

Old MacDonald Had a Farm
Variations: Add variations like:
An alarm clock that goes "ding, dong"
A saw that goes "buzz"
A fly that goes "bzzz"
Corn that goes "pop"

When You're Happy and You Know It Clap Your Hands
Variations: When you're angry and you know it, stamp your feet. When you're sleepy and you know it, start to snore. When you're silly and you know it, laugh hee-hee.

She'll Be Coming Round the Mountain When She Comes

Variations: She'll be slicing up red onions when she comes (wah-wah). She'll be riding on a horse fly when she comes (buzz, buzz).

This Is the Way We Wash Our Clothes

Variations: This is the way we wiggle our ears. This is the way we tickle our tummy.

Row Row Row Your Boat

Variations: Pump, pump, pump your bike, gently down the hill,
  Merrily, merrily, merrily, do not have a spill.
  Drive, drive, drive your car, gently down the street
  Merrily, merrily, merrily, pump it with your feet.

Teddy Bear Poem

(Act out motions)

Teddy bear, teddy bear, turn around,
Teddy bear, teddy bear, touch the ground.
Teddy bear, teddy bear, go upstairs,
Teddy bear, teddy bear, say your prayers.
Teddy bear, teddy bear, turn off the light,
Teddy bear, teddy bear, say good-night.

Variations: Change "turns around" to "touch your toes".
  Change "say your prayers" to "wiggle your nose."

Favorite Records for Toddlers

- *Music for One's and Two's,* Tom Glazer
- *And One and Two,* Ella Jenkins
- *Ann Murray Sings for the Sesame Street Generation*
- *Singable Songs for the Very Young,* Sung by Raffi
- *Homemade Band,* Hap Palmer
- *Playtime Parachute Fun for Early Childhood*
- *Getting to Know Myself,* Hap Palmer
- *Early, Early Childhood Songs,* Ella Jenkins

Art Activities

By eighteen months old, children enjoy arranging blocks in a row, or making a pattern in a sand box by raking the sand with their fingers. By two years old, they are intrigued with paint and clay, and are ready to experiment with paint brushes and other paint media. Between two and three years, children begin to arrange objects or materials in an order or array that is pleasing to them. While most children enjoy the sensation of spreading paint with their fingers, other children dislike getting their hands dirty and prefer to paint with a brush.

Materials for Painting

Types of Paint: Water colors, non-toxic tempera paints, finger paints

Surfaces for Painting: Young children enjoy variety. Try painting on an easel, painting on individual paper, and painting on a mural (either taped to the table or on the wall). Mural painting allows children to create something of their own which will decorate the room (see theme projects for specific ideas).

Paint Media: Toddlers can paint with brushes, fingers, sponges, Q-tips, cotton balls, eye droppers, and string. They also enjoy stamp painting. Potatoes cut in half with designs etched into the top work especially well. Even the young two-year old can make a pumpkin picture for Halloween using this method. Cookie cutters allow children to make holiday designs. Vegetable printing is also fun. Try carrots, string beans, cauliflower, and broccoli. On a sunny day, children can enjoy using large paintbrushes to paint with water on stone or concrete.

Painting and Pasting Activities

Finger painting: Finger painting can be done on a "messy play tray" (Childcraft), the table, or on individual floor tiles. When the children create something they want to save, make a print on newsprint. It is also fun to paint objects. Let the children collect and paint rocks, shells, pine cones, sticks, or scrap pieces of wood.

Shaving Cream Finger Painting: Use non-menthol shaving cream and a smooth surface. Add food coloring to make it even more interesting.

Ivory Snowflake Finger Painting: Add a little water to Ivory Snow Flakes and beat with an egg beater. This makes thick suds that can be used like finger paint. Food coloring can also be added.

Pudding Paint: For an extra special treat, let children finger paint with chocolate pudding.

Pasting: Once a child has learned to paste, all kinds of craft projects can be carried out. For little ones, large tongue depressors and individual portions of paste placed in baby-food jar lids work well. Another method of pasting involves watering down Elmer's Glue and painting it on with a brush. Children can create collages by pasting scraps of paper and other materials on heavy paper or cardboard. They can also draw with paste and then sprinkle on salt, colored sand, rice, or glitter to create interesting effects.

Sensory Activities

Sensory activity play is a favorite activity for toddlers. Toddlers enjoy water play, sandboxes, rice, oatmeal, and cornmeal bins. They are particularly fond of play-dough and enjoy a variety of textures.

Play dough: Kneading play dough aids in developing small motor skills and is a favorite among the younger children. You can make your own play dough with the following recipe:

Play Dough:
2 cups flour
2 tablespoons salad oil
1/2 cup salt
4 teaspoons cream of tartar
2 cups cold water
food coloring

Cook and stir over medium heat until play dough thickens. Color with food coloring (Make it very bright; but be sure to mix or knead it in well, as straight food coloring will stain hands and clothing). Cook and put in a ziplock bag.

Vary the implements presented with the play dough. Try rolling pins or dowels, tongue depressors, small cookie cutters, plastic knives, scissors, and small (non-swallowable) objects such as plastic letters, straws, poker chips, bottle and jar lids, and small toys.

Peanut Butter Play Dough:
1 cup of creamy peanut butter
1 cup light corn syrup
1 1/2 cups of dry powdered milk
1 1/2 cups of powdered sugar

Combine all ingredients in a mixing bowl and mix until smooth. Chill covered for 3 hours before use. Will keep fresh in a ziplock bag for about 3-4 weeks.

Building

Toddlers enjoy creating and experimenting with blocks. They are learning how to carry blocks, line up blocks, stack blocks, balance bigger blocks on smaller blocks, and nest blocks in unique ways. Use blocks of different sizes, shapes, and textures, provide cardboard blocks, nesting blocks, plastic blocks, and small unit blocks. Avoid large heavy wooden blocks because toddlers like to throw.

Pretend Play

One of the most exciting aspects of being a toddler teacher is to watch the gradual emergence of pretend play. Pretend play begins as imitation. Young toddlers love to imitate grown up activities. They enjoy babbling into a toy telephone, sweeping the floor with a child size broom, or mowing the grass with a bubble blowing push toy.

With most toddlers, we see gradual transitions from imitative play to pretending at around two years old. A little girl may insist on wearing a hat when she pushes her bubble blower. She is not simply imitating the act of pushing a lawnmower; she is pretending to be Daddy mowing the lawn. A boy may stir a pot with a spoon and then put it on a play stove. He is not just imitating a parent whom he has watched cooking; he is pretending that he is preparing dinner for the family.

Teachers can support the emergence of pretend play by providing the play space, the materials, the dress up clothes, and the furnishings that allow for the spontaneous emergence of pretend play. Basic props should include kitchen items, a steering wheel, a doctor's kit, dolls, and toy animals.

Objective 5: To describe sensory experiences, music, movement, art, building, story telling and dramatic play activities that encourage preschool children to express their creativity

> *One of the most exciting aspects of being a toddler teacher is to watch the gradual emergence of pretend play.*

M*iss Sue looked around the room sharply, a slight frown creasing her brow. Her glance seemed to rest briefly on each child.*

"We will not begin until everyone is absolutely quiet and still." A hush fell upon the room. Then, suddenly, twenty sets of small eyes turned in unison toward a loud crashing sound coming from the end of one of the long tables.

"Johnny, if you would sit like I told you, with both feet on the floor and both hands folded together on top of the table, you would not keep falling out of your chair."

Miss Sue rolled her eyes heavenward as if to say, "Why me, Lord,?" released a long sigh, and went on with her talking.

"I am giving each of you a sheet of paper to color. There are five flowers in a pot. Across each flower is written the word that tells you what color that flower should be. If you can't remember what the words say," she paused and glanced pointedly toward Johnny, "then look at the chart on the wall. Remember to work without talking and try to stay within the lines. When you finish, bring your paper to me to be checked. If you have colored neatly and correctly, you may then go outside to play. If not, you'll have to do the paper over until you get it right. All right, you may begin."

Miss Sue sat down at her desk and checked off "creative activity" on her lesson plan.

This story, of course, is an exaggeration of obvious "no-no's." Read through it again and see how many you can pick out. Now let's look at some productive ways of encouraging creativity in preschool children.

Sensory Motor Activities

The best way to encourage creativity is to have art materials available to children at all times. This keeps the focus is on the process, rather than the product, and encourages children to experiment with different kinds of materials.

- **Clay** (or dough) — for squeezing, pounding, rolling, kneading, punching, patting, molding, cutting, stamping, and sculpting

  - ▲ earth clay — buy in powdered form and mix with water
  - ▲ Play-Dough (commercial or home made)
  - ▲ salt/flour dough — the children will enjoy making it as much as using it

- **Finger paint** —keep a plastic can of water near by. Have children wet hands their hands before they begin.

- **Sensory materials** — to smear, hold, squeeze, make designs with, pour, sculpt, and use in art or building projects

- **Jell-O building** — Cut stiff Jell-O into cubes and give to the children on individual trays.

Creativity in Music

Interestingly enough, when we talk about creativity in arts and crafts, we talk about children's involvement in the creative process. When we talk about creativity in music, we are more apt to think of children as a participating audience, following the directions of an activity record or singing along with a song written by someone else. In both music and art, children need opportunities to be an appreciative audience and opportunities to create on their own.

Singing, dancing, and music making are favorite activities for all preschool children. Music activities provide opportunities for self-expression, creativity, fun, excitement, and comradery. Most important, music activities provide an opportunity for children to experience the joy and sense of power that comes from cooperation.

In this section, we look at three kinds of musical activities that are successful with preschool children. They include group singing, rhythm bands, and music and movement activities.

Group Singing

Preschool children love to sing. While many preschoolers are not very successful at carrying a tune or staying on key, most preschoolers are learning to recognize and repeat the contour and rhythm of a simple song. By limiting the number of different tunes and utilizing the tunes children know in a creative way, preschool teachers can provide children with a delightful repertoire of songs they know and love.

Favorite Songs and Variations
The Wheels on the Bus:

> *The wheels on the bus go round and round*
> *Round and round, round and round*
> *The wheels on the bus go round and round*
> *All through the town*

Variation: Suggest to the class that some farm animals have joined the children on the bus.

> *The ducks on the bus go quack, quack, quack*
> *The cows on the bus go moo, moo, moo*

Old MacDonald

> *Old MacDonald had a farm, ee-i-ee-i-o*
> *And on that farm he had a cow, ee-i-ee-i-o*
> *With a moo, moo here, and a moo, moo there*
> *Here a moo, there a moo, everywhere a moo, moo*
> *Old MacDonald had a farm, ee-i-ee-i-o*

Variation: Suggest that Old MacDonald decided to add some things to his farm, such as:

> *A clock that goes tick-tock*
> *A truck that goes vrum-vrum*
> *An engine that goes putt, putt*
> *A wagon that goes clappity-clap*

If You Are Happy and You Know It

> *If you're happy and you know it, clap your hands*
> *If you're happy and you know it, clap your hands*
> *If you're happy and you know it*
> *Then you're face will surely show it*
> *If you're happy and you know it, clap your hands*

Variation 1: Change the first stanza to include different emotions.

> *If you're silly and you know it, start to giggle.*
> *If you're thirsty and you know it, go slurp, slurp.*
> *If you're sleepy and you know it, start to snore.*

Variation 2: Change the second stanza

> *If you're happy and you know it, stick out your tongue.*
> *If you're happy and you know it, wiggle your nose.*
> *If you're happy and you know it, clap your elbows.*

Rhythm Bands

Rhythm bands provide opportunities for creativity, ingenuity, and the development of cognitive skills. They provide opportunities for making different instruments, for learning about different cultures, for developing listening skills, and for participating in a group experience.

Obviously most children of three, four, and five do not have the skill to write music or play a standard instrument. But this should not discourage a creative teacher.

Rhythm instruments can be created, improvised, or purchased. The simplest instruments to make are shakers, rhythm sticks, and drums. Shakers can be made out of juice cans, coffee cans, or well-washed Clorox bottles filled with

Rhythm bands provide opportunities for creativity, ingenuity, and the development of cognitive skills.

pebbles, rice, or beans. Rhythm sticks can be created from paper towel spindles, chop sticks, or dowels, and drums can be made from coffee cans, oatmeal cartons, and cereal bowls. The good part about homemade instruments is that children can bring their ideas home and the families can create their own rhythm band.

- Once children have created their own instruments, it is easy to encourage them to create their own rhythms. Try sitting a group of five or six children in a circle and letting each child have a turn being the rhythm leader.

- Provide children with an opportunity to smell a flower, taste a piece of fruit, feel a new texture, or watch a beam of light as it comes through a prism. Ask the children to describe their experience in words. When children select a descriptive phrase that seems to please them, ask them to say it over and over again. Inevitably their chant becomes a sing-song, their own original rendition.

- Equip your classroom with easy-to-play musical instruments. Montessori bells, xylophones, and kazoos are particularly appropriate. Encourage children to create their own songs.

Learning About Different Cultures

Almost every ethnic group has its own special music. Playing music from different cultures and helping children use an instrument to imitate or accent the beat provides a culture sharing experience.

Developing Listening Skills

There are many different ways of teaching listening skills through the use of rhythm instruments. The simplest way, of course, is to buy commercial records and commercial rhythm instruments. When programs can afford it, this is a good investment because instruments and records or tapes are unlikely to wear out. A second way to develop listening skills is to combine the singing of a familiar song with the use of homemade instruments.

Over the Mountain

Sit the children in a circle. Distribute home made instruments to the group, giving one section shakers, one section sticks, and one section drums. Explain to the group that they all have to watch the conductor so that they know when it is their turn to play their instrument. The group sings:

The bear went over the mountain
The bear went over the mountain
And what do you think he heard?
And what do you think he heard?
He heard the drums all playing (let the children with the drums play)
He heard the drums all playing (let the children with the drums play)
He heard the drums all playing (let the children with the drums play)
That is what he heard.

For the next stanza, sing:
He heard the sticks all playing

For the third stanza, sing:
He heard the shakers all shaking

For the fourth stanza, sing:
He heard the whole band playing (have everyone join in.)

Musical Games and Dances

Musical games and movement activities are traditional favorites in preschools around the world. They are wonderful for culture sharing, helping shy children participate, beginning and ending the day, and making productive use of waiting or transition time. Some musical games involve sitting or standing in a circle, while others work best if you choose a partner, or line up in twos.

Circle games that are all time favorites include "The Farmer in the Dell," "Go In and Out the Window," and "Ring around the Rosie." Favorite games that involve finding a partner include "Row, Row, Row Your Boat," "See Saw, Margery Daw," "London Bridge," "Miss Mary Mack," and "Little Brown Jug." Favorite dances include "Hokie Pokie," "Little Red Caboose", and "Skip to My Lou." Activity records where the children listen to the words and perform the actions are sure-fire favorites.

Creativity in Art

Preschool children, whether especially talented in art or not, love to engage in art activities. As teachers we can support this enthusiasm in many different ways.

- Encourage children to be spontaneous. Children's art products should be an expression of their own feelings and their own perceptions. When we give children stencils to color in or examples to follow, we make them dissatisfied with their own creations and stifle their creativity. Unfortunately, even under the best of circumstances, many children lose their spontaneity as they grow older, when their attention turns to copying reality.

- Recognize that the process is more important than the product. For young children, painting a picture or molding a piece of clay is an ongoing, dynamic activity. Young children love to watch the paint as it spreads over the paper or feel the texture of the clay as it slides through their fingers. It doesn't bother them at all if their multicolored pictures turns into a great big glob. The fun is in the doing.

- Don't persist in asking children to tell you about their picture. Often we hear teachers say, "Oh, I never ask a child to tell me what he has painted. I just ask him to tell me about his picture." Unfortunately, no matter how we phrase the question, when we ask a child to describe a picture we assume the picture is about something. Perhaps in order to please us, the child will look at his picture and give it a name, but that doesn't tell us about the picture. How can a child explain a painting that is a swoop of his arm, a twist of the brush, and a daring splash of paint, followed by a drip and a dabble?

Preschool children, whether especially talented in art or not, love to engage in art activities.

- Don't insist that a child complete the product, Because the child is concerned with the process, not the product, a picture is completed when the child has completed the process. Filling up the paper may not be important to the child.

- Try not to be overly exuberant about a child's creations. When we tell children that their picture is beautiful, we are making a value judgment that may not be appropriate. Sometimes children will contradict our judgment because they want us to repeat the compliments. At other times, however, the child may not be happy about the picture and the teacher's praise is distressing. What really matters is the way the child feels about his or her art.

- Provide opportunities to experiment in a variety of media. Each medium that children use — chalk, crayon, finger paint, water color, or poster paint, has its own special characteristics, providing a different kind of opportunity for creative expression. Finger paint is especially good for expressing feelings of exuberance. Poster paint affords an opportunity to express a feeling of power. Crayon or chalk gives children a sense of being in control. By allowing children to explore in a variety of media we give them a chance to match the media to their mood or discover the medium that feels best to them.

Planned Art Activities

While process art can be made available to all children at any time, planned art activities require special teacher preparation and/or direction.

Tearing and Pasting

Before a child learns to use scissors, tearing is a good fine motor activity. This can be an end in itself or part of a planned project. For example, as a part of a unit on food, the children could tear brightly colored tissue paper and paste them to fill in large outlines of fruits. The children could then arrange their fruits in a display.

Printing

Use sponges cut into various shapes attached to tongue depressors or Popsicle sticks with rubber bands. Finger prints, hand prints, and foot prints are also fun for children.

Vegetable prints

Potatoes are especially good.

Puppet Making
- Paper plate puppets on sticks
- Finger puppets
- Sock puppets
- Paper bag puppets

Collages
- Using materials found outside-leaves, twigs, acorns, small pebbles, shells, sand, bark, feathers.

- Using things to eat-rice, beans, cereal, macaroni, spaghetti, egg shells, popcorn, seeds.

- Using scraps of fabrics-lace, rick-rack, ribbons, yarn, buttons, beads, sequins.

- Using different types and colors of paper-construction paper, tissue paper, napkins, paper towels, cellophane, wallpaper, gummed circles, doilies, confetti.

- Using "odds and ends"— bottle caps, sponge bits, straws, cotton balls, etc.

Painting and Drawing
- Easel painting, on newsprint with large brushes.

- Finger painting — Try "foot painting" outside on large sheets of craft paper, or play a record with a march tempo and let the children dip their fingers in finger paint and "march" across the paper with their fingers.

- Magic markers — Use non-toxic colors that wash out and do not stain.

- Chalk — Try white chalk on black or dark blue paper for a night time picture or a snow scene.

- Crayons — Dittos and coloring books are great for teachers but not for children. Coloring within someone else's lines might be a good fine motor activity (although it is too advanced for three and four year olds), but it stifles creativity. Better to string beads or cut paper to develop fine motor skills, and let children use crayons to make lines, circles, and interesting arrangements with colors and space.

- String painting — Dip string in paint, lay on one side of the paper, fold over, and pull out string.

- Straw painting — Put a blob of thin tempera paint on a piece of paper and blow it with a straw for interesting effects.

- Blob painting — Use a small plastic spoon and drop several blobs of paint on the paper, fold it over in half, unfold and let dry.

- Sand painting — Drip glue over the paper and, while it is still wet, shake colored sand on the paper.

- Dry tempera painting — Dip cotton balls into dry tempera and rub on damp paper.

- Paint on a variety of materials to observe different effects: paper towels, tissue paper, rocks, wood, aluminum foil, shells, corrugated cardboard, cloth, etc.

- Computer art — Many children's software programs enable drawing, stamping, movement or placement of pictures, and artistic text effects. Computer "coloring books," where children select colors to fill in regions of a picture, can also be fun if the children are free to experiment, e.g., changing the sky from blue, to black, to green.

Creativity with Crafts

Although the product may not be important when the child is involved in an art activity, the exact opposite is true about crafts. Young children love the idea of bringing home a Mother's or Father's Day present, a Thanksgiving turkey or a school-made Valentine. But even a craft project can be counterproductive if it is a teacher, rather than a child, activity. No matter how beautiful a product is, it loses some of its value if the teacher has done the work.

Here are some guidelines for selecting crafts for three and four year olds.

- Select a craft in which the child can do most of the work.

- Choose something that is not too long or tedious. With a few exceptions, it is better to select a craft that can be completed in one sitting.

- Make sure that the craft has meaning for the child. Crafts are most apt to have meaning when they are tied in to a unit of study or associated with a life experience.

- Make sure that the craft is not too elaborate or fragile. Children like the idea of taking something home and get frustrated and unhappy if the craft falls apart before it gets there.

- Choose a craft that the children enjoy doing.

- Choose a craft that allows some leeway for individual ideas.

Craft Activities

There are many good books on the market containing ideas and instructions for making interesting objects from "throw-away" materials. Here are just a few examples:

Egg Carton Garden. Materials: Styrofoam egg cartons, soil, seeds. Punch a hole in the bottom of each small section. Remove the lid and set it on the bottom. Fill sections with dirt, and plant seed in each.

Fish in the Aquarium. Materials: Styrofoam tray, construction paper, sand, shells, plastic wrap, yarn, goldfish crackers. Have children glue on an aquarium scene and then cover it with plastic wrap.

Paper Plate Faces. Materials: Paper plates, construction paper, glue, yarn (or fabric scraps, buttons, bottle caps, etc.). For older children, holes can be punched around edge and yarn threaded through for hair.

The Teacher's Responsibility

- Set up an accessible art center with a variety of materials. Give the child time, space, and freedom to explore.

- Provide a creative climate. The classroom can be aesthetically pleasing, uncluttered, and colorful, reflecting the originality and individuality of the teacher and the children.

- Sensitize the children to the beauty and wonder of the world they live in — from a sweeping rainbow to a drop of dew on a blade of grass.

- Integrate art activities into the curriculum as a part of the learning experience, not something separate and apart. Example: After a field trip, let the children paint a mural to illustrate the things they saw, felt, smelled, and heard.

- Show an appreciation and enjoyment of creative expression.

- Use creative ways to introduce new concepts. Example: Make a "Hungry Lion" paper bag puppet with a slit for his mouth. The lion can "tell" the children that he "only wants to eat triangles today." Have a box of shapes for the children to choose from as they "feed" the lion.

- Clearly define responsibility and limits. If at all possible, teach the children how to mix dry tempera paints, wash the brushes they have used, hang their painting to dry, put away all materials, and clean up any spillage. The children should know what materials they can use, where they are to be used, and when they can use them.

Materials

Materials to Buy: crayons, glue or paste, tempera paint (liquid or powdered), easels, brushes (1/2 to 1 inch width, 10 to 12 inches long), scissors, magic markers (non-toxic, washable colors), paper (craft, white newsprint, construction paper and tissue paper in several colors), chalk

Or Make: paint containers (baby food jars set into cut down milk cartons), dough clay, finger paint

Materials to Save:

- Containers: egg cartons, berry baskets, cardboard food trays, empty cans, oatmeal cartons, milk cartons, plastic jugs, show boxes, pie pans, margarine tubs

- Good to have: tongue depressors, straws, paper towels, paper towel tubes, toilet tissue tubes, Popsicle sticks, pipe cleaners, toothpicks, cardboard boxes

- Don't forget: magazines, newspapers, paper bags, buttons, spoons, bottle caps, stones, shells, coat hangers, clothespins, paper plates, cards, wrapping paper, and ribbons.

Promoting Imaginative Play

One of the most effective ways to promote creativity in a preschool environment is to promote pretending. Pretend play allows children to give free reign to their imagination, to explore new ideas and invent new situations. In addition to promoting creativity, imaginative play:

One of the most effective ways to promote creativity in a preschool environment is to promote pretending.

- helps children develop prosocial behavior. It provides opportunities to communicate with each other, to plan cooperatively, to share responsibility, and to take a point of view that is different from their own.

- helps children cope with stress by giving them an opportunity to recreate actual life events. Not only can they replay happy experiences, but, in the case of frightening and disturbing events, they can assume the role of powerful people in a safe and new context.

- encourages creativity as children explore new ideas and invent new situations.

- benefits children socially, emotionally, and intellectually. It provides children with the opportunity to develop representations of reality that provide the basis for abstract thinking.

The Role of the Teacher in Promoting Imaginative Play

Imaginative play is promoted in the classroom when:

- The children are provided with a variety of real world experiences that can be recreated in pretend situations.

- The children are given time and space to develop their pretend play ideas.

- Children are provided with a variety of props that can be used for imaginative play.

- The adults in the environment encourage, model and join in imaginative play, but do not take it over In order for imaginative play to flourish, the teacher must be willing to let the children develop and extend their original play ideas.

Imaginative Play Prop Boxes

Imaginative play materials take up a lot of space, and many preschools and child care centers do not have space to spare. One solution is to limit imaginative play props to the housekeeping corner and the "dress-up" area. Another solution is to develop prop boxes, which can be changed from time to time.

Suggestions for Prop Boxes

Beach Play: Sun glasses, suntan lotion, pail, shovel, beach towel, swim ring, picnic basket, thermos, beach ball, thongs, sun hat, pretend food, shells, sand toys.

Doctor Play: Glasses, bag, sheets, white coat, stethoscope, spoon, hypodermic needle case, magic markers, tape, bandages, empty medicine bottles, otoscope, throat sticks, toy thermometer, prescription pad, pencil, toy money, hot water bottle.

Firefighter Play: Firehats, hose, siren, bell, pillows, rubber hatchet, lunch box, play walkie-talkies, megaphone, first aid kit.

Restaurant Play: Trays, menus, cash registers, order pads, aprons, dishes, glasses, silverware, pencils, play food, salt and pepper shakers, creamers and sugar bowl.

Other possibilities for prop boxes include Supermarket, Hairdresser, Post Office, Repairperson, Dentist, and Shoe Store.

The early childhood years have been called "The Magic Years," because this is the time when pretending is at its height. Take time to enjoy the children's natural creativity as they play with words, music, art materials, toys, found objects, and each other. Let them bring out your creativity and playfulness as you explore new experiences together.

Bredekamp, S. (Editor). (1993). *Developmentally appropriate practice in early childhood programs serving children from birth through age 8.* Washington, D.C.: National Association for the Education of Young Children.

Brickman, N.A. & Taylor, L.S. (Editors). (1991). *Supporting young learners: Ideas for preschool and day care providers.* Ypsilanti, MI: High/Scope Press.

Bronson, M.B. (1995). *The right stuff for children birth to 8: Selecting play materials to support development.* Washington, D.C.: National Association for the Education of Young Children.

Curtis, D. & Carter, M. (1996). *Reflecting children's lives: A handbook for planning child-centered curriculum.* St. Paul, MN: Redleaf Press.

Diffily, D. & Morrison, K. (Editors). (1996). *Family friendly communication for early childhood programs.* Washington, D.C.: National Association for the Education of Young Children.

Dodge, D.T., Koralek, D.G., & Pizzolongo, P.J. (1989). *Caring for school children.* Vol. 1. Washington, D.C.: Teaching Strategies, Inc.

Goodnow, J. (1977). *Children drawing.* Cambridge, MA: Harvard University Press.

Hirsch, E. (1996). *The block book.* Washington, D.C.: NAEYC.

Lasky, L., & Mukerji, R., (1980). *Art: Basics for young children.* Washington, D.C.: NAEYC.

McDonald, D. (1979). *Music in our lives: The early years.* Washington, D.C.: NAEYC.

Meisels, S.J., Marsden, D.B., & Stetson, C. (2000). *Winning ways to learn: 600 great ideas for children.* NY: Goddard Press.

Neugebauer, B. (Editor). (1987). *Alike and different: Exploring our humanity with young children.* Redmond, WA: Exchange Press, Inc.

Rice, J.A. (1995). *The kindness curriculum: Introducing young children to loving values.* St. Paul, MN: Redleaf Press.

Section IV:
The Performers

*S*amantha's mother and father were having dinner together. They had spent the whole day visiting Infant Care Centers. "We sure got an education today!" Samantha's Dad remarked. "I knew that finding a good nursery school wasn't going to be easy, but I didn't expect it to be this hard. Where do you think we should go from here?" "Let's go over our notes," Samantha's mother suggested. There were three places that we didn't put on the blacklist, Gentle Touch, Young Peoples' Paradise, and Kids' Place.

"We loved the staff at Gentle Touch, but the classrooms were dingy and there didn't seem to be much going on."

"The second school, Young Peoples' Paradise, wasn't too bad. We liked the fact that the rooms are attractive and inviting, and that there are plenty of things for the children to do. Our concern was that the caregivers seemed to lack warmth. We never saw a teacher bend down and talk to a child or give a child a hug."

"The third school, Kids' Place, came the closest to meeting our criteria. The teachers are pretty good, the classrooms are well equipped, the children play nicely together and there are plenty of things to do. The one negative we wrote down was that there seemed to be too many children in each room and too much going on at the same time. We were afraid that Samantha would be completely overwhelmed."

Samantha's Father continued the conversation. "Obviously we're not going to find the school of our dreams, but we've run out of options and it's time to make a choice. If we were choosing a place for my nephew, Mikey, there wouldn't be a problem. Nothing overwhelms that child, and he would do fine in Kids' Place. But with Samantha it's a different story. She needs to be in a quiet, low-key environment with a few kids and a loving teacher who has time for every child. I opt for Gentle Touch." Samantha's mother agreed.

Samantha's parents deserve a lot of credit. Not only did they visit every nursery school, and take careful notes but also they recognized the importance of selecting a school that would be the right place for a child like Samantha. Although they preferred the more stimulating setting, they recognized their child's need for a calmer, quieter environment. In this section we look at ways of recognizing each child's emotional needs, supporting each child's social and emotional development, and using positive guidance to help children manage their own emotions and respect the rights of others.

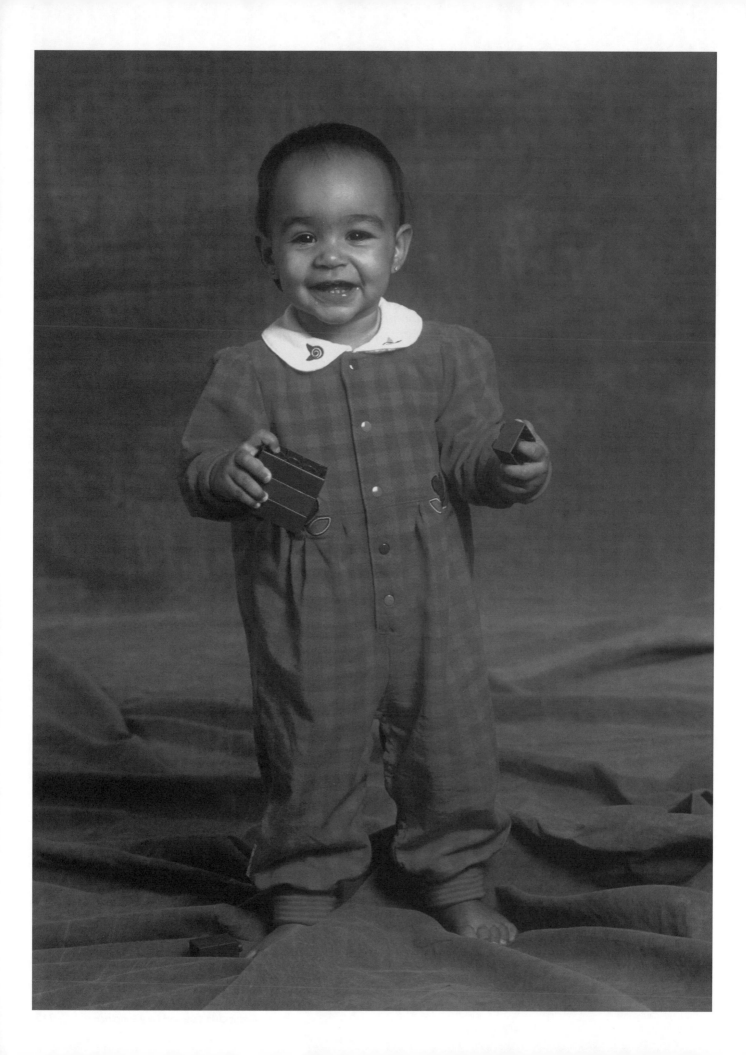

Chapter 10:
Developing a Sense of Self

Overview

elf refers to the inner experiences, thoughts, feelings, sensations, and emotions that constitute each person's unique identity. *Self-concept* is an individual's mental image of his own characteristics and capabilities. *Self-esteem* refers to the child's self-evaluation.

Rationale

The feelings that a child develops about himself and about the people around him help to form his emotional make-up and have a direct bearing upon his learning in school.

Infants vary in their inborn temperaments. Some are naturally easy-going and easy to soothe. Others are more sensitive, jittery, or feisty. Some quietly take in everything they see and hear; others seem to be always on the go. Some love novelty; others like predictability and are upset by too much change. When parents and caregivers respond sensitively, babies learn to calm and rouse themselves appropriately and to experience the joy of mastering new skills. They come to love and trust those around them and to feel good about themselves. They learn eagerly and constantly. Babies whose cues are missed — who are ignored, over-stimulated, or not given individual attention — fail to thrive. They may become depressed and withdrawn or constantly cranky and on edge. They may refuse to try new things, or give up quickly as if they expect to fail. The self is a combination of inborn tendencies and life experiences. Parents, other family members, and early childhood teachers and caregivers all play critical roles in shaping who a child will become.

Most children, regardless of family background, come to school with a sense of security and a rather well defined concept of self. These are learned during their few, short years living with a family that is generally giving and supportive. It is the responsibility of the school and the individual teacher to provide experiences that continually affirm these positive feelings. Each child must feel love, security, acceptance, and respect from the adults with whom he

The teacher helps each child to know, accept, and appreciate himself or herself as an individual.

or she interacts. The teacher helps each child to know, accept, and appreciate himself/herself as an individual. The teacher helps each child develop a sense of self-awareness and self-esteem, to express and accept her own feelings — both good and bad — and to develop pride as an individual and as a member of a cultural or ethnic group.

The teacher interacts with each child many times during the course of a typical day in childcare facility or school. It is critical that she be aware of the intimate relationship between self-concept and success in school, and indeed, success and competence in life. She must know that a child who feels incapable of success will not succeed and one who feels unworthy of affection or attention will not thrive. But the child who is made to feel "special," who is loved and listened to and appreciated, will put forth her best efforts because she experiences joy in learning and pride in achievement.

Objectives

1. To recognize the sequence of emotional development from birth to five years and the role of the caregiver in supporting this development.

2. To recognize ways in which infants develop trust and a sense of security.

3. To describe ways in which one-year olds develop self-awareness and learn to cope with separation.

4. To describe ways in which two-year olds develop a sense of autonomy.

5. To recognize ways in which caregivers can help preschool children develop a sense of personal identity and self worth and feel good about their heritage.

6. To describe ways in which caregivers can help young children develop a sense of responsibility.

Miss Trying had had a difficult day. Although she had only three babies assigned to her in the baby room, there was never enough time to relax and enjoy them. The basic problem was Jesse. "Jesse," Miss Trying explained to the director, "is the most difficult infant I have ever tried to look after. He's as taut as a violin string. If you move too fast or not fast enough, if you get his bottle a little bit too hot or not quite hot enough, he'll start to scream and it's impossible to soothe him. I wish I knew if he's like this at home, but I never get a chance to talk to his mother."

The director explained that she knew Jesse's mother quite well. As a matter of fact, she was the one who persuaded Jesse's mother to put Jesse in infant care. Jesse had been difficult since the day he was born. He would cry for no obvious reason, and once he started crying there was no way to calm him down. Just the other day she had met Jesse's mother in the supermarket. His mother thanked her effusively for keeping Jesse at the Center. She was beginning to see some changes in his behavior at home. He was becoming somewhat less irritable and a little bit easier to comfort. She attributed the change both to the fact that Jesse was maturing and to the fact that Jesse's caregivers at her center were so good with him.

All children are born into this world with unique characteristics and temperaments that define their individuality and affect the way they relate to other people, cope with stress, and develop self-control and self-confidence. Miss Trying's experience with Jesse demonstrates the importance of recognizing individual differences. As soon as she realized that Jesse's difficult behavior was a manifestation of temperament and not a reaction to her caregiving, she regained her self-confidence. Jesse, in turn, responded to this new self-assurance and his difficult behaviors diminished.

Temperamental differences are present in infants from the moment of birth. Some babies are even-tempered, alert, and predictable in terms of their sleep and nursing cycles. They adapt easily to change and enjoy new experiences. These children are described as having easy temperaments. Other children are irritable, difficult to distract, upset by new experiences, and unpredictable in terms of their sleeping and eating cycles. These children are described as having difficult or feisty temperaments. Because there is always interaction between infants and caregivers, it is difficult to know whether or not temperamental variables are really enduring or whether they initiate a chain of responses in the caregiving environment that maintain characteristic behaviors.

Recognizing that there are differences in individual temperament can help parents and caregivers be responsive to individual needs. Babies who are temperamentally slow to warm up need to be introduced to new experiences in a gradual way. Babies who are temperamentally irritable need their caregivers to be relaxed, gentle, and especially sensitive to their needs.

In this section we focus on the emotional challenges that every child must face in the first five years of life. We discuss ways in which children's success in meeting these challenges depends both on their inborn characteristics such as temperament and resiliency and on the kinds of emotional support they receive from loving and caring adults.

Objective 1: To recognize the sequence of emotional development from birth to five years and the role of the caregiver in supporting this development

Developmental Picture

The infant 0-8 months:
- Is developing a sense of trust and is learning to make predictions
- Learns ways of self-comforting
- Demonstrates a variety of emotions including sadness, anger, surprise, and joy

Recognizing that there are differences in individual temperament can help parents and caregivers be responsive to individual needs.

- Learns to return a smile with a smile
- Initiates interactions with parents and caregivers and signals the need for a break
- Shows emerging awareness of self by playing with her own hands or by touching her caregiver's mouth and then her own
- Develops preferences for certain sights, sounds, ways of being held, objects, and activities
- Enjoys active play but can get over stimulated

The caregiver:
- Provides environments and interactions that are interesting without being overwhelming
- Checks in with parents to learn what soothes, engages, and excites each child and what is overwhelming or tiring
- Helps the baby learn to soothe herself by offering a pacifier, a "lovey" or favorite blanket, a change of scene, or a favorite activity
- Engages in back and forth interactions with the baby
- Supports an infant's developing sense of trust by responding to his cries and recognizing and responding to his cues
- Uses words and smiles to let the infant know that he is loveable
- Accommodates the child's preferences for different levels of stimulation
- Recognizes the importance of maintaining a balance between quiet and active play
- Takes into account individual differences and responsively provides each infant with enough stimulation to keep her alert and interested without becoming overwhelmed
- Recognizes the importance of creating a balance between active and quiet play

The infant 8-14 months:
- Discovers that she is an agent who can make things happen
- Learns many different ways of getting adults to do her bidding
- Takes the lead in initiating interactions
- Responds to her mirror image by smiling and playing with the mirror
- Forms very special attachments to familiar people
- Shows self-awareness by putting a hat on his head or putting on a necklace
- Demonstrates shyness by hiding behind the caregiver

The caregiver:
- Interacts with the same babies on a consistent basis and with love, caring, and enthusiasm
- Expresses delight when the infant shows off a new accomplishment
- Recognizes when the infant is sad, angry, frustrated, or happy and talks about his feelings with words

- Provides toys that support infant's body awareness like mirrors, soft dolls, and large bead necklaces

The toddler 14-24 months:
- Recognizes herself in the mirror and wipes her own forehead if she sees a spot in the mirror
- Is very clear about he likes and dislikes
- Uses gestures, grunts, and some words to get adults to respond to her wishes
- Enjoys being praised, and is upset when scolded
- Shows delight when people clap for her or laugh at what she does
- Shows empathy when someone is hurt
- Expresses a whole range of emotions — happy, thoughtful, worried, frightened, jealous, angry, sad, surprised

The caregiver:
- Lets the toddler know in many ways he is good and worthy of love
- Expresses delight when the toddler shows off a new accomplishment
- Talks about different feelings like angry, sad, happy, or worried
- Responds positively when the toddler is playing nicely, supporting the toddler's self-image

The two year old:
- Asserts herself in many different ways, insisting on doing things her own way and on getting what she wants
- Is learning to make choices and to say "no"
- Is emphatic about doing things for himself
- Tests limits by doing what she has been told not to and watching the adult's reaction
- Has temper tantrums when she can't have what she wants
- Can use some words to express feelings
- Recognizes that some things belong to him, resists sharing and objects if someone takes something that belongs to someone else
- Enjoys being a helper

The caregiver:
- Recognizes that sharing is hard for two-year olds, and provides more than one of the same toy
- Provides opportunities for children to make choices
- Gives children opportunities to do things for themselves
- Provides opportunities for children to help with tasks and praises them for being helpful
- Recognizes that disobedience is a normal way for two-year olds to express their growing independence and selfhood
- Provides safe alternatives when children insist on doing something hurtful or dangerous

The preschool child:
- Is aware of her own individuality, and is able to express feelings, needs, and desires
- Evaluates his own skills and compares himself to others
- Recognizes her ability to make choices and control her impulsive behavior
- Responds positively to deserved praise and approval

The caregiver:
- Seeks out opportunities to praise children for genuine accomplishments
- Recognizes children who need special encouragement
- Finds ways to help children feel successful
- Offers children love and affection

Every baby needs to know that there is at least one person in her life who is always there for her, who can be counted on to respond to her needs and to find ways to relieve her distress.

Objective 2: To recognize ways in which infants develop trust and a sense of security

Amelia, a teen mother, was living with her own mother. Although Amelia felt fortunate that she could live at home and that her mother would help with the baby, she and her mother were always quarreling about what was good for the baby. "You've got to stop picking up that baby every time he lets out a little whimper," her mother insisted. "That baby is already spoiled and he's not even three months old!"

"I am not going to let my baby cry," Amelia insisted. "My teacher at school made it quite clear that you cannot spoil a three month old baby and I believe her"

"I bet that teacher, whoever she is, never raised a baby of her own. Just because she read a book she thinks she's an authority!"

Although other people may agree with Amelia's mother, Amelia and her teacher are absolutely right. Babies cry because something is bothering them. If you respond to their cries and find a way to comfort them, babies learn that they can trust you, and they will feel safe and secure.

Every baby needs to know that there is at least one person in her life who is always there for her, who can be counted on to respond to her needs and to find ways to relieve her distress. Through her interactions with this responsive person, the baby develops feelings of trust. She knows that she is safe so long as this person or one of these special persons is somewhere nearby. She also learns to associate this special person or these special people with playfulness and pleasure.

Between six and eighteen months, when babies are starting to move around on their own, they will not venture very far unless their special person is in sight. They are also likely to become wary of strangers. They know they can trust their special person or their special people, but they are not so sure about someone new. If a new person tries to pick him up, the baby will cling to his special person and turn away from the stranger. If his special person leaves the room, he will stop playing and is likely to burst into tears. When his special person returns to the room, he will greet her with his biggest smile. Infants who develop a strong attachment to at least one special person during their first year will be capable of developing strong and lasting relationships with many people in the years ahead.

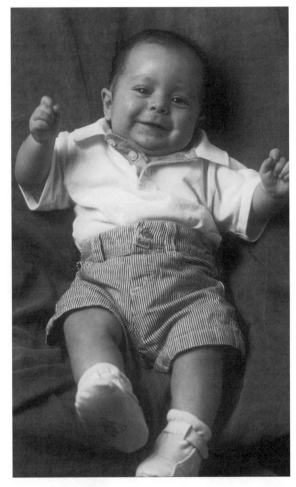

Babies who begin childcare at six months old or later are likely to have difficulty separating from their parent or primary caregiver. They may be perfectly happy in their new setting so long as their parent is in sight, but they do not want their parent to leave. Fortunately most babies are able to adjust to their new situation, as long as their new caregiver is warm, loving, and attentive. Before long they will learn that their parent will always come back and that there are substitute parents in child care who can anticipate and satisfy their needs.

Parents and caregivers can facilitate a baby's adjustment in several ways. The parent can help their baby feel comfortable in the new situation by letting the baby watch as the parent and caregiver talk happily together. Babies use their parents as a social reference. If she feels that her parent is friendly with her new caregiver, the baby senses that the caregiver can be trusted.

Parents and caregivers can find ways to reduce the difference between home and school. They can share information about how the baby prefers to be positioned at sleep-time or how the baby likes to be fed. The parent can also bring a favorite blanket or toy to school.

Caregivers can maintain a home-like atmosphere in the baby room. They can create small spaces, keep the lights relatively dim, and provide soft materials like cushions or stuffed animals. It is also very important to assign a primary caregiver to every infant. In other words, when two people are working together in the baby room, each should be responsible for a particular group of infants most of the time.

Objective 3: To describe ways in which toddlers develop self-awareness and learn to cope with separation

*M*iss Tightface was holding a conference with Melissa's mother. "I am a little concerned about Melissa," Miss Tightface began. "You know she is such a ham. As soon as the music starts, she starts to dance, then she looks around to make sure everyone is watching. It's the sort of thing that is cute when you are eighteen months, but I'd hate to see a child like Melissa growing up to be a show-off."

Fortunately, Melissa's mother was not ready to accept Miss Tightface's concerns. She recognized that Melissa's response to an appreciative audience was perfectly age appropriate, and not in any way suggestive that Melissa would grow up to be a showoff. In this section, we focus on the social-emotional development of children between one and two years old. We will identify the range of emotions they express, their expressions of attachment behavior, and their emerging ability to relate to and make friends with their peers. We will also suggest activities appropriate for a toddler class that will enhance emotional development and emerging social skills.

Emotional Expression and the Emergence of Self-Awareness

By the time-the baby is one year old she is able to exhibit a whole range of emotions including surprise, pleasure, delight, sadness, wariness, fear, and anger. She is becoming more interested in new people, although she will still react negatively to being picked up by a stranger. It is an age when the baby appears to be saying, "Don't come to me. I'll come to you."

While all one to two-year olds are capable of expressing a range of emotional responses, the intensity of emotional expression is an individual characteristic. Some one-to-two-year olds are wary by nature. They are slow to warm up in new situations and are easily frightened by sounds, sights, and people who are unfamiliar. Other one to two-year-olds are delighted with new situations and respond with exuberance to new and exciting events.

The Emergence of Self-Awareness

Around eighteen months old, most toddlers, whether slow to warm up or outgoing, are showing an increased self-awareness. They are developing a sense of identity, an awareness of being a person apart from and different from other people. An eighteen-month old recognizes herself in the mirror. If you tape a ribbon to her hair, she will notice the ribbon in the mirror and pull it off her head. It is as if the baby is saying that she recognizes the image in the mirror as a reflection of a body that belongs to her. Another indication of the baby's newly gained self-awareness is her use of the word "mine" to signify her own possessions. Finally, and most persuasively, the eighteen-month old demonstrates a special delight in assuming the role of a performer. If she dances to music and adults applaud the performance, she dances with increased vigor. Recognizing herself as the performer for an appreciative audience is a strong indication of awareness of self as an individual.

Exploration and Self-Control

The explorations of the one to two-year old inevitably increase the potential of hurting oneself or damaging property. She is continuously learning what kinds of explorations are permitted and what explorations are prohibited. "No, don't touch," or "Hot, don't touch," are familiar words to a busy and inquisitive one to two-year-old. Often we will catch a one to two-year-old who is about to touch a forbidden object saying "no, no" to herself.

In a home situation, parents have the option of putting breakable things away or leaving them within a child's reach and teaching her to touch them gently. In a child care situation, this option is not available. Anything that is breakable is also dangerous and must be taken out of the environment. Child-proofing an environment for a toddler means not only putting away breakable and sharp things and small parts that can be swallowed, it also means plugging up outlets, eliminating lamp cords, bolting outside doors, and removing chests that can topple over if the child stands on a drawer.

The toddler's ability to respond to a "no" is an important development in the second year.

The toddler's ability to respond to a "no" is an important development in the second year. It demonstrates the ability to inhibit an action that has been set in motion before it has been completed. But although we like to see children exhibit this control, we do not want to see a young child inhibited. If the child hears "no" too often or too sharply, she will over-generalize the prohibition and stop exploring with her hands. The child who is not free to explore with her hands is also not free to learn.

Expressions of Attachment and Coping with Separation

While one to two-year olds are developing increased awareness of self, they are also becoming increasingly more discriminatory of the people around them. Their world is no longer divided into only two sorts of people, preferred caregivers and others. For the one to two year old, there are dangerous people, like doctors, harmless people, like mother's friends, fun people to be with, like teachers and playmates, and special people who take care of them, like mothers or other primary home caregivers. While children may enjoy playing with playmates or other fun people, parents or primary caregivers remain their base of security. As long as they know where Mother is, they are willing to play and explore. Children who are sent to a child care setting for the first time when they are between one and two years old may have difficulty separating from the parents or primary caregivers who are their base of security. The fact that most young children have a limited understanding of language makes it difficult to explain in words the difference between a separation that is temporary and a separation that lasts forever. Keeping this in mind, here are some ways to make separation from a parent more understandable, if not easier, for a child.

- Accept the child's feelings. "You feel sad because your mommy left. We will play for a while and then Mommy will be back."

- Give parents the option of separating gradually from their children.

- Make sure that parents say good-bye to their children. Once they have said good-bye, they should leave without turning back. The quick look back to make sure the child is all right can destroy the child's confidence.

- Hold the child in your arms and encourage her to wave "bye-bye." Then engage her in a favorite activity or in something she finds relaxing, such as rice pouring or playing with play-dough.

- Stagger the times and/or days in which new children come to school. Children who are separating from a parent for the first time need extra attention.

Objective 4: To describe ways in which two-year olds develop a sense of autonomy

It was the first day of school and all the mothers had left except for Mrs. Hold-Tight and Mrs.Babylover. Kathleen, Mrs. Hold-Tight's two and a half-year old, was holding onto her mother's shirt and crying softly. Mrs. Baby-Lover was putting Chapstick on her daughter Theresa's lips.

Mrs. Hold-Tight: (talking to Kathleen) "I can't believe that a big girl like you would be scared to go to school. I'll tell you what — supposing I just stay and watch you while you go into the circle. See, I'll stand in this square and I won't move."

Mrs. Baby-Lover: "Okay Theresa, go with the other children. Make sure to let Miss Nancy put your sweater on if you go on the playground and ask your nice teacher to help you get your lunch box open. And remember, if you need help with wiping yourself in the bathroom, you just ask the nice teacher."

Poor Mrs. Hold-Tight and Mrs. Baby-Lover. They were embarrassed about the way their children were clinging to them but they didn't know what to do about it. Mrs. Hold-Tight was giving her daughter mixed messages. She was telling her that she would be okay at school, but that school was a place where you had to be big and brave. Mrs. Baby-Lover was telling her daughter that the teachers in school would take care of her if she would tell them what she needed. Obviously, Mrs. Hold-Tight and Mrs. Baby-Lover were having trouble separating from their children.

For older toddlers and preschool children, fear of separation may take several forms. One child may feign illness or succumb to illness in order to avoid separation. A second child may beg, cajole, plead, or have a temper tantrum. A third child may invent all kinds of elaborate manipulations such as "I'm afraid of my teacher," "I can't go to the bathroom at school," "I can't go to school because my dinosaur shirt is dirty and it's my favorite shirt."

Ways of Helping Children Separate

The time to prepare a child for separation is before a child is placed in childcare. Parents can give children practice with separation by arranging for short visits with family or neighbors where the child learns that she can manage without a parent and that parents always come back. Teachers can help pave the way for a smooth entry into childcare by providing different entry options that meet the needs of different families. Here are some options that are used in different child care settings.

- Children can visit the center for one or two days with their parents before being sent alone.

- Children become acquainted ahead of time with their teacher through home and/or school visits.

- Entry into childcare is staggered so that only one new child enters at a time and teachers can give the new child their full attention.

- During the first week of school, parents can stay with their child until the child is ready to say goodbye.

- Parents are instructed on the importance of saying good-bye cheerfully and then leaving without turning back.

The time to prepare a child for separation is before a child is placed in childcare.

While separation continues to be a major issue for older toddlers and their parents, two to three-year olds are struggling with another issue. They want desperately to hold on to the secure feeling of being cared for by adoring parents and caregivers. At the same time they have a strong need to assert their own will and make their own decisions. Their favorite word is "no" and their favorite phrase is "I do it myself." They are torn between their need to hold tight to a protective hand and their need to break away and explore the world in their own way and on their own terms.

Judith and her friend Marsha had decided to take their two-year-olds to the neighborhood park. When Judith told her son, Butch, that it was time to go home, Butch refused to leave. He pushed his mother away with both hands and ran to the slide with his friend. Marsha immediately agreed to stay in the park for a few more minutes with the two boys. The minute his mother said goodbye and started to turn away, Butch stopped playing, burst into tears, ran to his mother, and jumped into her arms. "He is a typical two year old," Marsha laughed. "That is exactly what my son would do."

Toddlers between two and three years old are torn between wanting to be a coddled and protected baby and wanting to be autonomous. Although parents and teachers may be exasperated by what appears to be negative behavior, the toddler is not being ornery. He is working hard to assert his independence and defend his right to make his own decisions and do things his own way. At the same time he is not ready to give up his dependency on adults, who are the base of his security.

Objective 4: To recognize ways in which caregivers can help preschool children develop a sense of personal identity and self worth, recognize and express their feelings, and take pride in their culture and ethnic heritage

Toddlers between two and three years old are torn between wanting to be a coddled and protected baby and wanting to be autonomous.

Brian started off the morning in high spirits. He was wearing his beautiful new Superman jersey that Grandma had sent for his birthday. Everything went fine until juice time when, somehow or other, grape juice slipped out of his hand and got all over his jersey.

From that time on, things went from bad to worse. At art time Brian finished his picture in a hurry so he could go over to the sink and wash the grape juice off Superman's face. "Come back to your seat," his teacher called. "I want us all to share our pretty pictures. Oh, look how beautiful Terry's picture looks. Would you like to tell me about it? Oh, Dimetria, look at what you've done. You made such a happy picture. I'd like to hear you talk about it." When she came to Brian's picture, she didn't say anything at all.

Then it was circle time and all the children were asked to put away their crayons and their papers and come to the circle. Brian started to put his crayons away, but then he looked at his picture. It really didn't look very pretty, he decided. Maybe he could add a few more strokes. Maybe some black lines going up and down would be a good idea. As Brian was fixing up his drawing, he heard his teacher saying, loud and clear, "What good children I have in my class. I like the way most of you put your crayons away so quickly."

Brian tried to hurry with his picture, but when he went fast with the black crayon, his paper started to tear. He crumpled it up, threw it on the floor, and walked over to the circle. "He threw his paper on the floor," Tommy tattled. "He's bad." "Yes, he's bad," agreed Ben. "He's got juice all over his shirt. His mommy is going to be mad."

The teacher paid no attention to these comments. "Come on now, let's sing in a pretty voice. 'If you're happy and you know it...'" At the end of the song it was dismissal time. All the children asked the teacher to stamp happy faces on their hands. "I'm good," Jerry asserted, as he stood in line for his happy face. Brian's mother came to the door and Brian dashed over to her. "Don't you want to get your happy face before we go?" Brian's mother asked. Brian burst into tears.

All of us, like Brian, have had days when one thing leads to another. We may feel grumpy or out of sorts, but we don't think of ourselves as bad people because we've had a bad day. With young children, it may be quite a different story. During the preschool years, children have their own unique way of looking at the world. Because they don't have the notion of "chance," they think that bad things happen for a reason. An accident, in their view, happens to them because they did something or thought something wrong. When a series of bad things happens to a child, he begins to think of himself as being a bad person. Brian's bad day was initiated by a minor, accidental spill. This started off a chain of behavior. By the end of the morning Brian was convinced he was a bad boy, unworthy of a smiling face.

Brian's teacher was clearly trying to make the children in her class feel good about themselves, but in Brian's case her techniques backfired. As she tried to engage the group with upbeat language, she missed Brian's distress over the spilled grape juice and didn't give him the opportunity to finish his picture. She praised the "good" children in a way that made Brian — and probably others — feel "bad."

During the preschool years, children are continually making judgments about themselves. The sum of these judgments constitutes self-concept, which is, in essence, the child's value judgment of himself. The preschool teacher can help children develop a healthy self-concept in a variety of ways.

During the preschool years, children are continually making judgements about themselves.

- By helping children develop a sense of personal identity.
- By helping children to recognize and express their own feelings.
- By helping children cope with separation.
- By helping children feel good about their ethnic and cultural traditions.

Developing Personal Identity and Self-Worth

All of us get upset when we meet someone we know and whose names we can't remember. We are concerned that this person will interpret our lapse of memory as a sign that we don't think of him as being important. For young children, their own names are especially significant. They expect everyone to know their names and they will often learn to recognize their names in writing before they can read anything else.

The more opportunities that we find to call each child in our class by name, the more we strengthen this sense of personal identity. But even though we recognize how important it is to call the children by their correct names, we may have problems in the beginning remembering all of the names of the children. Here are some suggestions:

- Become familiar with the class roster in advance, That way all you will need to do is attach faces to the names on the first day of school.

- Ask the parents to send in photos of their children in advance or use a Polaroid camera to take the children's pictures.

- Pin name cards on the back of each child.

- Sing songs in which the names of the children are repeated over and over again

Learning the names of all the children in the class is a good head start in helping children develop a sense of personal identity. Another way of helping children learn more about themselves is the development of the ME BOOK. A child can use a ME BOOK to record information about himself.

Me Book
Table of Contents
- This is my photo.
- This is my hand print.
- This is my family.
- My favorite food.
- My favorite color.
- My favorite animal.
- My best drawing of me.

Make time to have a private conversation with each child at least three times each day.

A child's ME BOOK is both a means of increasing his sense of personal identity and a record of the way he feels about himself.

More important than any activity, however, is ongoing personal attention. Make time to have a private conversation with each child, at least three times each day. It doesn't have to be formal. You can greet children individually when they arrive, then direct them to interest centers where you have set up simple and inviting activities. You can write down a child's story for him, admire the caterpillar he found on the playground, let him choose a book for story time, join him in a block-building project, or converse as you put out the snack together. What is important is that you let the child take the lead, that you really listen, and that you show him you are interested in what he has to say.

Helping Children Recognize and Express Feelings
Often children fail to distinguish between having bad feelings and actually being bad. The concept of feelings is not easy to grasp. Only when children have developed a firm idea of their own identity are they ready to understand what is meant by feelings. Younger children cry when they are sad, strike out when they are angry, and laugh when they are happy. As children grow older, they can use words that go along with these feelings, but it does take time. Once children have learned to express feelings in words, they are less likely to act out their feelings in ways that are inappropriate. Most important, they recognize that it is good to express their own feelings as long as they respect the feelings of other people.

Activities To Help Children Express Feelings
Feeling Wheel: Make a Feeling Wheel out of a paper plate. Put a pointer that can spin in the center and draw happy, sad, angry and sleepy faces around the perimeter. Give the children an opportunity to point to the way they are feeling.

Plate Puppets: Encourage children to express their feelings by using paper plate puppets with expressions of anger, sadness fright, happiness, surprise, excitement, etc.

How I Am Feeling Chart: With older children, prepare a chart with each child's name. As the child comes into the classroom in the morning he places a circular disc with a face that describes his feelings-happy, sad, angry, etc. At the end of the day at Good-bye Circle Time, each child is given a chance to change the disc beside his name if his feelings have changed.

Feeling Songs: Sing songs about feelings. One of the most appropriate songs is "If you're happy and you know it, clap your hands."

Feeling Stories: Read stories that describe situations in which a child faces anger, sadness or jealousy. Talk about the feelings that are aroused in the child.

Drawing to Music: Play happy and sad records. Let the children crayon along with the music. Talk with them about the difference in their pictures.

Helping Children Cope with Separation

Helping children cope with separation is a joint responsibility of parents and teachers. The techniques used to help with separation vary with the age of the child.

When children are able to understand language, teachers can ease the pain of separation by talking about it.

- Talk about the schedule of the day with the children. Show children where the hands of the clock will be when mommy comes to get them. (With some children, it helps to put up a tagboard clock with hands set on dismissal time. Children can compare the real clock time with the tagboard clock.)

- Pretend that a school teddy bear misses its mommy. Have the children say something nice to the bear during circle time to make him feel better. Children who comfort the bear will begin to feel better themselves.

- Encourage a child to make a picture or "write" (dictate or scribble) a "letter" to give to his parent at the end of the day.

- Ask parents to make a book of special people that the child can look at and can talk about with you.

Helping Children Feel Good about Their Ethnic and Cultural Heritage

James had just moved from a small southern town to a city in Connecticut. It was his first week in nursery school. James was happy to be with other children his own age and was excited about all the new toys and games in his classroom. At circle time he was the first one to volunteer to tell a story. "I aksed my mommy where we were," he began.

"James," the teacher stopped him, "You say 'asked,' not 'aksed.'"

"Aksed, not aksed," James repeated. He went on with his story "And mommy say we ain't got but a-"

> *Once children have learned to express feelings in words, they are less likely to act out their feelings in ways that are inappropriate.*

"You don't say 'We ain't got,'" the teacher explained firmly. "You say, 'We don't have.'" James stopped talking. The next day when it was time to go to school his tummy was hurting.

It is easy to understand why James had a tummy ache. Like all preschool children, he wasn't aware of grammar or articulation and he did not know why the teacher was correcting him when he was telling the truth. The one thing that he did sense was that the teacher didn't like the way he talked. Was there something bad about his talking? Was there something bad about him?

Most preschool teachers recognize that it is inappropriate to correct a child's grammar under any circumstances.

Most preschool teachers recognize that it is inappropriate to correct a child's grammar under any circumstance. It is especially harmful to correct a child's dialect. From the child's point of view, this may be a direct criticism of him and an indirect slur on his family. The best way to destroy a child's self-concept is to make him feel that he comes from a family that doesn't measure up to other families. A child whose ethnic, religious, or language background is different from the other children is always vulnerable. Even if the teacher is warm and accepting, the other children, through their words and actions, can make a child feel different. A sensitive teacher will make a special effort to make the child with a different background feel wanted and valued. She will check in with his parents to learn what makes him comfortable and how he is feeling about the classroom. She will learn all she can about the child's heritage and discover ways of helping the child feel proud of who he is.

Here are some ways of helping children appreciate their own ethnic and cultural heritage and the heritage of the other children in the classroom:

- Begin by examining your own feelings very carefully. How do you feel about children who are different? Do you have any built-in barriers or stereotypes that interfere with your ability to relate in a positive way to any of the children in your class?

- Invite parents from different backgrounds to prepare "ethnic" snacks for the class and to share folk stories, nursery rhymes, lullabies, and humor from their own traditions.

- Introduce children to music, chants, and games from different countries and different traditions.

- Have a multi-cultural pot-luck dinner where children are introduced to different foods.

- With the help of the parents, celebrate each of the holidays of the ethnic groups represented in your classroom.

- Select books, picture cards, and picture books that reflect the race, culture, and ethnicity of the children in your class and the children in the community. Be sure that children see people of their race and culture playing a variety of roles in everyday situations.

- Make sure that the photos and pictures on the walls, as well as the books in library and the dolls, clothes, and artifacts in the pretend play areas, represent children from different races and cultures.

- Plan parent/child programs in which children have the opportunity to meet the parents and grandparents of their classmates and parents have an opportunity to socialize with each other.

- Plan show and tell days in which children bring in and talk about a family artifact.

- Encourage open conversation in response to children's natural curiosity about differences in skin color, hair texture, language, food preferences, and family type.

- Talk with parents about what you are doing and solicit their ideas.

- Encourage inter-racial and inter-cultural friendships, and keep parents informed about their children's friendships.

Objective 6: To describe ways in which caregivers can help young children develop a sense of responsibility

One of the important ways in which parents and caregivers can prepare a child to enter kindergarten or first grade is to help children develop a sense of responsibility. School children are supposed to keep track of their own possessions. They are also expected to take care of their personal needs, to complete tasks assigned by the teacher, and to follow classroom rules like taking turns or helping with classroom clean up. When children have mastered the basic self-help skills and have learned to accept responsibility, they are primed for success in school.

Families, and cultures, differ in their ideas about how much responsibility young children should assume. In some families, children are fed and dressed by their parents until they are three or four years old. Parents feel that this gives their children a firm foundation of love and security upon which to build a sense of responsibility for self and others. In other families, parents encourage children to do as much as they can for themselves. They feel that this stretches children's capabilities and makes them feel good about themselves.

Both approaches can lead to happy, well-adjusted children who take responsibility for themselves and for helping others. In each case, the parent communicates respect for the child and an expectation that the child can — and will — assume more responsibility as she grows older.

Mastering self-help skills

Listing the self-help skills that children are expected to acquire by the time they are five years is an eye-opener. Helping children acquire and practice

One of the important ways in which parents and caregivers can prepare children to enter kindergarten or first grade is to help them develop a sense of responsibility.

self-help skills is a part of daily routine in child care or preschool settings. Many of the self-help skills that can be taught and practiced in school have been discussed already in the chapter on health. In this section, we discuss two of the many self-help skills that children need to master in order to be ready for school.

Eating

Often we think of children as having completed their eating skills when they have learned to drink from a glass or eat with a spoon without spilling. Actually, learning to use a utensil is just the beginning. The preschool child is expected to learn a host of customs and rules that have to do with eating. Often we scold a child for having poor manners without realizing all there is to learn and remember. Let us look at some of the eating rules that children have to learn.

The best way to teach children good table manners is not to teach them at all.

- Unfold your napkin and put it on your lap before beginning to eat.

- Wait until everyone is served before beginning to eat.

- Use the right kind of utensil for the food you are eating. Some food is eaten with fingers, some with a spoon, and some with a fork.

- Use the appropriate utensil or methods to put food on other food. Some foods are sprinkled on, some are poured on, and some are spread on with a knife.

- Some foods are all right to lick and some food cannot be licked.

- Some foods can be eaten directly and some foods can be eaten only if they are put on other foods (butter, sugar, jam, ketchup, gravy, salt, pepper).

- Some foods are cut with the side of the fork and some foods are cut with a knife.

- The mouth has to be wiped with a napkin whenever it gets dirty.

- Napkins have to be placed on the table after eating, but not during eating.

- If you want food that is across the table, you say "Please pass…"

- Once something is in your mouth you have to swallow it, even if you don't like it.

- Chewing has to be done quietly and with your mouth closed.

- It is not appropriate to draw a picture in your mashed potatoes or play with your food in any way.

- The glass has to be returned to the right side of the plate after drinking, not on the edge of the table or on top of the plate.

- It is all right to talk at the table, but not until you've finished a bite.

- You have to sit at the table, even if you have finished, until everyone else has finished.

Obviously, there are too many rules to expect a child to learn at one time, and much too many to remember at the same time. The best way to teach children good table manners is not to teach them at all. Instead:

- Make sure that mealtimes are happy times.

- Model good table manners.

- Explain reasons for certain prohibitions. "Eating a spoonful of sugar is bad for your teeth."

- Praise children for the rules they remember.

Independent Toileting

At many childcare centers, the criterion for entry is being toilet-trained. Although this is understandable from the point of view of a director, it may not always be in the best interest of either the school or the child. Parents who know that their children must be toilet-trained in order to enter school may become so tense about the process that their efforts are counter-productive. The unfortunate thing is that, in most cases, the easiest way to train a child is to take him to school. Many children are trained almost instantly when they watch other children use the toilet.

Although a child who has not learned to use the toilet may learn easily at school, it is also common for children who have good control at home to have accidents at school. A critical rule for all child care centers is to make sure that each child has an extra set of name-tagged clothing in his cubby. When a child does have an accident, he should be changed in a matter-of-fact way. No child, under any circumstances, should ever be shamed about an accident.

One of the questions that often comes up about toileting in nursery school is whether or not there should be a special time when all children go to the bathroom or whether children should simply have access to the bathroom whenever they need it.

In some situations, where the bathroom is not adjacent to the classroom, the teacher must take the children into the bathroom as a group. In other situations, where the bathroom is easily accessible, the teacher has a choice. Although it seems to be more reasonable and certainly more natural to let children go "on demand," there are several advantages to having bathroom times scheduled:

- The teacher without an aide does not have to choose between allowing a child to go to the bathroom alone, or leaving the rest of class while she takes the child to the bathroom.

- The teacher has an excellent opportunity to enforce sanitary rules such as using toilet paper, flushing the toilet, and washing hands after toileting.

- The teacher can watch the children as they practice appropriate hand washing.

- Other routines such as lunchtime or naptime are less apt to be interrupted if a set bathroom time has been scheduled.

- Children who are very busy playing or working may forget to use the bathroom.

In most cases teachers can schedule bathroom times, but still encourage children to use the bathroom when they need to.

Assuming Responsibility for Your Own Behavior

Adolph arrived in pre-school with a note to his teacher pinned to his shirt. "Please make sure that Adolph puts his sweater on when he goes out to the playground. If he does not eat all his lunch, put anything he did not eat back in the lunch box. Please find the tubby toy that he left in school yesterday and put it inside the lunch box. Thank you."

If we want children to assume responsibility for their own behavior, we need to be realistic in the demands we place on them.

"No wonder Adolph won't do anything for himself," his teacher grumbled, as she reminded Adolph to take his lunch box off the table and put it in his cubby.

We cannot find fault with Adolph's teacher for grumbling. Children cannot be expected to be responsible unless they are given responsibilities. At the same time, if we give children responsibilities they are not ready or able to assume, they will not learn to be responsible. They will either feel guilty because they let someone down, or else they will become very adept at finding an alibi.

Mrs. Neatnik gave her daughter, Candy, strict instructions not to get her party dress messed up in school. They were going to visit Grandma right after school and she had to look very pretty. Candy was very careful about putting on her smock before she finger-painted and she remembered to wash her hands so she wouldn't get the red paint on her dress, but then the class went out on the playground. Some of the children were digging in the mud searching for dinosaur bones. There was no way that Candy could resist the temptation to join the diggers.

If we want children to assume responsibility for their own behavior, we need to be realistic in the demands we place on them.

Mercer Mayer's book, *Just for You*, captures the dilemma of the preschool child who wants to be "good" and "helpful" but can't quite pull it off. In the book, Little Monster keeps trying to do something special to help her mother. Unfortunately, she keeps taking on tasks that are beyond her capabilities. When she tried to carry the groceries, the bag broke. When she tried to wash the dishes, she got soap all over the floor. When she tried not to splash in her bath, "there was a storm." Finally, she solves the problem by giving something her mother really wants — a kiss.

Other Self-Help Skills

Other self-help skills that may or may not be taught or used in child care settings include dressing, brushing teeth, falling asleep, and keeping track of personal possessions.

Dressing Skills: For children living in cold climates, putting on sweaters, jackets, boots, mittens, and hats in preparation for outdoor play can be a major chore. Most children five and under will need some help in putting on their outside clothes, but there are parts of the task that they can learn to do by themselves. Children as young as two years old can go to their cubby and gather up their outdoor clothes. At three or even younger, children can learn to lay out their jackets or sweaters in front of them, put in their arms and flip the garment over their head. Doing up buttons, snaps, and zippers can be more or less of a problem depending on the child's age and dexterity, and the size and type of the closure. Dressing boards can provide children with practice with zippers, snaps and buttons, but it is always more difficult to do up a closure when you are wearing the garment then when you are manipulating a dressing frame.

Brushing Teeth: Some child care centers include brushing teeth as part of their daily schedule. Children who resist brushing their teeth at home are likely to enjoy brushing teeth as a group.

Falling Asleep: When naptime is a part of the daily schedule, most children under five will fall asleep on their cot or mats when the lights are dimmed and soft music is played. A few children may need to have their backs rubbed. Allowing children to look at a picture book or do a puzzle may help them rest quietly even if they don't fall asleep.

Keeping Track of Personal Possessions: By at least three years old, children can assume the responsibility of putting their possessions into a cubby and of taking their things out of the cubby when it is time to go home. Problems are likely to arise when children are allowed to bring toys or other treasures from home. Some schools insist that children come to school with empty hands and empty pockets. Other schools take a compromise position. Items may be brought to school and shared with the group at circle time, but must be left in the cubby for the rest of the day.

Helping Others

Tammy was in tears. Her mother had insisted that she stay home, just because she had a fever. "But Mommy, I got to go to school. It's my turn to pass out the crackers."

Beginning in the toddler years, young children vie for opportunities to help out their parents or teachers. Helping out gives children a chance to feel grown up and powerful. At home children love to help with the cleaning, sort the laundry, wash the car, rake leaves, or even empty the trash. At school coveted chores may include passing out the crackers, feeding the goldfish, turning the dial on the weather chart, putting an X on the calendar to mark off the day, and leading the line out to the playground.

When children are told to do chores, like putting their jacket in their cubby, cleaning up a spill, or putting a puzzle together that they have just tossed on the floor, the same child who loved to do the "teacher helper" chores may resist the chore that she was asked to do. Helping the teacher makes you feel grown

Beginning in the toddler years, young children vie for opportunities to help their parents or teachers. Helping out gives children a chance to feel grown up and powerful.

up; being told what to do makes you feel like a baby. With a change of tone and a little finesse this kind of resistance is easy to overcome. "Please, hurry and pick up the puzzle, Hal. It's time for us to go outside and play some games on the playground."

Helping Children Learn to Care for Each Other

Karina, the new child in the Play Together Preschool, was totally blind. Miss Show-me, the preschool teacher, had been skeptical about accepting a blind child into the classroom. "I am afraid she might get hurt," Miss Show-me explained to her director. "Besides the other children might tease her, and she might feel badly if the other children are doing things she can't do." The director was sympathetic but firm. "I understand your concerns, but I would like you to give her a chance."

Miss Show-me had a prior appointment the next morning, so the director took over her class. When she arrived, Miss Show-me was amazed. Karina was sitting at the table with the other children, drawing in her daybook. Jose was holding her hand, helping her draw a circle for a face. Next he helped her make dots for eyes and a line for the mouth. "I made a face," Karina announced proudly as she felt the crayon marks with her finger. For the rest of the day, Karina joined in all the activities. When they went outside, one of the children held her hand and told her when to step down. When they played catch in a circle, the children told Karina to hold her arms out before they threw her the ball. When the ball hit her in the face at one point, Karina responded cheerfully, "I catch the ball next time."

At the end of the day, Miss Show-me went into the director's office. "It's hard to believe," she told the director. "How did you ever do it? Karina had a great day. The kids let her join in their play – they were amazing in the way they helped Karina without making a big deal."

"I didn't do anything," the director insisted. "You did it. You have helped your class learn to help each other. The nice thing about it is that your kids didn't make Karina feel as if she is different and they let her do as much for herself as she could. You have done a fine job."

The director of the Play Together Preschool was right in praising Miss Show — me. The children in her class knew without being told how to welcome a child with a disability and make her feel accepted.

The climate in a classroom is a reflection of the values promoted by the teacher, the example she has set, and the subtle messages she has sent to the children through her respect for their individual needs. Miss Show-me respected each child in her class, she emphasized the importance of cooperation, and she modeled trust, courtesy, and caring. Miss Show-me did not have to worry about including a special needs child in her classroom. The children she taught had already learned to value differences and to care for and about each other.

Objective 7: To describe ways in which teacher can create an inclusive classroom where every child is welcome

Prior to bringing Sunshine to the school, Mrs. Fairchild requested an opportunity to talk to her teacher.

Mrs. Fairchild: "You know, this is Sunshine's first experience with any kind of child care. Even since I found out about her cerebral palsy I have stayed at home and devoted full time to her. But now, my husband isn't well, and I have no choice — I have to go to work."

Mr. Up-beat: "I know that this is a difficult step for you. What can I do to make it easier?"

Mrs. Fairchild: "I guess what I really want to know is what you will do to help Sunshine make the adjustment."

Mr. Up-beat: "I have always worked in settings where children with special needs are included in the class. Over the years I have developed four guidelines that have worked well for me."

"First, I always begin by talking to the parents, just as I'm talking to you now. I ask what would they like their child to experience in the course of the year and what they can tell me about their child that would help me do a good job."

"Secondly, I try to determine the child's strengths and teach through those strengths."

"Third, through modeling and through talking, I help the children recognize how lucky we are to be in a class where every child feels welcome."

"Finally, I use every resource I have, including, of course, the parents, to find out ways of helping the child have a productive year."

Mrs. Fairchild: "I feel better already. Let me tell you about Sunshine."

Mr. Up-beat has had many positive experiences with including children with special needs in a preschool program for typically developing children. He recognizes that children with special needs are children first. Like all children, they have needs to be nurtured, to learn, and to be accepted as part of the "community." Like all children, they have their own set of needs and strengths.

An inclusive early childhood environment that is designed to meet individual needs and build on strength is appropriate for all children. Children with special needs benefit from being with other children who can serve as appropriate role models and can include them in their play. They gain opportunities to stretch their capabilities in multiple realms of development and to just "be a kid." The child without any diagnosed disability learns to be compassionate, helpful, and comfortable with all types of people and to see strengths as well as deficits. All children can learn from one another when they spend time together in a program that meets their individual developmental needs and supports their social interaction.

Welcoming the Family

Parents with children with special needs have the same needs that other parents do. They want their children to be in a safe, stimulating, and caring environment where they can learn, have fun, and make friends. If possible they would like it to be in the same place where they bring their siblings. Above all they want their children to be accepted and treated with respect.

Although many parents hope that their child will "catch up" to others of the same age, others recognize that this is an unrealistic goal. Their main hope for the child care or school experience is that their child will play with same-aged peers and have the happy experiences that all children enjoy. At the same time, they want to see their child making steady gains in physical, social/emotional, language, and cognitive development. They want their child to feel competent, confident, and proud of his accomplishments — whatever they may be.

Talking to the parents about their hopes, dreams, and realistic expectations, as well as about the child's strengths, preferences, and characteristic learning style, can help you plan for a special needs child. And, as with any parent, open, two-way communication about what is happening in the classroom and at home enables you to work as partners in fostering the child's development and providing a satisfying experience.

Many parents with a child with special needs have special needs for support. They often feel that they are being judged by society because their child does not look or behave the way other children do. These parents can grow from being around other parents who know their child as an individual and can support them and their family. Because they have had to fight harder than most parents to get their child's needs recognized and met, these parents can also be strong supports for each other and for parents whose children are developing more typically.

Modelling Inclusiveness and Helping Children Appreciate Each Others' Strengths

The teacher is the deciding figure when it comes to the attitudes in the classroom. The way the teacher handles herself around the children in the classroom will be reflected in the way the other children will react in the room. The teacher needs to think about the way he/she uses language, including body language. If she shows that she considers each child to be equally important and worthy of respect, the children will follow her lead. If she models kindness, good humor, a spirit of adventure, and a lust for learning, the children who look up to her will emulate these qualities. If she seeks creative ways to enable every child to participate, the children will get the message that no one should be left out. If she cheers children on as they struggle to master new skills, the children will join her in cheering on their friends. If her attitude toward difference and disability is one of matter-of-fact acceptance, the children will come to see these as facts of life and not as impediments to friendship.

The teacher is also in a position to highlight each child's strengths, both for that child and for his peers. She can choose a mix of activities that gives different children chances to excel. She can introduce cooperative activities that give every child an important role — such as parachute games, mural-making, cooking, and having a group of children act out a story that another child has told or written. She can praise and display work that children are proud of, noting each child's progress without comparing different children's products. She can enable a child who has difficulty to take his turn at helping, and thank him for his efforts.

Helping only when the child asks for help and keeping him safe without over-protecting

Every child has her own set of strengths and needs. Through observing the child in the classroom, you can determine the areas that can be addressed, just as you would look at any child in your classroom who needs more experiences with handling scissors or opportunities to use language. Recognizing what a child with special needs can do, you can make tasks easier without doing them for him. Like any child, a child with special needs must be able to fail on occasion if he is to taste the joy of success. If you let him try something challenging, he may surprise you with a new ability. If you provide help only when he asks, he will learn that he can trust you to assist him when he needs you but also that you trust him to do things on his own. Above all, all children need to feel successful in the program and to develop their self-esteem.

Many caregivers are afraid that a child with special needs may get hurt in their care. Be cautioned that overprotection can be damaging to the child as well. Children should be allowed to try activities, as long as it is safe, and encouraged to participate as fully as they are able. Most likely, if the activities are safe for typically developing children, then they will be safe for the child with special needs. There may be a few occasions where you may need to pay closer attention to a child. For example, a child who uses crutches may need a few seconds to get up and move to the next activity so that the children do not accidentally knock her over in the rush to be first.

When children ask questions about the child's disability, it is important to be open and honest with them. Remember that children are naturally curious and that noticing a difference is not the same as making a negative judgment.

Resources Available

The best resource available is the parent. The parent has lived with the child and knows the child best. The parent has probably been successful in trying

Like any child, a child with special needs must be able to fail on occasion if he is to taste the joy of success.

many ways of adapting the child's environment or dealing with behaviors. If the child is receiving early intervention services, her therapists may also be able to offer suggestions as to how to best work with the child. The child's pediatrician may be able to provide you with background information on the particular disability and with a list of local resources and support groups.

Individualized Education Plan

There is a possibility that the child may have an Individualized Education Plan (IEP) in effect, with goals that the family wants to accomplish with the child. An IEP summarizes the recommendation of an interdisciplinary team of specialists — including the child's parents and teachers — who have evaluated the child in key developmental areas. It states the services the child is receiving, the duration and amount of those services, how the child was assessed to determine the need for services, how the child will be evaluated to determine if progress is being made, and the goals that the child will be working on. Knowing some of this information can help in the classroom. For example, if a goal for the child is to use two to three words when speaking, then you will know that if the child just points to a toy car and grunts that it is especially important to encourage him to say "car," and to use it in a "sentence" such as "Want car." Along with the goal, the IEP may state how the goal will be accomplished. If the goal states that the child will learn to use language in social situations, the child will need to be around other children and have opportunities to practice this skill. The Americans with Disabilities Act (ADA) entitles all young children to an evaluation and, if warranted, early intervention services so that they can receive a "free and appropriate education."

Derman-Sparks, L. & the A.B.C. Task Force. (1990). *Anti-bias curriculum: Tools for empowering young children.* Washington, D.C.: National Association for the Education of Young Children.

Dodge, D.T., Koralek, D.G., & Pizzolongo, P.J. (1989). *Caring for school children.* Vol. II. Washington, D.C.: Teaching Strategies, Inc.

Heart Start: The emotional foundation of school readiness. (1992). Washington, D.C.: Zero to Three.

Lally, R.J. (Editor). (1990). *Infant /toddler caregiving: A guide to social-emotional growth and socialization*. Sacramento, CA: Far West Laboratory for Educational Research and Development.

Lieberman, A.F. (1993). *The emotional life of the toddler*. NY: The Free Press.

Meisels, S.J., Marsden, D.B., & Stetson, C. (2000). *Winning ways to learn: 600 great ideas for children*. NY: Goddard Press.

Neugebauer, B. (Editor). (1987). *Alike and different: Exploring our humanity with young children*. Redmond, WA: Exchange Press, Inc.

Rice, J.A. (1995). *The kindness curriculum: Introducing young children to loving values*. St. Paul, MN: Redleaf Press.

Riley, S.S. (1998). *How to generate values in young children*. Washington, D.C.: National Association for the Education of Young Children.

Roopnarine, J.P. & Johnson, J.E. (2000). *Approaches to early childhood education*. NJ: Prentice Hall, Inc.

Snow, C.W. (1998). *Infant development*. Upper Saddle River, NJ: Prentice Hall.

Zeitlin, S. & Williamson, G. (1994). *Coping in young children: Early intervention practices to enhance adaptive behavior and resilience*. NY: Paul H. Brookes Publishing Co.

Chapter 11: Social Development

Overview

Social development refers to the growth of the child's ability to make and maintain friends and to develop mutually supportive relationships with adults and children. It also includes learning to work and play cooperatively with children and adults and to assume the role of either leader or follower.

Rationale

Preschool children are egocentric. They see the world from their own point of view and have difficulty understanding a point of view that is different from their own. A typical example of this is the two-year old who holds a finger painting up to the phone and asks her Nana to admire it. Children's inability to recognize the point of view of someone else does not mean, however, that they are unable to be kind, cooperative, and empathetic. Children are natural mimics and talented actors. They can imitate the behavior of a kind and nurturant model and play the role of another person. The adult who is concerned with the development of social skills in young children must serve as a positive model and at the same time structure an environment in which children have the opportunity to learn how other people act and feel.

Objectives

1. To recognize the sequence of social skill development from birth to five years and the role of the caregiver in supporting this development.

2. To recognize ways in which infants and toddlers develop meaningful relationships with parents, caregivers, other adults, peers, and older children.

3. To recognize ways of encouraging preschool children to make friends and engage in social play.

4. To help children build on their strengths and overcome difficulties.

5. To describe ways in which caregivers can encourage respect, empathy, helping, sharing, and caring.

6. To design a classroom environment and curriculum that supports cooperative behavior.

It was Tina's first day at We-Are-Pals Country Day School. Mrs. Pusher, Tina's mother, gave her some last minute advice. "Now, Tina, I don't want you to be shy. You go right up to the children and ask them to play with you. You have to let the children know that you're friendly and you want to play." Tina said good-bye to her mother and went out to the playground. A group of children were climbing on the jungle gym. "May I play with you?" asked Tina. "No" said a big boy with a Ninja Turtle sweatshirt. "No girls allowed."

Next, Tina walked over to the sandbox. Three boys were busily building something in the sand. Tina dug a small hole on the other side of the box. "This is a neat fort," one boy announced. "We got to put guns in it." Tina handed him a stick "Here, take this, it's a machine gun." The boy took it and gave Tina further instructions. "Okay, it'll do. Now, find us some ammunition."

Despite her early rejection by the group of children on the jungle gym, Tina had a fine first day at We-Are-Pals. She played with the boys in the sandbox for several minutes, slid down the slide by herself, joined a bug hunt, and finally climbed to the top of the jungle gym with a group of new pals. Tina was a better authority than her mother on four-year old group entry techniques. She knew that it was appropriate to shrug off the first rejection and try a different method. She also knew how to participate in pretending without waiting for an invitation.

In this chapter, we focus on the development of social skills. We look at ways of helping children make friends, respect the feelings of others, and play cooperatively with other children.

Objective 1: To recognize the sequence of social skill development from birth to five years and the role of the caregiver in supporting this development

Developmental Picture

The infant 0-8 months:
- Maintains eye contact from the moment of birth
- Cries contagiously when another infant cries
- Enjoys watching another baby
- Engages in back-and-forth conversations with parents and other caregivers
- At 6 or 7 months, may show anxiety when approached by a stranger

The caregiver:

- Uses a low voice to quiet and comfort a baby and a higher voice to engage a baby in playful interactions
- Sings and plays interactive games with the infant like "peek-a-boo" or "patty-cake"
- Provides infants with opportunities to look at and babble with each other

The infant 8-14 months:

- Recognizes several different relatives and caregivers and reacts to different caregivers in different ways
- Can play alone for very brief periods
- May still show anxiety when approached by a stranger
- Enjoys being with other children and imitating what they are doing
- Forms attachments to transitional objects like blankets or play animals
- Is distressed when a special person like a parent or favorite caregiver leaves the room, and gives her a special welcome when she returns

The caregiver:

- Provides many opportunities for social interaction with children as well as adults
- Plays back and forth games that include opportunities for the infant to imitate actions and imitate interactions
- Engages babies in two-person and group games that involve music and movement

The toddler 14-24 months:

- Enjoys being with other children but does not understand taking turns or sharing
- Enjoys playing follow the leader games and may join others in throwing toys off shelves and making a mess
- Is likely to select one or two special friends
- May bite another child as an experiment, a way of getting attention, or as an expression of anger and frustration
- May join a friend in beginning pretending, such as making vroom-vroom sounds with a toy car or feeding a pretend cookie to a stuffed animal

The caregiver:

- Develops a special relationship with 4-5 toddlers
- Demonstrates affection by hugging, holding, rocking, and spending special time with each toddler
- Recognizes and reinforces early friend-making
- Recognizes that toddlers may seek to spend some time in solitary play

- Pays particular attention to a child who bites and takes note of what was taking place before the biting episode
- Recognizes that the young child does not have the concept of sharing and, when possible, gives the toddler a matching or similar object

The two-year old:
- May find a special friend
- Is likely to get into a quarrel with a friend over who gets to play with a particular toy
- Uses pretend play as a way of initiating friendship
- Uses transitional objects such as dolls or toy animals to overcome fears
- Enjoys playing running and chasing games with others
- Is learning to use words in pretend play and to converse with peers

The caregiver:
- Watches for and encourages the development of special relationships
- Uses pretend play as a way of enhancing empathy
- Provides duplicates of popular toys

The preschool child:
- Forms special friendships
- Initiates play and figures out ways of joining an established group
- Is learning to assume the role of leader and the role of follower, though she may have a preferred role
- Is learning to settle conflicts or disputes with words
- Engages in increasingly more complex games with peers
- Makes plans with friends

The caregiver:
- Recognizes that preschool children have their own play style and that they need opportunities to engage in the play they most enjoy
- Provides children with opportunities to be alone as well as to join groups
- Gives special help to children who are shy or fearful of joining a group
- Gives special help to children whose aggressive, impulsive, or bossy behavior causes them to be rejected by peers or is hurtful to other children
- Encourages cooperative play
- Helps children negotiate with each other and work out solutions to conflicts
- Models consideration, helpfulness, friendliness, and concern for others and for the environment

Objective 2: To recognize ways in which infants and toddlers develop meaningful relationships with parents, caregivers, older children, and peers

Noreen had just given birth to a baby girl and she and her husband, Daren were back in the hospital room. Daren called his mother to tell her she was a grandmother. "I can't even tell you in words what it was like. When the doctor handed Lisa to me just seconds after she was born, my knees turned to rubber. I know you won't believe it but she opened her eyes, looked up at me, and kept staring into my eyes. It was an awesome experience. I know that as a father I will never be free again and I wouldn't want it any other way."

Infants are born into this world primed to seek out social contact. Immediately after birth infants experience a period of alertness. The baby searches for her mother's eyes, and for a few magic moments mother and infant gaze lovingly into each other's eyes. The bonds between mother and infant are strengthened during the early months through every caregiving moment. As her mother responds to her cries, holds her close in her arms, speaks to her softly, and strokes her cheek, the bond between child and mother is strengthened. Soon the baby will learn that other people, too, can be trusted to meet her needs — a father, a grandparent or other consistent caregiver, even older siblings. She will develop a special bond with each caregiver who is in tune with her needs.

Babies who have developed secure relationships with adults in the first two or three months become quite social. They smile in response to a smiling adult and are ready to carry on a cooing conversation. Around three months old, a well-loved and cared for baby will smile spontaneously when she sees a new face and will engage in interactive vocalizations.

By six or seven months, caregivers may notice a change in their infant's social behavior. Rather than smiling spontaneously at every new face, the infant may be wary of new people who approach her. She may stiffen up, cling to her caregiver, and turn her head away when a new person tries to talk to her. While caregivers may be concerned that their nice friendly baby is becoming anti-social, the emergence of stranger anxiety is a healthy developmental sign. The baby has learned to recognize her primary caregivers even from a distance. She knows that they will play with her and respond to her needs, but she is not so sure about people who are not familiar.

By eight months old, most babies will demonstrate "attachment behavior". They will feel free to play with toys or explore new territory so long as their special person is in sight. The minute that person disappears, they will become sober or even distressed. Depending on their temperament, some babies will resume play in a few minutes and tolerate the presence of a new person. Babies who are temperamentally wary may continue to show distress until their attachment figure returns and will resist the overtures of an unfamiliar person. But, regardless of temperament, all babies who are securely attached

Babies who have developed secure relationships with adults in the first two or three months become quite social.

to a special caregiver will give that person an enthusiastic greeting when he or she returns to the room.

At twelve months old patterns of attachment are firmly established. Children who are securely attached to one or more caregivers are ready to move away from their attachment figure. In a new situation they will leave their caregiver's side and explore their surroundings, looking back from time to time to make sure their caregiver is watching. With one reassuring smile from their caregiver they renew their explorations with gusto.

The relationships that infants establish with their primary caregivers are the prototype for all relationships that babies will make throughout their lives. Babies who learn to trust and to love in their first year of life will have the capacity to make other meaningful relationships as their social world expands.

Babies who learn to trust and to love in their first year of life will have the capacity to make other meaningful relationships as their social world expands.

Between one and three years old there is a dramatic increase in the number of social relationships that children form. Toddlers make friends with members of their extended family, friends of the family, and friends of their older siblings. Toddlers who are placed in child care develop close relationships with their caregivers and make friends with other children in their group.

Making Friends with Siblings and Peers

Infants as young as three months old love to watch other children. An older sibling booing in the baby's face or jumping up and down is quite likely to elicit the baby's first genuine laugh. During the course of the first year the baby will engage in reciprocal play with an older sibling, knocking down a tower that their sibling has built or creeping after a wheel toy that their sibling is pulling around the room.

Although some authorities insist that babies and young toddlers are not ready to make friends, caregivers working with groups of youngsters attest to the fact that older infants and young toddlers are quite likely to select a favorite playmate. As soon as they arrive in the morning. some toddlers are likely to pair off and continue playing with each other for a good part of the day.

As we would expect, toddlers who spend a good part of every day playing with each other are quite likely to get into hassles. Most often these hassles are over toys. Hassles over toys can begin as a shouting match, "My bear!" "No, my bear!" and escalate into a battle with shoving, grabbing, kicking, and hitting. Often, these confrontations are short-lived. Before the teacher can intervene, the toddlers have dropped the toy and are off playing with something else. At other times the quarrel escalates and the caregiver has to step in.

Nathaniel and Rosia loved to play together and were usually quite compatible. One day they were playing with the class mascot, a threadbare, lanky monkey called Mimi. They were taking turns tossing Mimi into the air and trying to catch her. Nathaniel tossed Mimi a bit too high and she fell on the floor. Rosia and Nathaniel picked her up at the same time and started a tug of war. "My turn," shouted Nathaniel, "I get to catch her." "No, my turn," shouted Rosia in an even louder voice, "cause you just throwed her." Recognizing that the quarrel was escalating, the teacher decided to intervene. "Give me Mimi," the teacher insisted, "It's time for Mimi to rest." "Mimi," she said very firmly to the monkey, "You need to take a nap. You are feeling tired and cross." Rosia and Nathaniel forgot about the monkey and their quarrel and went off to play in the block corner.

The very fact that toddler twosomes get into hassles underscores the importance of encouraging early friendships. From the toddler's point of view, it is mine if I am playing with it and it is also mine if I want to play with it. Through interactions with a favorite friend and skillful interventions from a caregiver, toddlers gradually learn about sharing and taking turns. They come to recognize that the fun of playing with another child makes sharing and turn taking worthwhile.

Suggestions for Encouraging Friendships

- Because their play is largely imitative, provide toddlers with matching toys. Playing together for toddlers means playing side by side with the same toy.

- When you notice a friendship emerging, place the children together at mealtime or naptime. Budding friendships should be encouraged.

- Tell the parents about it when their children begin developing a friendship. The parents may wish to provide additional opportunities for the friends to play together

- Accept the fact that toddlers who play together are going to get into hassles. Before you intervene give the toddlers an opportunity to resolve the problem on their own.

- When a hassle gets out of hand and requires intervention, do not try to find out which toddler is in the wrong. Make the assumption that what is wrong is the particular situation and redirect the children to a different activity.

- Set up the classroom in a way that encourages making friends. Make sure that there are plenty of opportunities in each section of the classroom for children to play together in groups of two, three, or four.

Block Area: Provide enough of the same sort of blocks to allow children to work together. Add props like miniature animals, cars and trucks or miniature characters so that toddlers can play with the block structures they create.

Imaginative Play Area: Make sure that there are props in the imaginative play area that appeal to both girls and boys. Include props for doctor or rescue play, cooking, and pet care.

Art Area: Put up double easels so that two children can paint beside each other. Provide materials that encourage side-by-side play like water play, sand play and play dough.

Reading Corner: Make sure there are cozy spots where two children can read together.

Manipulative Play Area: Include large floor puzzles that two or more toddlers can complete together.

Introduce some simple cooperative games that the whole group can play together:

Parachute Play: Seat the toddlers around a parachute or a sheet and have each child grasp its edge. Play slow and then faster music, letting the children move the parachute up and down in time with the music. With older toddlers, place a beach ball in the center of the parachute and see if the children can make it bounce up and down without rolling off.

Egg Hunt: Before the children go outdoors, toss a dozen plastic eggs around the playground. At playground time bring out an egg carton and a stuffed animal. Ask the children to help their animal friend find all of the eggs that go in her carton. Encourage them to hunt in pairs or small groups "Why don't you three look in the sandbox? I think some eggs might be hiding there."

Punchinello: Have the children form a circle, then let one child go into the center. This child becomes "Punchinello." The whole group sings, "What can you do, Punchinello funny fellow? What can you do, Punchinello, funny you?" Punchinello then performs a simple trick, such as spinning around, putting his hands on his head, or walking like a duck. The whole group then imitates Punchinello as they sing, "Well we can do it, too, Punchinello, funny fellow. We can do it , too, Punchinello, funny you." Give each child who wants a turn a chance to be Punchinello.

Objective 3: To recognize ways of encouraging preschool children to make friends and engage in social play

Collegiate Preschool was located in a suburban area where the population was predominantly white middle class. When Bartholomew, a recent Haitian immigrant, was enrolled in the school, the director was both delighted and concerned. How could he get along with the other children when he doesn't know English? Will the other children reject him because his skin is a different color? Will he be behind the other children because he has had no experience in a preschool?

When Bartholomew arrived at the preschool two days later, the director was upset with herself. She had not told the mother to dress Bartholomew in play clothes, and Bartholomew was wearing a shirt with a collar and a tie. "How many strikes can one child have against him?" she thought to herself. As soon as she had dealt with the business of the day, the director went into Bartholomew's classroom. Bartholomew and another child were passing a truck back and forth underneath a tunnel made out of blocks. The director asked his classroom teacher if he had had any problems with Bartholomew. "Why should I have problems?" the teacher asked. "He's a fine kid. The only thing I did was to give him a t-shirt to change into. He was wearing a dress shirt and I didn't want him to worry about getting it dirty. I hope his mother won't mind."

When parents are asked what they would like their children to achieve in preschool, making new friends is always a top priority. Most parents recognize the importance of group acceptance. Some children, like Bartholomew, have a natural talent for making friends and can fit quite easily into a group. Other children, for a whole variety of reasons including temperament, experience, and self-confidence, need some extra help. There is clear evidence in the literature that preschool children who get along well with their peers tend to be well-adjusted when they enter elementary school, while children who are consistently rejected by their peers in preschool are at risk for later problems. Unquestionably, helping children make friends needs to be a top priority for teachers as well as parents.

The Teacher's Role in Helping Children Make Friends

Teachers play a critical role in helping children make friends. An effective early childhood teacher creates a climate and initiates activities that encourage the development of social skills.

Creating a Classroom Climate that Encourages Social Skills Development

A primary way in which teachers or caregivers create a friendly environment is by setting a good example. Teachers who are warm and friendly with parents, visitors, and fellow staff members are modeling social skills. When visitors are expected, make sure that the children help you prepare for the visit. You could help the children make a "Welcome" poster, prepare a snack, or practice a welcome song that they could sing to the visitor.

Other ways to encourage social skills include setting up an environment that encourages social interaction, planning a schedule that provides time for free play and for socialization, and planning activities that encourage social skills.

Setting Up an Environment that Fosters Social Skill Development

An environment that fosters social skill development provides spaces and equipment that encourages different types of social interaction. Sensory bins filled with sand or water or with unusual materials like "oobleck" (cornstarch and water) or shaving cream encourage small groups of children to carry on conversations as they play side-by-side or together in a non-competitive situation. Semi-enclosed areas, such as book corners or playhouses, provide opportunities for intimate play. Open spaces, indoors or on the playground, provide opportunities for children to play in larger groups.

Planning a Daily Schedule that Allows Time for Social Interaction

A daily schedule that provides large chunks of time for free play affords children ongoing opportunities to learn and practice social skills. During free play children have the opportunity to play together in groups. This is the time when children are most likely to play out favorite pretend scenarios with their old friends and also to make new friends as they join new groups.

Planning Activities that Encourage Social Skills

In preparing a curriculum for a preschool classroom, the teacher should make social skill development a priority goal. Activities that encourage social skill development include puppet play, cooperative art projects, book reading, cooperative games, and pretend play.

Puppet Play

Teachers can use puppet play in several different ways to encourage social skill development. The teacher can use puppets who talk to each other or to the children to suggest ways of making friends and resolving conflicts. Teachers can also encourage children to use puppets to build friendships to talk about troublesome issues.

Irene and Theodore wanted to play together but could not agree on what they wanted to play with. The teacher suggested that they use the class puppets to talk about different ideas.

Theodore: (talking for his puppet) "I wanna play with the clay and make a birthday cake for my uncle."

Irene: (talking for her puppet) "I don't wanna play with clay. It gets my hands all dirty and I don't even know your uncle! I wanna play in the housekeeping corner."

Theodore: "That's dumb. Housekeeping corners are for girls and I'm a boy."

Irene: "My daddy's a boy and he makes blueberry pancakes every Sunday morning."

> *In preparing a curriculum for a preschool classroom, the teacher should make social skill development a priority goal.*

Theodore: "I know how to make blueberry pancakes. You mix all the stuff in a bowl, stick in the blueberries and put it on the stove."

Theodore and Irene continued to talk back and forth with their puppets until it was time to go outside.

Cooperative Art Projects

Although we often think about art projects as individual activities, a creative teacher can find different ways to encourage cooperative art projects that allow for individuality. Favorite cooperative art projects include making collages, building a city out of different size boxes, and making a museum display. Children could make a science museum display by creating a planetarium with stars, moons, and planets, or a natural history museum with painted rocks or shells.

Book Reading

Book reading is a favorite activity in most preschool classrooms and books that encourage social skills are particularly easy to find. Children particularly enjoy books about animals that have problems with making friends, sharing their toys, taking turns, or doing their share of the work. Traditional favorites include the *Frances* books by Lillian and Russell Hoban, the *Little Monster* books by Mercer Mayer, the *Arthur* books by Marc Brown, and, for younger children, books by Rosemary Wells. Books about real children are equally helpful, and provide opportunities to show a range of families and neighborhoods and to address a wide range of issues. Ezra Jack Keats, Maurice Sendak, Stephen Kellogg, Alma Flor Alda, and Eloise Greenfield are among the authors who convey just what it feels like to be a young child.

Cooperative Games

Although older children are attracted to games that are competitive, preschool children are less concerned with winning a game then they are with having fun. From the point of view of most preschool children, the best games are games where everybody is the winner. Cooperative games are described in some detail in Objective 5.

Pretend Play

Pretend play provides children with a special opportunity to assume the role of important people and to see the world from the perspective of others. Children with good play ideas are very desirable companions. Teachers can encourage pretending by scheduling the day so that there is plenty of time for pretending, by joining in pretend play, and by arranging and equipping the classroom and the playground to maximize pretend play.

One classroom arrangement that encourages boys and girls to pretend together is setting up two pretend play spaces, a housekeeping area and a neighborhood place. The neighborhood place could be a convenience store, a fix-it shop, a doctor's office, a post office, a camera shop, or a restaurant. Encourage children in the housekeeping area to visit the store, or let the children who are manning the store make a home delivery.

Children with good play ideas are very desirable companions.

Objective 4: To help children build on their strengths and overcome difficulties

Children, like adults, have different social styles. Some children are outgoing while others are shy. Some children are leaders, some children are followers, and some children can assume the role of either leader or follower. Some children enjoy being a part of a large group, some children like to be a part of a small group, and some children prefer having one or two intimate friends. Some children enjoy engaging in active physical activities. Other children enjoy quiet play, creating an art product or carrying on a conversation. Some children love to stir up a controversy. Others enjoy being a peacemaker. Some children have strong preferences for group size and social role; others are happy to "go with the flow."

The Medieval Kingdom:
A Metaphor for the Social Structure of a Preschool Classroom

If you watch any preschool classroom over time, you will notice that there seems to be a distinct social structure. It is not exactly a "pecking order," nor is it the set of "in" and "out" groups or cliques that you are likely to see among adolescents. Yet it has some elements of both. In *Making Friends*, Don Adcock and Marilyn Segal use a medieval metaphor to describe the roles children play in their social groups as they play out dramas such as the following:

Melissa: "OK, children. I'm gonna make your breakfast. Gimmie those eggs, Cassandra. I gotta make an omelet."

Cassandra: "I don't want an omelet. I want regular eggs."

Melissa: "I told you – I am making an omelet."

Alexis: "May I mix the eggs, mother?"

Melissa: "No you may not. Your hands are dirty."

Shalimar: (Pretending to be a baby) "Wawa-wawa! I want breakfast!"

Melissa: "Be quiet baby. I gotta make it first."

Shalimar: "Wawa-wawa!"

Melissa: "Alexis — take that baby out of here. Who's got the garlic? I need it right now."

Cassandra: "We don't got no garlic."

Alexis: "Here is your garlic, mother."

Shalimar: "Wa-wa-wa!"

Melissa: "Cassandra, how many times do I got to tell you? Alexis, you take the baby out of here."

The basic social roles played out by the children are lords, bishops, vassals, and serfs. The lords, like Melissa, are the leaders of the group. They may be benevolent and easy going or they may be bossy and domineering. Melissa was a rather domineering lord, ruling her subjects with an iron hand. The largest group of inhabitants in the medieval kingdom is the serfs. Some serfs, like Alexis, are perfectly happy in serving their lord. Others, like Cassandra and Shalimar, are somewhat rebellious and disgruntled.

Other roles described in the Medieval Kingdom are vassals and bishops. Vassals are high status children who attach themselves to a lord and feel threatened when another child tries to usurp their position. In that case, the vassal may aggressively push the usurper away or urge the other children in the group to join him in excluding the interloper. Bishops, on the other hand, are peacemakers, who encourage cooperation, skillfully resolve conflicts, and tend to zealously promote the classroom's inclusive rules.

Prevention is the strategy of first resort. Keeping a running record of where and when problems occur can help you identify ways to prevent them.

These social patterns are interesting to observe, but what does the teacher do with the information? Whether, and if so how, a teacher should intervene, depends upon how the children are feeling. If they all seem happy in their roles and are able to resolve conflicts themselves in their play scenarios, then it is best to stay out of their way. The lord who seems obnoxiously bossy may also be full of fun ideas; in the give-and-take of group play he will learn to also incorporate the ideas of others. The loyal serfs who follow his ideas and those who cheerfully insist on being contrary within the boundaries of the game are learning how to cooperate to keep a project going. When things are working well, all the children including the serfs will contribute to their joint project and all, including the Lord, will learn to listen to each other's ideas.

But what if all is *not* well in the Medieval Kingdom? What if some children end up as "slaves" or victims, or are rejected altogether? What if a child wants to join a group, but doesn't know where to begin, or is too aggressive or socially inept to find a comfortable place within one? What if a child is cruel to others? In these situations, a teacher's intervention is essential.

Helping the Victims
A teacher's natural inclination is to protect the victim. There are generally three ways to do this effectively: prevent or minimize the problem, modify the victim's behavior, and modify the behavior of the victimizer.

Prevention is the strategy of first resort. Keeping a running record of where and when problems occur can help you identify ways to prevent them. You may find that children are restless or cranky at certain times of the day, that some classroom areas get too crowded or invite wild play, or that some groups of children have become stuck in patterns that are overly controlling or otherwise hurtful. You may then be able to reduce the problems simply by reconfiguring the schedule or the classroom space. Changing play props or introducing new themes may encourage children to form different groups. A cooperative curriculum (see below) helps create a classroom climate that prevents problems.

Despite our best efforts at prevention, there are one or two children in almost every preschool classroom who tend to be victimized repeatedly. Other children hit or push them, call them names, or say "we don't want you to play with us." Victims may be smaller children who cannot defend themselves or children who stand out as being different. Most frequently, the victim is a child who is timid and fearful and who cries and runs to the teacher whenever he is touched. An effective way to help the victim is to step in before the tears start (or simply ignore them if they have) and, deliberately ignoring the victimizer, give the child words with which to defend himself. "I know it made you really mad when John pushed you. I hope John remembers our no pushing rule. If he forgets again, tell him to stop. Nobody likes to be pushed." Focusing attention on the victim while preventing his tears is also an effective way to modify the victimizer's behavior.

Victimizers need help in gaining group acceptance without resorting to negative behavior.

Helping Children Who Are Loners

Before seeking out ways of helping the loner find a friend, it is important to know whether the child is happy being alone. Some children are easily accepted when they choose to join a group, but like to spend time pursuing their own interests. Other children are unhappy with their loner status. They may not be as socially mature as other children, or may be temperamentally slow to warm up. These children would like to have friends but they don't how to go about getting them. You might try pairing such a child with a more socially adept partner for a task like giving out snack or cleaning up the block area. Or you can help the child find a role that connects his talents and interests with what other children are doing. For example, you might ask a group of children who are building a block city if they need a police station, and, if the idea is accepted, help him get started in building it.

Helping Children Who Are Actively Rejected

Children who are rejected by other children are likely to be unhappy. Quite often the rejected child has tried too hard for group acceptance and has been labeled by the group as a pest. Unfortunately, preschool children do not want to befriend a low status child. Usually, the best bet in this case is to help the child find another group that will be more accepting. Another tactic is to include the low status child in a fun game or activity that you engage in with a small group. Try to choose a cooperative activity — such as putting together a floor puzzle, setting up a restaurant, or building a miniature zoo — in which each child's contributions will be valued. It is best, too, if the activity is one that the children can then do on their own.

Other children are rejected because they really are difficult to play with. They may be impulsive or destructive, or they may insist on having their own way. These children need positive guidance (see Chapter 12) to help them modify unacceptable behavior and learn social skills. When the problem is not within the child's control — for example, when a child who is clumsy or visually impaired tends to bump into others or knock down their constructions — you may also need to engage the other children in helping to solve the problem.

Helping Children Who Are Victimizers

Miss Right-Things was concerned about Adam, who often hit and kicked smaller children. She sensed that this victimizing was the only way that Adam knew of getting the other children to notice him. She decided to use the class puppet, Pinocchio, as a way of helping Adam. During circle time she had a conversation with the puppet. "Now, Pinocchio, if you want the children to like you, you have to stop hitting and kicking. What? They wouldn't let you play in the sandbox? Okay, I'll tell you what to do. If you find out that the children in the sandbox are baking a cake, bring them over some dark sand that they can use for icing. The children will see that you are a good helper and will let you join their play."

Very often children who victimize other children are concerned about being accepted by the peer group. Because the victimizer lacks adequate social skills, he plagues other children as a way of gaining prestige. Victimizers need help in gaining group acceptance without resorting to negative behavior.

Objective 5: To describe ways in which caregivers can encourage respect, empathy, helping, sharing, cooperation, and caring behaviors

Respecting the Personal Feelings of Others

Mr. Greene was eavesdropping in the dress up corner. He heard a dialogue between Mary and Ernest.

Mary: "I be the Mommy and you be the Daddy. You want some orange juice?"

Ernest: "Okay – I'm the Daddy. No orange juice. I got to work. Where's my lunchbox?"

Mary: "No you can't work. The baby's sick. He's got the chicken pops!"

Ernest: "No, he don't got chicken pops. He's just sick."

Mary: "I'm the doctor. Open your mouth, baby. You want a lollipop? Now you're all better."

Ernest: "No, poor baby. He's still sick. I give him medicine – okay?"

> *One of the qualities that we associate with social competence is the ability to express our own feelings and appreciate the feelings of others.*

Mr. Greene was glad he had eavesdropped. He had been worried about Ernest for a while because Ernest seemed to be unconcerned about the feelings of other people. Now Mr. Greene recognized that, at least in his pretending, Ernest could express empathy and concern and play a helping role.

One of the qualities that we associate with social competence is the ability to express our own feelings and appreciate the feelings of others. It can be quite difficult for young children to recognize and differentiate their own feelings. A child who is wound up and irritable may not realize that the real problem is that he is feeling tired. A child who becomes aggressive may not recognize that he is feeling frustrated and inadequate. A child who is exuberant and wild may not recognize that he is seeking an outlet for his happy feelings. Here are some suggestions for helping children recognize and describe feelings:

The essence of cooperation is the sharing of perspectives and the outcome of cooperation is making friends.

- Talk about happy, sad, and angry feelings and ask the children to think about times when they have happy, sad or angry feelings.

- Read a story like *I Feel Silly & Other Moods* and ask the children how each of the characters feels when something good or bad happens.

- Play a record and ask the children to tell you when the music is happy or sad.

- Ask the children to make a picture with colors that make them feel sad. Ask the children to make a picture with colors that make them happy.

- Use puppets to act out situations similar to those that children have experienced. Encourage the children to talk about how the puppet is feeling and how they should respond.

- Acknowledge children's negative feelings by reading books like *Alexander and the Terrible, Horrible, No Good, Very Bad Day* and referring to characters like Oscar the Grouch.

- Redirect negative behavior by giving children acceptable ways of expressing their feelings.

Objective 6: To design a classroom environment and curriculum that supports cooperative behavior

Mrs. Go-Getter was the first mother to sign up for a teacher's conference.

Teacher: "I am so glad you have come. Your son, Ulysses, is a real joy. I have been looking forward to meeting you."

Mrs. Go-Getter: "I'm glad to be here. Ulysses absolutely loves coming to school. The one problem that I have is he doesn't tell me much about what he does in school."

Teacher: "That's true of many of our children. At this age children think about parents as knowing everything. Ulysses probably figures that you know what he's doing at school. At any rate, what would you like to know about?"

Mrs. Go-Getter: "Well, how exactly is he doing? Is he keeping up with the other children? Would you say he's at the bottom of the class, top of the class, or somewhere in the middle?"

Teacher: "Well, you know, at this age we don't give grades and we don't compare children with each other. As a matter of fact, we try to downplay competition. We encourage children to cooperate, to work together, and to help each other succeed."

Mrs. Go-Getter: "That sounds all very good for right now, but what will happen to Ulysses when he gets out in the real world? You know, out there, it's dog-eat-dog and every man for himself."

Teacher: "I understand your concern but you know it's a changing world. Young people who can work well with other people will be at an advantage in whatever they undertake."

Nature of a Cooperative Classroom

When we talk about cooperation, early childhood teachers are likely to think of a developmental sequence. Children begin with parallel play where they play side by side, move to associative play where there is a sharing of play ideas, and eventually progress to cooperative play where they work toward a common

goal. In the context of this book, we take a much broader view. We think of cooperation as any social exchange where children take into account each other's point of view. Cooperation includes cooperative play, as traditionally defined, but it also takes place when children talk to each other in the art corner, negotiate turns on a tricycle or swing, or take part in a teacher-directed activity. The essence of cooperation is the sharing of perspectives and the outcome of cooperation is making friends.

Cooperative play in the traditional sense is most likely to occur in pretend play. Whether the children are acting out an exotic theme like space ship and astronaut or a more commonplace theme like eating dinner and going shopping, they are working toward a shared goal. Plans are made, roles are assigned, play ideas are exchanged, and conflicts are negotiated. The most common role-play theme for promoting cooperation is family play. This kind of pretending creates strong feelings of intimacy and group interdependence. Other themes, like monster play and superheroes, are more likely to create feelings of excitement and exuberance.

Whatever form it takes, pretend play generates cooperation that is emotionally intense.

At the other extreme, cooperation can be quiet and relaxing, and emotional expression can be muted. This kind of cooperative play occurs most often in manipulative play activities when children are rolling out play dough, shaping sand, or pouring water. A group of acquaintances casually share such sensory experiences. Their play is largely imitative, but as they play, the children watch each other and converse periodically.

Then there are activities where the natural outcome is a tangible product. Block building, artwork, and cooking fall into this category. Cooperation in these instances is dependent on good leadership, and frequently it is necessary for teachers to take an active role in organizing a group effort. Despite the fact that the cooperation is directed by teachers, the final product can give young children a strong feeling of pride and group achievement.

In the same vein, although distinct, are those activities that emphasize group discussion and an exchange of ideas. When successful, these activities also foster a feeling of group identity, a feeling of being at home in a familiar classroom. Typically, teachers encourage this kind of cooperation during circle time. For example, the children might cooperate in writing a story about a recent field trip, predicting what will happen next in a story they are reading, deciding what to put in the "science museum" they are making, or simply reflecting on the high points of their day.

A cooperative curriculum can extend to every part of the classroom. Each time of the day, each setting has its own possibilities for increased interaction and caring. Teachers who make a commitment to cooperation and friendship in the classroom will want to explore all these different forms of cooperative interaction. They will want to encourage social experiences that range from intimate to exciting to relaxing.

Whatever form it takes, pretend play generates cooperation that is emotionally intense.

Brickman, N.A. & Taylor, L.S. (Editors). (1991). *Supporting young learners: Ideas for preschool and day care providers.* Ypsilanti, MI: High/Scope Press.

Katz, L.G., & McClellan, D.E. (1997). *Fostering children's social competence: The teacher's role.* Vol. 8. Washington, D.C.: National Association for the Education of Young Children.

Lally, R.J. (Editor). (1990). *Infant/toddler caregiving: A guide to social-emotional growth and socialization.* Sacramento, CA: Far West Laboratory for Educational Research and Development.

Meisels, S.J., Marsden, D.B., & Stetson, C. (2000). *Winning ways to learn: 600 great ideas for children.* NY: Goddard Press.

Neugebauer, B. (Editor). (1987). *Alike and different: Exploring our humanity with young children.* Redmond, WA: Exchange Press, Inc.

Rice, J.A. (1995). *The kindness curriculum: Introducing young children to loving values.* St. Paul, MN: Redleaf Press.

Sokolov-Fine, E., Lacey, A., & Baer, J. (1995). *Children as peacemakers.* Portsmouth, NH: Heinemann.

Chapter 12: Guidance

Overview

Guidance involves helping children learn and practice appropriate behaviors that contribute to their own well being and the well being of others.

Rationale

One of the major challenges that teachers face is to create and maintain a climate within their child care setting where children are happy and productive and where stress and confrontation are limited. Teachers seek to achieve this goal in many different ways, depending on the age and characteristics of the children and the number of children they are responsible for. Infant caregivers recognize the importance of creating an environment that is basically quiet and soothing. Toddler caregivers recognize the importance of arranging and equipping the classroom to invite cooperative play and minimize disputes over toys. Preschool teachers find it helpful to develop classroom rules that emphasize responsibility and define acceptable behaviors.

A second challenge that all teachers face is identifying ways of redirecting behavior that is negative or non-productive. Again, the techniques that teachers use depend upon the age and characteristics of the children. The one rule of thumb for all child caregivers is that the guidance techniques we use must be positive. The goal of guidance is not to punish bad behavior, but to help children learn ways of achieving their own goals while respecting the rights of others.

New research has shown that "emotional intelligence" is the most important predictor of school readiness and of life success. Emotional intelligence involves the ability to handle stress without falling apart, to know right from wrong, to control impulses and exert self-discipline, to keep working in the face of challenge, to recognize one's own feelings and those of others, and to empathize with and take care of others. These abilities begin to take shape in the first year of life. Teachers and caregivers of infants, toddlers, and preschoolers play critical roles in guiding their development.

Objectives

1. To identify ways of helping infants achieve self-regulation and develop coping skills.

2. To identify ways of helping young toddlers explore their world and make new discoveries without being destructive or wasteful and without causing injury to themselves or others.

3. To help older toddlers cope with fear, anger and frustration and strike a balance between a longing for nurturance and a desire to be independent.

4. To learn ways of helping children recognize and value differences, resolve conflicts, express their feelings in words, and respect limits.

5. To recognize ways of using positive guidance techniques to reduce unwanted behaviors.

6. To recognize ways of helping children become self-directive.

We emphasize the fact that guidance is a constructive way of teaching that does not require punishment.

Mrs. Toe-the Line was interviewing for a job at the Heart Smart Preschool. The director asked her about the discipline techniques she uses. "I never have problems with discipline" Mrs. Toe-the-Line assured the director. "The kids in my class recognize that they can have lots of fun in my classroom so long as they obey the rules." "And if the children forget to follow the rules, what do you do next?" the director asked. "First, I talk to them and restate the rule in a firm voice. If they continue to act up after that then, the kids all know you have to pay the consequences," "Do you use physical punishment?" the director asked. "If you mean paddling, Mrs. Toe-the -Line replied, "I would never do that! I just give them a good smack on the back of their hands. Children need to know that when I say something, I mean it."

Mrs. Toe-the-Line did not get the job at the Heart Smart Preschool.

In this chapter, we focus on positive guidance as a way of enhancing desirable behavior and reducing behavior that is non-productive or disruptive. We emphasize the fact that guidance is a constructive way of teaching that does not require punishment. The caregiver who maintains a climate that encourages self-regulation, coping, and cooperation and who helps children accept reasonable limits and respect the rights of others is practicing positive guidance. She is helping children to develop skills and character traits that they will use their entire lives.

Objective 1: To identify ways of helping infants achieve self-regulation and develop coping skills

Mary brought her four-month old baby, Tina, to the family child care provider. The provider, Mrs. Totlove, asked her to stay for a while so that they could talk about Tina. "She's a sensitive little girl," Mary explained, "and she gets really upset if she is left alone in the crib. I know I'm not supposed to do it, but I put her in my bed at night. I let her sleep in her crib during the day, but the minute she wakes up, she starts crying." "What do you do when she cries?" Mrs. Totlove asked. "If my mother isn't there, I pick her up right away and she stops crying." "What happens when your mother is there?" "Well, my mother keeps telling me that if I pick Tina up every time she cries I will spoil her. So I try not to go to her too quickly when my mother is watching."

Mrs. Totlove thought for a moment before she responded. She knew about the research that made it quite clear that when caregivers respond quickly and consistently to an infant's crying, infants develop feelings of security and trust, and that you can't spoil a baby by responding to her needs. Later, perhaps, when she knew Mary better, they could talk about different child rearing beliefs, and she could help Mary find ways of talking about these differences with her mother. After a pause, Mrs. Totlove responded to Mary sympathetically without talking about spoiling. "I see that you feel badly when Tina cries. I am like you – I do not feel comfortable letting a baby cry. What else would you like to tell me about Tina? You know your baby so well, and the more I can learn from you about Tina, the more responsive I can be to her needs."

Mary, although still a teenager, was tuned in to her baby's individual needs. Although she did not want to contradict her mother, she felt instinctively that being responsive to her baby's needs would not spoil her baby. She felt that her baby was especially sensitive and needed constant reassurance that she was loved and that her needs would always be met.

Caregivers of infants are charged with an awesome responsibility. A caregiver must recognize the unique characteristics of each child in her care. She must modify the infant's environment in response to subtle cues, providing the infant with assurance that his needs will be met and that he can trust his caregiver. She must recognize that each infant has his own threshold for stimulation and must provide enough stimulation to keep each infant alert and interested. At the same time, she must recognize that too much stimulation is stressful for a baby, and she must look for telltale signs of overload, like changes in color, hiccups, body tension, or rapid breathing.

The caregiver must recognize that while some babies are disturbed by too much stimulation, others are not responsive unless the stimulation is intense and persistent. She must persist in her efforts to interact with a non-responsive infant by providing different kinds of stimulation. She must not assume that the non-responsive infant doesn't like her and give up her efforts to provide stimulation.

The caregiver must recognize that while some babies are disturbed by too much stimulation, others are not responsive unless the stimulation is intense and persistent.

Some Signs of Overstimulation
- The infant persists in avoiding the stimulation (whether sight, sound, or interaction) by turning his head away or falling asleep.

- The infant shifts suddenly from laughing out loud to whining or crying.

- The infant purses his lips and turns white around his mouth.

- The infant hiccups, has a bowel movement, or spits up in response to a caregiver's overtures.

- The infant tightens his muscles and curls his toes.

Some Signs of Understimulation

- The infant stares blankly into space.

- The infant seldom smiles or vocalizes.

- The infant spends more time asleep than other babies his age.

- The infant does not engage in a back and forth cooing conversation.

- The infant bangs his head against the crib as if seeking self stimulation.

...the way the baby behaves with the caregiver, is influenced by the baby, the caregiver, and the history of their relationship.

Like all relationships, the relationship between a caregiver and a baby is transactional. That means that the way the baby behaves with the caregiver is influenced by the baby, the caregiver, and the history of their relationship. A baby who is non-responsive may become more receptive to stimulation as his nervous system matures, but his caregiver may not be emotionally available if she has learned not to expect much of a response. By the same token, if a caregiver is emotionally unavailable during a baby's early attempts at interaction, the baby may be emotionally unavailable to the caregiver at a later time when the caregiver is ready and eager to interact with the baby.

Two of the most important behaviors that babies acquire in the first year are self-regulation and coping. Self-regulation is the ability to maintain equilibrium when exposed to stressors. Coping is the process of developing strategies to overcome or manage stress. In the early months, babies learn to calm themselves, or self-regulate, by putting their thumb in or near their mouth or by relaxing their muscles and cuddling with their caregiver. A baby who is cared for by responsive caregivers will continue to develop new techniques for self-regulation, such as sucking on a pacifier or her fingers, fingering a favorite blanket, or simply being still. As she learns new cognitive and physical skills, she will develop ways of coping with new stressors. A hungry infant stops crying when his caregiver approaches. A six-month old searches for the toy that he has dropped in the crib. A ten-month old seeks comfort from a new caregiver when his favorite person disappears.

Ways of Helping Infants Achieve Self-regulation and Develop Coping Skills

- Learn about the temperamental characteristics of each infant in your care by observing the infant intensely and over time.

- As new infants enter your program, ask their parent(s) to describe their baby's characteristics, preferences, and special needs.

- If a baby is overactive and excitable, use a quiet voice and soothing gestures to help him calm himself and control his impulses.

- If a baby is usually inactive and lethargic, introduce him gradually to new experiences that are stimulating and engaging.

- If a baby is unusually sensitive or jumpy, try engaging only one or two senses at a time. Talk to the baby in a soft voice without making eye contact, or hold the baby close and silently show him a toy.

- Increase the baby's ability to cope with novel situations by introducing him to new experiences when he is physically healthy and cheerful.

- If a baby appears to be withdrawn, observe him carefully and search for subtle cues that are indicative of his needs.

- Keep track of the kinds of stimuli that are either aversive (unpleasant) or pleasurable for each of the infants in your care.

- Keep track of the degree of change in activity and excitement that each infant can handle before becoming overwhelmed.

- Get to know each baby's cycles of sleep, quiet alertness, feeding, and crying.

- Help babies to achieve a quiet, alert state — prime time for play and learning.

- Slow down or stop interaction when a baby signals a need for a break or seems tired, before overload occurs.

- Help babies learn calming and coping skills. You might give a young baby a pacifier to suck or a favorite blanket to finger when he is mildly distressed, or help an older baby recover from a bump by playing with an interesting toy.

Objective 2: To identify ways of helping young toddlers explore their world and make new discoveries without being wasteful or destructive and without causing injury to themselves and others

There is no special magic in a baby's first birthday, but somewhere between ten and fifteen months, a remarkable change takes place. When the baby goes from creeping or scooting to walking, she sees the world from a new perspective. She can see more things, reach more things, and explore more places. Her emerging abilities provide new opportunities for investigation and, at the same time, make her world somewhat more hazardous.

Young toddlers as a group are fun, affectionate, curious, eager to please, and excited about learning new things. They can also keep you on your toes and exhaust the most energetic caregiver. Young toddlers can mess up a room in two minutes flat. They waste crayons, pads of paper, tissues, Band-Aids, and bottles of ketchup or paste. Before you can catch them, they will dirty their clothes, over-water a plant, or over-feed the goldfish as they try to do the things they have seen older people do. They can stick beans up their nose or in their ears, pull the pictures off the wall, climb up things that are not meant for climbing, or take a bite of another child who happens to be in their way. For the most part, toddlers are not malicious or even trying to be naughty. They just require constant watching.

In infancy, the caregiver provided guidance by recognizing and meeting the infant's needs, by helping the infant learn how to calm herself, by teaching her to cope with new stressors and challenges. With young toddlers, the guidance role of the caregiver takes on a new dimension. She must not only maintain an environment that provides toddlers with opportunities to engage in a variety of safe and fun activities; she must also limit the toddlers' opportunities of engaging in inappropriate behavior and redirect inappropriate behaviors when they do occur.

Situations That Require Intervention

The Situation: Pedro is an exuberant child who loves to make other children laugh. One day during lunch he opened his peanut butter and jelly sandwich and smeared peanut butter and jelly all over his face and hair.

The Caregiver's Response: Before the other children could imitate Pedro's antics, the teacher took him by the hand, told him in a firm but calm voice that peanut butter sandwiches are to eat, and cleaned him up in the bathroom.

The Situation: Rasheed took all the tissues out of the box, tore them in to small pieces and threw the pieces into the air. "Snowing, snowing," he shouted out gleefully.

The Caregiver's Response: Rasheed, I know you are having fun making snow. Here is one more tissue. The rest of the box is going up on the shelf. I will help you find something else that is fun to do.

The Situation: Bartholomew discovered the light switch and continued to turn the lights on and off.

The Caregiver's Response: The teacher takes Bartholomew's hand and says calmly and firmly. "The light switch is not a toy. Would you like to build a tower with the blocks or go up and down the slide with Patrick?"

The Situation: Henrietta pulled the tray of crackers off the table, dumped the crackers on the floor and stomped on them.

The Caregiver's Response: The tray of crackers belongs on the table. Here is the broom. We have to sweep up the crumbs so that our room stays nice and clean.

The Situation: Kayla would not lie quietly on her mat; she kept rolling around and getting up to bother her friend sleeping nearby.

The Caregiver's Response: The teacher explained to Kayla that it was quiet time and children need to rest on their mats. "If you are not sleepy you may choose to read three books or do a puzzle quietly on your mat." (If Kayla had been a very active child who did not need the nap, the caregiver might have taken her to another space where she could play quietly without disturbing anyone.)

Young toddlers as a group are fun, affectionate, curious, eager to please, and excited about learning new things.

Objective 3: To help older toddlers cope with fear, anger, and frustration and strike a balance between a longing for nurturance and a desire to be independent

Jeremy and Alicia were playing together in the park. Alicia's mother offered the children an animal cracker. "I want a 'yion'" Alicia stated emphatically. "I want a lion first," Jeremy insisted as he pushed in front of Alicia. "Watch your manners," Jeremy's mother cautioned, "I am sure that there are two lions in the box." Alicia's mother pulled two lions out of the animal cracker box and gave each child a lion. "I don't want this 'yion'. It's broken," Alicia whined as she handed the cookie back to her mother. Jeremy's mother tried to help. "Jeremy, why don't you trade like a big boy?" "No way," Jeremy growled, shoving the cookie in his mouth. By now Alicia was crying loudly. After dumping out all the cookies, Alicia's mother victoriously pulled out another lion and gave it to Alicia. "I don't want a 'yion', I want a tiger!" Alicia screeched, as she threw the lion on the ground.

Two-year olds can be stubborn, baffling and sometimes downright infuriating. Their sudden bursts into language allow them to be quite explicit about what they want. At the same time, their wants can be totally irrational and impossible to meet. The two-year old is trying out the limits of her power. Parents and teachers are faced with the challenge of helping the two-year old understand limits without destroying her spirit or dampening her desire to do things on her own.

A favorite word for most two-year olds is "no." The "no's" of the two-year old are not simply ways of saying "I don't want it" or "I won't do it." The "no's" are a way of declaring their right to make decisions. The two-year old wants to do it by herself, even when doing it by herself may not be in her best interest.

While "no" may be the two-year olds' favorite word to say, it is their least favorite word to hear. From the toddlers' point of view, "no" is more then a simple prohibition. It is an attempt by a grownup to limit their power. Their immediate reaction to hearing "no" is to throw a temper tantrum.

For the most part, the tantrums of the two-year old disappear as long as they are ignored. After all, it is not really worth having a tantrum if no one is going to pay attention. A few children at this age, however, have tantrums as a reaction to being tired, and leaving them alone does not change the behavior. For these children, it is usually a good idea to take them out of the situation, hold them quietly but firmly, and invite them back to play when the screaming stops.

While two-year olds are adamant about wanting what they want and will go to great lengths to get their own way, they are not always convinced that growing up is desirable. They want their parents and caregivers to recognize that they need to be grown up and independent and they also need to be cared for, cuddled, and treated like a baby. When a new baby arrives on the scene, the same toddler who has been insisting that he can do everything by himself may curl up in his mother's lap and ask her to nurse him or give him a bottle.

Parents and teachers are faced with the challenge of helping the two-year-old understand limits without destroying her spirit or dampening her desire to do things on her own.

One day Hans, who always enjoyed his lunch, strongly resisted when his teacher asked him to open his lunch box. "You always open your lunch box yourself Hans, why don't you want to open it today?" his teacher asked. "There is a dinosaur in my lunch box," Hans explained and immediately burst into tears. "I'll tell you what," said the teacher in a soothing voice as soon as the tears began to subside, "I'll take the dinosaur outside and put him in a cage so he can't hurt anyone, and then you can eat your lunch. OK?"

Although she handled the situation expertly, Hans' teacher was surprised by his sudden fear of his lunch box. Hans appeared to be a self-confident and independent toddler. Did something happen to Hans that could account for this change in behavior? In actuality, Hans' sudden demonstration of fear is not atypical. Many toddlers like Hans develop fears that adults might interpret as illogical or ridiculous. Lions and tigers may lurk in their closet, or a big bad monster could establish residence under the toddler's bed. Interestingly enough, the exaggerated fears of the toddler are part and parcel of his expanding view of the world. Not only might things exist even if they disappear from his sight, but things can exist that are not a part of his everyday experience and may be figments of his active imagination.

> *...the exaggerated fears of the toddler are part and parcel of his expanding view of the world.*

Objective 4: To learn ways of helping preschool children to value differences, resolve conflicts, express their feelings in words, and accept reasonable limits

Teresa entered the All Faiths preschool in the middle of the year. She seemed to settle in nicely with the group until snack time. Angelica, an African-American child, asked Teresa to sit beside her. "No, I can't," Teresa said politely. "Your skin is brown and I don't want to get dirty."

At first their teacher, Miss Right-It was taken aback, but she recognized that she had to intervene without being punitive. "You can sit beside Angelica," she told Teresa in an upbeat tone. "Angelica's skin is dark, but her skin is not dirty. Skin comes in lots of different colors." Teresa was reassured and sat down beside Angelica.

Young children like Teresa are not color-blind, but noticing differences is very different from being biased. Miss Right-it quickly recognized that Teresa didn't want to insult Angelica. It was just that Teresa had never seen a child with dark skin and assumed that dark meant dirty.

During circle that day, Miss. Right-it introduced a game. Each child was given a turn to hold hands with a person on her or his right and talk about one way they were like that person and one way they were different. "Do you know what that game is called?" she asked the children. "It is called 'We are all alike and we are all different.'"

Helping Children Use Words to Express Their Feelings

A very common problem that preschool children have is the inability to find appropriate words to express their feelings. When someone knocks down their block tower, their first instinct may be to lash out with fists or express their anger in a negative way. "You're a stupid dumbhead and I hate you!" is a common response. In these situations, the teacher can only make matters worse by scolding the child who knocked down the tower or berating the child whose tower was knocked down for using his fists or saying nasty things. The

appropriate solution is to empathize with the child's feelings and model appropriate language. "You are angry because your block tower fell down. You worked hard to make it big. Tell Manuel that it makes you mad when your block tower gets knocked down and ask him to help you fix it." Let's look at some other situations in which children need to find the right words to express their feelings.

- Sally was an attractive child with long blond hair that everyone liked to touch. She hated it when anyone stroked her hair. One day all the children were playing family in the housekeeping area. Sally was assigned the role of little girl. When the Mommy stroked her hair, Sally ran out of the housekeeping area and refused to go back. The next day in circle time the teacher enacted a similar scene using the class puppets.

Puppet: "I am going to stroke your hair. It's pretty."

Puppet: "I am glad you like it, but don't touch me. I hate to have my hair stroked."

- Bobby came to school in a terrible mood. He stomped on the daffodils that the children had planted in the garden, gave one of the girls a kick when she asked for a turn on the bike, and then came inside and knocked down a shelf full of blocks. His teacher walked with him to the quiet area. "You are having a bad day. First you need a few minutes by yourself to calm down. Then you need to find words to talk about how you feel."

"Go away. I hate you and I hate everybody and I hate my baby brother."

"You are feeling sad and left out. It is hard having a new baby brother who takes up so much of your Mommy's time."

"I'm going to throw him in the garbage and get him dead and send him back to the hospital."

"You are going to say to Mommy, 'I don't like you spending so much time with that baby. I need you to spend time with me.'"

- Melissa wanted to be first in line and tried to push her way ahead of Donald. Donald poked her very hard in the ribs, and Melissa started crying. Miss Controller spoke firmly to Donald. "Donald, I know you didn't want Melissa to get ahead of you, but next time use your words."

Objective 5: To recognize ways of using positive guidance techniques to reduce unwanted behaviors

Positive Ways of Resolving Problems

Mrs. Coat-tails was irate. "This is the third time that a child in your class has picked on my little Percy. On Tuesday, somebody got red finger paint all over his "Mommy's Little Angel" shirt, on Wednesday somebody ate half of his heart shape cookie, and today he came home with tears streaming down his cheeks because some nasty kid called him 'Mommy's boy!'"

Fortunately, Percy's teacher was a master of diplomacy. She talked about Percy's creative artwork and his story-telling talents before she discussed Percy's need to develop coping skills. By the end of the conference, Mrs. Coat-tails recognized that her son needed practice solving his problems and resolving his conflicts without adult intervention.

When preschool children come to us with a tale of woe — somebody knocked down their block tower, or somebody scribbled on their Halloween picture — our first instinct is to feel sorry and rush in to solve the problem. At times, our efforts to rescue children are more hurtful than helpful. We need to make a practice of helping children learn coping strategies and negotiation skills. In this section, we look at some common problems that are likely to emerge in preschool settings and describe positive strategies for preventing problems, redirecting negative behavior, and helping children develop social skills.

Reminding Children of the Rule

One of the first tenets of positive discipline is prevention. Most problems can be avoided by practicing sound classroom management techniques. A particularly effective technique is the development of classroom rules. For young children, a "rule" has a very special meaning. Rules are a part of the order of things and have to be obeyed. Because children accept rules without question, classroom teachers can use a set of simple rules as the backbone of classroom discipline. When rules are simple, clear, and understood by the class, many potential problems can be averted by reminding children about the classroom rules. Here is a set that has stood the test of time:

- We treat each other kindly.

- We take good care of our classroom.

- We share toys and take turns.

Simply referring to a rule is often all that's needed to avoid potential problems:

"Sue, please pick up that paper. Remember the rule 'We take good care of our classroom.'"

"Roger, give Enrique some of your clay. Remember the rule about sharing."

Anthony and Patrick were in the middle of a hassle.

Anthony: "Don't put your hands on me, you're dirty."

Patrick: "I am not dirty. You're dirty. And your mother has yucky yellow hair".

Anthony: "She does not. Your mother and your daddy have yucky hair and…"

Mrs. Comfort interrupted. "Oops, you two boys are forgetting the rule, 'We are always kind to each other.'" Because Anthony and Patrick were good friends, the quarrel ended with no further repercussions.

Reinforcing Positive Behavior

Another tried and true technique for changing children's behavior is the use of positive reinforcement. Children are likely to enjoy praise and covet attention. If we can catch children being good and give them praise, they are less likely to seek attention in negative ways.

Lorenzo was not very good about putting materials back on the shelf. Polite requests to help with clean up time had not been successful. Miss Coper had an idea. She put Lorenzo's favorite puzzle out on the table and, as he put the pieces back, she praised him for "putting the pieces away so nicely." As Miss Coper found more and more opportunities to praise Lorenzo for putting things away, his refusals to help with clean up became extremely rare.

Helping Children Resolve Their Own Conflicts

Although preschool teachers may feel that they spend a lot of their time arbitrating quarrels, the truth is that most preschool children try to solve their own problems directly without going to the teacher. In the following conversations, try to identify the strategies the children use to resolve a potential conflict.

Nathan: "I want the red crayon."

Alicia: "You can't have it because I'm using it and I got it first."

Nathan: "I'll be your best friend."

Alicia: "Okay, but give it right back."

Mavis: "I'm the mother and I'm making pesghetty and brownies for dinner."

Siri: "No fair, you always get to be the mother".

Mavis: "Well, you can be the other mother."

Kent: "Ha, ha, I got here first. I'm the leader."

Dennis: "You're too short. You can't be the leader."

Kent: "Can so!"

Dennis: "Can not!"

Kent: "Well I'll be the leader going frontwards and you be the leader backing up."

The strategies that children use to solve their conflicts are not very sophisticated, but they do seem to work. Children enjoy playing with each other and are not about to let a quarrel interfere with play. When children ask for help in a squabble, teachers have a good opportunity to strengthen social skills. Rather than arbitrating the quarrel and building up a dependency, the teacher can express confidence in the children's ability to find their own solution.

Olivia and Harry were building with blocks and were fighting over "who gets the long block."

Olivia: "I got it first!"

Harry: "You got it last time. It's my turn."

Olivia: That's no fair, I'm telling the teacher."

At this point, the teacher interrupted, "You two are good block builders. See if you can figure out a way of settling the problem. I will come back again when you have found a really good solution."

Focusing Attention on the Victim

Despite their best efforts to teach children to express feelings with words, classroom teachers recognize that some acting out is inevitable. When an aggressive incident occurs, inexperienced teachers are likely to focus attention on the child who did the aggressing. It doesn't work very well. Children who act out are reinforced both by the attention they are receiving and by the fact that their victim is temporarily ignored. Focusing attention on the victim while letting the aggressor eavesdrop is more likely to be effective.

Annette had an unfortunate habit of hitting children with her fist when she felt that they were in her way. The more Miss Henrietta talked to her about how it was wrong to hurt other children, the more likely Annette was to punch and hit and shove. Miss Henrietta decided to change her tactics. The next time Annette gave Gwendolyn a shove, Miss Henrietta arrived on the scene before the crying began. "Gwendolyn, you are such a big girl. You didn't even cry when Annette pushed you. I hope Annette remembers next time that we don't push other people." Annette was surprised about being left out of the conversation. She discovered that pushing other children wasn't much fun when you didn't get lots of attention.

Redirecting the Activity

In some instances, when children are either quarreling or exhibiting negative behavior, intervening with words is not very effective. This is particularly true with most children under three and when negative behavior is associated with boredom, hunger, or fatigue. Rather than focusing on the problem in these situations, distracting the child or refocusing his attention is both wise and effective.

Alonzo and Matthew had been chasing each other around the playground on their tricycles. As their excitement mounted, so did their speed and the inevitable crash occurred. Although neither boy was hurt, the two boys immediately accused each other of being stupid and not watching out. Miss Corvette intervened. "The bikes are tired. Hurry and put the bikes in their parking place so you can have a turn with the swings."

A related technique is allowing a child to save face by taking a break. This works especially well when a child is refusing to comply with a request from you. For example, when Yung Jin didn't want to pick up his toys before playground time, his teacher gave him another choice. "Ok," he said, "You can go put on your jacket and then come back and help me." By the time Yung Jin had gotten his jacket on, he had forgotten that he was refusing to pick up toys. "Let's see how fast you can pick up three toys so we can hurry and get out to the playground," his teacher called in a cheery voice. Yung Jin quickly picked up the three toys and rushed to the front of the line.

Special Words to Use With Children

Ways of Saying, "Good job!"
- I like the way you colored your picture.
- You look so pretty when you smile like that.
- You are a very good helper.
- Thank you for sharing such a good idea.
- You are very good at cleaning up.
- You are a super jumper.
- What a great idea!
- You did it all by yourself. That's fantastic.
- That was a good job you did.

Ways of Saying, "You could do it better"
- That was a good start. Let me see you do some more.
- I know you can figure out how to fix that puzzle.
- The room will look better when you pick up the toys.
- Let's put away the blocks quickly so we can go outside.
- Oops, don't forget the 'no standing on the table' rule.
- That's a hard puzzle, but I think you can do it.
- Terrance is sad because you hit him. Make him feel better.
- I really hear you better when you talk in your inside voice.
- Whining makes me feel cross. Could you say that in your grownup voice?
- I know you are feeling angry, but hitting is not allowed.
- Clara did not want her house knocked over. Help her build it back up.

Objective 6: To recognize ways of providing positive guidance for children whose families use styles of discipline that are different from those you have been taught

Ms. *U Can-do-it was frustrated. All of the three-year olds in her class were learning to put on their own coats and boots. All, that is, except Rosita. Rosita, who was usually a very sweet and cooperative child, wouldn't even take her own coat off the hook. If Ms. U Can-do-it insisted that she try to put it on, she was likely to burst into tears. At her wits end, Ms. U Can-do-it called Rosita's* *mother and explained the situation. Rosita's mother was startled. "But I always dress Rosita," she explained. "She's much too young to have to do this for herself. How will she know I love her if I don't take care of her when she's little?"*

The disciplining of children is one area where parents and professionals are likely to disagree. While some parents routinely use the techniques suggested earlier in this chapter, and others are eager to learn some of these techniques when they see how well they work in the classroom, many parents are convinced that the way they were brought up is the best way to bring up their children. Their style may not be yours, or it may be one that you used to use before you studied teaching. Yet you recognize that the parents are the child's first and most important teachers, and the discipline and positive guidance techniques they use are the ones the child is used to. How can you develop an effective partnership with parents that is respectful of their beliefs and their relationship with their own child, and at the same time not violate your own ethical code?

When parents' beliefs about discipline are very different from your own, especially if you come from different cultures, forging a partnership can be challenging. Here are some pointers that can help you be successful.

> *When parents' beliefs about discipline are very different from your own, especially if you come from different cultures, forging a partnership can be challenging.*

- Remember that children vary temperamentally in their responses to discipline and positive guidance. Some children may fall apart when they "run out of calories," and no amount of redirection or reminding of rules will help until the child is fed. Some children, even at two, will respond better to a long explanation such as "Please don't do that. I'm worried that you might fall and hurt yourself" than to a simple "No!" which is likely to send them into tears or provoke resistance. Others, of course, do better with the "No!" and will already have gotten in trouble by the time you finish the long explanation. Although you may be the expert on children in general, parents are the experts on their own children.

- Be a good listener and a good communicator. Ask parents about the techniques that they find work with their children. Ask not only what they do, but why. Share your own observations about the child's coping skills, the situations she finds difficult, and the kinds of things that seem to help her.

- Engage parents in frank discussions about your expectations for the child, and theirs. Explore differences together, in a spirit of curiosity and respect rather than judgment.

- When children come from cultures different from your own, seek advice from colleagues from those cultures. They may be able to explain fine points of approach, phrasing, body language, and intonation that will make the children more receptive to your suggestions.

- Pick your battles. You can agree to put on a coat for a child like Rosita until she feels comfortable doing it herself. But you can't violate your center's policy by spanking a child, no matter how much his parent insists that that is the only way "to make him mind."

- Explain your positions to parents. "Thank you for explaining what you do at home. It helps me understand Jack better. But when I'm working with a group, I find that a bit of humor works best because the children tend to copy each other."

- Although it is important to always be respectful and supportive of parents, there may be times when you need to draw a line. If you suspect a parent of neglect or abuse, you are required by law to report it.

Objective 7: Responding to Challenging Behaviors

Mrs. Contrite requested a conference with Dennis' teacher, Miss Knowing. Several neighborhood parents had approached her angrily, complaining that her two-year old son Dennis had bitten their children.

Mrs. Contrite: "I really don't know what to tell these parents. I don't blame them for being so upset, but I don't know what to say to them."

Miss Knowing: "Biting is a common problem with two-year-olds. It may be that some two- year-olds are still teething and like to bite down on something soft. More likely, two- year olds bite because they are angry or frustrated and can't express their wants or feelings with words. Also, two-year-olds are likely to bite children who get very upset when they're bitten."

Mrs. Contrite: "I know that biting is a common problem, but I don't know how to stop it. Is there anything that we're doing wrong at home or anything that we could do differently that could stop his biting?"

Miss Knowing: "Unfortunately, biting is a difficult behavior to control and I often think that the best way to handle biting is to wait for the child to grow out of it. Of course, in a preschool that's not a practical solution."

Mrs. Contrite: "Well, how do you deal with biting at school?"

Miss Knowing: "We observe the child carefully so that we can identify times and situations when he is most likely to bite. Then, during these times or situations, we watch him closely and try to redirect him before he gets a chance to bite. If he bites when we're not expecting it, we say firmly, "No biting! Biting hurts!" Then we sit him down in a quiet spot and ask him to chew on a teething ring."

Mrs. Contrite: "I appreciate the way you handle Dennis, but how can I explain his biting to other parents?"

Miss Knowing: "Just tell them that you are also very upset about his biting, that you have talked to me about it, and that we are hoping that we can get it under control."

No matter how hard teachers try to reduce troublesome behaviors, and no matter how cooperative parents are, young children do exhibit challenging behaviors that have to be managed. Challenging behaviors include spitting, stealing, biting, kicking, punching, using foul language, running away, destroying property or other children's work, and engaging in self-injurious behavior, such as head-banging.

Unfortunately, there is no one right way to manage challenging behavior. What works well in one situation may not work at all in a similar situation. Before deciding on a course of action, the teacher needs to ask another teacher or administrator to observe the child on several occasions and share his observations. She should also speak with the child's parents and then ask herself the following questions:

...there is no one right way to manage challenging behavior.

- Is the behavior typical for the child's age?
- Does the behavior occur frequently or just once in a while?
- What happens just before and just after the behavior has occurred? What does the target child do? What does the victim do? How do I react?
- When I spoke to the parents, did they describe any stressors at home that could explain the behavior? Does the child demonstrate this or other challenging behaviors at home? What ways have the parents used to reduce challenging behaviors?
- Does this child demonstrate any other challenging behaviors?
- Does the child have any friends or siblings who model this behavior?
- How well does the child get along with the other children in the class?
- Does the child recognize that this behavior is not acceptable?
- Does the child show empathy when other children are hurt or unhappy?

Once you have answered these questions, write up your impressions and potential course of action in a short paragraph. After you have written up the paragraph, develop an action plan. Here are some examples.

Jose: The destructive behaviors José is demonstrating may be a reaction to some stressors at home. He did not destroy his own and other children's work until quite recently when his parents adopted a baby. Most of the time he gets along quite well with the other children and appears remorseful when he realizes that he has upset one of his buddies. Time, extra attention and positive reinforcement may be all that José needs. It may also be a good idea to encourage him to talk about his feelings and to read books in circle time about children's reactions to the arrival of a new baby.

Action Plan
- Provide José with extra attention so that he feels wanted and loved.
- Use positive guidance techniques when José destroys his own work, the work of other children, or classroom property.
- Find books to read in circle time about new sisters or brothers.
- Share the books I find with his parents and encourage them to read to him at home.
- Keep a daily log of Jose's destructive behaviors.
- Reassess my plan in two weeks and make necessary changes or additions.

Janet: Janet has never really been a happy child. She craves attention from other children and, when they don't give her attention or invite her to play, she responds by spitting and pinching. Her parents are very concerned about her behavior and feel as I do that she will respond well to social training. I would like to refer this child to the Neighborhood Center where they have an excellent social training program for preschool children.

Action Plan

- Get a pamphlet from the Neighborhood Center for Janet's parents.
- Once Janet's parents have set up an appointment at the center, request their permission to discuss Janet's progress with the social training instructors.
- Use positive guidance techniques to help reduce Janet's undesirable behaviors.
- Ask Janet to help me with simple chores that we can do together. Use this as an opportunity to engage Janet in conversation and to praise her for being helpful.
- Pair Janet with Gail, an unusually gentle and socially-adept child, for some chores and partner games.
- Keep a weekly log of Janet's behavior.
- Reevaluate in six weeks and change approach if it is necessary.

Valerie: Valerie is worrisome. She doesn't even play with the other children. She spends much of the day sitting by herself in the corner of the room, rocking back and forth and mumbling to herself. Sometimes she chews on her own hand. I spoke to her grandmother, who is her primary caregiver, and she is also very concerned. Valerie exhibits the same behaviors at home as she does at school. Her grandmother feels that she needs to be seen by a psychologist and I agreed to help with the referral.

Action Plan

- Ask my director how I should go about finding the best person or program to evaluate Valerie.
- Share the information with Valerie's grandmother.
- Offer to discuss Valerie's behavior with the psychologist or provide a written description if the grandmother would like me to.
- Determine my next step after the feedback from the evaluation.

Alfred: Alfred has been a concern ever since his coming to the classroom. He is constantly punching other kids, grabbing things away from them, and using swear words. I have tried all the usual techniques; I praise him when he does something right, I reason with him, and I have even tried "time out," which I almost never use. His parents are not at all concerned. They told me quite bluntly that it's a tough world out there and they want their son to have guts. On the one hand, I believe that I should respect the child-rearing beliefs and values of his family, but at the same time I don't want him hurting or setting a bad example for the other kids. I am also concerned that Alfred is caught in a bind because he is getting mixed messages. I would like to bring this up at the next teacher's meeting; I know that the problem with Alfred is not unique and that we need to develop a strategy for dealing with this kind of problem.

Action Plan

- Continue to use positive guidance to help Alfred manage his behavior.

- Introduce some active, cooperative games and activities that will allow Alfred to be successful without having to prove his toughness.

- Discuss my next steps with my director, co-workers, and/or a consultant in accordance with the director's suggestions.

Nadra: Nadra is a bright child and a joy to have in the class, except when she starts to whine, which happens every time she wants something from me. I have always let her know that if she will just use her words, I will be happy to listen to what she is saying. This doesn't work. She continues to whine and I continue to ignore her and she bursts into a full pledged temper tantrum. I spoke to her mother about the whining, and she told me Nadra used to whine at home until a friend gave her a good idea. When Nadra starts to whine at home, I say in a calm voice, "I can't hear you because I am wearing my anti-whine ear plugs." I tried Nadra's mother's strategy at school, and she was right. It really works. After only two days, I think Nadra has just about given up whining.

Action Plan

- Use the anti-whine ear plugs technique suggested by Nadra's mother to help Nadra control her whining.

- Keep a weekly log of Nadra's whining.

- In two weeks, if the whining continues to lessen, call Nadra's mother and tell her of Nadra's progress.

- If there is no permanent change in Nadra's whining, continue to ignore it and try to decrease my own negative reactions to whining.

Ernesto: Ernesto has been trying to run away since the first day that he started school. In every other way, he has been a model child. He plays nicely with the other children and is making great progress with learning English. I have tried to talk with his parents, but they don't speak English and I don't speak Spanish. My director has promised to give me a Spanish speaking assistant, and I think that will be helpful. My hopes are that when he is able to communicate either in English or Spanish, Ernesto will feel more comfortable at school and will be less likely to run away.

Action Plan

- Continue to make Ernesto feel welcome in the class.

- Find children's bilingual books and tapes to share in circle time. Let Ernesto teach the children some of the Spanish words.

- Check with director to find out when I can expect a classroom assistant who speaks Spanish and who can talk to Ernesto and meet with his parents.

- Give Manuel crayons and paper after he has tried to run away. Maybe he can show me in pictures what he can't say in words.

- Re-evaluate in one month.

There is no one way to manage challenging behavior. When a child's challenging behavior persists or increases in either frequency or intensity, it is important to focus your attention on one target child, and craft a well-thought out plan to help the child. While it is tempting to look for a resource that lists each challenging behavior and how to deal with it, there is never a "one size fits all" solution. If we are concerned with individualization and with helping each child be the best that she can be, we need to give special attention to the children who need us the most.

———

Brazelton, B. (1992). *Touch points.* NY: Addison Wesley.

Brickman, N.A. & Taylor, L.S. (Editors). (1991). *Supporting young learners: Ideas for preschool and day care providers.* Ypsilanti, MI: High/Scope Press.

Dinkmeyer, D. (1997). *Parenting young children: Systematic training for effective parenting (S.T.E.P.) for children under six.* Circle Pines, MN: American Guidance Service.

Faber, A. & Mazlish, E. (1980). *How to talk so kids will listen & listen so kids will talk.* NY: Avon Books.

Fields, M.V. & Boesser, C. (1994). *Constructive guidance and discipline: Preschool and primary education.* Upper Saddle River, NJ: Prentice Hall.

Greenman, J. & Stonehouse, A. (1996). *Prime times: A handbook for excellence in Infant and toddler programs.* St. Paul, MN: Redleaf Press.

Honig, A.S. (1996). *Behavior guidance for infants and toddlers.* Little Rock, AR: Southern Early Childhood Association.

Neugebauer, B. (Editor). (1987). *Alike and different: Exploring our humanity with young children.* Redmond, WA: Exchange Press, Inc.

Rice, J.A. (1995). *The kindness curriculum: Introducing young children to loving values.* St. Paul, MN: Redleaf Press.

Slaby, R., Roedell, W., Arezzo, D., & Hendrix, K. (1995). *Early violence prevention: Tools for teachers of young children.* Washington, D.C.: NAEYC.

Sokolov-Fine, E., Lacey, A., & Baer, J. (1995). *Children as peacemakers.* Portsmouth, NH: Heinemann.

Stone, J.G. (1999). *A guide to discipline.* Washington, D.C.: National Association for the Education of Young Children.

Zeitlin, S., & Williamson, G.G. (1994). *Coping in young children: Early intervention practices to enhance adaptive behavior and resilience.* Baltimore, MD: Paul H. Brookes Publishing Co.

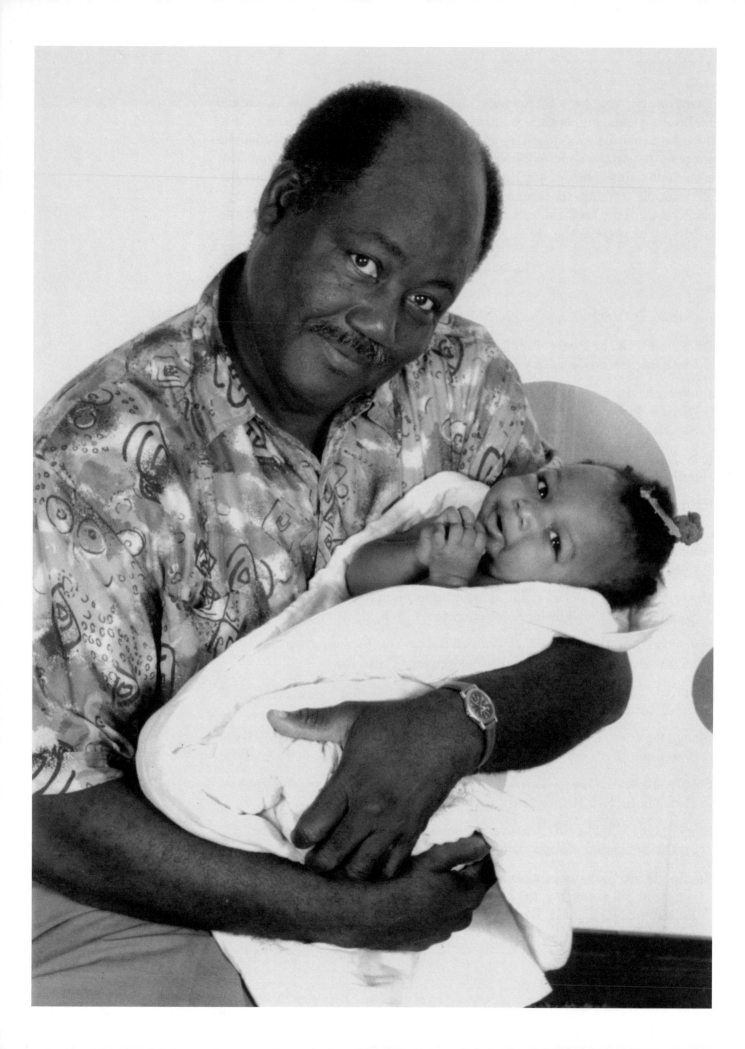

Section V:
Behind the Scenes

*M*rs. Many-Hats was managing a booth on Career Options in Early Childhood at the county Career Options Fair. The first person to approach her booth introduced himself as Mr. Undecided.

Mr. Undecided: "I have always been interested in becoming a preschool teacher, but I'm just not sure that it would be a good career choice. I love kids and, if I must say so myself, the kids love me, but I do have some concerns."

Mrs. Many-Hats: "Tell me about your concerns. I have been a preschool teacher for the last seven years and I know the profession like the back of my hand."

Mr. Undecided: "Well, the first thing that concerns me is that teaching can get you in a rut. You do the same things every day and you don't have an opportunity to assume new responsibilities and explore and expand your own capacities."

Mrs. Many-Hats: "No, teaching children is never just routine. I was just thinking about what I've done besides teach in the last two weeks. Last week, at the request of our director, I mentored a new teacher who was having difficulty managing her classroom. Then after school I met with a parent who was worried about her son's short attention span. We shared some ideas and came up with a good plan that we can work on together. This week I took the children on a field trip to three different ethnic grocery stores. I learned as much as the kids did. I also took part in a panel discussion on the importance of play that was sponsored by our local early childhood association. Then just yesterday I took part in a staff meeting at our center to plan our self-study for accreditation."

Mr. Undecided: "Well you have certainly answered my concerns about getting into a rut. But one other concern — supposing I want to advance my career in early childhood, what are the opportunities?"

Mrs. Many-Hats: "Early childhood is a growing profession. As long as you have the motivation and the commitment, the opportunities are waiting for you. You could direct your own center, become a teacher trainer, an accreditation validator, a college professor…"

Mr. Undecided: "Enough already. I'm sold. Just call me Mr. Decided from now on."

Mrs. Many-Hats is perfectly right. Early childhood is a growing field that has come into its own. Gradually, the country is beginning to recognize that if children are our future, then the teachers of children, especially the teachers of very young children, are our most important resource.

In this section, we talk about some of the behind-the-scenes work that Mrs. Many-Hats described, the critical connections with families, the individual and team planning, and the commitment to professionalism that support the high quality child care and early education that prime children for later success.

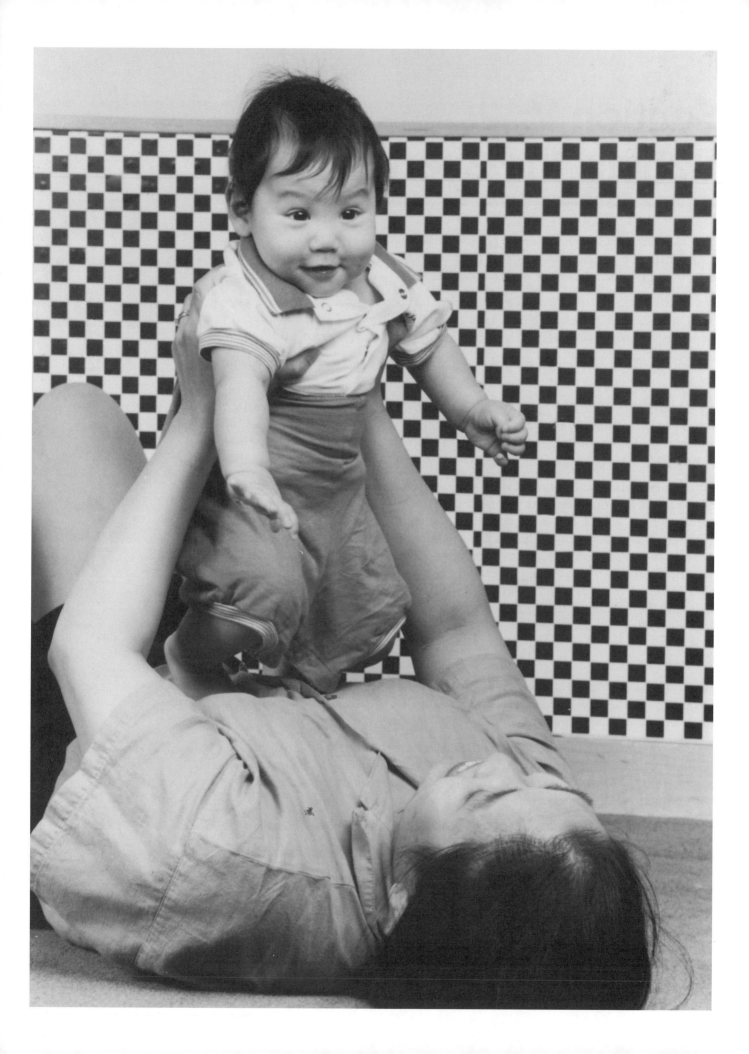

Chapter 13: Building Relationships with Families

Overview

The family can be defined as the person or people who have primary responsibility for the care, nurturing, and upbringing of the child. The family is the crucible for transmitting culture, heritage, and traditions across the generations. Families consisting of a single parent or of two parents or parent substitutes, along with a child or children, are described as *nuclear*. An *extended* family includes other relatives, whether or not they live together. Both nuclear and extended families can have important influences on children.

Rationale

It is widely believed that parents are, and in general should be, the single most important influence on the education and development of their children. It is the role of the teacher to maximize the impact of the educational experience by involving the parents and families in the life of the school or center. By encouraging involvement, by communicating frequently, by offering opportunities for input, and by exchanging information, the teacher creates an atmosphere of cooperation which benefits the child, his or her family, and the school or center.

Objectives

1. To understand the many purposes of establishing good communication with parents.

2. To learn how to set up a parent-school partnership.

3. To learn strategies for keeping parents informed about center activities and to encourage participation in parent meetings and volunteer opportunities.

4. To learn strategies for serving as a resource for families and for building a community that supports families.

5. To learn strategies for engaging parents in decision-making and advocacy.

Jim: "Want to come outside and play a game of catch?"

Dad: "No Jim, not right now."

Jim: "How 'bout a quick game of Nintendo?"

Dad: "Look, I said not now. Now bug off!"

Jim: (to Mother) "Did I do something wrong or something?"

Mother: "No, it's nothing you did. Dad just had a bad day at work. He'll be okay in a few minutes if we just leave him alone."

Like Jim, young children are often confused by their parent's behavior. They don't understand why a bad day at the office or a stack of unpaid bills would make their parents cross with them. From the point of view of a child, adults have only one role to play, that of a parent. If you are a teacher, you can't be a mother and if you are a father, you can't be a carpenter. The fact that adults function in many roles both within and outside of the family is beyond the understanding of many young children.

In this chapter, our focus is on families. Recognizing that the well-being of every child is intimately associated with the well-being of her family, we identify ways in which caregivers can establish partnerships with parents. We describe ways of enhancing communication between families and caregivers, of fostering parent participation in their child's school, of recognizing and meeting parent needs, and of promoting parent advocacy.

Objective 1: To understand the many purposes of establishing good communication with parents

Establishing good communication with parents is vital for many reasons:

- Parents have the right and the duty to be involved in the educational lives of their children. We must never forget that the ultimate responsibility for the child's welfare rests with his parents. A major thrust of our efforts in a sound educational program is to support the parents' role.

- Parents can provide information that aids our understanding of many aspects of their child's behavior in school. Learning that a child does not play with other children at home, for instance, helps us to understand his quiet, withdrawn manner at school. A sensitive teacher will work toward building this child's social skills by drawing him gently into interaction with other children.

- By sharing our knowledge of child development, we help parents establish reasonable expectations and goals for their children. A parent who is concerned about her four-year old's regression to infantile behavior since the birth of his sister can be reassured by the knowledge that this is a perfectly normal response.

- Regular contact with parents helps us to discover their talents. A wise teacher is always on the lookout for people with special talents or abilities or whose occupations or hobbies are of interest to the children. Although we must be sure to communicate that all parents have the skills necessary to assist in regular classroom activities, there are a few who can provide a special resource for the children.

- The unique perspective that parents can offer is an important ingredient in program development and evaluation. We must provide a system of input for parental thoughts, feelings, ideas, and reactions. Keeping a record of parent input can help us to understand parental needs and serve as a major benefit to the center's program.

- A healthy relationship with parents creates the best possible public relations and advertising program for the school. Satisfied parents, who are knowledgeable about the program, will be amazingly supportive.

- Parents are in an excellent position to assist our educational efforts at home. When they are aware of the goals and purposes of school activities, they can learn to recognize and then reinforce their child's emerging skills.

- There are many problems that can be solved better at home than at school. The establishment of healthy channels of communication ensures that parents will understand and support our requests for cooperation.

- Parents benefit by developing the knowledge and self-confidence necessary to function as advocates for their children.

- Children benefit from seeing that their parents and teachers work together on their behalf.

Objective 2: To learn how to set up a parent-school partnership

Parents are the child's first and most important teachers. They are responsible not only for what a child knows but for what he believes and values. From the beginning, a child's feelings about himself and the amount of confidence he has in his own abilities are an outgrowth of the experiences he has had at home. The child learns from a very young age the kinds of behaviors his parents value and the things they disapprove of. The child judges his self worth by the kind of feedback he receives at home as he meets or falls short of his parent's expectations. Teachers who develop a close relationship with the child's family can share information and perceptions of the child with the family. This shared knowledge can provide the basis of a school /parent partnership with long term benefits for the child.

Whether parents come to school on a regular basis or only on special occasions, a responsible early childhood teacher makes a special point of getting to know each one. Parents can give us insights into a child's feelings and concerns that cannot be derived from other sources. Parents also set the tone for what happens during a school day. Although we may not be able to reach every child's family, the more effort we as teachers make to establish a home-school partnership, the more likely we are to succeed.

Strategies for Getting to Know a Child's Family

Teacher: "Does anyone have something special to tell us about his or her family?

Fernandez: "Me! Me! Me!"

Teacher: "Fernandez would like to tell us something about his family."

Fernandez: "Maria got losted and she was all dirty and Mommy said she gots to stay outside."

Teacher (sounding incredulous): "Maria had to stay outside?"

Fernandez: "Yes, but then she meowed real loud and Mommy let her in."

Teacher: "Oh, Maria is your cat, not your sister!"

Fernandez looked confused. If he knows Maria is a cat, doesn't his teacher know too?

Preschool teachers recognize that young children expect them to know their families and understand their stories. The more familiar a teacher is with a child's home and family life, the safer and more comfortable the child feels at school. Here are some suggestions for getting to know the families of the children in your class.

Visit with Each Family Prior to the Beginning of School

An individual visit with the family, whether it is in school or at the child's home, is the ideal. Parents have the opportunity to share their intimate knowledge of their child as well as their hopes and concerns for him. The more you learn about a child in advance, the easier it will be to help the child adjust to school. Something as simple as knowing the name of a teddy bear or a family pet can comfort a frightened child.

Mrs. Handholder was concerned about taking Germaine to a childcare center. For two years before they moved, Germaine had been in a family childcare home with the same provider. "I'm concerned about putting Germaine in Tots-R-Ours," she told her husband. "He is not used to being with a whole group of children and with more than one unfamiliar adult."

When Mrs. Handholder brought her son to Tots-R-Ours center, she was pleasantly surprised. First, Germaine's teacher asked if she could visit Germaine at home before he joined the group so that she could have an opportunity to get to know him. Second, she showed Mrs. Handholder a new TV camera they had put up in the school. Children could go to the TV and watch their parents get into their car and send them a goodbye kiss.

Germaine's teacher's transition plan for him was successful. The home visit had worked out fine. At first Germaine hid behind his father's leg, but when his

> *The more familiar a teacher is with a child's home and family life, the safer and more comfortable the child feels at school.*

teacher asked about his dog, Bootie, Germaine joined the conversation. His teacher asked him if he would like to bring a picture of Bootie to school so that he could show it to his new friends. Germaine immediately asked his mother to find the picture. He had no difficulty separating from his mother on the first day of school.

At Circle Time he showed the children his picture of Bootie. The teacher suggested that other children could bring pictures of pets to school and they could create a pet gallery on the bulletin board. "I don't got a pet," one child complained. "But you have a panda bear. Bring a picture of Panny the Panda to school." For the rest of the day, Germaine played happily with the other children.

Have Parents Fill Out a Developmental Questionnaire

Information needed by the teaching staff can be collected through parent responses on a developmental questionnaire. The responses on the questionnaire should serve as the basis of a parent interview by the center director or teacher prior to the child's participation in the program. Additional comments for clarification of any of the parent responses can be recorded upon the questionnaire by the center director or the child's teacher. The purpose of a developmental questionnaire is to introduce the child to his teachers. It should be reviewed yearly for possible revision.

Developmental Questionnaire

Child's Name: _____ Birthdate: _____

Father's Name: _____ Occupation: _____

Mother's Name: _____ Occupation: _____

Marital Status of Parents: _____

Custody-Visiting Arrangements: _____

If the child is adopted, list age at adoption: _____ Is the child aware of adoption? _____

Give names and ages of other children in family, and names and relationship of other family members who live with you:_____
_____
_____

Is any language other than English spoken at home? _____

Is the child toilet trained? _____ Describe toilet assistance needed and list words used: _____
_____

What are your child's napping needs? _____

What are child's favorite activities? _____

Does your child have any special fears? _____

At present time, do you have special concerns in regards to child's development (i.e. speech, motor development, etc.)? _____

List the age at which your child:

Crawled on hands and knees _____	Named simple objects _____	Sat alone_____
Spoke in complete sentences _____	Walked _____	Slept through the night _____
Was toilet trained _____		

Does your child have any health problems, including allergies, that we should be aware of? ———

Explain: ——

Has your child had any serious accidents or operations? ————————————————

Explain: ——

List illnesses your child has had: ————————————————————————————

Does child take any medication regularly? ————————————————————————

Do you restrict your child's diet in any way? ————————————————————————

Has your child gone to preschool or child care before?————————————————————

If so, please describe previous experience(s): ——————————————————————
——

Has your child ever been cared for by someone besides the family? ————————————

Explain: ——

I have selected your program for my child because: ——————————————————

As a parent, I will participate in your program by (i.e. attending parent meetings, volunteering in the classroom): ——————————————————————————————————

Please use the back of the form to tell us anything else you think we should know about your child or your family.

Parent's Signature:_____Date: ————————

Build Bridges with the Family as Well as with the Child

The process of enrolling a child for a school or child care home provides many opportunities to build bridges.

- Registration forms can give parents the opportunity to share information about what is important to them and to their family, such as hopes for the school or child care experience, family holidays and traditions, and ways in which they would like to be involved in the center and with other parents.

- An open house can give families an opportunity to visit classrooms and meet their children's teachers informally and individually.

- Tours of the center for prospective enrollees can include an opportunity for teachers and parents to meet.

- Parents and teachers can get to know each other as they work together on a transition plan.

- Parents who have the time can stay with their children for a while, getting to know the caregiver and helping the caregiver and child get to know each other.

- A pizza party or potluck supper for families and staff can help everyone get to know each other in an informal setting.

- Parents can put family pictures on the child's cubby.

Strategies for Sharing Information about a Child

Getting to know a child's family is certainly a critical component of establishing a parent-school partnership. A second and equally critical component in developing a parent-school partnership is sharing information about the child with the parent. Of the many strategies that classroom teachers can use to keep the family informed, parent conferences are certainly the most effective.

Parent/Teacher Conferences

Father: "Before we begin this conference, I would like you get one thing straight. I do not want a wimp for a son. If you are here to tell me that my son is a bully and I should do something about it, then you are barking up the wrong tree."

Mother: "Herman, give the teacher a chance. Maybe he has something worthwhile to say about Dennis."

Mr. Wiseman (Dennis' teacher): "I am glad you were able to come today. It sounds as if you are both very interested in Dennis and the progress he is making."

Father: "Okay, get on with it. I have exactly fifteen minutes."

Mother: "Herman, take it easy."

Mr. Wiseman: "Dennis is a lot like you, Mr. Blowhard. He is an energetic child who loves to keep busy and get things accomplished."

Although parent conferences may not always start off smoothly, an emphatic teacher like Mr. Wiseman can find a way to make almost every conference a genuine sharing opportunity. Unquestionably, a carefully planned conference with parents is the most effective vehicle for sharing information.

...a carefully planned conference with parents is the most effective vehicle for sharing information.

Thirteen Commandments for Effective Parent Conferences

1. Know the objective of the conference. If you have initiated the conference, be clear about your agenda. What are your objectives? If the parent has initiated the conference, think about the parent's potential objectives.

2. Be very certain that you and the parent have agreed on time and place and that you confirm the conference the day before by telephone or written notice.

3. Gather all back materials, including all anecdotal reports and other records that are available. Contact all other people within your organization who work with the child. You may want to invite other personnel to the conference the day before by telephone or written notice.

4. Set up the conference room. DO NOT SIT BEHIND A DESK. Plan ahead for where the parents will sit. Have an extra chair in case both parents come. If you expect that the parents will bring along other children, set aside a play area with appropriate materials.

5. BE ON TIME FOR THE CONFERENCE AND BE READY. Any papers that are to be used in the conference should be in a folder with the child's name on it.

6. Unless there is an emergency, do not accept telephone calls during a conference.

7. Begin the conference by introducing yourself and your staff — USE FULL NAMES.

8. Following introductions, the initiator of the conference presents the objectives. If the parent initiated the conference, you may want to open with a statement like, "I am glad we are able to get together. Tell me what you would like to discuss."

9. Assume the role of listener. A good listener:
   • Maintains eye contact, shows interest through facial expression and body position.
   • Respects the parents' ideas, whether or not he agrees.
   • Resists the temptation to become defensive or get into a debate.
   • Recognizes that the real message may not be the same as the surface message.

10. Assume the role of facilitator. A good facilitator:
    • Creates a positive climate by emphasizing the child's strengths and good qualities.
    • Provides the parent with alternatives rather than solutions.
    • Describes ramifications of or problems associated with different alternatives.
    • Allows the parent to construct or help in the construction of a solution plan if there is a problem to be resolved.
    • Outlines steps for the implementation of the final plan.

11. End the conference on a positive note.
    • Repeat the objectives of the conference.
    • Summarize the solution plan (if applicable).
    • Detail the post-conference assignments.

12. Make plans, if appropriate, for a follow-up conference.

13. Do your homework after the conference.
    • Immediately, write a summary of the conference and any solution strategy.
    • Write a brief note to the parents thanking them for attending the conference.
    • Note on your calendar your own assignments and date-lines.

Other ways of keeping the family informed include the following:

Home Visits

So much information can be learned by visiting the child's home that this strategy should not be overlooked. In addition to what we learn by making a home visit, we are demonstrating our concern in a concrete, tangible way. A home visit puts school personnel on the family's turf, and provides an opportunity to make friends.

Telephone Calls

Although a telephone call is not nearly as effective as a conference for sharing information about a child, it can be used as an alternative when neither a school conference nor a home visit can be arranged. When possible make an appointment for a telephone conference at a time that is convenient for both you and the parent.

Class Parent

If one parent in each group will assume the responsibility to contact and coordinate the other parents of children in that group, the teacher's burden will be reduced significantly. The additional advantage of this strategy is that those parents who are reluctant to share real concerns with a teacher may feel more comfortable doing so with another parent.

Classroom Observation

Inviting parents to spend a day in the classroom is one of the best ways to create a strong bond between school and home. Parents learn about the program and develop an increased understanding of the difficult task faced by teachers daily. The teachers can prepare for an observation by preparing the children for visitors and by creating a system of feedback for parents in order to answer questions generated by the visit.

Send Home Notes

Contact each family at least twice a month to share something positive about their child. You may use a brief telephone call or send home a note.

Sample Notes

Becky had a wonderful day. She and her friend Alisa did a collage together and we put it up on the wall.

Jimmy is becoming much more confident about participating in Circle Time. Today he told us all about how much fun he had riding in the truck with his father.

I know that you have been worrying about Carlos, but he is doing very well. He cries when you leave in the morning, but he settles down and starts playing in about two minutes. All the children love him.

Send Home "Work" Samples

Another way to keep families informed about their children is to send home a drawing or a craft. If parents take an interest in their child's daily work (a point to emphasize at parent meetings and in your newsletter), they learn more about the program and create an opportunity to praise their child. You can also send home "happygrams" or stars in order to reinforce acceptable classroom behavior.

Create a Post-Office

Set up a file with a folder for each child and one for each teacher, where parents can receive and leave messages.

Create a Family Poster

Have each child bring in a photo of his family and lay out all the photos on a poster with each photo labeled. In circle time, you can talk about how there are different kinds of families and every family is special.

Keep Family Records

When you learn something important about a family, for example, that a new baby is expected or a grandparent is going to visit, make a note of it in your Family Album. This will help you and the children anticipate events before they happen.

Objective 3: To learn strategies for keeping parents informed about center activities and encouraging participation in parent meetings and volunteer opportunities

Teacher 1: "I have tried so many times to get Gary's mother to come to the center. I just don't know what to do any more."

Teacher 2: "Yes. It seems that it is most difficult to see those parents whose children have the greatest need. Sometimes I feel it is a lost cause. So many parents don't seem as if they care about their children."

This is one example of how teachers become discouraged with parents. This discouragement often leads to cynicism and a belief that attempts at parent involvement are doomed to failure. While it is easy to understand how this attitude develops, most of us know intuitively that the majority of parents care very deeply about their children. Many factors totally unrelated to degree of concern play a role in the involvement of parents in the school life and education of their children. For example:

- Some parents are consumed with problems of more immediate concern and do not have time or energy to devote to school.

- Many parents have negative impressions regarding their own school experiences and are reluctant to become part of the process.

- Many parents feel unequipped to deal with teachers. They may feel inferior educationally and/or financially, or feel that they have nothing to contribute.

- Some parents feel that they are blamed for their child's shortcomings and that any difficulties experienced by their children are a reflection on their knowledge, goodness, or abilities as parents.

- Some parents are kept away by difficulties with transportation, arranging substitute care for younger siblings or disabled family members, inflexible work schedules, or language barriers.

- Some cultures consider involvement with the school as interference in a realm that is best left to professionals.

Understanding parents' schedules, expectations for involvement, and concerns, as well as the ways in which they can and want to be helpful, helps you to design policies and strategies that welcome every family.

Strategies for Keeping Parents Informed

Sharing information about the program with parents is the responsibility of the program director and of every member of the staff. The responsibility begins before the child enters the center and continues as long as the child is enrolled. With today's busy lifestyles and multicultural communities, many programs find that they need to use several different approaches to keep parents informed and engaged.

Making Families Feel Welcome

Parents should feel welcome in the center at all times. They might linger at drop-off or pick-up time, come regularly to nurse a baby, join the children for lunch, stop in for a quick visit, or volunteer in the classroom. Whether or not they feel wanted depends not only on the center's policies but also on how these policies are implemented and communicated. Centers that are especially welcoming to families find them to be an enormous asset. Here are some strategies that can make diverse families feel comfortable.

- Welcome fathers as well as mothers. Introduce them to other families as well as to the children. Keep them informed, encourage their participation, and seek their advice.

- Make sure the center or family child care home reflects its families. Parents should see representations of their cultures, dominant languages, and neighborhood, as well as their children's work, photographs, and family mementos.

- Provide appropriate seating for adult guests.

- Provide a parent room, family corner, or family bulletin board.

- Greet parents by their formal names, then ask them how they would like to be addressed and introduced.

- Let parents know that you will be available for individual conferences if they would like to set up an appointment.

Parent Handbook

The development of a parent handbook is a good way to answer parental questions and address common concerns. Items to include in a parent handbook are the following:

Centers that are especially welcoming to families find them to be an enormous asset.

- introduction to the history of the center and its educational philosophy.

- information on policies, hours, fees, enrollment procedures, lunches, snacks, late- arrival and pickup, sick child and bad weather policies, etc.

- list of supplies and clothing parents must purchase or bring to the center.

- frequency of reporting to parents, parent-teacher conferences, phone conversations, home visits, etc.

- schedule of parent meetings and other activities.

- a section with frequently asked questions and concise answers based on the center's philosophy and policies

- a sample daily schedule.

- volunteer opportunities and parent committees

- important phone numbers and e-mail addresses (Some centers also include parent contact information, with parent permission)

Newsletters

The regular distribution of a newsletter is an excellent way to communicate with parents. It demonstrates the center's concern for sharing information and reaches those parents who might otherwise have little direct contact with the center. Items to be included in the newsletter are:

- information on field trips or special events.

- notification of meetings.

- requests for donations of useable junk.

- requests for volunteers and expressions of recognition and gratitude to those parents who have assisted the program

- craft suggestions

- reports on school "happenings"

- introduction of new staff members

- tips for teaching skills at home

- recipes for nutritious snacks

- weekly menus so that parents can plan complementary home meals

- special parent section with articles provided by parents

Parent Meetings

Large group parent or family meetings should be held on a regular basis. These meetings provide opportunities for parents to meet, share ideas, discuss problems, and learn from each other. They also serve as a vehicle for effective communication with many people at one time. Here are some suggestions for organizing group meetings:

- Notify parents and include an RSVP card that can be mailed back or dropped in a box at the school. In this way, you have an idea of the number of people who will attend. Also, you can follow up on those who don't respond.

- Provide childcare.

- Survey the parents for the best time.

- Schedule evening as well as daytime meetings to insure attendance by the greatest number. Some centers find that breakfast or Saturday meetings work best.

- Provide refreshments.

- Develop the program according to the needs of the parents and involve parents in the planning:

  ▲ Offer information about the school program.

  ▲ Present films or speakers on child development, toilet training, sibling rivalry, eating habits, discipline, etc.

- Evaluate meetings using anonymous questionnaires submitted at the end of the meeting and informally, through the grapevine.

- Use the information gained from the evaluations to plan the content of subsequent meetings.

- Encourage parents to create their own parent organization with officers, by-laws, and a formal agenda.

Parents as Volunteers

The use of parent volunteers has an impact on two important areas. It can supply an extra pair of hands to an understaffed center. In addition, it provides a systematic route for involvement of those parents who have special skills or talents or who enjoy donating their time and working with children. You can recruit volunteers at the time of initial enrollment, through regular contact with parents, and by using a parent activity chart. Place a simple sign-up list on the bulletin board, enlisting parents' help as volunteers and offering them a choice of dates, times, and types of contributions.

Parents can help by:

- sharing something from their work or cultural heritage

- arranging for other visitors whose work is related to something the children are exploring

- reading to children

- introducing special activities

- helping with activities like cooking, woodworking, and field trips that require extra supervision

- making educational games and toys for the classroom

- fundraising

- acting as substitute teachers

- serving on parent committees such as long range planning, diversity, fundraising, evaluation, and policy committees

- coordinating parent/teacher activities and classroom celebrations

- helping with the newsletter and other communications

- translating for other families

- bringing in recycled materials such as paper towel spindles, cards, wrapping paper, boxes, food packaging, dress-up clothes, magazines, and other items that can be used for art projects, pretend play, or to make toys and games

- preparing meals and snacks

- sharing family photos

- loaning books, toys, and other materials

- helping to repair books, toys, and other materials

- helping with clean-up days, gardening, and playground repair

- sharing special talents

- recruiting, hiring, and evaluating teachers

- planning curriculum and special projects

- ensuring that the center's policies are family-friendly

- letting others know about the program's special strengths

- completing parent surveys required for accreditation or other special recognition

- serving as liaisons to other parents

- letting teachers know about their children's interests, friendships, concerns, and perceptions of school experiences

- informing the school about community events of interest to families with young children

- participating in advocacy

- letting teachers know when they have done an especially good job

Parents are almost always helpful. Occasionally, however, their "help" can create problems. These can be minimized with advance planning:

- If you are counting on a parent to come in for a special activity or field trip, confirm it the previous day or evening.

- Remind parents who plan to help in the classroom or office that all information about children and families is confidential. And be discreet.

- Resolve any disagreements over educational philosophy or classroom management in private, not in front of the children.

- If a parent's presence in the classroom is disruptive or her child is unduly upset when she leaves, hold a parent conference to discuss the pattern and work out a solution.

Objective 4: To learn strategies for serving as a resource for families and building a community that supports families

Strategies for Serving as a Resource for Parents

Teacher: "I am so pleased with Cornelius. He is doing so many things for himself these days. You know, he's my best helper at clean-up time."

Parent: "I'm glad he's being good at school but, you know, I'm still having problems at home. When he makes his bed, it looks worse than when he began, and if I depended on him to feed the dog, Rover would be dead from hunger."

Teacher: "Many parents of four-year olds share your concerns about helping children learning responsibility. As a matter of fact, we are having a workshop on responsibility that you may want to attend."

In addition to involving parents in the program and sharing information about the children, a family oriented preschool seeks out ways of meeting the needs of parents. Parents may need information on child growth and development, guidance with child-rearing issues, or leads on community services and resources that could be of help to the family.

In situations where parents express or demonstrate a need for increased knowledge of child development, it is important for the classroom teacher to follow up by discussing the need with the director and other staff members. Setting up a family education program can be a benefit to the teachers as well as the parents.

A good way to identify parental needs and interests is to send home a parent survey.

Sample Parent Survey

I would be interested in attending parent workshops: ❑ Yes ❑ No

I would be able to come to a talk on: (Please check available day)
❑ Monday ❑ Tuesday ❑ Wednesday ❑ Thursday ❑ Friday

The following topics would be interesting to me:
❑ Sleeping problems and solutions   ❑ Ways of handling biting
❑ How to handle sibling rivalry   ❑ Bad dreams and other fears
❑ Getting my child interested in   ❑ Other
   books and reading

I would need child care if the workshop is scheduled on the week-ends
or in the evenings: ❑ Yes ❑ No

Parent workshops are most successful when they focus on the topics that parents have identified as being important to them.

Once you have identified the parent's needs and interests you can set up creative strategies to meet these needs. Strategies that have been used successfully in many centers include:

Parent Workshops

Parent workshops are most successful when they focus on the topics that parents have identified as being important to them. Child management issues are a prime concern for most families. Other topics that can be suggested to parents include using the community as a resource, health, safety, nutrition, and preparing your child for kindergarten and beyond.

Parent Resource Center

Although space is often a priority in a child care setting, a shelf or section of a room devoted to materials for parents is always a good investment. This section could include books on child management, information pamphlets on community resources, and pamphlets on health, safety and nutrition. In many cities free magazines on issues related to child care are available for distribution.

You will also want to provide parents with information about other services for which they may be eligible. You may be able to arrange with the appropriate agencies to distribute their application forms. Such services may include:

- WIC: a nutrition supplement program for pregnant women, infants, and new mothers

- CHIP: the Children's Health Insurance Program. (This goes by different names in some states.)

- Food Stamps: food purchasing assistance for low income families

- Medicaid: health care for low income families

- Earned Income Tax Credit: tax credit or refund for low-income working families with children

- Dependent Care Tax Credit: tax credit for some child care expenditures

- Section 8 Housing: housing assistance for low-income families

- Parents as Teachers and other home visiting programs that provide parenting education and support

- Early Intervention screening and services

- Health and dental screenings and other services provided by your local public health department

- Kindergarten enrollment and transition services

- Voter registration

Contact your local Resource and Referral agency, public library, school, Department of Public Health, or licensing agency for information on these and other family-serving programs.

Family Bulletin Board

A good place for the family bulletin board is near the entrance to the center or your classroom. You may want to include:

- Calendar and information on upcoming events

- Copies of notices and newsletters

- Pictures of children at work and play

- Notices of community events

- Advertisements by individual parents

- Requests for volunteers

- Parent activity chart

- Interesting articles from newspapers and magazines

- Weekly menus

- Information on family or center projects such as a food drive, fundraiser, or toy and clothing drive

Parents may also want to use this bulletin board to sell or exchange infant equipment or clothing and to exchange information related to babysitting, carpooling, or sick child care.

Parents look to professionals for child-rearing advice, but they also look to each other for advice and support.

Community Building and Parent Empowerment Strategies

When Dawn, five-year old Rachel's mother, was suddenly diagnosed with a brain tumor, the parents at Rachel's faith-based after-school program organized themselves to help. They agreed to provide dinners for the family during Dawn's hospitalization and chemotherapy. A schedule was posted in the center, and families signed up for days when they could provide a meal. Meals were brought to the center and sent home with Rachel. Five months later, when Dawn received a clean bill of health, everyone celebrated with a family pot luck supper.

Parents look to professionals for child rearing advice, but they also look to each other for advice and support. Who is the best local children's dentist and how far in advance do you need to make appointments? Where can you get bargains on snowsuits? What are the strengths and weaknesses of different kindergarten programs and teachers? These are the kinds of questions that other parents are best equipped to answer. But the kind of community where parents know and trust each other enough to ask for and receive help doesn't just happen. It needs to be intentionally built.

Parent Support Programs, based on a model developed by PSP, Inc. in Fairfax, California, are parent to parent programs that use the child care center as the base of operations. The child care center provides organizational leadership, meeting space, and child care while the parents organize recreational and educational programs in accordance with the interests of the families. PSP programs are likely to sponsor holiday celebrations and outings. In addition, PSP programs can sponsor stress management and parenting workshops, vocational education, revolving loan funds, and respite care.

Other community-building activities include:

- informal get-togethers for parents and staff, with or without children

- parent work days: some parents can volunteer to provide child care in their homes while others work in teams to give the center a thorough spring cleaning, build new playground equipment, create materials for the classrooms, or make needed repairs.

- baby sitting co-ops and other barter and mutual assistance programs such as shopping clubs and exchange banks where parents exchange toys and furniture for money or services

- fundraising and center beautification projects that reflect families' talents and traditions

Parents and teachers get to know each other as they play and work together. When a special need arises — such as the birth of a new baby or a parent's unexpected hospitalization — a support system is already in place. Parents are less likely to feel isolated or depressed and more likely to feel empowered as they help each other in small, and occasionally very large, ways.

Objective 5: To learn strategies for engaging parents in decision-making and advocacy

Helping Parents Advocate for their Own Children

A first step in helping parents become advocates for children is to endorse their role as advocates for their own child. Parents need to feel that when they have concerns about their child, these concerns will be taken seriously and actions will be taken to address them. Let's look at some examples:

> Gina's mother was upset about the fact that Gina was having accidents at school. When Gina's mother and teacher discussed the problem, they were both convinced that Gina would get so engrossed in her play that she would wait too long before going to the bathroom. The teacher agreed to arrange the schedule so that Gina would go to the bathroom before going out to the playground.

> Although Timothy had not been identified as having a problem in the hearing screening, his mother felt that on certain days Timothy had difficulty hearing when there was any kind of background noise. She discussed the problem with his teacher who agreed that Timothy should be referred to Child Find for a full evaluation of speech and hearing. Next, the teacher arranged for a follow-up conference to discuss the outcome of the evaluation.

Open channels of communication, as previously discussed, help make parents comfortable in sharing concerns about their children and becoming partners in solving problems. It is important to recognize, however, that some parents look to the teacher as the expert and expect her to solve problems on her own, while others want very much to be involved. Parents who defer to teachers may hesitate to be vocal, especially in public. You will need to find tactful, culturally appropriate ways of soliciting their input. If you are unfamiliar with a parent's culture, try to find a colleague from that culture who can give you advice.

A first step in helping parents become advocates for children is to endorse their role as advocates for their own child.

Encouraging Parent Participation in Center Governance and Advisory Groups

Just as it is essential to involve parents in decisions that primarily affect their own children, it is also important to involve them in decision-making that affects the program as a whole. The more parents know about the program's curriculum, policies, finances, long-range plans, dreams, and challenges, the more helpful they can be.

A parent/teacher advisory council or board of directors can meet monthly and take responsibility for center governance. This elected group can solicit the opinions of other parents through surveys, informal get-togethers, and phone trees when controversial issues need to be decided. A committee structure allows many parents to contribute in their areas of interest and expertise. The leadership and advocacy skills that parents develop through these kinds of involvement will stand them — and their children — in good stead for years to come.

Some parents will need little prodding to join advisory and decision-making groups. They have clear ideas about what they want for their children, and are eager to have a hand in anything that affects their children's education and upbringing. Other parents may need more encouragement. In order to get a representative group and to make all families feel that their input is valued, you and the parents you are working with can try some of these techniques:

- Provide information about governing and advisory boards and committees in the parent handbook and at the first parent meeting. Encourage current board and committee members to share why their work is important, what they have learned, how much work is involved, and what challenges and opportunities are currently at the top of the agenda.

- Seek out the natural leaders. These are not necessarily the most vocal or educated parents, but the ones who are looked to by others for information and guidance, who have strong opinions but are willing to listen to those who disagree with them, and who have a talent for building bridges and smoothing over differences.

- Try to ensure diversity of opinion, gender, race/ethnicity, income level, and age of children, as appropriate.

- Create a nominating committee to recruit new board members.

- Hold meetings that are open to all. Publish the agenda in advance, and summarize the meeting in your newsletter.

- Be sure to provide child care, food, transportation, and translation serves when needed and to hold meetings at times that are convenient for families.

- Use the committee structure to nurture next year's leaders.

Once parents have become comfortable about serving as advocates for their own children, they are ready to broaden their horizons and become advocates for all children.

Empowering Parents as Advocates for Children

Once parents have become comfortable about serving as advocates for their own children, they are ready to broaden their horizons and become advocates for all children. Recognizing that the critical tool for a child advocate is information, teachers can play an important role in keeping parents informed about issues related to children. Here are some ways to keep parents informed and committed:

- Maintain a bulletin board that includes updated pamphlets, periodicals, and news releases that focus on children's issues at the federal, state, and local levels.

- Inform parents of television specials that are related to children's issues.

- Invite parents to participate in workshops and study sessions devoted to child issues that are relevant to your center.

- Post reminders to vote as Election Day approaches.

- Invite elected officials to visit your center when an issue affecting young children is on the agenda. Ask parents to join you in highlighting how the issue affects their family.

- Invite candidates for local office to speak at a parent meeting.

- Get involved yourself! Work with your local child care provider association, a state or local child advocacy group, or a national group such as Stand for Children.

Parent involvement is an effort toward the establishment of common aims and goals, so that the labors of home and school are consistent. The greater the congruence between the values and objectives of home and school, the greater the impact of each and the greater the benefit to the child.

Finally, and perhaps the most important, is your realization that you are the child's teacher for only one or two years. The effect that you have during that time, however great, cannot match that of the parent, who influences the child throughout his formative years. The parent is the child's real teacher. We professionals have the greatest impact when we share our knowledge and ability with the child's family, extending our influence into the child's future.

Brickman, N.A. & Taylor, L.S. (Editors). (1991). *Supporting young learners: Ideas for preschool and day care providers.* Ypsilanti, MI: High/Scope Press.

Diffily, D. & Morrison, K. (Editors). (1996). *Family friendly communication for early childhood programs.* Washington, D.C.: National Association for the Education of Young Children.

Dodge, D.T., Koralek, D.G., & Pizzolongo, P.J. (1989). *Caring for school children.* Vol. II. Washington, D.C.: Teaching Strategies, Inc.

Drawing Strength from Diversity: Effective Services for Children, Youth and Families. San Francisco, CA.: A California Tomorrow Publication.

Greenman, J. & Stonehouse, A. (1996). *Prime times: A handbook for excellence in Infant and toddler programs.* St. Paul, MN: Redleaf Press.

Lally, J.R., Griffin, A., Fenichel, E., Segal, M., Szanton, E., & Weissbourd, B. (1995). *Caring for infants and toddlers in groups: Developmentally appropriate practice.* Washington, D.C.: Zero to Three.

Stone, J.G. (1987). *Teacher-parent relationships.* Washington, D.C.: NAEYC.

Chapter 14:
Program Management

Overview

Program management in center-based child care refers to the role of the teachers in promoting the smooth running of the child care center. It includes observing, recording, and tracking the development and behavior of each child, following administrative policies and procedures set by the center, working as a team with other members of the staff in program and curriculum planning, and participating with the director and other staff members in evaluating the strengths and needs of the center. In family child care, program management includes curriculum planning, record-keeping, business management, and other administrative duties.

Rationale

The level of cooperation evidenced by staff members is a critical component in the development of a healthy, productive center. In the best of circumstances staff members share resources, materials and ideas. In addition, time is set aside for joint planning and problem solving. Staff meetings are devoted to discussions of problems and identifying opportunities. Being a good program manager requires both interpersonal skills and managerial skills. The teacher with program management skills can work cooperatively with other adults – sharing ideas, resources and expertise. In addition, a good program manager maintains individual records on all of the children in her class or home and uses these records as the basis of program planning and curriculum development.

Objectives

1. To work cooperatively as a member of a team.

2. To follow the policies and procedures set down by the center.

3. To maintain a record keeping system that serves as the basis of individual and group program planning.

4. To manage your own classroom efficiently so that you devote most of your time to working directly with the children.

The director of We-R-Caring Nursery was having a conference with one of her teachers.

Director: "I am pleased with the way you are interacting with the children. The one thing I would like to work on is improving your management skills."

Teacher: "Oh, that's no problem. I don't even plan to go into management. If there is any managing to do in the school, I'll leave that up to you."

Despite this new teacher's lack of concern, program management is a part of every teacher's job. The classroom teacher is responsible for participating with other teachers in program planning. She is responsible, too, for tracking the progress of children in her classroom, for knowing the policies and procedures developed for her center, and evaluating her own performance as a classroom manager.

The most effective sharing comes about when teachers plan together on a regular basis.

Objective 1. To work cooperatively as a member of a team

During a staff meeting, Miss Spontaneity made her position quite clear. *"I am happy to cooperate in any way I can, but I am very much against the idea of a shared monthly calendar. How can I possibly know now what kind of field trip I am going to plan for next month? I like to plan field trips that either emerge from the spontaneous interests of the children, or take advantage of some unplanned event that is going on in town, like last year when we found out two days before it happened that there was going to be a parade of old and new fire engines, or the time when the new yogurt store had its opening and they passed out mini cones with frozen yogurt to all the kids."*

The director praised Miss Spontaneity for recognizing the importance of expanding on the children's interest and taking advantage of unplanned events. The monthly calendar, she assured her, is not a document written in stone. It is a way of identifying events that affect some or all of the classes, of knowing in advance when we need to get permission slips or arrange for transportation, a way of coordinating open houses so that parents with more than one child do not run into conflicts, and it is also a way for teachers to share their good ideas. Miss Spontaneity had to agree that a monthly calendar wasn't such a bad idea.

Planning as a Team

While a director can create a climate for team building by her leadership style and the policies she promotes, it is up to the rest of the staff to make team building happen. The ingredients of a successful staff team include a shared philosophy about children and how they learn, mutual trust and respect, and an ongoing commitment to planning together and sharing ideas and resources. Although some sharing of information can come about informally, as teachers eat lunch together or meet after school, the most effective sharing comes about when teachers plan together on a regular basis.

While it is up to each teacher to plan her own weekly plan sheets and class schedules, it is helpful for teachers to collaborate in the development of the yearly calendar and monthly plans.

The Yearly Calendar

A yearly calendar describes the major events taking place during the year that affect the whole center. While teachers may feel pressure in the beginning of the year to get their rooms set up and their individual curriculums planned, the time spent before classes begin in setting up the yearly calendar sets the tone for cooperation throughout the school year. In addition to regularly scheduled holidays and vacations, the yearly calendar should include major school-wide events like parent nights, field trips, community events, health related activities, annual fundraisers and food drives, and graduation.

Monthly Plans

While the yearly calendar alerts classroom teachers to the major scheduled events, monthly planning meetings provide the opportunity of outlining tasks and dividing responsibilities associated with these events. Monthly planning meetings also give teachers a chance to talk about new opportunities for joint projects and events. Two classes may decide to get together for a Mother's Day breakfast or one of the teachers may suggest a school-wide recycling project.

Sharing Ideas With Other Teachers

Once teachers discover the advantages of joining forces with other teachers, sharing will take place on a spontaneous basis. One idea that works well is setting up a shelf in the teacher's room where teachers can display crafts that worked well in their class. Other ways of sharing include:

- Participating in weekly or bi-weekly staff meetings

- Making up activity boxes (with a lesson plan, directions, and all of the necessary materials for an activity) that can be rotated through the classrooms

- Developing a library schedule where teachers take turns checking out library books for the center

- Placing a large carton in the storage area where teachers can put left over scraps or craft materials that can be shared with other teachers

- Inviting another class in to share a celebration or performance

- Letting two classes exchange greeting cards that they make in class

- Sharing ideas, lesson plans, and useful websites via e-mail

- Writing brief articles for the center newsletter

Objective 2. To follow the policies and procedures set down by the center

*M*other: *"I am sorry about Bruce acting up in class. You know I always say, "Spare the rod and spoil the child." If you would give him a rap on the knuckles now and then you wouldn't have any more problems."*

Mrs. Toe-the-Mark: "I agree with you but you know we're not allowed to hit kids. It's a stupid rule but I have to follow it or I lose my job."

Mrs. Toe-the-Mark was quite pleased with herself. She had managed to placate this mother without violating the policies of the center. Or had she?

> *A teacher is responsible for supporting the policies of her center in word as well as deed.*

Obviously Miss Toe-the-Mark did not understand her responsibility for following the policies and procedures of the center. Even when a teacher is not in agreement with a center policy, she is responsible for supporting that policy in word as well as in deed. This does not mean, however, that teachers should simply follow policy without question. If a teacher understands the reason for a policy and still disagrees with it, it is important to talk over the policy with the director. Almost inevitably an open discussion of a policy will lead to a modification in which everyone is satisfied. If a teacher feels she cannot support a center policy after a thorough discussion, she really needs to find another position.

A child care teacher who supports the policies and procedures of a child care center is thoroughly familiar with its written and unwritten policies and procedures and is conscientious in their implementation. Policies and procedures operational in a child care center fall into three categories: personnel, families and children, and the center.

Personnel Policy

In larger and/or well-established centers, policies and procedures related to personnel are likely to be written up in a personnel handbook. Typically, a handbook describes the rights and responsibilities of employees, and includes sections on salary and benefits, evaluation procedures, release time, policies related to liability, and policies related to termination. In small centers, personnel rights and responsibilities may not be written out. In the absence of a written document it is important for every staff member to be familiar with his or her job description and discuss job-related benefits and responsibilities with the director.

Policies Related to Families and Children

Centers that have a personnel handbook are also likely to have a parent handbook. This handbook may describe policies related to fees and service charges, health, drop off and pick up, class visitation, insurance, field trips, and clothing. Other policies that may be written or unwritten related to children might include: maintenance of child-related records, accident, late arrival, and absentee procedures, and procedures to follow in cases of suspected abuse and neglect. Policies related to discipline, safety, use of facilities, curriculum and lesson-planning, television-watching, and inclusion of children with special needs are also child-related. Policies related to families may include the number and types of contacts the teacher must initiate, the maintenance of confidentiality, policies related to minor illness, and procedures to follow when a non-custodial parent attempts to take a child from the center.

Policies Related to the Center

Policies related to the center fall into two categories, health and safety, and inventory maintenance. Policies under health and safety include fire drill practice, emergency procedures, and upkeep of health records. Policies under inventory and maintenance include inventory maintenance, reports on consumables used, and reporting on furniture and equipment that needs repair.

From Knowledge to Implementation

While being knowledgeable about policy and procedures is extremely important, it is equally important to know how and when to implement a policy. It is helpful to practice filling out forms like inventory time sheets, accident reports or contagious disease exposure forms before doing it for "real." It is also helpful to mark down on the yearly calendar the dates for turning in reports or evaluations.

Objective 3: To maintain a record keeping system that serves as the basis of individual and group program planning

Mrs. Carefree was surprised to find a note in her box from Melissa's parents. It said, "We would like to set up a conference with you in order to find out how Melissa is progressing."

"That's the most ridiculous thing I ever heard of," Mrs. Carefree remarked to another teacher. "Melissa is a perfectly okay kid. She's not having any problems as far as I can tell, and her parents keep wanting to know how she is doing."

Despite Mrs. Carefree's disparaging remarks, Melissa's parents' request was not unreasonable. A classroom teacher with good management skills monitors the progress of the children in her classroom on an ongoing basis. She maintains checklists based on curriculum objectives as well as anecdotal reports to keep track of individual progress. She may also use behavioral observations when children exhibit special needs or problems.

Checklists

Checklists developed by the teacher and based on the curriculum objectives are the simplest way of tracking the progress of all children in the class. Checklists should be age specific and should include a place for the date, the child's name, age and date of birth. The specificity of the checklists depends on the curriculum that is used in the classroom. A classroom with a highly structured curriculum and sequenced behavioral objectives requires an elaborate checklist. A simpler checklist is more appropriate for a curriculum that is relatively flexible and developmentally oriented. Checklists should be filled out at least three and preferably four times a year.

Birth to Six Months Developmental Check List

	Yes	At Times	No
Follows a moving rattle with her eyes for a short distance			
Turns her head toward source of sound			
Smiles in response to a smile			
Brings thumb to mouth			
Watches own hands			
Engages with caregivers in back and forth babbling			
Holds own head up when lifted			
Reaches and grasps rattle			
Lifts head and chest when on stomach			
Rolls over			
Picks up a toy			
Crawls Chuckles out loud			
Transfers toy from hand to hand			
Sits with support			
Sits without support			

Anecdotal records are the most effective way of personalizing a record-keeping system and providing parents with a real picture of how a child functions in typical class situations.

Anecdotal Record

Anecdotal records are the most effective way of personalizing a record keeping system and providing parents with a real picture of how a child functions in typical class situations. Anecdotal records should be short and precise, describing what the child is saying or doing. The anecdotal record should not include the teacher's impression or an analysis of the behavior. It is especially important to record the date, time, and setting for each anecdotal record.

Sample Anecdotal Record

Date: February 12
Time: 9:30 a.m.
Setting: Block Corner

Situation: Betty is building a block tower. Jonathan knocks it down.

What happened: Betty said to Jonathan in a firm voice, "You knocked down my chocolate factory. Help me build it up." Jonathan sat beside Betty and the two children rebuilt the block structure.

Anecdotes, such as this one are very useful for sharing with parents the good things that their children are doing. Betty's parents were concerned about Betty's tendency to let other children take advantage of her. By sharing this anecdote, Betty's teacher was able to show how Betty could be appropriately assertive without being confrontational, or stepping out of her role as peacemaker.

Anecdotal records can also be used to discuss behaviors that may be of concern. It is important, however, that when we share worrisome anecdotes with parents, we also share anecdotes that demonstrate their child's strengths.

Anecdotal records are also useful for developing an anecdotal portfolio, which serves as an assessment of the child's progress. The portfolio should include anecdotes that demonstrate a child's salient

characteristics and her performance and understanding in various areas. If areas of concerns are identified in the beginning of the year, anecdotal reports can describe incidents where the child has shown progress in the targeted area.

Objective 4: To manage your own classroom efficiently so that you devote most of your time to working directly with the children

*A*t the suggestion of the director, Miss Scatterbrain was visiting Mrs. Got-it-Together's classroom. In the morning, the children all went to circle time. They listened to a story about spiders, sang some songs, including "There's a spider on my leg," and after circle time, the children selected a token from the choice board. Each token represented an interest center, and the children were asked to choose a token. One of the children explained to Miss Scatterbrain that each token was an admission ticket to an interest center. When Miss Scatterbrain asked what happened when there were no tokens left for the interest center she wanted, the child answered matter-of-factly, "You just choose a different interest center."

During the course of the day, children went out to the playground, completed a collaborative art project, made Jell-O, put on a puppet show, had snacks and lunch, napped, acted out a story, met with their teacher in small groups, picked up their toys, and joined in a circle to talk about the day. There were no incidents, and Mrs. Got-it-Together seemed perfectly relaxed.

Miss Scatterbrain was incredulous. "How do you manage fourteen children by yourself and keep them all busy and happy without getting frazzled. You must have a magic formula."

"No, its not magic," Mrs. Got-it-Together explained. "I just have a place for everything so I don't spend time looking for things, and I plan each day in advance so that I don't have to scramble around getting things ready the last minute."

Although Mrs. Got-it-Together made managing a classroom seem like a piece of cake, it takes a while for every teacher to develop classroom management skills.

Organizing the Classroom

Following Miss Scatterbrain's visit to Mrs. Got-it-Together's classroom, the director asked Mrs. Got-it-Together to visit Miss Scatterbrain's classroom. Miss Scatterbrain began the day with circle time. She read a story to the children and they seemed to really enjoy it. After the story, the children asked her if she would play the Hokey Pokey tape. Miss Scatterbrain agreed but she had to get the tape recorder from the other side of the room and then she couldn't find the tape. When she finally found it, and returned it the circle, two of the children were engaged in a wrestling match and three others had left the circle and were racing across the room. Miss Scatterbrain called everyone back to the circle and put on the Hokey Pokey tape. After two rounds of Hokey Pokey, Miss Scatterbrain told the children that she had a special surprise. "Find a chair and sit down at a table and see if you can guess what it is."

Miss Scatterbrain showed the children a big jar of peanut butter. "I know," Cecile shouted out, "We're going to have a peanut butter snack" "Maybe later," Miss Scatterbrain responded, "but right now we are going to do something else."

Several children raised their hands. Miss Scatterbrain called on Peter "We're going to feed it to Hammy."

"I don't think so, Peter. Hamsters hate peanut butter."

After a few more guesses and lots of laughter, Miss Scatterbrain told the children that they were going to make peanut butter play dough. Miss Scatterbrain gave each child a sheet of wax paper and a big glob of peanut butter. "Okay, now, get ready to work," she told the children. "Everybody gets one tablespoon of flour and — "Miss Scatterbrain interrupted herself. "Oh dear," she said out loud, "I seem to have forgotten the baking soda!"

At that moment the director summoned Mrs. Got-it-Together to come into her office. "So what do you think of Miss Scatterbrain?"

"Oh, she's a great teacher," Miss Got-it-Together responded. "She is full of fun and the children seem to love her. The only thing is that she is a little bit disorganized?"

"You mean she's a real scatterbrain. Do you think she's salvageable?"

"Of course she is," Mrs. Got-it-Together replied. "She just needs a little help with organization. I'll be happy to help her."

While some teachers are by nature more organized than others, caregivers and teachers in child care settings need to know where to find things when they need them. A good way to think about how you would like to reorganize your classroom is to think back over the last two weeks and make a note of each item that you needed but couldn't find without a search.

Well organized teachers offer the following suggestions:

- Place the things that you use on a daily basis on one shelf. This would include items such as scissors, staple gun, hole puncher, paper clips, note pad, pens, tissues, first-aid kit, and planning book. Also keep a notebook that includes children's birthdays, a list of children with allergies, parent contact information, and any other vital information that you need to keep at hand.

- Place the special items that you are planning to use for the week on a second shelf. This should include the weekly plan, the books and tapes you are planning to use, samples of crafts, home-made books, and a box of materials you will need for working with individual children as described in your weekly plan.

- Give the children visual clues so that they can help maintain classroom organization. You might post the daily schedule, make a job chart that shows who's turn it is to pass out snack or feed the pets, use pictures and labels to show what belongs on a shelf or in a bin, or put stickers on the wall or floor to show how many children can be in an interest center.

- Look at your classroom from a child's point of view. Does everything have a logical home? Are items placed near where they will be used? A good way to think about how you would like to reorganize your classroom is to think back over the last two weeks and make a note of each item that you or the children needed but couldn't find without a search.

- Strike a balance between following your plans to the letter and "going with the flow." Remember that you can accommodate children's wishes without gratifying them immediately. For example, you can keep a list of books the children want you to read, and read one or two at nap time or circle time.

- Balance activities that require lots of preparation with ones that you can do on the spur of the moment. Introduce only as much variety as you and the children can comfortably handle.

- Plan some activities that evolve over time. For example, you and the children could build a store in the classroom, adding new items each day. Later, you can introduce play money, add a new department, or even invite visitors from another class.

- Keep a file with all the blank forms you use on a regular basis placed in manila folders, labeled and organized alphabetically. These might include the following forms:

▲ Observation forms	▲ Weekly plan forms
▲ Daily attendance forms	▲ Contagious Disease exposure forms
▲ Accident reports	▲ Field trip permission slips
▲ Supply requests	▲ Time sheets

- Keep a folder for each child. Include anecdotal records and observations, work samples, notes and follow-up plans from parent meetings, and any observations or recommendations by consultants.

- Keep a "to do" list in the back of your plan book. Check of items when you finish them.

- Schedule time for yourself. Give yourself time for planning, collecting materials, arranging, and just thinking. Schedule separate times for reading, visiting other teachers' classrooms, and searching out new ideas.

- Share the work and share the fun. Ask other teachers or parents to help you with big projects. Celebrate your success by doing something fun and relaxing together.

Weekly Plans

Weekly plans are a way of mapping out the daily activities that take place in the classroom. An effective weekly plan for preschool children describes the theme of the week, the special activities planned around the theme, and the kinds of preparation that the teacher needs to do in order to carry out the activities. In addition, a weekly plan can describe special games or activities designed for children who have special needs. What a weekly plan should not be is a detailed description of what you plan to do in your class everyday. The activities you do on a daily basis are described in your daily schedule. Unfortunately, some centers do require extensive weekly plans and it takes much teacher time to complete the plans. Here is an example of a simplified weekly plan:

Weekly plans are a way of mapping out the daily activities that take place in the classroom

Weekly Plan

Theme: Animals

Day	Special Activities	Teacher Responsibilities	Target Children
Monday	Read A Children's Zoo By Tana Hoban	Arrange for transportation to zoo.	Help Jerome with one-to-one correspondence using counting bears.
Tuesday	Play activity record "We're Going to the Zoo".	Send home field trip permission forms.	Liz-continue to reinforce sharing.
Wednesday	Use cookie cutters to make zoo animals.	Prepare clay table. Collect permission forms.	Give Marcel 14 piece zoo puzzle.
Thursday	Zoo play in block area and in imaginative play area.	Set up block area and pretend area with zoo theme. Check camera.	Let Jerome distribute animal crackers at snack time.
Friday	Field trip to zoo.	Take pictures at zoo.	Give Alphonzo the special job of holding Liz's hand during the field trip.

Resource Files

Keeping a well-organized and up-to-date resource box is a great timesaver. Although it is quite possible to use a carton to keep your individual resource files in, it is easier to keep your file organized if you use a file case with large hanging files.

A resource file should contain two categories of files. The first category should be organized according to topic: e.g. field trips, parent programs, classroom visitors, articles about special needs children, and advocacy material.

The second category includes activities that you have done with the children: e.g. health and safety activities, creative art projects, science activities, etc. If you use themes in your classroom, you may want to add a theme category; e.g. all about me, children from around the world, celebrations, and growing things.

Volunteers in the Classroom

Volunteers in the classroom can be either a great help or a bother. When volunteers are prepared and willing to take on a job that needs to be done, they can be quite useful. If volunteers either take on jobs that they were not requested to do or continually ask how to do each task and what they should do next, they could become a burden.

The most willing and most useful volunteers in the class are the children. Children love to be helpful and may vie to wash the tables, sort out the puzzle parts, or pass out the snacks.

Whether your volunteers are parents, college students or seniors, it is always helpful to orient them ahead of time.

...a well-managed classroom tends to run itself.

Your next best volunteers can be parents. They have a stake in what happens in the classroom and have experience with young children. They often bring special skills and talents, and can share their family and cultural heritage. Occasionally, however, parents overstep their bounds. They may usurp the teacher's role in disciplining children, introduce an unplanned activity, make a promise that can't be kept, or hover over their own child. They may find out information about another child or family and forget to keep it confidential. Unfortunately, concerns over these excesses have prompted some centers to limit the use of parent volunteers.

Whether your volunteers are parents, college students, or seniors, it is always helpful to orient them ahead of time. Find out about their skills, their time commitment, and the tasks they enjoy doing. It often helps volunteers if they are given a list of tasks that need to be done, such as updating bulletin boards. The list could include:

- writing down the words children use to describe pictures

- reading to the class, to a small group, or to an individual child

- arranging the children's art work on the wall

- helping individual children with tasks they are having difficulty with like cutting with scissors

- playing informally with children in an activity area

- helping children put on outer garments when they go on the playground

- giving extra attention to a child who needs it

- working with a small group of children to prepare a meal or snack

- teaching a song or game

Before inviting volunteers into the classroom, check your center's policies. Some centers require that every volunteer must be fingerprinted and go through a background check.

Behind the Scenes

Organization and preparation may take a lot of work, but they save time in the long run. Over time, you will find that a well-managed classroom tends to run itself. As children learn the routines, they will need less direction, leaving you more time for real communication and teaching. With a well-organized set of resources at your fingertips, you will be prepared to build on the children's emerging interests and spontaneous questions. As you read over your well-kept records, you will most likely be delighted with what you and the children have accomplished.

Bredekamp, S. (Editor). (1993). *Developmentally appropriate practice in early childhood programs serving children from birth through age 8.* Washington, D.C.: National Association for the Education of Young Children.

Brickman, N.A. & Taylor, L.S. (Editors). (1991). *Supporting young learners: Ideas for preschool and day care providers.* Ypsilanti, MI: High/Scope Press.

Curtis, D. & Carter, M. (1996). *Reflecting children's lives: A handbook for planning child-centered curriculum.* St. Paul, MN: Redleaf Press.

Dodge, D.T., Koralek, D.G., & Pizzolongo, P.J. (1989). *Caring for school children.* Vol. II. Washington, D.C.: Teaching Strategies, Inc.

Greenman, J. & Stonehouse, A. (1996). *Prime times: A handbook for excellence in Infant and toddler programs.* St. Paul, MN: Redleaf Press.

Lally, J.R., Griffin, A., Fenichel, E., Segal, M., Szanton, E., & Weissbourd, B. (1995). *Caring for infants and toddlers in groups: Developmentally appropriate practice.* Washington, D.C.: Zero to Three.

Meisels, S. & Fenichel, E. (1996). *New visions for the developmental assessment of infants and young children.* Washington, D.C.: Zero to Three: National Center for Infants Toddlers, and Families.

Chapter 15: Professionalism

Overview

Professional is defined in the *American Heritage Dictionary of the English Language* as "one who has an assured competence in a particular field or occupation." The professional early childhood teacher/caregiver has a strong knowledge of early childhood theories and effective practices. This ever-growing knowledge base informs her judgement and guides her daily activities.

Rationale

Because the developmental course of the child is determined in large part by early experiences, caregivers and teachers of young children play a critical role in shaping the future of our country. Recognizing the importance of our professional role, we must not only follow best practices and maintain the highest ethics of the profession, but must continually strive to increase and share our own knowledge and serve as advocates for children.

Objectives

1. To seek opportunities to increase professional knowledge and improve professional skills.

2. To serve as an advocate for children and families.

3. To maintain the ethics of the early childhood profession.

4. To build a professional support system.

Angelica had just graduated from high school and was talking with a girl friend about what she would like to do with the rest of her life. "One thing is for sure," she started off, "I am not going to college. I hate studying. I tried waitressing for a while but I didn't like it. Too much work and some of those people are real nasty. Last summer I had a pretty good job in a department store selling cosmetics. I would have stayed with it but they gave me all this boring stuff I was supposed to learn. You know what I think I would really like? Working in a child care center. I love kids and at least when you work with children you don't have to keep learning stuff."

Obviously, Angelica needs career guidance. It takes more than a love for children to be successful in child care.

Taking care of children is a professional commitment. It requires energy, dedication, and a commitment to professional growth. In this section we identify four components of professionalism: continuing to improve our competency, serving as an advocate for children, maintaining the ethics of the profession, and creating a personal system or network to provide professional support.

Objective 1: To seek opportunities to increase professional knowledge and improve professional skills

Every early childhood professional has an obligation to seek self-improvement.

Early childhood is a growing profession. It is growing in terms of the amount of material there is to learn, the status of the early childhood professional, and the career opportunities that are opening up. The increased recognition that is being given to early childhood professionals stems from a growing awareness of the importance of the early years and the increased demand for quality child care as mothers return to the workforce.

Every early childhood professional has an obligation to seek self-improvement. The basis of quality child care is a well-trained and competent staff. As the field grows in knowledge and expertise, it is incumbent upon all personnel to keep current with new knowledge and continually upgrade their skills. The process of self-improvement includes five critical steps: *assessing your strengths and weaknesses, identifying your goals, identifying educational resources, implementing a self-improvement plan, and sharing your new expertise with others.*

Step 1: Assess your strengths and weaknesses

Miss Driven had just spent an hour with Michael's parents. Michael had been diagnosed as mildly autistic. The psychologist who tested Michael felt that he should be placed in a classroom with typically developing children. Based on the psychologist's recommendation, Michael's parents had decided to enroll their son in the Wee Care Preschool. Michael's parents were extremely satisfied with the progress Michael was making. Miss Driven's toilet-learning routine had been successful, and Michael seldom had an accident. Also, he had completely stopped biting his hand and had learned several new words.

Following the conference with Michael's parents, Miss Driven scheduled a conference with her director. Despite the fact that Michael's parents were pleased with their son's progress, Miss Driven was convinced that she was not helping Michael enough. "He is such a nice kid," she complained to the director, "but he is still a loner. There must be something I could be doing to help him play with the other children."

Miss Driven is being too hard on herself. She is so focused on where she has failed that she hasn't taken credit for all she has accomplished. Some practitioners, like Miss Driven, are not very good at self-evaluation. They are either so focused on their areas of deficit that they lose sight of their strengths or are so focused on their strengths that they overlook areas of weakness. Fortunately, most practitioners are quite accurate in their self-assessments.

One way to begin the process of self-assessment is to prepare your own report card. This report card will help you develop a self-improvement plan.

Sample report card

	Always	Sometimes	Desired Growth Area
I am conscientious in following the guidelines and procedures of the center including work hours, record keeping, punctuality, appearance, attendance record, safety and health rules, and curriculum planning.			
I am a team player. I work cooperatively with all members of the staff and am willing to assume additional tasks when called upon.			
I have the knowledge, skills, and commitment to work effectively with children with special needs and with children from different ethnic and cultural backgrounds.			
I am fully competent in the areas of classroom management and curriculum development and implementation.			
I have excellent relationships with the families of the children in my class and have been successful in partnering with families and finding creative ways of involving families within the program.			
I seek out information, reflect on my practice, and consult with others to improve my professional knowledge and skills.			
I am an advocate for children and families and for my profession.			
I am committed to sharing my knowledge and skills and assume an active role in my center, my community, and my professional organizations.			
I am familiar with the options for careers in early childhood and am either comfortable with my current role or am open to pursuing another option.			

When you have completed your report card, it is important to share your self-evaluation with your director as well as your teammates. If everyone agrees that your report card is a fair assessment of your competencies, you are ready to take the next step, the identification of your own career goals.

Step 2: Identify your goals

As you look at your self-assessment, you will see areas of strength and areas in which you would like to improve your skills. At this point, you can set two kinds of goals, goals for improving skills related to your current position and goals for career advancement.

If your self-report indicates room for improvement, you may want to search out workshops, readings, mentorship, and other learning opportunities that will help you improve your performance. It is best to start with just one or two goals that you can achieve within a year. Your success in meeting these self-selected goals is likely to fuel your desire for further learning.

If your self-assessment indicates that you are at the top of your form, you may want to stay in your current position but take on new challenges in mentoring others or sharing your expertise through conferences and workshops. Or you might decide that it is time to move on.

As the number of early childhood programs continues to grow in the 21st century, the supply of child care personnel cannot keep up with the demand. The country is desperately short of child care givers who have the knowledge and skills to fill the job vacancies in infant and toddler care, in preschool programs, in public and private pre-kindergarten and kindergarten programs, and in programs for young children with special needs. Perhaps even more serious is the desperate shortage of personnel who can manage and direct new programs, train personnel, train the trainers of personnel, license child care facilities, mentor family providers and relative caregivers, provide specialized coaching in areas such as literacy promotion or child assessment, or provide technical assistance to new child care programs and to programs seeking accreditation or self-improvement.

Not too long ago, child care was considered a dead-end profession. At this point in time career ladder options are plentiful, and the quality of child care in this country depends on our ability to find personnel who are ready to ascend the ladder.

Step 3: Identify educational resources

Mrs. Here-to-Stay was attending an in-service session required by her center. A consultant had been invited to the session to describe educational opportunities for child care providers. Mrs. Here-to-Stay had no interest in the topic. She sat herself in the back of the room and pulled out her knitting. Unfortunately, her knitting needles made a clicking sound that caught the director's attention. During a break the director approached Mrs. Here-to-Stay and suggested that she put the knitting away. As soon as the director left, Mrs. Here-to-Stay whispered to a co-worker. "I don't know why we had to come to this stupid meeting. I have been taking care of babies for twenty-seven years and the last thing I need is an education."

While no one can quarrel over the value of experience, being experienced does not necessarily mean that you are well-informed. Mrs. Here-to-Stay had some valuable skills. She could change a baby's diaper faster than any one in the center, and she had great skill when it came to quieting a crying baby. Unfortunately, Mrs. Here-to-Stay knew nothing about the new brain research, refused to sit on the floor and play with an infant, and continued to give parents misinformation on nutrition, immunization, and developmental screening. Even if Mrs. Here-to-Stay had no interest in seeking a degree or in ascending a career ladder, her refusal to keep informed was interfering with her ability to provide quality care.

Educational Resources

Early childhood personnel interested in furthering their education have many different options. These include:

- reading newsletters, articles, chapters, and books

- attending conferences, lectures, and workshops

- watching videotapes or listening to audiotapes

- networking with other personnel through meetings, telephone calls, e-mail, or Internet bulletin boards, listservs, and chat rooms

- surfing the Internet

- visiting other early childhood programs

- participating in leadership training or fellowship programs

Professional Organizations

Early Childhood professional organizations provide many valuable resources in the form of workshops, conferences, magazines and journals, web sites, videotapes, colleagues, and mentors.

Here is a partial list:

National Association for the Education of Young Children (NAEYC)
1718 Connecticut Avenue, NW
Washington, DC 20009
www.naeyc.org

NAEYC is the largest professional organization in the country. It has 100,000 members and 360 affiliate groups that are located in different states and regions. In addition to sponsoring an annual conference, NAEYC publishes a bimonthly journal, Young Children, and many other excellent publications on early childhood issues.

National Association for Family Child Care
525 S.W. 5th Street. Suite A
Des Moines, Iowa 50309-4501
www.nafcc.org

NAFCC seeks to promote quality in family child care and advance the family child care profession. The national association advocates for family child care providers, provides technical assistance to local provider associations, runs a national conference, and promotes family child care accreditation.

National Black Child Development Institute (NBCDI)
1463 Rhode Island Avenue, NW
Washington, DC 20005
www.nbcdi.org

NBCDI is an early childhood organization that supports the healthy growth and development of black children. It sponsors an annual conference and publishes the *Black Child Advocate*.

National Head Start Association
1651 Prince Street
Alexandria, Virginia 22314
www.nhsa.org

The National Head Start Association (NHSA) is a membership organization representing the 835,000 children, upwards of 170,000 staff, and 2,051 Head Start programs in America. It runs training conferences, provides distance education via satellite TV, promulgates new research, and publishes *Children and Families, NHSA Dialog,* and other resources for teachers.

National Institute for Hispanic Children and Families
2000 Rosemont Avenue, NW
Washington, DC 20010

This Institute focuses on legislative issues related to the needs of Hispanic children.

Southern Early Childhood Association (SECA)
P.O. Box 5403
Brady Station
Little Rock, AR 72215

SECA is comprised of 13 State Associations concerned with promoting professionalism and advocacy in Early Childhood Education. It hosts an annual conference and publishes a quarterly journal.

ZERO TO THREE: National Center for Infants, Toddlers and Families
734 15th Street, NW, Suite 1000
Washington, DC 20005
www.zerotothree.org

ZERO TO THREE is the nation's leading resource on the first three years of life. Zero to Three provides information to professionals in many disciplines and to parents through its web site, an annual conference, the *Zero to Three Bulletin,* growth chart posters, and other publications.

Early Childhood Education Courses

Formal coursework is available online from sources such as the National Association of Child Care Resource and Referral Agencies' *Learning Options* (*www.learningoptions.org*), Nova Southeastern University (*www.nova.edu*), and Lesley College (*www.lesley.edu*).

Courses may also be available at your local community college or university, through your local resource and referral agency, or through Head Start, military base child care programs, or other federal or state programs.

Try to choose courses that will help you climb the early childhood degree ladder.

Child Development Associate Credential

One way to improve your educational status is through the Child Development Associate program. A CDA is a professional who has been assessed by the CDA

National Credentialing Program and judged to be competent as an early childhood teacher.

Associate, Bachelor's, and Advanced Degree Programs

Colleges may offer an AA or an AS degree in early childhood. In most community colleges an AS is a terminal degree, while an AA "articulates" with a Bachelor of Arts in Early Childhood Education, allowing you to receive credit for the first two years of the bachelor's program. Students who complete their bachelor's degree in early childhood or a related field may pursue a graduate degree in Early Childhood Development or Education on a masters or doctoral level. Many bachelor's programs in Early Childhood Education offer college credit to candidates who have received a CDA or candidates with documented life experiences. Because an increasing number of colleges are currently offering distance education degrees, it is now possible for early childhood personnel to earn advanced degrees without giving up their jobs.

Continuing Education Units (CEU'S)

Whether you are teaching in a licensed early childhood setting, or whether you hold an advanced degree and are teaching in a public or private school, most states require that you renew your skills within a prescribed period by receiving a set number of C.E.U credits. C.E.U's are also required to maintain your status as a Child Development Associate or as a certified teacher. Some CEU courses can be counted for undergraduate or graduate credit if you complete extra assignments and pay an additional fee.

It is important to recognize that career opportunities in early childhood are not automatically available to people who hold an undergraduate or graduate degree in early childhood. Every state has a system for certifying early childhood educators. In order to be certified as an early childhood teacher, it is necessary to meet the certification standards of the state where you are seeking employment. In most states, a candidate must be certified in early childhood education in order to be eligible to assume a pre-kindergarten or kindergarten teaching position within the public school system.

Financial Support

Financial support for furthering your education through courses or conferences may be available from several sources:

- T.E.A.C.H. scholarships in several states underwrite educational costs and provide stipends for graduates who agree to stay on the job.

- PELL Grants support college education for students of modest income.

- Many Resource and Referral Agencies provide free courses and administer scholarship programs.

- Professional conferences are often partially underwritten by corporate sponsors, who provide scholarships for some attendees.

- Many centers will pay all or part of your tuition for work-related study.

Step 4: Implement a self-improvement plan

A meaningful professional plan is based on a self-evaluation and describes the resources you will use to reach your self-improvement goal(s).

Mr. Coolit: "What are you doing now? Can't you for once in your life leave work at school so that we can spend some time together?"

Mrs. Coolit: "Don't worry. This won't take more than five minutes. My evaluation is tomorrow and the director and I have plans to write these professional improvement plans."

Mr. Coolit: "That's stupid. I like you just the way you are."

Mrs. Coolit: "I know it's silly. We go through this every year. These plans are like New Year's resolutions. You make these great plans, stick them in the drawer, and promptly forget about them."

Mrs. Coolit has described exactly what a professional plan should not be, and what you should not do with it.

A meaningful professional plan is based on a self-evaluation and describes the resources you will use to reach your self- improvement goal(s). Here is a sample professional plan that states a goal and lists steps toward its achievement. Notice that the plan includes both learning (through reading and a workshop) and initial ideas for applying that learning in the classroom and in work with parents.

Sample Self Improvement Plan

Goal: Expand the curriculum to include a greater focus on multicultural and anti-bias education.

June: Order materials for the classroom that are culturally appropriate: multi-ethnic dolls, play foods from different cultures, multicultural books

July and August: Read materials on anti-bias and cultural responsiveness.

Valuing Diversity — The Primary Years by Janet Brown McCracken
Anti-bias Curriculum by Louise Derman-Sparks
Including All of Us by Merle Frosch
In Our Own Way — How Anti-bias Work Shapes our Lives, Redleaf Press

September: Re-do the curriculum for the year and include one activity per month that teaches children to value diversity

October: With the children and parents, develop a showcase in the classroom with artifacts from all of the different cultures that are represented in our classroom.

December: Use *We Celebrate Holidays* as a theme. With the help of parents, plan different holiday celebrations. Ask parents and/or grandparents to help prepare holiday fun around the holiday they celebrate at home.

March: Participate in a professional workshop on celebrating diversity.

April-May: Gather recipes from the different families in the class. Reproduce the recipes. Let the children make cookbook covers in the class and give their mothers cookbooks for Mother's Day.

Step 5: Share your new expertise with others

Whether you have researched an area, made changes in your classroom, or qualified for a new career, you can find many opportunities to share what you have learned.

- Share what you have learned informally with colleagues.

- Invite other teachers to visit your classroom.

- Share a book or videotape that you found valuable with parents and colleagues.

- Plan a presentation or discussion for a staff or parent meeting.

- Contribute an article to a newsletter or journal.

- Join with colleagues to present at a workshop or conference.

- Mentor a colleague.

- Assume an office in a professional organization.

Objective 2: To serve as an advocate for children and their families

When the director of the Growing Together Nursery School asked the staff if they would attend a legislative hearing supporting higher subsidies for childcare, Miss Not-me, a new teacher, was annoyed. "Why should we spend our good time supporting child care. It is bad enough that we have to take care of kids for the kind of money they pay us. If parents want the government to pay for their child care, it's up to them to attend the hearings!"

The director of Growing Together was taken aback by this attitude. She had taken for granted that all teachers were concerned about the welfare of children and would seek out opportunities to serve as child advocates.

Although the director of Growing Together may be expecting a lot of a brand new teacher, she is certainly right in stressing the importance of early childhood teachers becoming involved in advocacy issues. Teachers of young children have firsthand knowledge of the needs of children and families. When they share this knowledge with legislators or government officials, it is likely that they will be listened to. Just as important, teachers are in a good position to share their knowledge with parents and associates who in turn can become child advocates.

Miss Not-me needs to do some hard thinking. She is absolutely right when she complains about poor wages. She is also right when she asserts that parents should advocate for child care subsidies. But an underpaid child care workforce and a scarcity of parent advocates are good reasons for her becoming a child advocate and poor reasons for sitting on the sidelines. Child care givers know the importance - and the cost - of quality care for young children and are in a prime position to educate policy makers. Child care givers who have earned the trust of parents are also in a prime position to help parents advocate for their children.

Many caregivers, like Miss Not-me, would rather stand on the sidelines and complain than join the ranks of the advocates. Let us look at some of the reasons caregivers give for shying away from being advocates, and some of the ways in which directors and co-workers could overcome their concerns and win them over.

"I get up at 5:00 in the morning, get the kids off to school, get home at 6:00 p.m., make dinner clean the house, help the kids with their homework. I don't have time to breathe, let alone do this advocacy stuff."

"I am not one for mixing into politics. I don't care which party they belong to, they're a bunch of crooks and I wouldn't give them the time of day."

"I never was much of a reader and I don't know one candidate from the other. If I start giving them advice about what they should vote for, I'd sound like a bumbling idiot. I once went to one of those political open houses and I was supposed to tell a candidate about why he should vote for a children's board and I started stuttering and I turned red in the face."

"They told me I should write this letter about market rates and that I should use my own words. I really tried, but I get tongue-tied when I have to write something. By the time I have my letter written, the legislative session will be over."

"I think voting should be private and I'm not going to tell anybody what or whom they should vote for."

"I wouldn't mind so much going to a town meeting or rally but my husband works nights and I hate to go places alone."

"Legislatures get hundreds of calls. One little call for me is not going to make a difference."

Ways of Overcoming Concerns about Being an Advocate

As we read through the reasons caregivers offer for shying away from advocacy, it is relatively easy to identify the underlying reasons for their reluctance. These include feelings of being over-extended, lack of confidence and experience, fear about being uninformed, lack of motivation, feelings of futility, distrust of government, and fear of going out alone. If we want child care givers to assume an advocacy role, we need to find ways of overcoming these concerns. The director of Growing Together, Miss The-Buck-Stops-Here, discovered several different ways of inspiring reluctant caregivers to become committed advocates.

- *"When teachers tell me that they don't have time for advocacy, I make the time for them. I take over their class for five minutes while they make their advocacy calls. I also pass around post-cards at teachers meetings, explain the cause we need to support, and write several short sample notes on the board. At the end of the meeting, I collect and mail the postcards."*

- *"When teachers lack confidence and/or experience with advocating, I invite them to accompany me to a public hearing, a rally, a visit to a legislator, or a school board meeting. One year I used the school bus and took several staff members up to the state capital. We walked the halls and talked to several legislators about the need for subsidized child care slots. Not only did we have a blast, but we became part of a larger group that got more money than had been originally earmarked for child care subsidies from the legislature."*

- *"When teachers are fearful about being uninformed, I write short blurbs about issues that affect children, and we discuss the issues at our Friday teacher's meeting."*

- *"When teachers seem to lack motivation, I find an issue that hits home for them, and we talk about it. One approach I use all the time is to find an issue that relates to our school, like the need for a stop sign on the corner. Then we plan an advocacy campaign together. I even encourage my staff to advocate to me as the manager for more vacation days or better classroom supplies."*

- *"When teachers tell me that their one call to a legislator or their one vote doesn't count for anything, I remind them that we wouldn't be living in a democracy if everyone thought the way they did."*

- *"When teachers tell me about their distrust of government, I remind them that our government is no better than the people we put in office. If people don't get interested in supporting good candidates, the government will not become any better."*

- *"When teachers are fearful about going to a political event alone, I make it my business to find them someone to go with."*

Objective 3: To maintain the ethics of the early childhood profession

Mrs. Quickreader was visiting with a child care provider, Mrs. Lean-on-Me.

Mrs. Quickreader: "As I told you on the phone, I am looking for a family day care home where I can place Jason, who is now sixth months old."

Mrs. Lean-on-Me: "I am glad you have come here. We do have an opening for a six-month old. Talk to me a little bit about your son."

Mrs. Quickreader: "He's a wonderful baby — social, outgoing, and full of smiles and laughs. I am sure he will make a good adjustment wherever I put him, but I am especially interested in finding a caregiver with whom I can build rapport."

Mrs. Lean-on-Me: "Again, you have come to the right place. I make a practice of keeping parents informed about everything their baby is doing and I listen carefully when parents have concerns. As a matter of fact, the reason why I have an opening is that Mrs. Yellow-tail, who also has a six-month old, is moving to Arizona. The last day her baby was with me she gave me a hug and told me that she felt as if she was losing more than a caregiver, she was losing her best friend. I feel so sorry for Mrs. Yellow-tail. Her husband never helps her with her son, and when she moves to Arizona, she'll have no support system at all."

Mrs. Quickreader thanked Mrs. Lean-on-Me and went to another interview. Needless to say, she did not place her son in Mrs. Lean-on-Me's home.

> ### A code of ethics is a set of principles that describe the behavior expected of a professional.

A code of ethics is a set of principles that describe the behavior expected of a professional. In some situations that occur in a child care setting ethical behavior can be clearly identified. It is not ethical to share confidential information, to misrepresent our credentials, to put extra hours on a timesheet, to talk to one parent about problems with another parent, or to withhold information on an accident report that may be incriminating. In other situations, the ethical course is harder to determine. Should we report a parent for abusing a child when we are pretty sure but not positive that the abuse occurred? Should you tell a nervous parent that her child fell down on the playground when her child wasn't hurt?

While many different codes of ethics have been written, the following five principles are inherent in the code of ethics for early childhood professionals:

Ethical Principle I: Professionals always maintain the confidentiality of the parents and co-workers in the child care setting. When Mrs. Lean-on-Me divulged personal information about another client, she was violating an important ethical principal.

Ethical Principle II: Professionals are honest, dependable, and reliable in performing all duties related to the center. This includes following all procedures related to the health, safety, and well-being of the children and of adhering to the program philosophy.

Ethical Principle III: Professionals are truthful with children, parents, co-workers, and directors. They do not make promises that they cannot keep and they do not commit to a course of action that they know they cannot follow.

Ethical Principle IV: Professionals treat all children and families with respect regardless of gender, ethnicity, culture, sexual orientation, or economic status. Being respectful to parents includes respecting differences in beliefs and child rearing philosophies, while maintaining your calm even if parents attack unfairly.

Ethical Principle V: Professionals treat each child as an individual. They recognize the importance of building on each child's strengths, of providing realistic challenges, and of providing opportunities for each child to be successful. They are concerned with making each child in their group feel wanted, welcome, and successful, regardless of their level of competency.

As you read through the following vignettes, identify the vignettes where there is a clear violation of an ethical principle and those vignettes where the ethical course of action is difficult to determine.

Mrs. Yellow-Belly was a newly hired teacher assistant assigned to a seasoned teacher, Mrs. Do- it-my-way. One of the first things that Mrs. Do-it-my-way told her assistant was not to let a child named Dorothea play on the playground. "One of the parents," she explained, "told me confidentially that Dorothea was exposed to AIDS. If she happened to get scratched on the playground, her blood might get on another child and it could start an epidemic."

Mr. Corner was telling his co-worker about the telephone call he had received from Naomi's mother. "I know you won't believe it but Naomi's mother told me that Naomi is not allowed to participate in the Christmas pageant. Well, her Mother can keep her home on the day of the pageant, but I'm certainly not going to keep her from taking part in the rehearsals!"

Mrs. Cantelli had requested a conference with her daughter's teacher to discuss the reading curriculum. "I know that it doesn't hurt to expose children to reading and writing, but I don't think you should be teaching phonics to preschool children. Do you really think these children are ready to learn phonics?" Mr. Carter didn't know how to respond. He felt that Mrs. Cantelli was right, but the director of the school had made it quite clear that everyone had to teach phonics.

Cuddle Care is the only licensed childcare facility available to the migrant camp. During harvesting, Cuddle Care is often over-enrolled. The director realized that if she does not take the children into her center, many of the infants might be left in the care of preschool children. When the health department arrived unexpectedly one day, the director was afraid that she might be shut down for over-crowding. She asked one of the teachers to take ten of the children on a walk so the health department wouldn't find out how many children there were in the center. The teacher was not sure whether or not to follow the director's instruction.

Objective 4: To build a professional support system

Being a professional means that, to some extent, you operate independently. You make judgements and decisions every day and are responsible for their consequences. This can be empowering; it can also feel lonely and even, at times, intimidating. That is why teachers, like all professionals, need to reflect on their practice, find colleagues with whom they can discuss new ideas and "tough calls," and build a network for personal and professional support.

Making Time for Reflection and Discussion

In addition to planning and preparation time, early childhood teachers and caregivers need time to think: to reflect on what they are doing and what is and isn't working, to puzzle out what is happening with individual children and why, to read about new research and explore what it might mean for their classrooms, and to dream up new ideas. Some of this thinking is best done alone; some is best done through conversations with colleagues, parents, supervisors, and consultants.

With all of the demands on your time, how can you make time for reflection and discussion?

Whether you are working in a family child care home, in a small center, or in a large organization, you need adult work-based relationships. Here are some things you can do to build supportive relationships.

- Set aside at least fifteen minutes each day for "kid watching." Use this time to observe individual children and make notes about behaviors that impress, intrigue, or puzzle you. Some teachers like to keep a journal on each child, including observations, photographs, and samples of the child's work. These journals can be shared with parents, who may also make entries.

- Set aside at least an hour each week for learning. Read early childhood journals, attend a class or workshop, search out early childhood Internet sites, exchange e-mail with colleagues, browse through catalogs and activity books to get ideas, research a topic that you are studying with the children.

- Insist on regular staff meetings and breaks. Use these times to discuss issues and ideas with your colleagues, as well as to relax and socialize.

- Arrange with colleagues to visit each other's classrooms.

- Use professional days to visit other centers, attend conferences, and participate in advocacy events.

- Meet regularly and as needed with your supervisor or with a colleague who can support you. Bring *your* goals, issues, and questions to these meetings.

- Find a mentor — A more experienced colleague who can show you the ropes, answer your questions, and help you think through your plans and ideas.

- Enlist parents as partners. They can help you understand their children, their family, and their culture. They may also have special skills and ideas that can enrich your classroom.

- Look at your classroom through the eyes of a child and through the eyes of a parent. What new things do you notice?

Building Relationships

The staff at the We're a Family Center were proud and elated. They had just put on a very successful conference for parents and professionals in their community. Teachers and directors from other centers had joined them to hear about the latest research on language development and to see some of the things they were doing in their classrooms. Now that the conference was over, they went out for dinner to celebrate. They were each other's best friends, and they didn't want this day to end too soon.

Relationships like those at We're a Family don't happen overnight. The teachers there had been working together for more than ten years. They knew each other's dreams and foibles, joys and burdens. They had spent time with each other's families and had supported each other through challenges and triumphs. They shared in-jokes and memories. They had gone together to professional conferences, both as learners and as presenters. They had worked together to improve wages and working conditions, to earn accreditation for their center, and to figure out how to meet the needs of new immigrant families and of several children with challenging disabilities. Through shared work and shared play, they had become a team.

Whether you are working in a family child care home, in a small center, or in a large organization, you need adult work-based relationships. Here are some things you can do to build supportive relationships:

- If you are working alone or with few colleagues, take advantage of community resources and events. Bring your group to the library, playground, or local drop-in center where you can meet other colleagues.

- Plan parties and other social events. These can be for staff only, staff and parents, or staff and families.

- Plan special days when you can all have fun together. You might put on a carnival as a fund-raiser, celebrate Halloween with costumes (no masks) and special treats, have a family picnic, or go on a field trip together.

- Celebrate accomplishments and milestones: birthdays, graduations, individual and center achievements.

- Start a "learning circle" or peer mentorship relationship. Meet regularly in person or on the phone with a few colleagues to discuss your work.

- Spend some time with colleagues when work is not on the agenda. Just have fun together.

- Advocate for your needs. You may wish to join a union (parents and directors can join, too) or form a task force within your center to investigate ways to improve communication, working conditions, or wages and benefits.

You and your local colleagues may want to join a professional organization together, or even found your own chapter. Joining a professional early childhood organization provides you with access to current publications, opportunities to attend conferences and conventions, opportunities to network with other professionals, and opportunities to join working committees and plan workshops.

As you take your place within the ever-widening circle of the early childhood profession, remember that you not only have a lot to learn and live up to. You also have a lot to contribute.

Bellm, D., Whitebook, M., & Hnatiuk, P. (1997). *The early childhood mentoring curriculum: A handbook for mentors.* Washington, D.C.: National Center for the Early Childhood Work Force.

Bloom, P.J., Sheerer, M., & Britz, J. (1991). *Blueprint for action: Achieving center-based change through staff development.* Beltsville, MD: Gryphon House, Inc.

Curtis, D. & Carter, M. (1996). *Reflecting children's lives: A handbook for planning child-centered curriculum.* St. Paul, MN: Redleaf Press.

Dodge, D.T., Koralek, D.G., & Pizzolongo, P.J. (1989). *Caring for school children.* Vol. II. Washington, D.C.: Teaching Strategies, Inc.

Guidelines for preparation of early childhood professionals. (1996). Washington, D.C.: National Association for the Education of Young Children.

Guillebeaux, A.J. (1998). *More is caught than taught: A guide to quality child care.* Montgomery, AL: Federation of Child Care Centers of Alabama, Inc.

Harms, T., Cryer, D., & Clifford, R.M. (1990). *Infant / toddler environment rating scale.* NY: Teachers College Press.

Phillips, C.B. (Editor). (1991). *Essentials for child development associates working with young children.* Washington, D.C.: The Council for Early Childhood Professional Recognition.

Provider's self-study workbook. Quality standards for NAFCC accreditation: Pilot study draft. (1997). Boston, MA: The Family Child Care Project, Wheelock College.

Pawl, J., & St. John, M. (1998). *How you are is as important as what you do...in making a positive difference for infants, toddlers and their families.* Washington, D.C.: Zero to Three.

Snow, C.W. (1998). *Infant development.* Upper Saddle River, NJ: Prentice Hall.

The child development associate: Assessment systems and competency standards. Preschool caregivers in center-based programs. (1996). Washington, D.C.: The Council for Early Childhood Professional Recognition.

The child development associate: Assessment systems and competency standards. Infant / toddler caregivers in center-based programs. (1997). Washington, D.C.: The Council for Early Childhood Professional Recognition.

Index